Valley of the *Kings*

A HISTORY OF THE W.S. COX PLATE

RHETT KIRKWOOD
& BRIAN MELDRUM

"For a scribbler casting around pearls, the Cox Plate has become a tease. The problem is: how do you write about the race without appearing to slobber? I'll explain. The Moonee Valley Racing Club, rather like that good colt Shakespeare in his Classic year, insists on staging masterpiece after masterpiece. They gave us the Kingston Town trilogy; that used up a few pearls. Then as a variation, they staged the Bonecrusher-Our Waverley Star slug-feast. And how do you follow that?"
– *Les Carlyon, Chasing A Dream*

First printed in 2000
Updated and reprinted in 2015

Published by:
Equus Marketing Pty Ltd
(ACN 058 139 898)
1/22 Summerhill Road
Glen Iris Vic 3146, Australia
Tel: +613 9889 7741
Web: www.pharlap.com.au
Email: equus1@bigpond.net.au

and

Bas Publishing
ABN 30 106 181 542
PO Box 335
Dromana Vic 3936, Australia
Tel/Fax: +613 5988 3597
Web: www.baspublishing.com.au
Email: mail@baspublishing.com.au

The National Library of Australia Cataloguing-in-Publication entry:

Creator: Kirkwood, Rhett, author.

Title: Valley of the Kings : a history of the W.S. Cox Plate /
                    Rhett Kirkwood, Brian Meldrum.

ISBN: 9781921496394 (hardback)

Subjects: Moonee Valley Racing Club--History.
                    Cox Plate (Horse race)--History.
                    Horse racing--Victoria--Moonee Valley--History.

Other Creators/
Contributors: Meldrum, Brian, author.

Dewey Number: 798.40099451

Design and Layout: Ben Graham

ANOTHER PHAR LAP – COX PLATE RECORD

Almost seven decades after his death, Phar Lap was still setting records.

In November, 1999, his 1931 Cox Plate trophy, which was actually a Cup, bought a record $420,500 at auction.

Of 18 carat gold, the Cup is believed to be the only surviving trophy won by Phar Lap.

Sold by Sotheby's in Melbourne, it achieved a record for any piece of sporting memorabilia sold in Australia when bought by a South Australian tuna fisherman.

A FARM TRANSFORMED

Robert Hoddle, senior surveyor for the new colony of Melbourne, obviously liked what he saw after instructing assistant surveyor Smyth to plot "Mone Mone Creek", a few miles north of the new settlement, in December 1837.

After Smyth had finished mapping what we now know as Moonee Ponds Creek, Hoddle instructed a draftsman to define a boundary for a new Parish to be called Doutta Galla, and thereafter to divide the land adjoining the creek "into sections agreeable to the usual regulations".

The tracts were clearly agreeable to Hoddle, who acquired three such Crown Allotments (Nos 3, 4 & 5) totalling 152 acres, abutting the Creek which Smyth had surveyed, for a cost of £573/16/-. His neighbour, who bought Allotment 6 (covering an area of 53 acres) for £212/-/-, was a former British soldier settler, who was listed in the electoral roll under the names of John Mooney or John Moonee. Considering the land was in the area now known as Moonee Ponds, it is logical to think that the latter version of his surname is correct, establishing a connection between him and the name of the area. However, there are other more credible theories on the derivation of the name "Moonee Ponds", the most popular being that "Mone Mone Creek" changed in time to Moonee Moonee Ponds and finally to Moonee Ponds. (Such name changes were not uncommon, another example being the transformation of the original title of Pascoeville to Pascoe Vale.)

Robert Hoddle ....
obviously liked what
he saw in the area now
known as Moonee Ponds.

Three years after his original purchase, Moonee increased his holding when he bought Allotment 5 from Hoddle, with the extra 48 acres taking Moonee's land parcel to 101 acres.

After subdividing and selling several lots along Pascoe Vale Road, Moonee still had a large tract of arable land extending to the creek, which he sold to farmer Richard Feehan for £9,000. Legend has it that the deal was brokered as the two were riding to the nearby town of Keilor, but what is known is that the sale was concluded exactly one week before Christmas Day, 1855.

Some 20 years later, Gippsland farmer William Samuel Cox, who hailed from Scotland, bought a property at Kensington, only a 10 minute canter from Feehan's farm, which by now was producing prize winning cattle. Cox (who was commonly known as Sam) was a keen racing man and was preparing to convert his holding, situated near the Kensington Railway Station, into a private racetrack. It was to become Melbourne's second proprietary racecourse, following in the hoofprints of the Croxton Park track near Northcote, which had closed in July, 1873.

The small Kensington Park Racecourse, with a seven furlong circuit, opened in October 1874 attracting about 3,000 spectators who saw a program which included flat and jumping races. Only 12 months after opening Kensington, Sam Cox had more good news on the racing front when his horse Imperial won the Sydney Cup.

Sam Cox's new course quickly won acclaim as, being adjacent to the railway station, it was easily accessible and, because of its compactness, ensured a good view for all. Taking advantage of the growing popularity of Flemington's Spring Carnival, (which was already a four day Carnival by 1869) the shrewd Cox decided to add a Spring meeting to Kensington Park's program. He chose the Saturday before the Victoria Derby – which to this day remains the key date for Australasia's greatest weight-for-age race, Moonee Valley's W. S. Cox Plate, which honours William Samuel Cox.

Ironically, the popularity of Kensington Park brought about its demise. It

Run over a mile, and won by the filly Castaway, the Moonee Ponds Cup was one of five races on Moonee Valley's first program, which carried total stakemoney of £180. Though she ran the very slow time of 1 minute 48.7 seconds for the mile journey, Castaway still holds the record for the Moonee Ponds Cup because the race was not run again. The following year, the Cup had assumed the same name as the racecourse, with the result that Meteor became the first winner of the Moonee Valley Cup under that name.

was too small to cope with increasing crowds, so Sam Cox was forced to look further afield for an alternative site, eventually settling on the 98 acres of Mr Feehan's farm. Being a natural ampitheatre, it was an ideal site for his second racing venture – it allowed for a bigger track than Kensington and could also cope with bigger crowds, while still permitting people to be close to the action. After negotiating a seven-year lease with an option to purchase, Sam Cox closed the gates on Kensington Park on December 16, 1882. It was to take him nine months to turn Feehan's Farm into his new racing dream.

Though based in the heart of Moonee Ponds, Cox opted for the euphonious title of Moonee Valley when selecting a name for his new 1¼ mile track, which opened on September 15, 1883. However, such consideration did not extend to the name of the main race on day one – it was called the Moonee Ponds Cup. Run over a mile, and won by the filly Castaway, the Cup was one of five races on the program, which carried total stakemoney of £180. (Though she ran the very slow time of 1 minute 48.7 seconds for the mile journey, Castaway still holds the record for the Moonee Ponds Cup because the race was not run again. The following year, the Cup had assumed the same name as the racecourse, with the result that Meteor became the first winner of the Moonee Valley Cup under that name).

Opening day at the Valley started in spectacular fashion when the fillies Eveline and Pyrette dead-heated in the first event, a six furlong Maiden Plate. One racegoer, obviously keen to ensure he had a perfect view of proceedings, tried to take a box through the gate. The patron was stopped by the gatekeeper, after which an argument developed and the gatekeeper's hat was knocked from his head. As a result, charges were laid and the racegoer finished up £5/15/- out of pocket.

The new venue proved extremely popular and Sam Cox was quick to make utmost use of it, by also conducting trotting races on the grass track during the 1890's. Testament to the success of the new location was when 10,000 people saw Little Bob win the first of two successive Moonee Valley Cups in 1891.

No doubt buoyed by the success of Moonee Valley, Cox was quick to expand his racing business by opening a new course at Maribyrnong in December, 1891. This course, with a mile circuit, was on the site which formed part of the famous Maribyrnong Stud farm. The stud was owned at various times by the brothers Hurtle and C. B. (Charles Brown) Fisher, who were to have a significant influence on the formation of the VRC. Hurtle was a founding Committeeman of the Club while C.B. was Chairman from 1883-1895. Their stud/training establishment, regarded as Victoria's showpiece racing property, comprised some 350 acres on the flats of the Saltwater River (now Maribyrnong River) and such was its vastness that Hurtle Fisher was referred to as the "Squire of Maribyrnong". Samuel Cox's race Club there lasted some 15 years. It was to close in 1905 when the Victoria Racing Club, by then racing's controlling body, sharply pruned the number of metropolitan meetings allocated for the season, resulting in only the "strong" tracks surviving.

Sam Cox did not live to see its demise, as within four years of this second racecourse purchase, the racing patriarch was dead. Cox died on October 2, 1895, aged 64, bequeathing real estate worth £70,872/-/- and cash and personal effects to the value of £3,784/6/6 in trust for his widow Mary and his family of five daughters and two surviving sons. Cox appointed one son Archie and daughter Alexandra as Trustees to operate Moonee Valley and his farming property as separate businesses for the benefit of his family.

It was his wish that the Trustees operate the businesses (officially termed as being those of racecourse proprietor, grazier and farmer) for 10 years, but such was the obvious prosperity of the businesses that the beneficiaries and

Trustees agreed to a 10 year extension to the arrangement at the expiration of the first 10-year term.

Cox had left an indelible mark on the history of racing in Victoria. Apart from what he had achieved with his racing ventures, he was the founder of a racing dynasty which was to be closely involved in a century-long association with Victorian racing.

His first son, W. S. Cox Jnr, was a famous amateur rider who piloted his father's horse, The King (50/1), when he finished midfield in the 1878 Melbourne Cup. He is best remembered, however, for his association with Redleap, one of Australia's greatest jumpers, on whom he won the 1889 and 1892 Grand National Hurdle as well as the 1892 Grand National Steeple, thus becoming the first jockey to win Victoria's feature jumps racing double. W. S. Cox Jnr later became a successful trainer. His best horse was Realm, who won the 1907 Australian and Sydney Cups for VRC Chairman Lachlan Mackinnon after winning the 1906 Grand National Hurdle the previous year.

Another son, Albert, died in his late teens after suffering a broken back when a horse he was riding reared, while the third son was A.H. "Archie" Cox, who succeeded his father as manager of Moonee Valley. Archie switched roles in 1906 after being appointed one of only two VRC Stewards, whose duties had been carried out previously by Members of the VRC Committee.

With Archie's departure from Moonee Valley, his brother-in-law, A.V. Hiskens (who had married Archie's sister Alexandra) took over as manager, and quickly set about improving amenities. The old grandstand which had served at Croxton Park, Kensington, and then Maribyrnong, was re-erected for a fourth time at Moonee Valley and renovations were also made to the track.

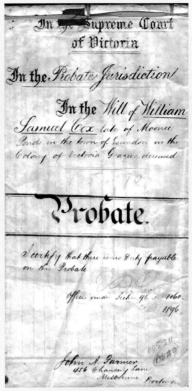

"Ribbleden" captured the situation this way in *The Australasian* of January 12, 1907:

> *"The Moonee Valley racecourse is very popular with the multitude, it is so accessible and when the improvements now in progress are completed it promises to be more popular than ever. Improvements have long been needed, and it is no wonder that the hon. secretary, Mr. A. V. Hiskens, is dissatisfied with things as they are, and is determined upon an alteration in the interest of his patrons.*
>
> *Mr. W. S. Cox, the original proprietor of the property, was a diligent student of 'Every man his own architect', and what was more – or rather, what was worse – he put these theories into practice. The visitors to Moonee Valley are familiar with the result – a number of odds and ends of buildings of little use and less ornament – a blot on the landscape. But these eyesores – these monuments of false economy – are fast disappearing, and will be replaced by more suitable and more convenient structures.*
>
> *The old stand has seen long service. It first did duty at Croxton Park; then it was shifted to Kensington Park and thence to Maribyrnong; but the accommodation was not equal to the requirements. So when the VRC squelched the Maribyrnong Racing Club Mr. Hiskens conceived the idea of transferring the Maribyrnong stand, which will seat a thousand persons on a pinch, to Moonee Valley.*
>
> *It will be placed on the site of the mound between the old stand*

Sam Cox left real estate worth more than £70,000 and personal effects worth almost £4,000. It was his wish that the Trustees operate the businesses (officially termed as being those of racecourse proprietor, grazier and farmer) for 10 years, but such was the obvious prosperity of the businesses that it was agreed to extend the initial arrangement by a further 10 years.

and the weighing enclosure and the old betting ring will know the bookmakers no more.

The lawn, sloping gradually toward the outer fence of the racecourse, will be 500 ft. long and will extend towards the carriage paddock, giving everybody a fine view of the racing. The neighbouring pavilion, Stewards' room and stand, luncheon-rooms etc – all new buildings – will be situated to the right of the Judge's box, and there will also be a sort of visitors' reserve.

The waste ground at the back of the stand will be utilised as a saddling paddock, which will be considerably enlarged, and it is intended to erect a large frame for the horse numbers and the jockeys' names will be attached. The proprietary has not forgotten its patrons. There are two sorts of meetings at Moonee Valley. Besides the meetings of the MVRC there are the Hunt Club meetings – Oaklands, Findon and Melbourne and the votaries of Diana have to be specially catered for.

On such occasions, hitherto, the ladies have been provided with afternoon tea in a large marquee in the carriage paddock; but there is to be no more suggestion of circus. Instead of the canvas tents, which were inconvenient, large permanent pavilions will be set up, containing picnic tables and seats, something after the plan adopted at fabulous Flemington. This is an improvement indeed and will be appreciated not less by hunting men and their lady friends than by the lovers of polo.

The patrons of the hill, or outer reserve, will also appreciate the improvements which have been effected in their part of the course. The hill has been cut down to within 2 ft. of the course, and while affording accommodation for one third more spectators, will give each and every one an uninterrupted view.

It is, of course, steeper than it was; but not quite as steep as the hill at Flemington, which falls one in four; this falls one in four and a half. More shelter will also be provided. The proprietary is also preparing a new seven furlong course, which will start just underneath the hill. The entrance to Moonee Valley is not like unto the gates of Paradise; but in course of time, when the land is available, the place will be entered by a fine street, 66ft wide, the street going down behind the saddling paddock, and sweeping by the graceful curves right into the carriage paddock. (**Ed Note**: This street is now known as Alexandra Avenue.)

These improvements, which will run into a thousand pounds or thereabouts, will bring Moonee Valley right up to date – in fact, right up to the day after tomorrow; and the proprietary deserves well of the sporting public. Moonee Valley has been the scene of many a stirring contest, and, under the present capable management, it cannot fail to maintain its popularity as a racing rendezvous.

The work, which is being carried out under the supervision of Mr. Tuxen, is as yet rather rough, but there will be a tidying up before next Saturday and those who patronise the S. G. Cook benefit meeting – and I hope there will be a bumper attendance – will be able to form an excellent idea of the proprietary's intentions."

The "proprietary's intentions" obviously worked when put into effect as, before the expiration of the second 10 year contract, the beneficiaries agreed in July 1914 to continue their arrangement via a Company structure, known as Moonee Valley Proprietary Ltd.

An insight into how Moonee Valley had fared financially to that point can be gained from correspondence in *The Age* newspaper on June 20, 1916. It began with a Letter to the Editor, from *"One of the Public"*, who claimed that figures proved proprietary racing was too expensive; with the writer asking Mr Hiskens to reveal the Balance Sheet and divulge the amount of capital he had put into Moonee Valley.

Two days later Mr Hiskens' reply was published, stating that Moonee Valley racecourse was the property of Moonee Valley Pty Ltd, a Company consisting of eight persons. He said the course had been in existence for 33 years with varying fortunes; the capital invested in the racing venture was in excess of £100,000; and that the distribution to shareholders was £300 per year. He added that the racing track had been remodelled three times, including an occasion in the last decade when 16 acres were purchased (which included about half a mile of street frontage) to make the track nine furlongs in circumference. He also noted that in the previous year £8,000 was raised at Moonee Valley for "charitable or public funds."

Like other sporting clubs at the time, Moonee Valley was loudly promoting such charitable contributions to assuage the Government which, by mid 1915, was bringing increasing pressure on raceclubs to support the war effort. Even the VRC came under close scrutiny to curtail its operations, so considering the principal Club was under the microscope, the future of racing was even more bleak for lesser credentialled clubs – and that included a proprietary club like Moonee Valley.

The VRC argued that many people would be unemployed if racing ceased, and, to further boost its chances of being able to conduct meetings, decreed that all net profits from Flemington would be paid into patriotic funds. The VATC was quick to adopt the same strategy, but Victorian Premier Sir Alexander Peacock still considered that too much manpower and money was tied up in racing. After a review, many race clubs – particularly the pony clubs and lesser known proprietary courses – lost dates. The VRC and VATC escaped without any changes – but Moonee Valley had three of its meetings curtailed. It was in this climate – and fearful of further Government cutbacks – that the Cox family decided in 1917 to abandon the track's proprietary status and make a positive step for its survival by making Moonee Valley a fully fledged Club.

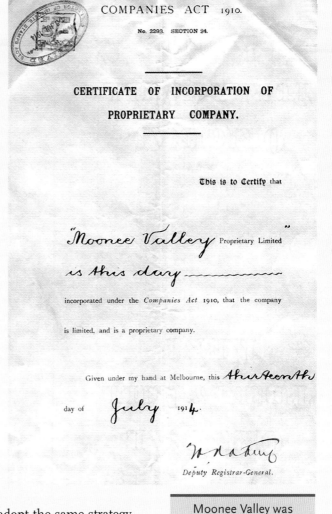

COMPANIES ACT 1910.

No. 2293. SECTION 24.

CERTIFICATE OF INCORPORATION OF PROPRIETARY COMPANY.

This is to Certify that

"Moonee Valley" Proprietary Limited

is this day

incorporated under the *Companies Act* 1910, that the company

is limited, and is a proprietary company.

Given under my hand at Melbourne, this *thirteenth*

day of *July* 1914.

W. J. Raking

Deputy Registrar-General.

Moonee Valley was incorporated as a Proprietary Company in 1914.

A CLUB IS BORN

Alister Clark ...
inaugural Chairman of
Moonee Valley Racing
Club.

The inaugural Moonee Valley Racing Club Committee was formed at Hosie's Hotel on March 26, 1917.

World-renowned rosarian Mr Alister Clark was elected Chairman and Arthur Hiskens was appointed Secretary, with an annual salary of £700 and a residence at the racecourse. Mr J. F. Feehan (a son of Richard Feehan, who had owned the racecourse site) was appointed Vice-Chairman with other Committee Members comprising Messrs J. B. McArthur, A. Anderson and T. R. Bloomfield.

General conditions under which the Club was to be conducted were read and approved by the Committee at their next meeting a week later. It was resolved that the new Club, which would take control forthwith, would consist of "about 30 Effective Members (later to be known as Executive Members) and an indefinite number of 'Stand Members' or 'Reserve Members'."

It was also agreed that the exact number of Effective Members would be determined at a later date and that a Committee would be formed from this segment of Membership to "administer the affairs of the Club". The Reserve Members were granted the same privileges as the Effective Members except that they had "no vote or voice in the administration and affairs of the Club". The subscription fee for both groups of Members was £5/5/- (including Amusement Tax), but this was subsequently reduced to £4/4/- after further Committee discussion later that year.

The Committee decreed "that in the event of any one of the Effective Members resigning or giving up his Membership, his place shall be filled by a ballot of remaining Effective Members".

It was also decided that "half of the number of the Committee will retire each year but will be eligible for re-election. Should any Member of the original Committee of the Club lose his position as a Member of Committee through resignation or by being defeated at an election of Committee, he shall be appointed a Life Member of the Club."

The new Club agreed to lease the racecourse on racedays from Moonee Valley Pty Ltd for a term of 21 years with the Company having the use of the land when it was not being used for racing. Should any other club wish to use the course, it would be charged at the rate of 25% of nett profit, "except in the case of charity meetings, pure and simple".

The general conduct and policy of the Club was to be on the "same lines as during the past 15 years, except for any innovation that in the opinion of the Committee will improve the status of the Club". The rental for the 21 year period was not to exceed ten percent of the capital value of the racecourse which had been fixed at £80,000 for a seven year term, with Moonee Valley Pty Ltd having the right to a re-evaluation of the land – apart from improvements – every seven years.

Other topics for the inaugural Committee included a gymkhana to be conducted at the track on May 24 to celebrate the proclamation of the City of Essendon and Empire Day. It was to be staged in conjunction with Oaklands Hunt Club to aid Lady Stanley's appeal for the British Red Cross.

Such was the interest in the impending gymkhana (complete with "spinning jennies", being a version of the lucky spinning wheel) that a Mr Geo. Horn wrote to the Committee seeking permission to run a match race between his draught horse "Alawa" and "Polly Crate", owned by Mr C. Knapes, for a £25 side wager. On obtaining advice from the Club's solicitor, Secretary Hiskens advised Mr Horn that the race could be conducted "under conditions approved by Committee". Unfortunately, we are none the wiser as to who finished £25 the richer as the result does not appear in official records!

Other "business" included donations of £25 for "soldiers at Langwarrin" and £10 "for tobacco for soldiers in France".

The fledgling Club held its first Annual Meeting on April 18, 1918, in the Boardroom of the Victoria Racing Club, when it revealed that the Club had donated its profit of £4,885 to "patriotic and charitable purposes". Figures produced for the second AGM in 1919 showed that profits had increased to a total of £10,973.

Profitability continued in 1920 with the Club achieving gross revenue of £27,000. After allowing for contingencies such as rent (£8,000), donations (£3,600) and expenditure of £2,000 on improvements, the new Club had asset backing in excess of £16,000. Income included £3,000 in advance fees from bookmakers and Chairman Clark, who had visited the pro-Totalisator environment of New Zealand during the year, closed the annual meeting with a comment that would have brought ringing endorsement from Victoria's bookmaking fraternity.

His final comment at the third Annual meeting was: "I hope we avoid getting the Totalisator."

It was a message that he would continue to preach even when it became obvious that the Totalisator was indeed the Golden Egg for racing.

Trotting, which had been conducted on grass at Moonee Valley when it was under the control of Sam Cox – who also agreed to polo and Plumpton (greyhound) racing as well at his course –

became a topic in 1921 when representatives of the trotting fraternity sought permission to race there again. They were told that trotting facilities would be unavailable "at present". (Little did they realise it would be a wait of some 55 years!) But polo was well and truly on the agenda with the Club agreeing at the 1921 AGM to build a first class polo facility so that "we shall be able to have the best and most spectacular game possible – a game that people will go a long way to see".

Chairman Clark added : "This little game of polo is one of the things that make one regret getting old."

As an afterthought, he also made reference to a proposed new race when he told Members:

"I did desire to touch upon one thing that slipped my memory. We have been hoping to get a weight-for-age race at Moonee Valley.

"*I think there is no doubt that in our next Cup program we will be able to have a good weight-for-age race. The distance has yet to be decided, but the stake will be £1,000.*

"*I think you will all be glad to hear that.*"

It was the first official reference to what was to become Australasia's

Moonee Valley Racing Club's first letterhead. The Club was based at Kirk's Bazaar, a well known horse-trading market in Bourke Street West. Established by James Bowie Kirk in the early 1840's, Kirk's Bazaar was quickly adopted as a rendezvous by the racing fraternity in general. (Note the above message was signed by Archie Cox.)

greatest weight-for-age race – a race which would eventually become part of an elite international racing championship.

The Chairman also provided further comments on the introduction of a Totalisator, again relying on his experiences after another visit to New Zealand.

"Having been in New Zealand during the Summer I saw some racing there and I really felt on returning home it was a pleasure to be on our little course instead of having to battle with the Tote.

"The Tote may have its advantages but it also has its disadvantages, I know it has one in particular. All those fine horses were taken out onto the course, and the boys also, 20 minutes at the very least before the start – simply to induce the public to put their money on the horses. That is one thing we escape by not having the Tote."

While the Moonee Valley Cup was still the biggest race for the Club, the Committee was true to its word in introducing the new event in 1922. Run over 9½ furlongs, and carrying a stake of £1,000, it was called the W. S. Cox Plate, in memory of Moonee Valley's founder. The Cup was worth £500 more than the inaugural Cox Plate, which attracted a good field of 14. The imported Violoncello, who had won the Caulfield Cup the previous year, won the inaugural Plate, so from the outset the race was won by a class horse.

Easingwold continued the trend in 1923 when he made amends for his second the previous year, but the Moonee Valley Cup still clearly held the limelight. The Cox Plate continued to be won by good horses and, even early, it was establishing a format of quality over quantity. The race in 1924 (won by the Governor's horse, The Night Patrol) attracted a field of only nine but two were scratched, while the following year (Manfred's) only seven runners accepted, and one of those did not run.

However, it was not the paucity of runners which attracted the attention of Chairman Clark when he reviewed activities for 1924 – rather the Chairman preferred to wax lyrically about the Earl of Stradbroke's victory with The Night Patrol:

"The demonstration when the Governor won was the most cordial that has ever been seen on a racecourse.

"It began in the grandstands and on the lawn and finished on the Flat where it was equally enthusiastic. This shows that the Governor, who is a true English gentleman and a thorough sportsman, was most popular and that everyone seemed to realise what a sportsman he is.

"We are extremely honored and pleased to have him win the race."

(**Ed Note:** Many years later Moonee Valley Chairman Bill Stutt was advised by Sir Phillip Payne-Galway that the artefacts owned by the Earl of Stradbroke were being auctioned in England. Among them was The Night Patrol's Cox Plate trophy, which the Club secured for about £7,000. It is now on display in the MVRC Committee Room.)

The Chairman's seeming obsession against the Totalisator (again drawing on his New Zealand experiences) continued with comments such as:

"I do not think the people who go to racing there find it any more profitable than they do here with regard to being able to bet. Seeing that you have to toil into and wait in the (Totalisator) queue eight times to get your money on and then repeat the process another eight times to collect I think you are fortunate in having bookmakers. (Hear, hear)

".... I think we are better off with the bookmaker than with the Totalisator."

The "toil" of being in a collect queue eight times in a day aside, the Chairman reported work was progressing well on a new grandstand worth £54,000, with plans afoot to erect a new public stand and ultimately link the two.

Heroic continued the run of class Cox Plate victors in 1926 – but the trend of small fields also continued as he had only three other runners to beat.

If the MVRC Committee was concerned, it was not documented in official Club Minutes. They continued to report on matters such as good profits and improvements in amenities. Such was the progress that one Member commented "the whole of the course available to the public is now covered with stands and other accommodation which enable all to view the race in complete comfort and without interruption. This new stand enables persons after seeing horses in the paddock, even if they are caught napping, to see the race without any discomfort – and to see it well."

Another lauded the track by noting that if he had a horse "it would always be running at Moonee Valley".

A clue that the Club was concerned about the number of Cox Plate runners in previous years is evident from the comments made by Alister Clark after the running of the race in 1927, which attracted 12 entries for 10 starters, a notable increase on numbers in previous years. Clark noted that the Cox Plate comprised a "really good field" and was "an excellent contest". He had made no such public comments about any Cox Plates previously and, from this distance, the fact that he saw fit to praise aspects of the 1927 race suggests that he had not wanted to draw attention to some of the earlier contests.

And of course, he could not let pass an opportunity to say he was "more confirmed than ever in my belief that we are very well off without the Totalisator".

In giving evidence before a Legislative Council Committee in November, 1928, Mr Hiskens told of the arrangements the Club entered into about leasing the course and improvements from the Cox family Company. During the hearing he also revealed that the Club had a Membership of 1270, including 60 Executive Members. The Committee, which also heard evidence from the representatives of the VRC, VATC, and the proprietary clubs of Epsom and Mentone, ruled that the VRC should control all racing; profits from racing should be used to boost facilities, stakes and amenities, and that there be a general rationalisation of the number of clubs, with particular emphasis on the closure of proprietary clubs.

Even though Moonee Valley was now wholly controlled by the Moonee Valley Racing Club and the eight shareholders in Moonee Valley Pty Ltd had no further control in racing at the track, a plan was conceived to better shore up the Club's chance of survival.

In what Chairman Clark described as "one of the most important events in the history of the Club", the MVRC purchased the racecourse and "attached lands" from Moonee Valley Pty Ltd for the sum of £160,000 in February, 1929. One of the conditions of the purchase was that the Cox Estate would keep £50,000 from the sale proceeds available in liquid assets for five years in the event the Club wished to borrow money for any new structures, such as a Totalisator building.

Alister Clark said at the annual meeting in April that the Club could pay more than "half cash and we can pay the balance, on which there is a very low rate of interest, whenever we are ready".

The property comprised the racecourse, the motor parks, some land on Pascoe Vale Road and several acres in West Brunswick, totalling more than 100 acres. In further justifying the decision, Mr Clark said that the money the Club had spent on improvements was practically no use to the Club unless it owned the course.

He said it was a "capital arrangement" – the Club had made a good bargain and "no harm has been done to the Estate in selling the property".

To ensure that no individual could profit in any way in the event the Club had to be wound up, the Committee resolved that all assets of the Club, after payment of all liabilities, would be "divided amongst and between such charitable institutions in Victoria" as the Committee saw fit. There was a further rider – if the Committee defaulted in its duty, the assets would be paid to the VRC Benevolent Fund Association.

The Club Treasurer, Mr W. Thomson, noted that the sale included all improvements made by the Club and the Cox family, which amounted to approximately £65,000. The Club now owned its own property and other assets worth £20,000 and had a liability of $70,000 at an interest rate of "only 6 percent".

With exquisite timing, Mr Thomson then said that from hereon those wishing to become Members would have to pay for that privilege. He said that there had never previously been an entrance fee, because "the persons paying the entrance fee would have the same claim on the assets of the Club.

"Now that this Rule has been passed that no person can get any benefit, the Committee has taken the necessary steps to charge an entrance fee, and that fee has been fixed at £10/10/-.

"I do not think anyone will cavil at that."

The Sun News Pictorial summed up the purchase in the following manner:

"The Moonee Ponds course gains the distinction of being the headquarters of the only leading Club with the exception of the Australian Jockey Club, which owns Warwick Farm, that owns its own course."

The Cox Plate, unchanged in value at £1,000, though attracting some quality runners, was still lacking in quantity. Only nine faced the starter in 1928, while Nightmarch's success in 1929 was in the second field of four in four years.

At the time, the Government was discussing the (on-course) Totalisator Bill, but not everyone was looking forward to its introduction. One such person was Executive Member Mr R. E. Hayes, who said at the 1930 annual meeting that a "very heavy expenditure will be incurred in establishing the Totalisator – and that is one of the chief objections to it".

That other well known Tote objector, Mr Clark, added "whatever the Totalisator does it does not increase betting". However, obviously realising its imminent introduction, he noted that "it is recognised that we have the right class of bookmaker and I do not see why they should not work in conjunction with the Totalisator".

By now feeling the effects of the Depression, with a considerable decline in attendances, the Club was forced to reduce some admittance prices and make reductions in stakemoney. Moonee Valley's racing revenue had shown a marked decline, being down from £26,000 in 1929 to only £11,646/10/- in 1930. This prompted Treasurer Thomson to say: "This is a time when politicians and individuals have to look at their balance sheets, and they have to balance the ledger, and until they do that, then God help Australia."

Ironically, despite this negative trend, it was also a time when Moonee Valley had to find £30,000 to install the new on-course Totalisator.

"Club Stallion" dies

Moonee Valley Racing Club sustained a serious loss when the thoroughbred stallion, Headwind, met with injuries which necessitated his destruction. Headwind, whose wins had included the 1919 Standish Hcp, had been secured by the Club on his retirement, at a high price as a stallion "in furtherance of a commendable scheme to improve the general utility horses of the district. Headwind's services were placed at the disposal of owners of mares other than thoroughbreds, at a low fee". The report added that Headwind had carried off the highest honors at the Royal Agricultural Show on several occasions.
– *The Australasian, July 1, 1922*

A PERIOD OF CONSOLIDATION

Totalisators – legal and illegal – had been a point of contention within Victoria for many years.

The first Bill for a legal Tote was introduced in 1880 but was defeated. Amazingly, considering (with hindsight) the fortunes that both Governments and the Racing Industry have received from Tote operations, it was to take about 50 years before the Victorian Government passed the legislation. This meant that Victoria became the last State in Australia with such a facility.

Illegal Totes of all dimensions abounded in Victoria from the 1880's. The most simple was a one-person operation requiring the customer to select one of the runners penned on a sheet of paper, by putting a mark next to the runner. After the race, the operator would deduct his 10% commission from the total pool. He would then declare a dividend by dividing the remainder of the pool by the number of marks on his sheet against the winner. (As likely as not the operator might add a couple more marks after the result was known and give himself some of the dividend as well!)

The most famous illegal Tote was that of John Wren, which started in Collingwood in the 1890's, with Wren allegedly funding the operation from money he won on Carbine in the 1891 Melbourne Cup. Wren's commission was 10%, which provided the basis for his fortune. This included successful racehorses (Murmur won the 1904 Caulfield Cup); pony tracks in Melbourne; private racecourses in Queensland and boxing/wrestling stadiums in Sydney and Melbourne. All of these businesses continued well after his Tote was finally closed down in 1906.

Prior to the Government passing the necessary Tote legislation, representatives of the VRC, VATC, MVRC and the Williamstown Racing Clubs met to discuss the issue. They agreed that VRC Secretary Arthur Kewney, who had previous experience as an administrator in Western Australia and South Australia – which had Totalisator operations when he was there – be sent overseas to determine the best Tote machine for Victoria. He returned with a recommendation to use what was known as the Julius machine, named after English-born inventor George Julius, who came to Australia as a baby.

Julius, who became Chairman of what is now the CSIRO, was educated in New Zealand and began his professional career in Western Australia in 1896. He stumbled upon the Totalisator after developing a vote-counting machine which would give an election result "without any human intervention". Julius decided to adapt it for use as a racecourse Tote after the Government failed to recognise it as a vote counting machine.

A history of Julius, "*From Tote to CAD*" says the inventor had never seen a racecourse, but found the project "of great interest". After forming Automatic Totalisators Ltd in Sydney, his first Tote was installed at Ellerslie racecourse in Auckland in 1913. Many other overseas countries were quick to also use his invention.

In the biography, Julius' son, Awdry makes reference to how the continuing design work kept the engineering firm of Julius Poole & Gibson in the black during the Great Depression. It was at this time that Victoria was installing his machines.

It was estimated that Victoria's new Tote machine – which required a room of 10 x 10 metres – would cost £60,000, to be divided by the number of

Arthur Vaughan Hiskens
.... the "worthy Secretary who will carry us through".

North Hill Opened

Among the innovations to be introduced at Saturday's meeting is the full use for the first time of the new reserve at the north west corner of the Club's property to be known as the North Hill. This has been in use merely as a place from which to view a race .. but on Saturday it will be a fully equipped reserve capable of accommodating 8,000 onlookers. A charge of four shillings will be made for admission to the North Hill as compared with three shillings to the flat.
– *The Age, October 19, 1927*

clubs using the machine. Apart from the shared cost of the equipment, the individual clubs also had to erect Tote houses where people could place their bets.

The deduction for all bets was set at 10%, to be shared equally between the Government and the club conducting the meeting. (Earlier the Federal Government had proposed that it would take a separate 13% slice, deeming totalisators to be lotteries, but this was overturned by a ruling from the High Court.) The base betting unit was set at five shillings, which, amazingly, is still the minimum some 70 years later. By comparison, the Cox Plate stake has risen from £650 to $1.5 million in the same period.

The MVRC Committee approved plans to start building its Tote-house in February 1931 and only months later – on August 19 – the Totalisator was used legally for the first time in metropolitan Victoria at a Yarra Glen and Lilydale Hunt Club meeting held at Moonee Valley. It operated from three sites – in the Stand enclosure, on the North Hill and on the Flat.

The Argus reported the day after the meeting:

"The Totalisator acted as a magnet to racing patrons and the attendance was the largest at a Hunt Club fixture for years.

"Long before betting opened on the first race, a large crowd had gathered to study the new betting medium and as soon as the selling windows were opened for business there was a rush of speculators."

Despite the fact that the newspaper praised the betting initiative – and the public quickly accepted it – Chairman Clark noted "that except for the delays in both investing and collecting, it has worked fairly well. Perhaps these will be modified, if not eliminated, in time."

Proof of the Club's true feelings about the future of the Tote was literally uncovered more than 40 years later.

It occurred when the original Tote house on the Flat was demolished to make way for the new trotting track in 1976. Upon demolishing the old Tote house it was discovered that it had been erected using "railway sleepers and used building material". George Nye, MVRC Racing Manager for 10 years between 1974 and 1983, said that former Assistant Secretary Les Vivien (who worked under A.V. Hiskens and W. S. Cox III) had told him that such materials were used because neither Chairman Clark nor Secretary Hiskens "believed the Tote would last more than 12 months".

Despite the public fervour with the new betting machine, away from the racetrack there was no such optimism. Instead of improving, the general economy was getting worse with the result that the Club's profit for 1932 was less than half that of the £6,700 the previous year. Treasurer Thomson said that he had heard that the deduction from the Totalisator was going to be increased and, if that were true, racing would be ruined.

Typically, Alister Clark did not have kind words for the Tote, with the sarcastic comment "However fast it works you will realise that it cannot possibly be as fast as the bookmakers".

But there were much greater issues than the Tote affecting racing. The grip of the Great Depression was tightening. The price of Australia's main exports such as wheat and wool were to be slashed by almost 50 percent and by 1932 the unemployment rate had hit 30%. People in their hundreds were applying for one job and roaming the countryside looking for work. This naturally had a flow-on effect on racing – in attendances and betting – and clubs were forced to prune prizemoney levels. Not even the Melbourne Cup was immune, as the stake dropped from £12,429 in 1930 to £7,200 from 1931-34, while the Cox Plate stake, which had remained at £1,000 until 1930, was cut to £650 in 1931. The actual prizemoney (not including the £100 trophy) did not get back to the 1930 level for another 11 years! Such was not the case, however, for the jewel in the crown, the Moonee Valley Gold Cup. While its stake was reduced by £500 in 1930, it was back up to a record level of £3,000 in the Club's 50th Anniversary year of 1934.

Not even the appearance of Phar Lap in the Spring of 1930 could boost attendances – less than 20,000 saw him win, whereas, in previous years, Moonee Valley Cup/Cox Plate day was attracting crowds in the order of 27,000. Given Phar Lap's enormous profile, this was a clear indication that the racing public was hurting.

On the other hand, Alister Clark was confident that Moonee Valley had the answer.

While admitting that some Club Members had been forced to economise – temporarily, he hoped – his positive spin was: "We have not got our backs to the wall and, even if we had, we need not worry as our worthy Secretary, Mr Hiskens, would carry us through." If only Prime Minister Lyons had known!

Surprisingly, Mr Clark by now had some praise for the Tote. He noted it was operating a lot more smoothly and such was its popularity that the investments per head at Moonee Valley were considerably larger than even in Sydney. Further proof of public acceptance was that Tote facilities had been extended and extra staff had been put on.

Indeed, such was its popularity, that new Club treasurer, Mr W. S. (Bill) Cox – the grandson of the founder of Moonee Valley, and a son of W. S. Cox the amateur rider – pointed out that the Government share from the Totalisator revenue in 1933 was almost £27,000.

Bill Cox, who was to play a dominating role at Moonee Valley in future years, announced the following year that the Club was now the absolute owner of the racecourse having paid the balance of the loan outstanding to the beneficiaries of the Cox estate. In addition, it had managed to pay off "a little" of the cost of installing the Totalisator. It was a remarkable financial feat for the Club to have achieved in such a short space of time, particularly considering the negative economic impact of the Depression.

The Club was rocked by the death of Arthur Hiskens, their indefatigable Secretary, in 1935. He was described as "a man of great ability and intellect and one who has given great service to Moonee Valley Racing Club ... one of the kindest and best fellows you could meet ... a man who could see room for improvements and then have them executed and bring everything into one harmonious whole."

Treasurer Bill Cox, who had been trained by Hiskens, was promoted to Secretary on a wage of £900 a year plus £100 allowance. At his first annual meeting, it was announced that Club Membership fees were to rise from 10 guineas to 15 guineas and that Members' medallions would be issued for the 1936 racing season in lieu of leather tickets. The Committee also voted to perpetuate the memory of Arthur Hiskens by naming the £1,000 steeplechase run in September, after him.

General community confidence was improving by the late 30's – evidenced by the fact that some 29,000 attended the Moonee Valley Gold Cup meeting in 1937 betting a record £57,000 through the Totalisator. The Club was also making extensive improvements to amenities, including the purchase of five houses in Thomas and Wilson Streets, which were demolished to improve the traffic flow from the Members' Motor Paddock, while at the same time giving more room to North Hill patrons. Chairman Clark made particular reference in his review of 1937 to "ladies, in particular, becoming great supporters of ours in the last few years". This was because the Club now had a "ladies' Tote", a move which was lauded by Executive Member, Mr T. M. Burke.

Cold vegies get the cold shoulder

The topic of vegetables was tabled at a recent Committee meeting. It was decreed that vegetables were to be served more promptly at Committee Luncheon and only one man was to be in charge of the wine at the Luncheons.
- *Committee Note, Sept 1928*

"Ring Ins" in the Ring

In view of the fact that a number of spurious £10 notes are at present in circulation, no notes of that denomination will be accepted at the ticket offices or change offices at Moonee Valley today.
- *Argus, October 27, 1928*

He said at the annual meeting:

"As a Member and frequent patron of the Club it is gratifying to me to hear the Chairman say the attendance of ladies has increased.

"I confess it caused me some dismay, as I suppose it did many others, to have the ladies ask me to invest a small sum of money for them when I was betting. There is now nothing to prevent the fair sex from entire participation in the racing business.

"It does my heart good to see a long queue of ladies, particularly at the pay-out windows collecting their thousands and enjoying the sport."

Committee also made a big decision in 1937 with regards to the broadcasting of information from the course, ordering that no starting prices or Totalisator dividends could be relayed.

Given the figures produced by the Totalisator, the Committee had no qualms in acting on a submission by Automatic Totalisators for a new main Tote house incorporating 40 selling windows facing the betting ring and an equal number of paying windows at the rear. Patrons at the main Spring meeting the following year were greeted with the longest Totalisator house in Victoria – all 196 feet of it – with every selling window a winner for the Club and the Government.

The last Committee meeting for the 30's also decided to honor their Chairman by changing the name of the March Quality handicap to that of the Alister Clark Stakes "as a small token of appreciation for the wonderful work that our Chairman has devoted to the Club".

Further improvements at the Valley were soon put on hold with the outbreak of World War II as, like other racing clubs, the MVRC announced its intention to subscribe as much money as it could towards the Patriotic Funds. Caulfield and Williamstown racecourses were taken over by the Federal Government for military purposes and, at one stage, Moonee Valley, too, was being earmarked for the same purpose, but was deemed unsuitable because of possible flooding.

Victorian raceclubs again acted quickly to appease the Federal and State Governments. They used the same strategy as had been used in 1914, proclaiming that racing was a big employer; it could generate money for Patriotic Funds and also provide a vital recreational outlet.

Once again, they would minimise spending and maximise donations to the War effort. Such was the feeling that the MVRC Committee set aside specific meetings from which all profits were directed to War funds. In a further display of cost cutting, in 1940 the Club decided to discontinue official luncheons for the duration of the War. Not even the course floral arrangements escaped scrutiny! Concerned that upkeep of the flowerbeds was costing money the Club could not spare, Secretary Cox informed Members that this was the reason they "are possibly not quite so good as usual".

The Club pledged to "contribute the greatest amount possible to such worthy funds as the Red Cross and Comforts Fund, and to all War Loans. All these things help to make the lot of our soldiers, sailors and airmen as free as humanely possible from hardships and discomforts".

By way of showing support for the VRC's reasoning to the Government to allow racing to continue, Alister Clark said: "I am not asking for anything for Moonee Valley but surely the Government must realise that every additional race meeting held at Flemington means more money for our local hospitals and also more money for the VRC to distribute to funds helping the War effort?"

Mention was also made of the example set by "His Majesty, who has manifested his views on the matter (of racing during war time) by continuing to race horses."

The MVRC Treasurer, Mr E. G. Brook, announced that operations for 1941 had resulted in about £8,200 being donated to Patriotic Funds and charitable institutions, making a total contribution of almost £17,000 since the War commenced. The Club had also permitted the Deputy Director of Recruiting to use course amplifiers at the November meeting in 1941 for recruiting purposes.

As the intensity of the War increased, with Singapore falling and Darwin being attacked – combined with horrific reports of the tens of thousands of troops who had been either killed or taken captive – it was no surprise to see racing further reined-in by order of Federal and State Governments. Racing in Victoria was prohibited on Public Holidays and midweek, and then, by edict of Prime Minister Curtin in September, 1942, no racing was permitted in any Australian capital cities on the first Saturday of the month.

Alister Clark said that the purpose of race-less Saturdays each month was hard to follow but the Club recognised the difficulties of the Prime Minister and hoped that the ban would be lifted as soon as possible. He said that racing was in fact "in a very flourishing condition" – a record 30,410 attended Moonee Valley Cup day that year. He said the Club's distribution to the War effort in the 12 months was £9,600 taking the total to £24,667 – and another £13,000 had been placed in War Loans during the year.

However, the Club adopted a further austerity measure by omitting the word "gold" from the Moonee Valley Cup title with a "£100 trophy" being substituted for the traditional £200 gold cup. Such prudent financial "housekeeping" was paying off as Club treasurer Brook reported in 1943 that stakes had been maintained at a record level; a record 33,250 saw Amana win the 22nd Cox Plate; and ever increasing donations were being made to Patriotic Funds and War Loans.

In an effort to appease owners during those trying times, Moonee Valley reduced Acceptance fees for all races in 1944 to "well under" 1% of the stakemoney "to make racing as cheap as possible for the hard pressed owners".

The word "gold" was back in vogue for the first peacetime Moonee Valley Gold Cup and W. S. Cox Plate in six years, on Saturday October 27, 1945. Despite it being a rainy day, it didn't stop 31,060 seeing the first "leg" of a unique double in both feature races. Valcurl, who won the £3,500 Gold Cup, was to repeat the effort the following year, while Flight took the £1,500 Cox Plate, a feat she emulated two years later.

As improvements to course amenities had been deferred during the War years, Moonee Valley quickly set about upgrading facilities, with the Committee agreeing to expenditure of £100,000, about which Alister Clark said: "It sounds incredible to me to be able to approach that amount." Secretary Cox was sent to the USA to gain ideas from American and English tracks including the "Camera Eye (photo finish), starting gates, TeleFilm (Stewards' Patrol film) and car parking". At home, the course amplifying system was replaced at a cost of £1,453 – and the ice chest in the office was upgraded to a gas refrigerator!

Course Broadcasts

In addition to more amplifiers around the racing track, MVRC will install 27 amplifiers in refreshment rooms, bars and on the Tote house and at other vantage points. They will serve as a warning that a race is about to start, but if persons taking refreshments prefer, they will be able to remain seated and listen to a description of the race by the Course Broadcaster.
- *Sun, September 17, 1946*

TAXES, TOTES AND TOUTS

Now the austere times were over, the Club also looked at avenues of increasing revenue – as did the Government, which increased its share of Tote revenue from 5% to 7%. Alister Clark said that while the Club had spent £45,000 on Totalisator buildings and machinery it was now faced with a return "not at all commensurate with this outlay".

Showing that things have not changed much over time, he also observed that he had no idea where the extra money from the new Tote deduction would go.

"We know it is in the hands of the Government, but, as in the case of money for taxes, such as the automobile drivers' licences, which amount to £80,000, the Country Roads Board, to whom it is really due, does not get it.

"Speaking for myself in this matter ... it strikes me that having spent that huge amount on the Totalisator and taking all the risks of failure, we should have been allowed to handle that money, because every penny we receive from it ... absolutely goes to Charity or to the benefit of racing."

He added that he did not think the Government "would have jumped in and helped us if we had had a dead loss on the Totalisator".

The Federal Government, too, was criticised by Club Treasurer Brook, who said that Prime Minister Curtin had "clapped a very punitive" tax rate of 4/7d, called an Entertainment Tax, on entrance charges during the War to act as a deterrent for people to attend and now that the War was over it was "particularly obnoxious" that the tax was continuing.

He then added that Moonee Valley alone had contributed more than £80,000 to the War effort, and "certainly the racing public should not be penalised by taxes and knocked about by the taxing authorities".

It was shown that the six city clubs (VRC, VATC, MVRC, Williamstown, Mentone and Epsom) had paid more than £900,000 in State and Federal taxes for 1944-45, and that did not take into account the taxes paid by country clubs nor the trotting associations.

However, the Club, too, didn't mind upping the ante to suit itself – bookmakers' fees were raised by £5 to £30 in the Stand Reserve, while those fielding in the North Hill had to pay £15 for the right – an increase of £2/10/-. Another change for the bookies was that betting boards were to be introduced in the Stand Betting Reserve – and it was compulsory for every fielder in that area to use them. Not even Servicemen escaped the eye of Club accountancy staff. During the War, people in uniform had been permitted free admission but from July 31, 1946, that privilege was rescinded.

Among the innovations introduced upon the return of Mr Cox from America was the "Photo Patrol", which would eventually film a complete race. The system prototype took a film of the final stages of all races from the home turn to the winning post and thereafter Stewards could view the film 10 minutes later – once it had been developed in the specially equipped darkroom.

"If the film confirms the Stewards' opinion that a rider has broken any racing rules the Stewards will have little difficulty in determining whether the infringement was accidental or wilful and make their decision accordingly."

Racing quickly found a new confidence with Moonee Valley Cup day drawing a record crowd of nearly 46,000 in 1947. As crowds went up, so did prizemoney. The Cup went to £5,000 and the prize for the Alister Clark Stakes, first run in 1939, shot up to the same amount, making it the richest mile race in Victoria. In explaining the prize boost for the Alister Clark Stakes, it was "to honor our loved and esteemed Chairman who has been our inspiration and

Captain of the Ship for 29 successive years". The trophy for the winner was to include for the first time a silver rose bowl and a bouquet of flowers grown by Mr Clark, a world–respected rosarian. Meanwhile, the Cox Plate, which had been won by some of the best horses of the era, languished around £1,500. Unfortunately, neither the Federal nor State Governments had rescinded the Entertainment Tax or the extra levy on the Tote.

Another of Mr Cox's overseas "imports", the wooden starting stall – which could be dismantled in only 45 seconds – was gaining in popularity in 1948, to the extent that several clubs had copied them. The stalls had been used for the first time at Moonee Valley in April that year when 13 starters had been "sent away in perfect order" in the Epping Handicap.

Starter Mr Frank Dempsey said: "There was no delay and the stalls also eliminated a certain amount of interference which occurs at a start when some horses jump in and other horses jump out."

The stalls were in effect wooden framework partitions being 3ft. 11in. high with a 3ft. space between them in which to place the horse. The horses walked into their barrier and jumped once an "elastic strand" was released at the front of the stalls. At the time, no other clubs in Victoria were using starting stalls, preferring to wait for the introduction of the "American Gate" style stalls, which were the forerunners to those on racecourses today.

One club to copy the system of the stalls was New Zealand's Canterbury Jockey Club – but Moonee Valley also "imported" an idea from the Dominion that year. It was described as "the New Zealand system of pumping beer through plastic tubes" which was installed in several racecourse bars "with considerable success". And for any patrons who might have lingered there too long, thus affecting their judgment in a close finish, the new photo-finish camera was operating, and had in fact recorded the first dead-heat for first in Victoria in a race at Moonee Valley.

Some other fruits of Mr Cox's overseas visit were also in place by 1948. Special fire sprinklers had been installed in the wooden stand and the Public Tea Room, which Mr Cox said made Moonee Valley the only racecourse in the world with such a system fully installed.

The Photo Patrol was also in daily use, involving five trained cameramen in specially built towers at strategic positions around the track to take the film.

Bookmakers' fees also shot up again – to £115 on the Rails and £50 off the rails – and there were plenty of them swinging their bags at the Valley that season. They numbered 314 – and all of them were paying 10/- for the right to use their betting boards.

The Club's founding Chairman, Alister Clark, died suddenly in January, 1949, aged 84. In acknowledging his contribution to the Club the Committee recorded: "It is largely due to his wisdom, foresight and his extensive knowledge of racing that the Club is in the position that it is today. Mr Clark's charm, courtesy and kindness endeared him to all who knew him and most of all to the Members of his Committee."

Mr John F. Feehan, who had been Vice-Chairman of the Club since its formation was elected new Chairman. The Committee deemed in May of 1949 to rename the Glenroy Stakes, run in September, after their new Chairman. However, Mr Feehan was never to see the race carrying his name as he died, aged 85, in June, 1949. New Chairman Mr C. F. (Charlie) Taylor described Mr Feehan as someone who had been connected with Moonee Valley all his life.

"His father farmed the land in the early days and when it was made into a racecourse in the 1880's John took such great interest in the racecourse that in 1901 he became a Steward. When the present Club was formed in 1917 he was elected to the original Committee, of which he remained a Member until he died. No more courteous, kindly and upright man ever lived."

Photo finishes

Permission has been granted for the construction of camera apparatus for race finishes on top of the stand (sic). Films of races from start to finish were another innovation looked for in the near future. At present, a race could be filmed from the home turn and the objective was to have the negative available to the Stewards in 10 minutes and avoid delays when protests had to be considered.
- *The Age, May 31, 1947*

Photographs were developed in 51 seconds during tests with the photo finish camera at Moonee Valley yesterday. The camera will be used at the Valley for the first time today.
- *Argus, January 24, 1948*

The Judge or the camera could not separate El Faloos and Gay Silhouette at the finish of the second division of the Seaside Handicap at Moonee Valley. It was the first dead heat for first since the camera had been installed in Melbourne.
- *Argus, May 10, 1948*

On a sterner note, the Government "grab" of Totalisator money was still a very sore point and Club Treasurer Brook outlined very clearly what was intended when the Totalisator Act had been introduced.

He said the commission the Clubs retained had to be used in the following manner:

Firstly, defraying the cost of:
- Installation of any Totalisator/s;
- The construction of the necessary buildings to be used in relation thereto;
- The upkeep and working or such Totalisator/s;
- The maintenance of the racecourse on which such Totalisator/s is installed.

Secondly, providing prizes for horseracing, trotting racing or pony racing.

He said that after the War finished – during which time all racing Clubs had contributed all their profits to War Funds – the Government considered that as societies such as the Red Cross and Comforts Fund no longer needed the help of the racing clubs, it was an excellent opportunity for the Government to secure additional revenue from racing. The Government had promised to return the extra 2% they had taken once clubs were in a position to reconstruct their courses. Despite a deputation to Premier Dunstan, this had not been forthcoming. The Club provided figures which clearly illustrated the massive hidden costs. In 1949, for example, when Moonee Valley raced on 14 days, it paid more than £13,500 per day in taxation and other costs – about double what was distributed daily in stakes.

The breakdown was: 7% Totalisator Tax (£112,000); Totalisator fractions, i.e. the money left after dividends are rounded down (£16,000); while Entertainment, Licence and Income taxes amounted to £62,000.

Regardless of these imposts, the Club was still able to continue with improvements, which included a new centre car park in 1950 and new betting ring. In addition, looking to the future, the Club had purchased a property of about 830 acres at Roxburgh Park, Somerton, for £42 an acre. It was described as a property that "would be an investment and in addition could be used as a racecourse if the Club ever had to vacate Moonee Valley". Initially, it was leased for farming purposes by brothers W. M. ("Murray") and J. M. (John) Cox, great grandsons of Moonee Valley's founder, "Sam" Cox. Subsequently, it was operated as a commercial farm by the MVRC, with Murray Cox as the farm manager until he took over an administrative role at Moonee Valley, which led to him becoming Club Secretary. The land was then again leased to a private farmer before eventually being sold some 40 years later for a massive profit by the Club for housing development. Ideally accessible by train, the land was well drained, situated in attractive surroundings and was "large enough for anything ever likely to be required".

In the interim, the Club was doing very nicely where it was, extending Tote facilities and increasing the bet denomination windows, with only minimum bets of £5 being permitted at one of them. At that stage, the average bet per head, per meeting was £4/10/-.

Chairman Taylor used a different tack in the ongoing snipe over the Tote tax grab – this time it was that the tax had reduced attendances and driven many punters to patronise the illegal Starting Price bookmakers. He said: "If the Government had wanted to increase Starting Price betting they could not have done it in a better way. Big bettors now place their bets without going near a racecourse and get a 10% discount if their horse loses. We hope some sanity prevails soon."

Sydney clubs had been using the "American Gate" starting system by 1950 but Moonee Valley was still unprepared to change to the newer system when the VRC called a meeting about starting stalls in 1952. To that stage, the stalls had been successfully used in all weathers with less than a half percent of mishaps or accidents "none of which were in any way serious". Defending its decision not to use them, the Club said its stalls enabled 19 horses to start at most barriers and it did not want the new mechanised system because fields would be limited to 14 and the track would be affected by the new heavier gates which were towed by a tractor. (The Club inevitably bowed to "progress" in the mid 1950's, and their maximum field size was cut to 16.)

The sudden death of Chairman Taylor, about three weeks before the 1952 Cox Plate, resulted in Major General Sir Samuel "Ginger" Burston being elected Chairman with Mr A. J. Moir as Vice-Chairman. It was during their reign that the Cox Plate finally received some due recognition – in terms of both prizemoney and public acknowledgment. This came about when the Club announced a massive boost in Cox Plate stakemoney in 1953 – virtually doubling it to £4,000, making it the richest weight-for-age race in Australia. From a prizemoney perspective, the Cox Plate was now on a par with the Moonee Valley Cup. In making the announcement, Sir Samuel Burston said that in the past it had been the policy of the Club to give a large stake for the Cup and less than half to the Cox Plate. He said that his Committee felt that the field for the Cup would be the same, irrespective of the stake, and had decided, therefore, to take £1,000 from the Cup prize (reducing it to £4,000) and adding this amount, plus another $1,000, to the Cox Plate. This made the Cox Plate a race worth £4,000, which "is fitting to the class of horses competing".

He pointed out that, since its foundation, the Cox Plate had drawn the best fields in the land with winners such as Phar Lap (twice), Manfred, The Night Patrol, Amounis, Chatham (twice), Ajax, Heroic, Beau Vite (twice), Flight (twice), Tranquil Star (twice), Delta and Hydrogen (who won the race when it was worth £2,100 in 1952 and saluted again in 1953 when it was worth £4,000).

In announcing the stakes boost the Chairman said that the rollcall of Cox Plate winners was "a list that no other race in Australia can excel".

The Chairman also announced an increase in the number of Members from 1,500 "which has stood for some years" to 1,550, hoping that current Members would not be "inconvenienced in any way by this action". A determining factor in settling upon Membership numbers was the number of motor cars used by Members. Noting that the Members' Motor Park was usually filled to capacity on big race days, a section of the Flat Motor Park was set aside for use by Members, being a convenience for those "arriving after the commencement of racing or wishing to leave before racing ends".

Public amenities were not overlooked either, with plans to improve the public luncheon and tea room "which has long been inadequate for our requirements".

Like most Victorian race clubs, falling attendances were a growing concern for Moonee Valley, with crowds having fallen steadily since the peak year of 1948/49, when 491,000 attended the Club's 14 meetings – an average of more than 35,000 per meeting. In 1952-53 this figure had dropped to around 25,000 per meeting.

In the absence of Sir Samuel Burston, Acting Chairman, Mr A. J. (John) Moir, blamed the downturn in crowds on "Starting Price betting and taxation, including Winning Bets Tax". He said the stay-at-home punter was being given more information than ever before by radio stations – "in fact, race broadcasts have been taken from the racetracks to give off-the-course bettors the latest information and tips in just sufficient time for a backer to make a phone call to a Starting Price bookmaker".

"How can racing in Victoria be prosperous with so much money going out of racing?", he asked. "Should a race morning turn out wet or cold the

Protest Siren

MVRC has installed a siren to help punters save money. It will be sounded immediately after a protest has been lodged, or something unusual has occurred which might affect the result of a race.
- *Argus, December 4, 1951*

chances of the Club making a profit are now slender. On the other hand, the Government, without spending one penny, is always a winner.

"The Government takes, in all, 10% from the Totalisator, and when the Federal Government relinquished the Entertainments Tax, the State – very unwisely – reimposed this tax. In my opinion this was a very short-sighted policy because the more people attending race meetings the more money there is for the Government, hospitals and the (race) clubs."

To illustrate how much the Government was potentially losing, Mr Moir said that the average investment at Moonee Valley was £5 per head per day. Therefore, a reduction of 1,000 people per meeting meant a loss of £500 per day to the Government, "which is nearly double the amount raised by the State Entertainments Tax".

However, the Club did have one method of gaining extra funds – it became the first Victorian Club to operate a Doubles Totalisator, from which the Government had allowed the Club to take an 8% slice of turnover.

It was not the illegal off-course bookies – but instead finance companies – which were cited as a cause for declining attendances in 1954, when Sir Samuel Burston blamed the "rapid growth of finance companies and the consequent increase in the use of the Hire Purchase system" for people staying away. He said that they were putting their money "into purchasing necessities and luxuries for their homes and have not got the same amount of money to put into racing". Another factor was the opposition from the Tattersall's sweep, in which people bought tickets, enabling them to win big prizes if their ticket number was drawn from a barrel.

Prior to this time, the Sweep had been run from Tasmania with the Tasmanian Government receiving all taxation revenues. Eager to grab a slice of this, the Victorian Government wooed Tattersalls to Melbourne, resulting in greater interest in Victoria in this form of gambling. Naturally, this had an impact on the expenditure on race betting.

However, the balance sheet for the year showed some financial improvement with a profit 50% higher than for the previous 12 months due to the abolition of a 3% State Government Tax, and notwithstanding a 1% increase in Totalisator commission for part of the year.

Just how serious the Club was about the future of the Cox Plate became evident when it was announced in February, 1956, that the MVRC Committee had decided on a long range plan to make the Plate a £10,000 race. As a first step, prizemoney for that year was boosted by £1,000 to £5,000 plus a £250 trophy. It was now worth £1,000 more than the Moonee Valley Cup.

The Club was also spending money on facilities. Some innovations were new mobile starting stalls (which meant maximum field sizes had to be reduced from a previous maximum of 19 to 16); the new Doubles Tote; minor improvements to public stand amenities and plans for a new £200,000 public grandstand honoring Club Chairman Burston. The new stand, which provided seating and standing accommodation for about 5,000 people, was to include reserved boxes and seats, which hitherto had not been available on Victorian tracks. (Such was their popularity that the number had to be increased from an original 45 to 120.) The new facility was used for the first time at the Cox Plate meeting of 1958, drawing a crowd of more than 37,000. Outsider Yeman won the Plate that day when it was worth £5,200, still well under the £10,000 stake which had been mooted three years earlier.

The 50's closed in grand style with average attendances rising by more than 2,000 to 25,874 in 1959; Tote holdings were up by 19% and bookmakers' holdings had shown a 12% rise – and the total amount wagered was almost £10 million.

SP? NOT ME, TAB!

The decade of the 60's heralded racing's best news. The birth of the TAB, which was to become the industry's biggest benefactor, was just around the corner.

Unlike the situation with the on-course Tote – when it was the last State to have legislation approved – Victoria was to become the first in Australia to establish the TAB. A Bill to establish the off-course betting service had already been passed in the Legislative Council and Moonee Valley "sincerely hoped" it would follow the same pattern in the Upper House. The persistent lobbying for the TAB – which had been operating in New Zealand since 1948 – had been led by VRC Committeeman and subsequent Chairman, Sir Chester Manifold. Fittingly, Sir Chester, who was tireless in gaining racing and Government approval for the proposal, became the first Chairman of the TAB.

Sir Chester began lobbying for a TAB in the early 1950's with the result that in 1958 the State Government had convened a Royal Commission to inquire into off-course betting. The Commission, conducted by retired Supreme Court judge, Mr Justice F. R. B. Martin, took evidence from racing officials, bookmakers – legal and illegal – police, church representatives and even small punters. It found that illegal S.P. betting was rife and that such activity was also the cause of crime and corruption.

An example about which the Commission was informed, involved a "fortress" out of which 12 illegal bookmakers operated in separate rooms, each with an admitted annual turnover in excess of £500,000. This one location handled bets in excess of £6 million a year and Justice Martin observed that the turnover figure was likely to be underestimated because of Income Tax implications.

In their submissions the Racing Industry was represented by the four city race clubs – the VRC, VATC, MVRC and Melbourne Racing Club – and the Trotting Control Board. They said they were prepared to advance £200,000 on loan to the proposed Board for the establishment of the off-course betting scheme. The Commission recommendations were handed down in January, 1959, and after an early Parliamentary defeat – the bookmakers and churches had strong lobby groups – the Bill which led to the establishment of the TAB was passed on June 1, 1960.

While the Royal Commission was being conducted, Moonee Valley, like the rest of the Victorian Racing Industry, planned carefully for the impending off-course betting medium.

In July, 1960, MVRC Secretary Bill Cox was authorised by his Committee to commit the Club to an expenditure of £125,000 for the establishment of the TAB. Such was the confidence in some quarters about the potential success of a TAB, the following month Mr Cox reported to his Committee that the National Bank of Australasia Limited was prepared to provide funding for clubs to the tune of £650,000 to establish the TAB. The maximum amount of Moonee Valley's liability would be £123,000. Chairman Burston, who had also been closely involved in the preparations for the TAB, did not live to see its introduction, passing away in August, 1960.

The first meeting on which the TAB operated was the Newmarket Handicap fixture at Flemington on March 11, 1961. Using only about a dozen metropolitan and regional offices as well as providing a limited Telephone Betting service, day one turnover was £34,325/10/-. By comparison, a single day's turnover at the end of the TAB's first financial year (four months after opening) – when

Sir Chester Manifold
... he worked tirelessly to gain approval of the racing industry and government to establish the TAB.

there were now 29 off-course betting outlets – was £90,787/5/-. Punters, the Government and the race clubs were on a winner! This was beyond dispute when off-course turnover the following year exceeded £13 million from a network of just over 80 outlets. Horse owners were on a bonus too, when Moonee Valley introduced fourth placed prizemoney. Stakes were split 70% for first; 18% for second; 8% for third and 4% for fourth. In addition, it was decided that from July, 1962, Moonee Valley would pay float charges up to

£3/10/- per horse and, in addition, farrier fees incurred each race day would be picked up by the Club.

Into year three of the TAB, Moonee Valley attendances were beginning to decline, being down almost 12%, and new Chairman, John Moir, sounded a warning which was still ringing in the ears of racing administrators some 40 years later. He said that his Committee was determined to do all within its power to make racing a sporting spectacle with popular appeal and within the means of the "man in the street".

"After all, we are competing with football and we have got to produce something more attractive," he said.

He also said that the TAB was responsible for a "large percentage of this reduction in attendances".

"But, on the other hand, it has provided finance to assist in the improvement of racing facilities and in the development of the bloodstock breeding industry, without which we cannot hope for the champion horse, and without that horse we cannot get attendances."

A calculation done by the Club indicated that one visitor to the course contributed as much to racing as 12 people who did not attend but used the TAB. Chairman Moir said: "If we cannot get the public to attend racecourses then the sport of racing tends to deteriorate into an exercise solely for the purpose of determining who takes the pool provided by the TAB."

As part of the solution, Moonee Valley reduced admittance charges – and the following year crowds were up by 13%. TAB betting was also booming with the amount wagered on Moonee Valley meetings averaging £335,000 a day – an increase of 60%.

The new TAB Off-course Daily Double was proving a great success with a pool "rarely less" than £100,000 a day – and legislation had been passed to permit sales on-course as well. The other big on-course betting news of the day was that an Interstate Totalisator was in operation, allowing punters to bet on Adelaide and Sydney fixtures.

Even bigger things were in store with the Metropolitan clubs agreeing to purchase new Tote equipment – Moonee Valley's share was £100,000 – which would include new approximate dividend barometers which would show price changes within seconds.

Also on the rise was the prizemoney for the Cox Plate. The £10,000 stake which had been mooted in 1956 was achieved in 1964 – and the race was now worth £4,000 more than the Moonee Valley Cup.

The Club lost another stalwart when Bill Cox died in April, 1966, aged 73. He had been on the Committee for almost 40 years and had served as Secretary for more than 30 years. His son, W. M. (Murray), who had acted as an assistant to his father in the 12 months preceding his death, continued the Cox lineage at Moonee Valley when he took over as Secretary.

One of his first major projects involved negating the impact which construction of the new Tullamarine Freeway had on Moonee Valley boundaries. The project resulted in some 7 acres of Moonee Valley land being used for the new road to the airport, necessitating extensive alterations to the track and a car underpass beneath the course proper – all proceeding without interrupting use of the course.

Another big issue involved a Report on racing which proposed the merger of the VRC and the MVRC.

The 1967 Report claimed :

"The Racing Industry should benefit substantially if the MVRC and VRC merged their interests and identities.

"Terms could no doubt be worked out to suitably recognise the contribution of each Club and to provide for the reasonable representation of each on a reconstituted Committee."

In rejecting the assertions, MVRC Chairman Moir said that the MVRC had reason to be proud of its status in Victorian racing and of its standard of administration at all levels.

"All this, built up over many years, would be sacrificed to no purpose since our financial contribution to a merged Club would not alone retrieve the position", he said.

The Report also stated:

"With the merger and mid-week racing it would be possible to transfer some Saturdays from Moonee Valley to Flemington and in this way use both courses to near capacity with advantage to the Racing Industry. It is estimated 12 mid-week days in the financial sense would offset the loss of 6 to 8 Saturdays at Moonee Valley."

In response to this Mr Moir said: "Your Committee would not entertain a proposal that the Moonee Valley Racecourse, with its long tradition of spectacular racing since 1883, should be converted to a mid-week course. By a loss of seven Saturdays the course would only race on seven Saturdays and holidays in a year. No mid-week poorly attended meeting would make up for this."

The Home Straight?

Essendon City Council wants MVRC to cease racing at the end of the 1964-65 season and for the Housing Commission to take over the area for home development. A decision to ask the State Government to rescind the Club's permit to race was made by a five to four vote of the Council last night. Councillors claimed that the five year period of grace would allow the MVRC sufficient time to develop a modern racecourse at its Somerton site.
- *The Age August 16, 1960*

The Premier (Mr Bolte) yesterday rejected Essendon City Council's proposal that the Housing Commission would acquire MVRC at the end of the 1964-65 season. He said it would be uneconomical to buy the course and suggested that the Williamstown Rifle Range might be taken over for housing.
- *The Age, August 22, 1960*

Essendon City Council decided last night not to carry on its fight to have Moonee Valley Racecourse closed.
- *Sun, July 4, 1961.*

THE HIGH-FLYING KIWI

Ian McEwen ... he quickly realised that Moonee Valley had to be brought up to scratch .... and set about doing it.

The January of the 70's began with the resignation of Secretary Cox to take up the equivalent role with the VRC, resulting in the appointment of a New Zealand journalist/racing administrator to the position vacated by Mr Cox.

It was the first time that a person outside the "Cox clan" had filled the role of Secretary of Moonee Valley. However, with the names of Ian Stuart Campbell McEwen, the new Secretary could, at least, clearly lay claim to continuing the Scottish heritage established by old Sam Cox.

McEwen, whose father was racing editor of *The Dominion* newspaper, began in the same department of the same paper in 1949. After a clash over the belief that he could do better than his father, McEwen joined *Truth* in New Zealand as racing editor. He left in 1964 to take up a position as Managing Secretary of the Bay Of Plenty Racing and Trotting Club and Whakatane Racing Club all of which raced on the Gate Pa course at Tauranga.

While there, McEwen was responsible for the development of New Zealand's biggest weight-for-age race, the *Stars Travel Invitation Stakes*, over 1¼ miles. It was restricted to 10 runners, comprising the two best three and four-year-olds of each sex; and the best two older horses. The initial stake was $10,000 but, seeking to increase it, the entrepreneurial McEwen approached Bob Owens, who was owner of a Company called Stars Travel, for sponsorship.

"He was a big sponsor of golf and I pointed out he would get much better exposure in racing than he would in golf," McEwen said.

As a result, prizemoney for the race increased from $10,000 to $25,000 in three years and the insular McEwen – who had never been to an Australian race meeting – believed *The Stars Travel Invitation* was more valuable than the Cox Plate. All he knew about the Cox Plate was that it was a weight-for-age race in Australia.

"I was quoted in some racing publication about the value of the Stars Travel race and then some bloke in NZ wrote to me and said to me: 'Haven't you heard about the Cox Plate in Australia? It is worth $30,000'," McEwen said.

Regardless, the *Stars Travel* was New Zealand's richest weight-for-age race and under McEwen's guidance the Bay of Plenty Racing Club had gone from about 30th in ranking to the fifth highest on and off-course turnover club of about 80 in New Zealand.

Aged 39 and "full of enthusiasm", McEwen acted promptly when an advertisement appeared in the NZ Racing Calendar in November, 1969, for a position as Secretary of MVRC. The time was perfect for him to take on the Australian challenge. Chairman John Moir asked Bill Stutt – who had filled the Committee vacancy caused by the death of Sir Samuel Burston – to interview McEwen when Stutt was in New Zealand for the Trentham yearling sales.

After preliminary discussions, McEwen made his first visit to an Australian racecourse – at Flemington – the day after his final interview which resulted in his MVRC appointment.

"Looking back now it was really a day out of history," Mr McEwen said. "It was a formal Committee lunch and everyone wore suits, ties and hats and they toasted the Queen! Such formalities aside, it appeared to me that the racing was professionally organised.

"Another initial impression was how the racing scene was dominated by bookmakers. It was the volume of the betting and the intensity of the people involved and the bookies calling the odds, doing their business so differently from what it is today."

McEwen also realised, soon after beginning his new role, that Moonee Valley was very much the minor of the metropolitan clubs; it raced 15 times a year and apart from those race dates the gates were shut.

He recalled: "It had an antiquated Members' grandstand (built in 1925), the Tote was out of the 1930's and, given the VRC push against Moonee Valley three years earlier, my view was that if you don't do something to this place, McEwen, its going to be closed."

The "new kid on the block", who was to become the driving force behind significant enhancements to the way Moonee Valley conducted and promoted racing, had not been with the Club long enough to be involved in a ground-breaking Club initiative announced at the Annual Meeting in 1970. The introduction of Quinella betting on all races in May, 1970, helped boost on course turnover to a record level for the year. Previously, the Quinella had operated on the last race only, because it was the only time there was a "spare" Tote window. At the time, punters had to place Win and Place bets at one window and use another for Doubles. Come the last race, there was no other event on which to operate a "Double", so rather than waste the window capacity, the clubs would operate a Quinella on the last event. However, such was the popularity of the bet that it was Moonee Valley which added the third all-day color-coded window – being that of the Quinella – to join the Win and Place and Doubles windows.

Stakes for the year were also at a record high, but rather than increase them for 1971 the Committee decided to reduce acceptance fees to a flat $6 per race and to pay a losing riding fee on behalf of owners who did not receive prizemoney. The theory was that it was "better to improve the lot of the losing owner rather than contribute more money to the owners of winning horses. Only 36 horses may earn stakemoney in a nine race program (the Club paid prizemoney back to fourth) but it takes another 90 horses to make a race meeting."

The administrator of one country club voiced concern about his club implementing the losing riders' fee, but in responding Chairman Moir said: "The mere fact that Moonee Valley has implemented these things does not mean that country clubs, nor any other club in Victoria, must follow Moonee Valley."

Aviation magnate, Sir Reginald Ansett, who was Chairman of Mornington Racing Club, praised Moonee Valley's bold move.

"I am sure that the problem that my friend has mentioned will be solved by consultation among the (racing) industry. Being an owner of some magnitude, I think it is marvellous. Certainly it will be introduced by all clubs and therefore I think it is a wonderful move which I must congratulate you on because it takes this sort of thing to set the wheels in motion from time to time. I congratulate Moonee Valley," Ansett said.

The first full year of paying such fees cost the MVRC $10,400, but these costs were offset by increasing Tote receipts. True to McEwen's initial thoughts about upgrading facilities, extensive alterations were made to the main Totalisator house, enabling the demolition of the old facilities. A simple ploy of allowing two people to queue side by side at the Tote window instead of one person at a time was also introduced, resulting in up to 1,000 extra tickets being sold at Win and Place windows. For the comfort of punters, a verandah extended the full length of the selling windows and illuminated signs indicated the type and value of betting at each window. The general betting ring was also re-designed with the rails ring incorporating for the first time two Sydney and two Adelaide fielders.

The Committee decided, in 1972, to embark on a large upgrading project,

£ foolish – $ wise

The introduction of decimal currency in 1966, which "doubled" the amount in pay packets – with each £1 being worth $2 – was blamed as the reason for the smaller increase in bookmakers' holdings that year. Bookmakers said that big bettors were tending to cut their bets by investing the same amount numerically in dollars as they previously invested in pounds.

extending the (Public) Burston stand by 120 feet. Estimated to cost around $500,000, the extension would provide accommodation for an extra 2,700; a Totalisator hall with 29 windows; provision for bookmakers on one floor; improved dining and bar facilities and the demolition of a small, old, concrete stand and some wooden buildings behind it.

In short, Moonee Valley was taking on a new look.

The Cox Plate was also obtaining a new lease of life – rising from $30,000 to $45,000 in 1972, thanks largely to money from the Spring Stakes Fund. Established to maintain the supremacy of Victorian racing, the Fund's source was one quarter of one percent of TAB turnover. That year's race was won by the crowd favorite Gunsynd, who had attracted an enormous following because of his ability and raceday antics. Gunsynd seemed to know how to play a crowd and would prop and nod his head in acknowledgment before and after races. He was at his crowd-pleasing best on Cox Plate day playing to the crowd of 42,000, attracting massive publicity for himself and trainer Tommy Smith, racing in general and the Cox Plate in particular.

This did not go unnoticed and McEwen believes that Gunsynd's year was a turning point in the way the Cox Plate was to be promoted in future.

"I think that the success of the Gunsynd promotion was the thing that stirred the Committee to say 'Here we have got something we can market'," McEwen said.

From that point, the Club made a more concerted effort to promote the Cox Plate. An immediate step was to increase its prize for the following year by $30,000 to $75,000, with the additional $30,000 being half financed from the Spring Stakes Fund and half from Club funds. In announcing the sharp boost, the Club said it had been done to "keep the Cox Plate in its rightful place as the most important weight-for-age race in Australia".

The completion of the extension of the Burston Stand in 1973 finalised the first major project in Moonee Valley's forward planning program. The next project was much more far reaching, and behind it was the Government's intention to transfer trotting from the Showgrounds site at Ascot Vale to Moonee Valley.

It began as a result of a suggestion to Secretary McEwen from the Minister for Youth, Sport and Recreation, Mr Brian Dixon.

McEwen recalls he received a call from the Minister who asked: 'Why couldn't you put a trotting track inside Moonee Valley?'.

"The thought was that the first thing we had to do was to plan a new grandstand, so there was an association between trots, the new grandstand and generally rebuilding Moonee Valley," McEwen said.

The Committee, which deliberated long and hard, eventually took the lesser of two evils by agreeing with Minister Dixon – providing it was on Moonee Valley's terms.

The decision also forced the Committee's hand on upgrading facilities, with the result that plans for a new $5.5 million grandstand – "the ultimate in comfort for Australian racegoers" – were publicly announced in April, 1974. To cater for the Members and public, it would seat more than 4,000 people, three times the capacity of the 1925 stand, and it would link the Burston and South Hill stands. Providing all manner of dining and bar facilities as well as covering the main betting ring, the new project was to be financed by the proposed sale in June of the Club's Roxburgh Park property at Somerton. The property had been rezoned as "Reserved Living" and was described as a "bonanza" for real estate developers.

It was noted that the announcement of the new facility, coupled with the extensions to the Burston stand the previous year, "quashes for all time the rumour about the Club being ousted from its present site or being forced to merge with the VRC".

In line with his philosophy of using a racecourse on occasions other than race days, the canny McEwen didn't miss the opportunity of gaining local support by saying said that the new building would provide the Moonee Ponds area with a new facility for community purposes. Tenders were to be called in September.

However, all plans were put on hold when the Roxburgh Park property did not realise the Reserve. Bidding for the block, which had cost £35,000 in 1950, started at $3 million but stopped at $4.1 million, at which price the Club would not sell. It was announced two months later, in August, 1974, that plans for the grandstand had been suspended. At the Annual Meeting the following month, Chairman Moir said he would not be a candidate for re-election as he wished to make way for a younger man. After announcing his resignation, he added: "I am reminded that we have the plans here of the new stand. Of course, there will be no new stand until we can finance it and we cannot finance it until we sell that property (Roxburgh Park) and there will be no further commitment until we do sell it."

New Chairman, Mr Ian Macdonald announced the following year that all betting records had been broken in the previous 12 months and that for the first time the Club had achieved the highest per-capita daily average on-course Tote turnover of the three City clubs. The Cox Plate was a big beneficiary of all this with its prize being boosted by $50,000 to $125,000 in 1975 and such was the Club's commitment to weight-for-age racing that the minimum stake for all such events at Moonee Valley would rise from $20,000 to $25,000.

The massive increase in prizemoney for the Cox Plate meant it was now richer than the Caulfield Cup and only the Melbourne and Sydney Cups and the Golden Slipper were worth more. The push for night trotting had not subsided. All plans had been completed and tenders for the new track and lighting had closed, but its future depended on the outcome of a Town and Country Planning Appeal Board hearing.

Mr Macdonald said that, subject to the Appeal Board outcome, the new grandstand would be built in two stages. The first stage, to cost $4 million, would be financed by the Club's bankers, with the interest being funded from income generated by the Trotting Control Board's use of the racecourse. This stage would provide seating for 4,000 which would be divided about 50/50 between Members and the public.

He anticipated that this stage of the construction, costs for which would eventually be met from the sale of Roxburgh Park, would be completed in about 18 months so that it would be functioning by May of 1977.

"At a later date, when finance is available, the building will be completed by the addition of four floors extending over the general betting ring", the Chairman said.

After night trotting received the green light, the Committee reviewed the construction contract some months later and decided that one contractor would complete the whole project rather than have it done in stages. The cost would be $5.2 million and the work would be completed by the end of November, 1977. The Club had been forced to borrow to meet the costs, as "the financial climate has not been conducive to the sale of Roxburgh Park".

Night trotting began at the track in October, 1976, though attendances were initially affected because of the grandstand construction, which had blown out to a cost of $6.7 million. Moonee Valley racing was also affected by the construction which forced the closure of the track for three months and the transfer of three meetings to Sandown and Flemington.

Gloomy Surroundings

Everyone was left in the dark for about an hour during the Cox Plate meeting on October 23, 1976.

An eclipse of the sun resulted in the crowd of nearly 40,000 huddling under lights or studying the form at the bar while waiting for the re-appearance of the sun, permitting the meeting to continue.

The Cox Plate that day went to the champion Surround, first filly to win the event.

The building works meant that facilities were more cramped than normal, but this led to another Moonee Valley "first" – the breaking down of the segregation barrier between sexes in the Members' area. This century-old taboo was signified by a white line painted in an area of the Members' – a line over which women were not permitted to cross.

Chairman Macdonald said that the mixing of men and women in the Reserve had worked well while the new stand was being built so the Club would initiate an official policy on the matter. In effect the "white line" was to be abolished and sexes could continue to mix freely wherever they wished. The decision took the other two clubs by surprise. Initially, they baulked at the idea of following suit, but, as with the payment of losing riding fees, they soon did.

Opened in December, 1977, the stand was an immediate hit with the racing fraternity and external organisations.

Behind the scenes, however, there were plastic smiles. Having a grandstand – and having to pay for it – were two different matters. Roxburgh Park had still not been sold and the Club desperately needed money to finance the stand.

Ian McEwen takes up the story:

"In 1979-80, we could have been bankrupted with the stroke of a pen. The only reason we were saved was because we had a great relationship with our bank.

"We were at the stage then when we couldn't generate enough money to repay any of our loans. One year, we had to borrow about $700,000 from the bank, which represented the whole interest bill. The bank had to actually lend us money to pay their interest bill.

"Another year, we had to borrow half of what we owed in interest. Normally, when you have to do that you're gone."

Little wonder the new venue was actively promoted for business and social functions with the Committee anxious to generate maximum revenue from as many sources as possible to defray the debt. But that was not as simple as it seemed either.

Knowing the Club's desperate need for money, McEwen determined that the Club could do its own catering. After a rocky start with the new project in 1979, he eventually managed to get the food-only component working smoothly and very profitably.

The liquor side of the business was another story. At that stage, every sporting/social function that was not run on licensed premises was operated under a Booth Licence. The Club's former caterers, O'Briens, held that licence and, when they departed, so did the right to serve liquor under the Booth Licence arrangement.

McEwen then arranged for the nearby Grandview Hotel to take out a Booth Licence which McEwen operated on the hotel's behalf at Moonee Valley – until he was told one day that he was breaking the law. At that stage, Moonee Valley was selling 2,500 gallons of beer a day at a good race meeting.

The entrepreneurial Chief Executive then hit upon a brainwave. He invited the whole of Parliament to Moonee Valley for lunch; to show them the facilities; show them the kitchens and the way the Club operated its liquor sales. He also explained that he felt the Club was breaking the law as it stood.

Such was the effect that the Liquor Control Act was changed permitting special liquor licences for such functions.

Bill Stutt, who had deftly overseen the precarious financial arrangements regarding the stand, was elected Club Chairman just weeks after it opened. Mr Justice W. (Bill) Crockett was elected Vice-Chairman.

THE COX PLATE "PUSH"

The new Chairman was a blue-blood racing man, having been involved with racing and breeding since he was a lad, eventually becoming manager of Wright Stephenson's Bloodstock Agency. Such is his passion for all things racing that Bill Stutt scoffs: "I only learned to read so that I could decipher pedigrees."

His interest in horses began when, as a youngster, his mother would play bridge with Lily Fisher, the wife of Flemington trainer Elwood Fisher. Young Bill and his brother Jack would beg their mother to let them go along so they could look at the horses. Aged about seven at the time, the boys became regular visitors, asking all manner of questions about the horses' names and breeding, to the point that, on one occasion, the trainer said to them: "You two kids know more about my horses than I do."

Studying law before the outbreak of the War, Bill Stutt intended to resume his studies on his return from Service, only to be offered a chance of employment with prominent breeder E. A. (Ted) Underwood as his stud manager.

With the arrival of family, Mr Stutt decided he needed to be closer to the city so he joined the bloodstock firm of Mackinnon and Cox which was eventually sold to Wright Stephenson's, who appointed Mr Stutt their Australian Manager. (The "Mackinnon" in the original firm was related to former VRC Chairman Lachlan Mackinnon, while the "Cox" was in fact W. S. Cox III, who, although he was Secretary of Moonee Valley, also acted as the auctioneer for the Company. Fortunately, he was never far away from either role, as the offices of both the bloodstock Company and Moonee Valley Racing Club were only two floors apart at 482 Bourke Street, Melbourne. Indeed, they were so closely linked that the MVRC switchboard had a direct extension line to the bloodstock office, in case the partners had to contact each other in a hurry. This was particularly helpful when it was necessary for cheques to be signed by them both.)

Even before he joined the Committee, Mr Stutt had a firm conviction that weight-for-age was the true test of racing, ahead of Handicaps. His theory was – and still is – that all the best sporting events are 'off scratch'.

"In the Olympic games, for instance, no-one is given a start. I mean I could win every Olympic race from 100 yards to the Marathon if I was given the right handicap – and that, I hasten to add, would have to be within a yard of the finish line. But my point is, no competitor is given a start in the ultimate athletic test of the Olympics – and so it should be with racing."

He also has a theory on why most of Australia's richest races are Handicaps, and not weight-for-age events.

"In the early days of Australian racing, it was not possible for horses to easily travel long distances and they kept pretty much to their own areas," he said.

"If big races had been run at weight-for-age, one horse could easily have scooped the pool, winning all the main races, which would have been a big disincentive for other owners and trainers. To prevent this, Handicap races were framed. This meant that the better a horse became the more weight it received, to the extent that the horse could not keep winning race after race.

"We have now inherited that system for our major races and are unable to change it, even though it does not mean that the best horse will win.

Bill Stutt ... his belief that weight-for-age is the real test of racing had a significant impact on the W. S. Cox Plate in particular, and racing at Moonee Valley in general.

"However, only the best horse will win at weight-for-age and to my mind it is the real test of racing," he said.

That was the lore according to Stutt before he joined the Committee – and nothing has changed some 40 years later. Once appointed to the Committee, he diplomatically let others know of his feelings.

"I didn't make a song and dance and carry on, I just quietly made my views known. When the opportunity was there, I would say that the weight-for-age races are for the best horses and they should carry the best stakemoney, otherwise why would anyone try to have the best horse in the land?

"I was very keen to get the weight-for-age stakes up but it was a matter of quietly speaking about it where I could," Mr Stutt said.

However, after his elevation to Chairman in January, 1978, he was in a position to have significant influence on the future direction of the Cox Plate, in conjunction with other "weight-for-age allies" on the Committee, who included his new Vice-Chairman, Mr Justice Crockett, and Ian McEwen.

At the time of Bill Stutt's appointment, the Cox Plate was worth $150,000 – only $60,000 less than the Melbourne Cup – and it had taken over the mantle from the Moonee Valley Cup as the Club's feature race. People were now referring to Moonee Valley's main race day as "W. S. Cox Plate day".

Two years later, the Cox Plate was worth $175,000 and then, in 1980, it hit $200,000. The stakes "push" continued to the extent that in 1982 the Cox Plate had leapfrogged to $275,000 to be within only $35,000 of Flemington's famous "two miler". Three people who were certainly behind the "push" were Chairman Stutt, Vice-Chairman Crockett and Chief Executive McEwen.

"We led the march on the Moonee Valley Committee that the Cox Plate had to become the No. 1 race in Australia, if not the No. 1 race in the world," McEwen said.

"This was because we all believed in weight-for-age racing being the only real test of good horses. The Cup was left to stagnate on about $100,000 as there was no point in competing with the Caulfield and Melbourne Cups.

"The main competition for the Cox Plate was handicap racing at Flemington and Caulfield.

"There was no direct competition in a weight-for-age sense apart from the Caulfield Stakes and the Mackinnon Stakes, which complemented the Cox Plate."

Two years later and another quantum leap saw Cox Plate prizemoney increased by $125,000 to $400,000 for 1984 – which McEwen admitted caused "some skirmishes" with some Members of the Committee.

"We had a resolution that the Cox Plate stake should keep pace with that offered by the VRC for the Melbourne Cup. We also decided that every feature race at Moonee Valley would be at weight-for-age or set-weights, with the minimum stake for any such race to be $100,000. Weight-for-age racing attracted the best fields so it meant whatever the best horses were, they would race at Moonee Valley.

"Basically, the Cox Plate was the leader of the band and, having set a principle for the Cox Plate, we set a principle for the other weight-for-age races."

That rule for the Cox Plate did not include toppling the Melbourne Cup from its number one prize status.

"Bill Stutt insisted it was not our role to beat the VRC," McEwen said.

"While he was highly competitive, and always allowed me to be highly competitive, he said to me 'There is one thing you can't do, you can't pay more money for the Cox Plate than the Melbourne Cup. The Melbourne Cup is Australia's race. The Cox Plate can be up there with it but it can't be ahead of it'.

"I now realise that such a decision showed that Bill knew Moonee Valley's place", McEwen said.

Further proof of the Club's stand on quality racing was provided by Chairman Stutt at the 1984 Annual Meeting when he said a survey had shown that "Gimmicks merely offer the public a short-term incentive ... we need to get back to racing related promotions ... our biggest days are the days we offer the stars."

By now, interest in the Cox Plate was matching its soaring prizemoney. The stake rose a further $100,000 in 1984 and then hit $500,000 the following year. While its status on the national racing calendar was unchallenged, it was not so for other main races at the Valley.

Chairman Stutt made this point when he said the only Group 1 events approved for Moonee Valley were the Cox Plate and the William Reid Stakes, which was elevated to Group 1 status in 1987.

"Events such as the Manikato Stakes, Feehan Stakes, Moonee Valley Stakes, Veuve Clicquot, and A. J. Moir Stakes are still only allotted Group 2 status," Mr Stutt said.

"Many inferior handicap events throughout Australia are rated either Group 1 or Group 2. The whole principle of the Group classification of races in Europe is to award Group status to weight-for-age or set-weight events. While Australia may see fit to award Group 1, 2 or 3 status to handicap events, the Principal Clubs should at least recognise that Moonee Valley is following the true tradition of Group racing by providing weight-for-age events. At the stake levels – a minimum of $100,000 – all Moonee Valley's weight-for-age races should be awarded Group 1 status."

The prize for Moonee Valley's main Group 1 race went through the roof by another $250,000 to reach $750,000 in 1986, which McEwen says was the "defining moment" for the Cox Plate.

The 1986 race, which was promoted around two New Zealand horses – Bonecrusher and Our Waverley Star – was billed as *"The Race of the Century"*. Few who saw it would disagree, as the two horses who, as predicted months earlier, would own the race, cleared out from the rest 600m from home. From thereon they went to the line head and head, running on empty over the final 100 metres, surviving on only fresh air and willpower. The official verdict went to the aptly named Bonecrusher, though Our Waverley Star was certainly no loser.

The hype for the race had begun in February that year, when the two horses had been racing neck and neck in NZ and effectively taking turns in winning. At that time, Chairman Stutt and Vice-Chairman Crockett were in the Dominion for the Trentham yearling sales.

"The New Zealand newspapers kept reporting after each encounter that the showdown to determine which horse was the best would be decided in the Cox Plate at Moonee Valley in October," Ian McEwen said.

"Bill Stutt and Bill Crockett brought these cuttings back and the story just kept on being repeated in both NZ and Australian papers."

McEwen was in a quandary as to how to keep up the publicity momentum.

"In those days, you wouldn't dare suggest that I should even pick up the phone and say come over to the Cox Plate.

"The money was certainly there; the race had sufficient importance so they (Bonecrusher and Our Waverley Star) just came.

"The only thing I did about it was to say to the Committee that we had to keep the heat on in Melbourne to ensure we got maximum publicity, so we engaged a Melbourne Company, *Raceplay,* to market the race. It really led to a new way of marketing racing here."

By now, the Cox Plate was a major talking point of Spring Carnival events – and the fact that the race was worth $1 million in 1987 only added to its reputation. Leaving little doubt about its future, Mr Stutt said after Rubiton had won the event that year that it was the Committee's intention to "maintain the pre-eminent position" the race had achieved.

He had full reason to be "bullish" as attendances were up by more than 4%; the on-course Tote holdings at Moonee Valley were up $5 million to $37 million, while the off-course sales had increased by $29 million to $182 million. Stakemoney for the year was $2 million ahead of the previous year, while owners had received subsidies of more than $200,000 for jockeys, farriers, float rebates and WorkCare fees.

Furthermore, Roxburgh Park, which had been earmarked for sale to pay for the new Grandstand in 1974 but had been passed in for $4.1 million, had been sold to the Urban Land Authority for $11.3 million for housing development.

By then, the Club had made many improvements to the Members' and Public stands. The track had been upgraded; the Club's own catering department was showing spectacular growth in function business, with turnover exceeding $1 million; and the main betting ring had been covered with a "space dome".

Given the rosy report, it was no surprise when the Cox Plate prize soared by 50% to $1.5 million in 1988. During that season, another big change was the purchase by the racing industry (which included Moonee Valley) of radio station 3UZ. This was to ensure the continuation of race broadcasting when radio station 3DB ended its contract with the TAB to broadcast races, in July 1988. Off the track, Moonee Valley's new catering department showed spectacular growth with function centre business alone providing turnover in excess of $1 million. The year also marked the retirement of one of the Club's main weight-for-age protagonists, Mr Justice Crockett, who stood down in August.

In what was to be Bill Stutt's last Cox Plate as Chairman, prizemoney for the Cox Plate of 1989 was increased by $200,000 to a record $1.7 million, plus $6,500 in trophies. It was a fitting tribute to Mr Stutt, who had been a key player in seeing the value and status of the Cox Plate soar. He stood down after 12 years as Chairman because he was approaching the compulsory retiring age. The future of the Cox Plate was indelibly assured, due in no small part to his efforts.

While the 1989 Cox Plate attracted around 30,000 people, overall attendances in Mr Stutt's last year dropped, mainly because of a fall-off in midweek crowds, when numbers fell by almost 1,000 people a meeting compared with the previous year. Despite the fall in crowds, on-course Tote turnover increased – but bookmakers were feeling the pinch. Their turnover had dropped from $106 million the previous year to $103 million. In an endeavour to assist bookmakers, Moonee Valley continued its policy of not issuing new licences to help the remaining bookmakers become more competitive.

A year later, the Club was rocked again, this time by the resignation of Ian McEwen. No-one saw it coming, but he knew the time had come after Better Loosen Up had crossed the line to win the 1990 Cox Plate some weeks earlier. It related to what had become an annual involuntary reaction for the (at times) gruff, no-nonsense Chief Executive. He was always so overcome with emotion as the horses crossed the line in the Cox Plate that he would have to wipe away a tear as he soaked up the atmosphere he had frenetically encouraged.

In 1990, he did not need his handkerchief. After all this time, the spark was fading. McEwen, 60, said the decision had come about following the continuing pressure of Spring Carnivals and "before the ravages of diabetes really hit". A diabetic for 40 years, he said he would continue in his role as National President of Diabetes Australia.

While his reflex emotion had deserted him on Cox Plate day, such was not the situation when he read out his letter of resignation to the Committee. He sobbed as he announced he was cutting his ties from his passion for 20 years. New Chairman, Norman Carlyon, could not tempt him to re-consider.

During his time at the helm, McEwen had been head-on and hands-on; he'd trodden on plenty of toes and crushed many egos; he had also questioned long-held traditions and changed them to suit the times; but no-one could question his enthusiasm nor his devotion. To his staff, he was the best boss in the world; to the media, he was the best racing contact in The Little Black Book; to those who sought racing advice, he was peerless. Mostly though, he was relentless in his pursuit of lifting the status of anything connected with Moonee Valley. Under his reign, the Club had created many "firsts". These included the introduction of losing riding fees; the desegregation of the sexes in the Members' area; twilight race meetings; Trifecta betting (from Trios); interstate Quinellas; free parking; and the first live telecast of racing. (This was, naturally, of a Cox Plate, which McEwen sneaked in a week before the VRC was to do the same with the Victoria Derby.) He also saw the facilities and décor at the Valley become the equal of many of the best racetracks in the world.

McEwen easily surpassed what he set out to achieve when he first saw the track and realised that "something had to be done, and quickly".

He went on to ensure, forever, the security of Moonee Valley; he elevated the Cox Plate to a state of virtual enshrinement; and he led the way for Australian racing administration.

Incoming Chief Executive, Michael Classon, had big shoes to fill.

The Valley "Specialist"

While Ian McEwen had trodden on plenty of toes, he still had the respect of his peers when he stepped down.

Typical reaction was:

"Ian was a one-off. His job was to always do his best for Moonee Valley, and he did."
- *VRC Secretary Rodney Johnson*

"It has come as a bombshell to me; I didn't know anything.

"I don't always agree with what he does but he's been very good for Moonee Valley."
- *VATC Chief Executive Jim Conway*

"Ian's era has been one of prosperity and progress for the Club.

The past 20 years will be known at Moonee Valley as the 'McEwen era'."
- *MVRC Chairman Norman Carlyon*

NOW FOR THE WORLD!

Norm Carlyon ... ensured minimum stakemoney remained high.

At a time when the Cox Plate was worth $1.7 million, Chairman Norman Carlyon announced that the Club was committed to ensuring minimum stake money remained high. In line with this philosophy, the Club increased minimum prizemoney from $25,000 to $27,000 in 1991, with midweek stakes rising by $2,500 to $15,000.

Carlyon commented that the increases were made possible by a reduction in stakemoney in several of the Club's feature races. The Cox Plate was not one of them that year, but nor did its stake increase. In fact, it too, was soon to see its stake reduced.

While Tote turnover was continuing to reach record levels, bookmakers were finding things a lot tougher. Their turnover for 1992-93 fell from $66.4 million the previous year to $53 million -- a drop of some 20%. In the previous five years, they had seen their turnover decline by almost 50%. So concerned was the Club that it agreed to reduce bookmakers' fees.

Not helping bookmakers – nor racing – was the opening of a casino in Melbourne, which only added to the already tough competition for the leisure dollar. The introduction of poker machines compounded the problem. Fortunately, the Racing Industry was able to share to some extent in the profitability of poker machines through an arrangement with TABCORP Holdings Ltd, which was formed upon the privatisation of the TAB in August, 1994. In addition to its exclusive licence to continue regular TAB betting activities, TABCORP also held one of only two licences to operate poker machines in hotels and clubs throughout Victoria. The Racing Industry had close links with the new Company, entering into a Joint Venture arrangement with TABCORP through an entity called VicRacing Pty Ltd, which was to receive 25% of TABCORP's nett profits. The Racing Industry would now receive a distribution of TABCORP profits not only from traditional wagering markets, but also from the booming poker machine sector.

Moonee Valley quickly took advantage of the poker machine boom, becoming the first racing club to be granted a gaming licence. Situated on the North Hill, the new gaming complex, which incorporated a TAB outlet and dining facilities, was to prove a valuable revenue source for the Club. In its first full year, the gaming machine facility, built at a cost of $2 million, showed a profit of nearly $730,000, ranking it among the top venues in the State.

Unlike the Melbourne and Caulfield Cups – which had been sponsored by Foster's since 1985 - the Cox Plate was still solely under the banner of the Moonee Valley Racing Club. There had been approaches to sponsor the race, but the Club preferred to wait until it found a sponsor whose product was in keeping with the status of the race. Prestige auto manufacturer BMW provided that perfect fit when the race became the BMW Cox Plate for the first time in 1994.

That Cox Plate was the last to be run on the Course Proper as it had been known by racegoers. The track was refurbished after the race that year; turns were altered, the track widened and cables laid in preparation for the introduction of night racing. New Chief Executive, Paul Brettell, who commenced duties only a month before the track was dug up, had to oversee a massive project. The grass track surface, known as StrathAyr, was to provide better drainage, improved cushioning for horses and improved turf growth. At the completion of the work, more than half the course was a minimum of 23m wide (previously 16m-19m). The project involved laying more than

4 km of stormwater drainage and 12 km of sub-surface drains; and 55,000 square metres each of sand, netlon mesh and Blue Grass and rye with sprigs of Kikuyu grass. Its construction led to a lay-off in racing at the Valley for about 12 months, resulting in 19 meetings being transferred to the other three metropolitan tracks.

The StrathAyr surface, known for its ability to withstand even the wettest conditions, lived up to expectations in its first full year of operation in 1995-96, when 23 meetings were conducted and the track was not rated "heavy" at any time. The worst rating for the track that Winter was "slow" – on only two occasions, during a period when the Club had conducted three meetings in 11 days.

Night racing was ushered into Victoria to the sounds of rock musicians at Moonee Valley on Australia Day, 1998. More than 30,000 packed the Valley to experience racing's "new frontier", which attracted many new (and younger) patrons. Maybe they were there for the rock concert, or the disco after the races; in any event they were also experiencing racing, which certainly had a bright new look.

There were flashing lights above the starting stalls to indicate race start; the color of jockeys' caps was standardised with each colored cap representing the same number in each race; and the time between races was cut to 30 minutes to keep the action rolling. To complete the scene, all of this was beamed live in brilliant color on a huge infield screen. Racing had caught up with the football and cricket in providing visual excitement to new and committed audiences.

Such was the success of early night racing, Chairman Geoff Torney reported, that due to its popularity, Moonee Valley was the only metropolitan track to increase overall average attendance, outside of Spring Carnival time.

Subsequent Moonee Valley directors and executives have continued to ensure the club prospers, with the Cox Plate, now considered "Australia's weight-for-age championship", becoming a $3 million race in 2002.

Old Sam Cox could never have envisaged what he started. The "eyesore", that "blot on the landscape", will be further dramatically improved in a multi-million dollar rebuild of the track and amenities after 2020 under the direction of chairman Robert Scarborough and his committee and CEO Michael Browell. Apart from a new track and grandstands, the project will also include a residential development on the 98 acre site.

CEO Browell said that the residential and commercial components of the project would help the Club to fund a new grandstand and track upgrades, delivering a modern, multi-function facility that would secure the racecourse's future as a major state, national and international racing venue.

"The project is expected to take 10-15 years to complete. The construction of the new Moonee Valley racecourse and grandstands is planned to commence following the staging of the 100th W S Cox Plate in October 2020", Browell said.

Ribbleden's florid prose of 1907 is still just as apt some 110 years later:

"Moonee Valley has been the scene of many a stirring contest, and, under the present capable management, it cannot fail to maintain its popularity as a racing rendezvous."

Only now the boundaries of popularity extend beyond Melbourne, beyond Victoria and beyond Australia. The race honoring Sam Cox is now truly an event of the world after the success of Irish star Adelaide, who became the first international winner for Aidan O'Brien in 2014.

Old Sam Cox could never have envisaged what he started. Feehan's Farm is now the site of a $3 million race watched globally by millions. The "eyesore", that "blot on the landscape" has been transformed into a world-class racing venture, soon to be dramatically enhanced even more.

Michael Browell ... the multi-million dollar refurbishment will secure Moonee Valley's future as a major state, national and international racing venue.

THE PLATES

1922 — SWEET MUSIC FOR PLATE'S DEBUT

The crowds that flocked to Moonee Valley on October 28, 1922, were probably as oblivious to the fact that history was about to be made, as were the thousands who at the same time were lining the banks of the Yarra for the Henley Regatta.

But, just as it was nostalgia for the Mother Country that led to the naming of Melbourne's annual boat races, then so it was to England that the first ever running of the W.S. Cox Plate will be irrevocably linked.

It was won by the imported stallion Violoncello, a nine-year-old who the previous year had won the Caulfield Cup at only his fifth start in Australia after being brought out from England.

Just as the Cox Plate today is recognized as Australia's premier weight-for-age race, so too is the Melbourne Cup its greatest handicap. Fitting then, perhaps, that the first running of the Cox Plate should have an indirect link with Australia's most famous race. Some 12 years earlier, the imported galloper Comedy King, a stallion who upon retirement embarked on a highly successful stud career, had won the Melbourne Cup.

The 1919 Melbourne Cup was won by Comedy King's son Artilleryman, part owned by Sydney businessman Sir Samuel Horden. Sadly, Artilleryman died later that season, leaving Sir Samuel determined to find a replacement. His quest took him eventually to England, where he purchased Violoncello for 4,000 guineas. The then seven-year-old had raced just six times for three wins – all at Newmarket. More likely though it was the knowledge that Violoncello's half brother, Quinologist, had won the 1916 AJC Metropolitan that influenced Sir Samuel to buy him.

In winning the 1921 Caulfield Cup, Violoncello defeated Purser, a horse whose name for various reasons is etched in Australia's racing history. In the race book the winner appeared as "Violincello" but it was established the more odd spelling of his name was correct. (Coincidentally, less than an hour after Violoncello consolidated his place in racing history by winning the first ever Cox Plate, Purser came out and won the 1922 Moonee Valley Cup.)

1922
(Saturday, October 28)

£1000 Weight for Age 9½ furlongs

1.	VIOLONCELLO	C. H. Bryans	9.4	J. King	2/1
2.	Easingwold	W. Marks	9.0	F. Dempsey	8/1
3.	Furious	F. J. Marsden	8.9	R. Lewis	9/4

Winning details

Margin: 1½ len x nk. **Time:** 1.57.5 14 started.

Breeding: Valens – Catgut – Lactantius (ch h 7) **Owner:** Sir Samuel Horden

Winner's Colors: White, red sash, pale blue cap

Winning Numbers: 6, 12, 13

ALSO RAN

David	J. Holt	A. Wood	9.4	10/1
Salatis	P. T. Heywood	C. Boyd	9.0	7/1
Tangalooma	J. Holt	H. Cairns	9.1	6/4f
Wirraway	C. H. Bryans	W. Duncan	9.1	20/1
Caserta	A. Foulsham	V. Sleigh	7.11	20/1
Anton King	J. M. Cummings	R. Medhurst	7.11	40/1
Prince Charles	F. J. Marsden	J. Munro	9.4	33/1
Kingsfield	F. Musgrave	A. Wilson	7.11	100/1
Prince Minimbah	F.J. Marsden	J. Mulcahy	7.11	40/1
Basella	C. Star	J. Toohey	9.4	100/1
Brilliant Sunshine	J. J. O'Toole	E. O'Sullivan	9.4	100/1

Scratched: Eurythmic, Kenneppil, Harvest King

VIOLONCELLO ... a classy import who set the standard for Cox Plate winners from the outset. – Picture: HWT

At that time, the Moonee Valley Cup was considered more important than the Plate, for it was seen as one of the most influential lead up races to the Melbourne Cup. That said, it is clear no one who witnessed that first running of the Cox Plate doubted the impact the event would have on racing in the future.

Writing in the *Sun News Pictorial* on race day, *Vigilant* had this to say about the new race:

"It seems likely to make a brilliant debut .... as most of the best horses in Australia are among the 17 acceptors."

The pre-post favorite was the Jack Holt-trained Eurythmic, the 1920 Caulfield Cup winner who had graduated into the best weight-for-age company, but he was scratched on race morning. Instead, the Holt stable ran Tangalooma, inferior to Eurythmic but a weight-for-age winner just the same. Although nominated for both races, Tangalooma in fact had seemed certain to start in the Moonee Valley Cup, but such were the racing rules then he was able to be switched to the Plate just hours before start time.

Holt's genius – not for nothing was he known as the Wizard of Mordialloc – decreed Tangalooma should start favorite at 5/2, with Violoncello next best at 7/2. Violoncello performed brilliantly, Tangalooma ran ingloriously, the race was as simple as that. Jockey John King always had the imported stayer close to the lead and turning into the straight he urged him up to the pacemaker, the West Australian Easingwold.

Violoncello quickly gained the upper hand and raced away to win by 1½ lengths from Easingwold, with the smart NSW mare Furious running home strongly for third.

And so began the W.S. Cox Plate which would become synonymous with Moonee Valley hosting the weight-for-age Championship of Australasia.

1923 — THE GOLDFIELDS CHAMPION

If ever the Moonee Valley Racing Club wondered about how long it might take for the W. S. Cox Plate to cement its place as one of the country's premier weight-for-age races, then its mind was soon put at rest.

Just a year after its inception, Melbourne's *Herald* had this to say of the 1923 field:

"With such a wealth of talent engaged the W. S. Cox Plate, run at weight-for-age, almost eclipses the Moonee Valley Cup in importance."

It is a significant statement, for it should be remembered the Moonee Valley Cup then enjoyed a status not much less than that of the Caulfield Cup, with both events considered prime lead-up races to the Melbourne Cup. And the big handicaps then were the glamour races of the Australian turf, to which the weight-for-age contests generally played second fiddle.

That said, while in the eyes of those expert in horse racing matters the Cox Plate was perhaps a match for the Cup, in terms of prizemoney it still lagged well behind. Total prizemoney for the 1923 Cox Plate was £1,000, two-thirds of the overall stake for the Moonee Valley Cup.

It could hardly compare with the money on offer in the Melbourne Spring Carnival's two major races, with the Caulfield Cup in 1923 worth £6,500, and the Melbourne Cup more than £13,000.

Still, it was a classy field of 11 runners that left the mounting yard for the second running, and it included the tough, former West Australian galloper Easingwold, runner-up to Violoncello in the inaugural contest, and Purser, the 1922 Moonee Valley Cup winner and a hardy campaigner at the highest level for several seasons. They were joined by the 1922 Caulfield Cup winner Whittier, classy New Zealand stayer Rapine, and the highly promising three-year-old filly Frances Tressady.

It is hard to imagine now that a Kalgoorlie Cup winner could one day be good enough to win the Cox Plate, and that's in no way meant to denigrate the pride and joy of racing in the Goldfields. But Easingwold was a much, much better than average galloper, whose credentials first came to notice in Western Australia. As a three-year-old in the 1921-22 season, he won the West Australian Derby and the WA St. Leger and, at the

1923
(Saturday, October 27)

£1,000 Weight for Age 9½ furlongs

1.	**EASINGWOLD**	J. Holt	9.4	*G. Harrison*	6/4f
2.	**Whittier**	H. McCalman	9.0	*L. Franklin*	3/1
3.	**Purser**	C. T. Godby	9.1	*H. Cairns*	6/1

Winning details

Margin: 1½ len x len. **Time:** 1.57.25 9 started.

Breeding: Eaton Lad (GB) – Bahloo – Maltster (ch h 5) **Owner:** W. Marks

Winner's Colors: Red, purple spots

Winning Numbers: 1, 5, 4

ALSO RAN

Cliffdale	A. Inkpen	J. Toohey	8.11	20/1
Rapine	J. H. Jefferd	R. Reed	8.11	10/1
Frances Tressady	W. Vauxhall	F. Dempsey	7.6	16/1
Stormy Day	P. McCarthy	J. Gardiner	7.11	33/1
Royal Roue	R. C. Stanton	J. Munro	7.11	33/1
Stare	P. Guinane	E. O'Sullivan	9.4	8/1

Scratched: Harvest King, Shrapnel

beginning of the following season, in August, 1922, he was taken to Kalgoorlie for three starts for three wins, including the Cup.

Brought to Melbourne by his owner-trainer W. Marks, he ran a strong fourth in the Toorak Handicap and was unplaced in the Caulfield Cup before finishing runner-up in the Cox Plate. By the Spring of the following year, Easingwold, although still owned by Marks, was in the care of legendary trainer Jack Holt. A consummate horseman, Holt prepared horses according to their individual traits. Easingwold was a tough, durable campaigner and so he was given plenty to do in the lead up to the Cox Plate.

He started on all three days of the Caulfield Cup Carnival, and on each occasion produced stirring efforts. He finished a close third in the Caulfield Stakes (1800m) on day one, won the Herbert Power Stakes (2200m) on the middle day, and carrying 9.1 (57.5kg) ran a gallant second to the mare Wynette (carrying 6.11) in the Caulfield Cup (2400m).

A natural leader, Easingwold took the lead early in the Cox Plate, but always had Whittier worrying him on his outside. The pair took the field along at a great rate, to the extent the remainder of the field could never muster a proper challenge.

As Easingwold gained the upper hand from Whittier nearing the turn, it appeared for a few strides that Purser's strong challenge from the ruck might carry him past the leaders, an opinion voiced by Holt who was watching the race in the company of Purser's trainer, Cecil Godby. Purser, though, could not sustain his run and, at the same time, the gallant Easingwold dug deep and found the necessary reserves to draw away again and win by 1½ lengths from Whittier, with Purser a length away third, in a then track record time of 1.57.2.

Perhaps because of his origins, Easingwold was never really accorded the distinction he deserved in the Eastern states, which probably prompted the Letter to the Editor from *"Easingwold"* which appeared in *The Herald* on the Monday after his great Cox plate win.

"Am I any good?" he asked. *"Have I pace? Have I stamina? Is there a horse in Melbourne who can outstrip me from one furlong to 12?"*

On Cox Plate day, 1923, there wasn't.

1924 — SCANDAL CUTS PLATE FIELD

Even as nominations were being declared, a racing storm was brewing. Eventually, it would engulf the 1923 Cox Plate to the extent the race would be but a fleeting diversion in a series of events that rocked the racing world, culminating in an inquiry that was to rank as one of the most sensational in Australian turf history.

Because the first two runnings of the Cox Plate had attracted so much interest, it was right to assume the 1924 running of the fledgling weight-for-age race would be a talking point of the Spring Carnival that year.

Entries for the race suggested as much. The 1923 winner Easingwold was there, presumably to defend his crown against the likes of Caulfield Cup winners Whittier and Purser. To add to the class of the field, other entries included the outstanding three-year-old Heroic, and a highly respected imported galloper, The Night Patrol.

But even as nominations were being declared, a racing storm was brewing. Eventually, it would engulf the 1923 Cox Plate to the extent the race would be but a fleeting diversion in a series of events that rocked the racing world, culminating in an inquiry that was to rank as one of the most sensational in Australian turf history. Given who most of the main players were – plus those on the periphery – it is a story that must be re-visited.

At the centre of it was the seven-year-old gelding Purser, that durable stayer who'd won the 1922 Moonee Valley Cup and who'd finished third behind Easingwold in the 1923 Cox Plate. He was owned by prominent racing men Jack Corteen and George Tye, who early that year had combined their racing interests in the care of astute trainer, Cecil Godby, to form a triumvirate which was much feared, in particular, by bookmakers.

Purser had been placed in both the 1921 and 1922 Caulfield Cups, but early in the week leading up to the 1924 Cup, trainer Godby declared the old campaigner a non-starter, saying The Monk would be his Cup representative. This plan seemed well founded when Purser ran in the Coongy Handicap on the middle day of the Caulfield Carnival and, after racing second for much of the way, faded badly in the straight to finish 11th.

Nevertheless, Purser was an acceptor for the Caulfield Cup, but even as late as Cup morning was not expected to run. It should be explained that in those days horses could be scratched right up until what was called Payment Time, usually about 1½ hours before a race. Thus it came as a complete surprise when, at 1.55pm, Godby declared Purser a Caulfield Cup runner and, at the same time, scratched The Monk. There was a further surprise when Purser was

---

1924
(Saturday, October 25. Attendance 27,540)

£1,000 Weight for Age 9½ furlongs

1.	**THE NIGHT PATROL**	J. Scobie	9.4	*G. Young*	7/2
2.	**Whittier**	H. McCalman	9.4	*F. Dempsey*	6/4f
3.	**Demades**	L. J. McCann	7.11	*J. Daniels*	100/1

Winning details

Margin: ¾ len x 2 len. **Time:** 1.59.25 7 started.

Breeding: Stedfast – Dark Flight – Dark Ronald (b h 7) **Owner:** H. E. The Earl of Stradbroke

Winner's Colors: Red and white quarters, black cap **Barriers:** 6, 5, 1

Winning Numbers: 1, 3, 8

ALSO RAN

The Hawk	J. M. Cameron	L. Franklin	9.1	7/2
Lilypond	J. Holt	G. Harrison	8.11	4/1
Frances Tressady	W. Foulsham	A. Cooper	8.9	50/1
Solidify	D. Lewis	J. Harris	7.11	100/1

Scratched: Easingwold, Polycletan

THE NIGHT PATROL ... owned by the Governor of Victoria, Lord Stradbroke, the imported stallion was one of the Plate's most popular winners. – Picture: HWT

backed from 50/1 to 15/1, a show of confidence that belied his Coongy form. Then it was announced Hughie Cairns, Purser's regular rider, would be replaced by New Zealand hoop George Young, who'd been listed to ride The Monk.

And then the biggest surprise of all. After trailing the 23-strong field for about 1000m, Purser was set alight by Young and almost effortlessly rounded up the opposition to hit the front early in the straight and win hard held by 2½ lengths. His win elicited few cheers and widespread conjecture, yet it wasn't until the following Tuesday the VATC stewards announced they'd opened a retrospective inquiry into Purser's Coongy performance.

On Thursday, just two days before the Cox Plate, all parties to Purser's Coongy Handicap run were questioned, as well as a number of witnesses. Shortly after lunch, the stewards announced their verdict. Godby, Corteen, Tye and Cairns all were disqualified for 12 months, charged with being party to Purser not being allowed to run on his merits in the Coongy. The horse, too, was banned for the same period. An appeal was lodged immediately, but VRC chairman L.K.S. Mackinnon ruled it could not be heard until the following Monday.

In those days there was no such thing as a stay of proceedings, and so the Cox Plate field was thrown into turmoil. Purser naturally could not run, but neither could Heroic, who was owned by Corteen and trained by Godby. The field was further depleted when it was decided Easingwold would not defend his crown, but instead would tackle the Moonee Valley Cup.

Come race day and only seven runners went to the barrier, with Whittier a strong favorite at 6/4, with The Night Patrol at 7/2 along with The Hawk, while Lilypond was at 4/1. The rest, including Frances Tressady, were 50/1 or better.

The Night Patrol had made the pace in the Caulfield Cup to the home turn a week earlier, so jockey George Young – yes, the same man who won the Caulfield Cup on Purser – had no hesitation in taking the imported galloper to the front around Moonee Valley's turning circuit. Before the halfway mark was reached, Whittier had moved up to sit at The Night Patrol's girth, but try as he might in the last 400m, the favorite could not get past the brave English galloper, who held him at bay to win by three-quarters of a length.

The Night Patrol's win briefly illuminated what were dark days in racing, for Lord Stradbroke, the very popular Governor of Victoria, owned him. He'd raced The Night Patrol with success in England and, following his appointment as Victoria's head of State, had arranged for the horse to come to Australia.

The Sun News Pictorial reported:

"When it was obvious The Night Patrol was going to win a great roar of applause and cheering went up. It continued and swelled as the horses swept past the post, and was taken up again and again."

When all of the tumult and shouting had died, there was still the matter of the Purser case to be decided.

The VRC committee listened to the Appeal by Purser's connections – and others – for 2½ hours on the Monday after the Cox Plate, but took all of 15 minutes to reach their decision. Appeal dismissed.

1925 — MANFRED JUMPED AT THE CHANCE

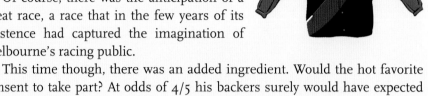

That Manfred was an outstanding galloper, possibly a champion even, was not in doubt. However, he'd inherited from his great sire, Valais, not only the ability to gallop, but also a stubbornness that on racedays frequently translated into "barrier rogue".

In fact, it is fair to assume that had the barrier behaviour standards of today been in force in Manfred's time, then almost certainly he would have been banned from racing.

The breathless hush that invariably casts itself over the crowd just before the start of a Cox Plate held extra meaning in the seconds leading up to barrier rise for the 1925 running of the event.

Of course, there was the anticipation of a great race, a race that in the few years of its existence had captured the imagination of Melbourne's racing public.

This time though, there was an added ingredient. Would the hot favorite consent to take part? At odds of 4/5 his backers surely would have expected to at least get a run for their money. But with the three-year-old Manfred, this was no certainty.

That he was an outstanding galloper, possibly a champion even, was not in doubt. However, he'd inherited from his great sire, Valais, not only the ability to gallop, but also a stubbornness that on racedays frequently transformed him into a "barrier rogue".

In fact, it is fair to assume that had the barrier behaviour standards of today been in force in Manfred's time, then almost certainly, he would have been banned from racing, costing Australia one of its true turf greats.

His exceptional ability shone through as a two-year-old when he won the Champagne Stakes at Randwick by eight lengths. Six months later the colt returned there for the AJC Derby. His reputation suffered a little when he started at 1/3 in a lead-up race, the Hill Stakes at Rosehill, but had his colors lowered by the handy, but not exceptional, weight-for-age performer The Hawk.

Two weeks can be a long time in racing, so when he stepped onto the track for the Derby, Manfred again was next to unbackable at 2/5. "Bank teller" odds, as they say, ("borrow" from the till on Friday, hopefully put it back on Monday) but when the tapes flew up any tellers that might have "taken a loan" must have almost died with fright.

Manfred swung around and charged sideways across the track, chased by a clerk of the course waving his whip. The colt sidled off at half pace, but by the time jockey Bill Duncan convinced him to take up the chase, Manfred was giving his five rivals a start of more than 100m.

Fortunately perhaps, the leaders went slowly through the first part of the race, enabling the wayward colt to tack onto the field. Inside the last 800m Manfred ranged alongside his chief adversary, Amounis, and together they swept into the lead. Surely the effort of

1925

(Saturday, October 24. Attendance: 30,320)

£1,000 Weight for Age 9½ furlongs

1.	MANFRED	H. McCalman	7.11	F. Dempsey	4/5f
2.	The Night Patrol	J. Scobie	9.4	G. Young	9/4
3.	Pantheon	F. Williams	9.1	S. Cracknell	14/1

Winning details

Margin: Short ½ hd x 3 len. **Time:** 1.57 (Course record) 6 strs.

Breeding: Valais – Otford – Tressady (b c 3) **Owner:** Ben Chaffey

Winner's Colors: Black, blue sleeves, red sash and cap

Winning Numbers: 6, 1, 3 **Barriers:** 6, 3, 2

ALSO RAN

Royal Charter	J. Holt	W. Duncan	8.11	20/1
Valimita	F. Taverna	A. Reed	9.0	50/1
Hampden	F. Foulsham	J. Daniels	7.9	50/1

Scratched: Whittier

making up the lost ground would tell upon the favorite? Far from it!

Manfred soon shook off Amounis, and raced away to win being eased down by 1½ lengths from Petunia and Tibbie. The time of 2min 35.5secs was relatively slow, but because of the enormous start he gave away, Manfred was timed to have run the 2400m in 2mins 28.5 secs, an extraordinary gallop given the then Australian record for the distance was 2mins 30.5 secs.

The big Sydney crowd wildly cheered the colt, but the vast number of punters who ventured to Caulfield Guineas day two weeks later found no cause to similarly applaud the colt. Again a 2/5 chance, Manfred dug his toes in for good at the start of the Guineas, and defied Duncan's increasingly frantic efforts to kick him into action.

The ultimate Spring mission for Manfred was the Melbourne Cup, and therefore a run in the Cox Plate was always going to be optional. His genial owner, Mr. Ben Chaffey, also owned Whittier, a highly talented but injury plagued galloper who'd won the Caulfield Cup in 1922 and a week after Manfred's Guineas disgrace, won it again. In the previous two years, Whittier had finished second in the Cox Plate, and indications after his Caulfield Cup win were that he would contest the race for a third time. But Chaffey and trainer Harry McCalman felt that possibly the only way to cure Manfred's barrier behaviour in time for the Cup was to race him as often as possible, and so it was decided he would be the stable representative in the Cox Plate.

Twice the colt was taken to Moonee Valley for barrier practice, on both occasions giving no trouble. More importantly, the connections decided on a change of rider, the mount going to Frank Dempsey, recently returned from England. In all of the hullabaloo surrounding Manfred, sharp-eyed punters did not miss the report on the eve of the race, to the effect that The Night Patrol, the defending Cox Plate champion, had established a 1200m record on the tan track at Flemington in his final track gallop.

Still, general feeling on raceday was that Manfred would win the race IF he consented to jump away. Despite that risk, there were plenty of takers when bookmakers offered a shade of even money before sending him off at 4/5, with The Night Patrol at 9/4, the only other one of the six starters in the market.

There were many at Moonee Valley that day who believe Manfred was given a "flying start," although his exit from the barrier was more of a sideways jump, rather than a clean getaway.

At the first attempt to get the field away, Manfred backed out at the last moment. As the field lined up again, Dempsey kicked the colt forward. The starter Mr. Wood released the tapes at that second, but Manfred gained little, if any, advantage. However, he DID get away cleanly. Soon after, The Night Patrol took up his customary position at the head of the field. Thereafter unfolded a race that surely must have been the equal of a Cox Plate run 61 years later, the contest dubbed the Race Of The Century between Bonecrusher and Our Waverley Star.

Dempsey had been informed that on occasions The Night Patrol would give up when challenged for the lead, so with this in mind, he took the leader on with all of 1000m left to run.

Far from throwing in the towel, The Night Patrol responded to Manfred's challenge, and the pair went stride for stride to the home turn. Even then it appeared both horses were still full of running. In the end, perhaps, it was the pull in the weights – under the scale The Night Patrol had to give his younger rival 9.5kg – that enabled Manfred to gain the upper hand. Still, his time of 1min 57secs created a new record for the distance and wasn't bettered until 1938, coincidentally by a grandson of Manfred's sire Valais, the mighty Ajax.

Dempsey was fulsome in his praise: "He is the gamest colt I have ridden," he said.

The following year, although refusing to jump on several occasions, Manfred confirmed his greatness by winning the Caulfield Cup with 60kg and setting a weight-carrying record.

1926 — HE WAS HEROIC BY NAME AND NATURE

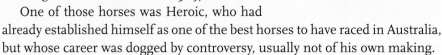

Heroic had already established himself as one of the best horses to have raced in Australia, but his career was dogged by controversy, usually not of his own making.

Even when he put the seal on a great career by winning the 1926 Cox Plate, there were those intent upon downplaying his performance, given he had only three rivals.

But to cast an eye over Heroic's career record reveals a horse who on his day was capable of beating all-comers, be they good, bad or indifferent.

It would be fair to say that in the mid-1920's the depth of weight-for-age competition in Australian was unprecedented.

Maurice Cavanough, in his history of the Caulfield Cup, says "a strong case can be made out for the contention there never has been another season in which so many good horses raced against each other as in 1925/26."

One of those horses was Heroic, who had already established himself as one of the best horses to have raced in Australia, but whose career was dogged by controversy, usually not of his own making.

Even when he put the seal on a great career by winning the 1926 Cox Plate, there were those intent upon downplaying his performance, given he had only three rivals. On the face of it, Heroic's opposition in the Cox Plate that year did not reflect the strength of weight-for-age racing that was so evident the previous season.

But to cast an eye over Heroic's career record reveals a horse who on his day was capable of beating all-comers, be they good, bad or indifferent. And what is more, he did it over four seasons, having shone as a two-year-old, excelled as a three-year-old, and proved himself a high class performer at four and five.

Heroic originally was owned by Jack Corteen, and trained for him by Cecil Godby at Caulfield. There was nothing controversial about the two-year-old Heroic, just a brilliance that enabled him to win major juvenile races including the Maribyrnong Plate in Melbourne, and the Champagne and Breeders' Stakes in Sydney.

In the Spring of 1924, he was taken to Sydney for the AJC Derby and, heavily backed to start favorite at 10-9, scraped home by a head from Nigger Minstrel, with Spearfelt, later to win the 1926 Melbourne Cup, a head away third.

The event though was shrouded with sinister mystery, for rumors abounded in Sydney BEFORE the race that it was to be fixed for one of the runners. Such was the backing for Heroic, and the fact several of his rivals including the two placegetters did not have the best of runs, fuelled speculation that Heroic was IT.

Nevertheless, the colt returned to Melbourne to win the Caulfield Guineas, to confirm his position as odds-on favorite for the Victoria Derby, and a 4-1 top pick for the Melbourne Cup.

Pre-post betting, because it is "all in", has about it

1926
(Saturday, October 23. Attendance: 28,500)

£1,000 plus £100 trophy Weight for Age 9½ furlongs

1.	HEROIC	J. Holt	9.4	H. Cairns	4/5f
2.	Limerick	F. D. Jones	7.8	T. Green	2/1
3.	Metellus	J. Holt	9.1	J. Winks	14/1

Winning details

Margin: 3 len x 3 len. **Time:** 1.58 4 started.

Breeding: Valais – Chersonese (GB) – Cyglad (ch h 5) **Owner:** C. B. Kellow

Winner's Colors: Yellow, green sleeves and cap

Winning Numbers: 1, 4, 2 **Barriers:** 3, 1, 4

ALSO RAN

Cromwell	L. McCann	W. Duncan	7.11	8/1

All started

an element of risk, but those who backed Heroic to win those races were entitled to feel cheated when he failed to appear in either.

As was referred to in the story of the 1924 Cox Plate, both Corteen and Godby were among those disqualified over the running of Caulfield Cup winner Purser in the Coongy Handicap of that year. Thus horses owned by Corteen could not fulfil their engagements, and so Heroic was forced out of the two races for which he'd been heavily backed by punters throughout Australia.

A disillusioned Corteen sold many of his horses, including Heroic, who passed into the hands of an equally well-known owner, Charles Kellow, for the considerable sum of £16,000.

The wisdom of the buy came in the Autumn of 1926, when Heroic produced a superb performance to win the VRC Newmarket Handicap over 1200m. He was unlucky not to have completed a rare double, suffering severe interference before finishing fourth in the Sydney Cup behind Murray King.

Not for nothing had trainer Jack Holt earned a reputation as the "Wizard of Mordialloc" but it took all of his magic to have Heroic ready to run and win the Cox Plate. The colt suffered a leg injury in the weeks leading up to the race, forcing Holt to ease him in his work. In so many instances an interrupted preparation has been the downfall of even the best gallopers. But the wily Holt made up for Heroic's period of relative inactivity by in effect doubling his workload in the week leading up to the Cox Plate.

In his last serious workout at Mentone on the Thursday morning, Heroic galloped 1600m with his stablemate and Cox Plate rival Metellus, and astounded clockers by breaking the track record. To their added amazement Heroic, after slowing for several hundred metres, suddenly picked up the pace again and sprinted 600m in a cool 37 seconds.

It could be said the Cox Plate of 1926 was tailor-made for an upset win. Only four horses went to the barrier, and so often in small fields the unexpected result occurs.

Not this time. Punters saw it as a two horse race, between Heroic, the favorite at 4-5, and the former New Zealander Limerick at 2-1. Limerick then was a good galloper, but didn't really find his best form until the following season, when he beat the likes of Windbag, Amounis and Gothic at weight-for-age.

Given he'd missed work, it came as no surprise to find Heroic looking a trifle big in the mounting yard, but most importantly he showed no signs of any soreness. Limerick and Heroic duelled in front for most of the journey but Heroic eventually broke away to win easily by three lengths.

Once again Holt's "wizardry" paid off, although it is testament to Heroic's durability and courage that he was able to put the seal on a great career by winning the weight-for-age championship.

The following Autumn, Heroic won five races – including the VATC St George Stakes, which brought up his sixth win on end, and the two mile VRC King's Plate – before being sent to stud, with a career record of 21 wins and 15 placings in 51 starts.

An outstanding success at stud – he was leading Australian sire on many occasions – his progeny included Gallantic (VRC and AJC Oaks), Melbourne Cup winner, Hall Mark, and Nuffield, winner of the Victoria and AJC Derbys and the Caulfield Guineas.

1927 — AMOUNIS CONQUERED THE VERY BEST

The son of Magpie beat the mighty Phar Lap on two occasions, in the 1930 St. George Stakes at Caulfield, and later that year in the Warwick Stakes at Warwick Farm. Amounis, who raced with distinction for the best part of six seasons, was a classy, game and versatile competitor.

The late 1920's and early 1930's must rank as a golden age in Australian racing, featuring as it did some of the greatest names to grace the turf in this country.

Phar Lap, of course, stands alone at the top, but the likes of Peter Pan, Nightmarch, Manfred, Windbag, Hall Mark and Chatham, to name but a few, would have challenged any horse in any era.

So too, would have Amounis, the 1927 Cox Plate winner, who both before and after his win in the weight-for-age classic, provided formidable opposition for many of the above named gallopers.

Indeed, the son of Magpie beat the mighty Phar Lap on two occasions, in the 1930 St. George Stakes at Caulfield, and later that year in the Warwick Stakes at Warwick Farm. Amounis, who raced with distinction for the best part of six seasons, was a classy, game and versatile competitor.

Sold as a yearling for 300 gns, Amounis won twice as an early three-year-old but was then sold for 2,500 gns, and promptly won several races including the 1925 Rosehill Guineas for his new connections. For reasons unknown – perhaps his owner found himself in some financial strait – Amounis was sold again, this time for just 1,500 gns to Walter Pearson, and entered the stables of astute Sydney trainer Frank McGrath.

A former jockey, McGrath almost lost his life in an horrific 16-horse fall in the 1885 Caulfield Cup, which saw an extraordinary 41 runners face the starter. One jockey was killed, but McGrath recovered to become one of the best trainers in the country.

He ranked Amounis as one of his favorites, and understandably so. For the next five years the brown gelding raced in the best company, in handicaps and in weight-for-age contests, and when he won the 1930 Caulfield Cup, he surpassed the mighty Gloaming as the then greatest stake-winner in Australian racing history.

A genuine "miler", he won the Epsom Handicap at Randwick in 1926 as a four-year-old beating the very talented sprinter Fuji

1927

(Saturday, October 22. Attendance: 26,300)

£1,000 plus £100 trophy Weight for Age 9½ furlongs

1.	**AMOUNIS**	F. McGrath	9.1	*J. Toohey*	3/1ef
2.	**Avant-Courier**	F. Foulsham	7.11	*J. Daniels*	7/2
3.	**Gothic**	L. Robertson	9.1	*A. Reed*	3/1ef

Winning details

Margin: Nk x len. **Time:** 2:00.5 10 started.

Breeding: Magpie – Loved One – Duke of Melton (br g 5) **Owner:** W. Pearson

Winner's Colors: Purple & yellow diamonds, purple sleeves & cap

Winning Numbers: 3, 8, 2 **Barriers:** 4, 1, 8

ALSO RAN

Thracian	J. Pengilly	V. Sleigh	9.0	20/1
Merry Mint	F. McGrath	E. Bartle	7.10	8/1
Metellus	J. Holt	W. Duncan	9.1	25/1
Sacedon	S. B. Ferguson	F. Dempsey	7.11	20/1
Charlot	W. Foulsham	H. Foster	7.8	33/1
Statesman	W. Kelso	S. Davidson	7.12	50/1
Bacchus	W. Kelso	H. Cairns	9.1	50/1

Scratched: Pantheon, Silvius

AMOUNIS ... a dual victor over Phar Lap, he was embroiled in Phar Lap's Melbourne Cup doubles betting sting, but made a name for himself for another reason with this Plate win in 1927. – Picture: HWT

San, and the same season defeated a high class weight-for-age field, including Windbag and Limerick, in the Chipping Norton Stakes.

In more recent times horses in their lead-ups to the Cox Plate generally have followed what many have believed to be a traditional preparation, starting off over short trips and building up to the now 2040m of the Valley race. Traditional perhaps in modern times, but not so back in the early part of this century, when the options were not so varied.

Amounis began his 1927 Spring preparation by beating all but the talented Limerick in the Warwick Stakes over 1600m at Warwick Farm, then finished third to that horse, split by Gothic, in the 1600m Hill Stakes at Rosehill.

Next on the agenda was an attempt at back-to-back wins in the Epsom Handicap, in which he ran an honest sixth with the steadier of 61.5kg. It seems the training methods of the time dictated that good horses such as Amounis contested the Metropolitan Handicap, despite it coming just two days after the Epsom. It proved too much of a test for Amounis, and he finished in the back half of the field.

Wisely perhaps, McGrath rested the gelding for a week or so before sending him to Melbourne, and then resisted the temptation to give Amounis a run before the Cox Plate. Although a field of 10 lined up for the race, the general feeling was it would be a three-way contest. Few would split the talented five-year-olds Amounis and Gothic, and indeed at post time they shared favoritism at 3-1.

Gothic's versatility was typical of so many of the great horses that raced in the two decades before World War II. His best was yet to come when he contested the 1927 Cox Plate, but he'd already proved himself capable of winning the Newmarket Handicap the previous Autumn. The Caulfield Guineas winner Avant Courier was seen as the horse most likely to upset the favorites, being very much in the market at 7-2. The only other runner at single figure odds was another three-year-old, Sydney-trained gelding Merry Mint.

Under his light weight, Avant Courier was determined to make his older rivals work hard for victory, and set a solid gallop, with both Amounis and Gothic settling in the mid-field. The order changed little until nearing the 600m, when long-shot Charlot tried to put pressure on the leader but was quickly shaken off. Approaching the turn, jockey Jack Toohey urged Amounis forward and upon straightening he had joined forces with Avant Courier, with Gothic angling for a run between them.

The *Melbourne Herald* report of the concluding stages of the race is interesting. It describes how Avant

Urged on by jockey Frank McGrath, Amounis just lasts from the dogged Avant Courier. McGrath ranked Amounis as one of his favorites. – Picture: HWT

Courier fought courageously when tackled by Amounis and only relinquished the lead close to the post to be beaten a neck.

Then it states: *"Gothic was sandwiched between the pair of them at the distance (200m mark). Just as Gothic was making an effort to get through Amounis cut across in front, and (jockey) Reed had to ease Gothic, who finished a length away third."*

The report gives the impression there might have been grounds for an objection. Perhaps because a successful protest would have promoted Gothic into only second place, there wasn't one.

Both Amounis and Gothic found Silvius too good for them in the Melbourne (now Mackinnon) Stakes the following week, but five days later Amounis scored a convincing win in the Linlithgow Stakes over 1600m.

The following Spring, Amounis began his preparation with wins in the Tramway Handicap, the Epsom Handicap (with 60.5kg) and the Craven Plate, before finishing second to Gothic in the Caulfield Stakes. He ran equal favorite but finished a disappointing seventh to Highland in the Cox Plate on a heavy track, but after twice being beaten by Gothic at weight-for-age, bounced back to win the Williamstown (now Sandown) Cup.

The next season this great horse was again a force at weight-for-age, beating Phar Lap in the St George Stakes and also winning the Futurity Stakes at Caulfield and the Canterbury Stakes in Sydney.

Five months later, in the Spring of 1930, he again beat Phar Lap, in the Warwick Stakes, and later scored an easy win in the Caulfield Cup, although therein lies a story. Phar Lap that year appeared to have a mortgage on both the Caulfield and Melbourne Cups, and consequently combinations in doubles betting on the events were almost any odds bar the obvious one.

Phar Lap's trainer Harry Telford never had any real intention of running "Big Red" at Caulfield, but legendary punter Eric Connolly convinced him not to scratch the horse until just five days before the race. His presence scared away much of the opposition, including talented New Zealander Nightmarch, the previous year's Victoria Derby and Melbourne Cup winner whose connections became sick of playing second fiddle to Phar Lap in Sydney weight-for-age races, and took him home.

Only hours before Phar Lap's scratching, Connolly's agents backed the Amounis-Phar Lap Cups double with bookmakers all around Australia at odds of up to 20-1. Amounis had little trouble in beating a sub-standard Caulfield Cup field, and when Phar Lap romped home at Flemington the bookies lost an estimated £200,000, which translates these days into several million dollars.

1928 – 'WIZARD' WEAVES SOME HIGHLAND MAGIC

Not for nothing was legendary trainer Jack Holt dubbed the "Wizard Of Mordialloc." From his beachside stables he sent out many champion gallopers to win Australia's greatest races.

They included Melbourne Cup winner Hall Mark, Caulfield Cup winners Eurythmic, Maple and High Syce, and five Cox Plate winners Heroic, Highland dual winner Young Idea and Chanak.

Much of Holt's success stemmed from the fact he possessed an exceptional eye for a horse, and the manner in which he acquired Highland, the 1928 Cox Plate winner – and a much underrated galloper – is testimony to this great attribute.

In his book *The Caulfield Cup*, Maurice Cavanough explains how Holt at Randwick one day in 1927 had a substantial bet on star sprinter Fuji San to win the Railway Handicap.

On the advice of a friend, Holt had a "saver" on a Queensland-trained six-year-old named Highland. But, as the runners filed onto the track, Holt commented that Highland was too light to do himself justice.

Fuji San won, but Highland ran well to finish third, so immediately after the race Holt sought the owner of Highland and made an acceptable offer of £700 for him.

One of Holt's leading patrons was a young woman named Rita Buxton. Upon his advice she took over the purchase of Highland, a high class handicapper who'd won back-to-back Stradbroke Handicaps in 1925 and 1926, and a horse which Holt obviously felt had scope for even further improvement.

Highland showed a glimpse of weight-for-age class in early 1928 when third in the William Reid Stakes, but it was the following Spring the gelding emerged as a far better racehorse than perhaps even Holt could have imagined. His first-up run was nothing startling, an unplaced effort over 1200m in an apprentice handicap at Flemington.

Highland made a quantum leap at his next

> Much of the success of trainer Jack Holt stemmed from the fact he possessed an exceptional eye for a horse, and the manner in which he acquired Highland, the 1928 Cox Plate winner – and a very much underrated galloper – is testimony to this great attribute.

1928
(Saturday, October 27. Attendance: 27,400)

£1,000 plus £100 trophy Weight for Age 9½ furlongs

1.	HIGHLAND	J. Holt	9.1	*W. Duncan*	9/2
2.	Ramulus	G. Price	7.11	*E. Bartle*	3/1ef
3.	Fourth Hand	J. Scobie	9.1	*A. Wilson*	15/1

Winning details

Margin: Short hd x 2 len. **Time:** 2:06.75 9 started.

Breeding: Highfield – Regulator – Havoc (br g 7) **Owner:** Mrs L. R. Buxton

Winner's Colors: Purple white stripe, sleeves & cap

Winning Numbers: 3, 6, 2 **Barriers:** 7, 9, 8

ALSO RAN

Winalot	J. W. Cook	J. Toohey	9.0	4/1
Statesman	W. Kelso	M. McCarten	9.0	25/1
Oatendale	J. P. King	J O'Brien	7.11	15/1
Amounis	F. McGrath	J. Munro	9.1	3/1ef
Strogoff	A. Skirving	F. Cameron	7.11	50/1
Prince Humphrey	J. T. Jamieson	A. Reed	7.11	15/1

All Started

assignment, in the weight-for-age Underwood Stakes, then run over 1600m, at the long defunct Williamstown track.

The only weight-for-age winner in the field was the 1926 Melbourne Cup winner Spearfelt, but he was not expected to be forward enough to win, and so the favorite's mantle fell upon the sprinting mare Lady Beth.

In the event she made the pace but did not quite run the journey, with the result Highland raced past her in the straight to win by a length. Adding merit to the feat was that Highland ran the trip in 1min. 39secs. to break the course record by half a second, despite the dearth of genuine weight-for-age horses in the field.

At his next outing, Highland was unplaced behind English-bred sprinter-miler Gothic, a dual Newmarket Handicap winner owned by leviathan bookmaker Sol Green, in the 1800m Memsie Stakes at Caulfield. Astute judges noted, though, that Lady Beth, beaten by Highland in the Underwood, managed to finish second on this occasion.

At his next start, Highland again ran unplaced, this time behind Kalloni in a Quality Handicap over 1400m at Moonee Valley. Only fair form on paper, but in hindsight highly significant.

Three weeks before the Cox Plate, Highland went out a 10-1 chance for the October Stakes over 1600m at Flemington. Only one opponent counted, the high class and very versatile galloper Gothic.

Most, if not all, considered Gothic unbeatable. "It should be a simple matter for Gothic to defeat his seven opponents ..." stated the Melbourne *Herald's* turf correspondent, an opinion apparently shared by bookmakers.

The majority didn't bother to frame a market on the race, and the less than handful that did, had Gothic at prohibitive odds of 1-10. He was also a firm pre-post favorite for the Caulfield Cup.

Highland beat him, by a half neck. The defeat promoted a greater gnashing of teeth among bookmakers than it did among punters, for by not betting on the race the bagmen denied themselves of a real "killing".

Many blamed Gothic's defeat on jockey Jim Pike, saying he'd taken Highland too cheaply. In fact Gothic took the lead in the straight but was unable to hold the challenge of the Holt-trained horse, upon which the strength and skill of one Bill Duncan was very apparent.

Both horses stepped out at Caulfield the following week, Gothic in the Caulfield Stakes and Highland in the Toorak Handicap. Gothic redeemed himself – and more – by soundly defeating Amounis. Highland was beaten into second place by his old foe Kalloni, but it was an outstanding performance considering Highland was conceding his rival a whopping 12kg.

Gothic was beaten into third place in the Caulfield Cup at his next run – it was won by the Holt-trained, Duncan-ridden Maple – which probably influenced Green not to run him in the Cox Plate. Amounis was there though, trying for back-to-back victories, and with the right form on the board. The horse considered his biggest danger was the three-year-old Ramulus, runner-up in the Caulfield Guineas.

The pair started equal favorites at 3-1, with Sydney Cup winner Winalot at 4-1 and Highland the only other runner under double figures at 9-2. Perhaps the very heavy track was against Amounis, but whatever the reason, he was never a force in the race.

A muddling pace was set by Fourth Hand, who made play until the home turn, when he was overtaken by Ramulus. In the straight the only challenger to Ramulus was Highland, but it took all of Duncan's immense strength to force the gelding ahead of his younger rival in the very last stride.

The win left most racegoers nonplussed. However, it appeared they had all but forgotten the effort three weeks earlier, when Highland had beaten Gothic – obviously a performance which many had considered a fluke. As if to prove his Plate win was not in fact a fluke, Highland stepped out two weeks later and won the Cantala Stakes over 1600m at Flemington.

In the Spring of the following year, he confirmed his rating as a horse of exceptional quality by winning in succession the Underwood Stakes, the Memsie Stakes, a Quality at Moonee Valley, and the Toorak Handicap with 9.10 (61.5kg).

Highland also defended his Cox Plate crown the next year and, in typical fashion, ran a game race to beat all but the outstanding four-year-old Nightmarch.

1929 — NIGHTMARCH DESERVED THE "CHAMPION" TAG

It could be argued a horse that beats only three opponents in any race has not been stood the full test, but in the case of the 1929 Cox Plate nothing could be further from the truth.

It was won by a horse of immense stature, but one who needed to call on all of his great attributes to claim the prize. His name was Nightmarch, a genuine champion of the turf.

Owned and trained in New Zealand, he came to Australia in the Spring of 1929 with eight wins to his credit and a reputation forged against the best of the Kiwi three-year-olds the previous season. A first-up win in the Spring Stakes at Randwick confirmed his standing and he lost no admirers with a subsequent third in the Hill Stakes over 1600m at Rosehill.

His connections had targeted the AJC Metropolitan as his Sydney mission, but were convinced by Australia's biggest and best punter Eric Connelly – he offered them £8000 to nothing – to start Nightmarch in the AJC Epsom Handicap as well. Of course they agreed, whereupon Connelly proceeded to back the four-year-old from 20-1 to 3-1 favoritism for the big Randwick "mile".

Two days before the Epsom, Nightmarch worked over 1200m at Randwick, and clocked a sizzling 1min 13secs for the gallop, an effort which could well have flattened him for the race. To the contrary, Nightmarch overcame a wide barrier to score an authoritative Epsom win, and two days later ran a gallant second under 62.5kg to Loquacious in the Metropolitan.

On the same day Nightmarch won the Epsom, another son of Night Raid, a three-year-old named Phar Lap, bolted away with the AJC Derby. It was inevitable their paths would soon cross. In those heady days horses were for racing, so five days after his Metropolitan appearance Nightmarch returned to Randwick to contest the 3200m Randwick Plate, and established his staying credentials with a strong two length win.

It would be almost unthinkable now for a horse, in his last two outings before the Cox Plate, to run over 2600 and 3200m respectively, but his next stop was the Plate. Throw in the fact Nightmarch was racing at the tight Moonee Valley circuit for the first time, and was coming off five starts racing the opposite way, and you would surely expect to obtain good odds.

At one stage it was expected Phar Lap would contest the Cox Plate, but

In those heady days horses were for racing, so five days after his Metropolitan appearance Nightmarch returned to Randwick to contest the 3200 metre Randwick Plate and established his staying credentials with a strong two length win.

It would be almost unthinkable now for a horse, in his last two outings before the Cox Plate, to run over 2600 and 3200m.

1929
(Saturday, October 26. Attendance: 28,230)

£1,000 plus £100 trophy Weight for Age 9½ furlongs

1.	**NIGHTMARCH**	A. McAulay	9.0	*R. Reed*	5/4f
2.	**Highland**	J. Holt	9.1	*W. Duncan*	5/2
3.	**Mollison**	F. Foulsham	8.11	*W. Cook*	9/1

Winning details

Margin: ½ nk x 2½ len. **Time:** 2:01.5 4 started.

Breeding: Night Raid – Marsa – Martian (br h 4) **Owner:** A. Louisson

Winner's Colors: Purple, yellow spots, purple sleeves, yellow cap

Winning Numbers: 3, 1, 5 **Barriers:** 2, 1, 3

ALSO RAN

Black Duchess	J. King	J. O'Brien	8.13	15/1

Scratched: Amounis

early in the week leading up to the race he was notified as a non-starter. While the opposition to Nightmarch amounted to only three other runners, two of them, Highland and Mollison, were of the highest quality.

Highland in fact was the reigning Cox Plate champion, and came to defend his title in what can only be described as scintillating form, having won his past four starts, the Underwood and Memsie Stakes, the Quality Handicap, and the Toorak Handicap carrying 61.5kg. Also, he had the services of a master jockey in Billy Duncan who, by performing at his brilliant best, all but stole the prize from the New Zealand champion.

When the race came on in earnest with 700m to run, Mollison just led Nightmarch on his outside, with Duncan on Highland gambling on gaining an inside run on the turn. As Mollison wobbled his way into the straight, forcing Nightmarch even wider, Duncan pounced and drove Highland through and into the lead upon straightening up.

It was then Nightmarch revealed his true colors. Despite having difficulty in getting on to his right leg and thus giving his New Zealand jockey Roy Reed a torrid ride, the brown horse gradually overhauled the local champ and in the last 50m gained the upper hand to win by a half neck.

Said *"Ascot"* in the *Melbourne Herald*: "Champion racehorses have won the Cox Plate in the eight years the race has existed, and the victory of Nightmarch compares favorably with those of the brilliant thoroughbreds that have gone before him."

In a sense, they were prophetic words. A week later, on the same day Phar Lap was annihilating his opposition in the Victoria Derby, Nightmarch, his speed blunted, finished third to Caulfield Cup winner High Syce and Mollison in the Melbourne (now Mackinnon) Stakes.

Three days later though, in the Melbourne Cup, Nightmarch carried 58kg to a resounding three length victory, relegating the lightly weighted Phar Lap (47kg) into third place, although the three-year-old pulled very hard and gave jockey Bobby Lewis a nightmare ride.

That said, to win an Epsom Handicap, a Cox Plate and a Melbourne Cup all in the space of just over five weeks truly was the mark of a champion.

1930-31 – PHAR LAP IS STILL THE PLATE STAR

Phar Lap is Australia's best known and best loved horse. Even some seven decades after his death he is still revered.

On the track, he won 37 of his 51 starts (which included an international success in Mexico) but, in addition to his amazing race record, he also became a hero off the track. Enhancing the romance about Phar Lap was the fact that he kept overcoming obstacles introduced by racing administrators and, on one occasion, perpetrated by gangsters. Racing rules were invoked to stop him winning and gunmen tried to maim him to prevent him running in the 1930 Melbourne Cup, for which he was a hot favorite after he was the centre of a Caulfield-Melbourne Cups double betting "sting".

But nothing could stop him. He just kept winning. All this occurred during the Great Depression when public morale was at its lowest ebb, and so it was that the public looked to Phar Lap as a symbol of hope in such harsh times; he was seen as an example of how adversity could be overcome.

A cheap purchase at only 160 gns, he was considered the people's champion, going on to win more than £55,000 and setting time and weight records. Adding to the appeal of "Big Red" was the faithfulness of his gentle strapper Tommy Woodock, in contrast to the harsh manner of his trainer Harry Telford.

Telford bought Phar Lap at the Trentham (NZ) sales because of his breeding but, not having the money to pay for the purchase, convinced Sydney-domiciled American, Mr David Davis, to buy the horse. On checking his appearance when he arrived after crossing the Tasman, Mr Davis did not fancy his purchase, and leased a half share back to Mr Telford.

So began the fairy tale of a horse whose world wide fame now transcends racing.

Early in his career, it appeared that Mr Davis'

MR DAVID DAVIS ...
paid 160 gns for Phar Lap.

Trainer Harry Telford bought Phar Lap at the Trentham (NZ) sales because of his breeding but, not having the money to pay for the purchase, he convinced Sydney-based American Mr David Davis to buy the horse. On seeing him when he arrived after crossing the Tasman, Mr Davis did not like the look of his purchase, and leased a half share back to Mr Telford.

So began the fairy tale rise to fame of a horse whose world wide fame now transcends racing.

1930
(Saturday, October 25. Attendance: 19,490)

£1,000 plus £100 trophy Weight for Age 9½ furlongs

1.	PHAR LAP	H. R. Telford	8.11	J. Pike	1/7f
2.	Tregilla	C. O. Battye	7.11	E. Bartle	10/1
3.	Mollison	F. Foulsham	9.1	J. Daniels	10/1

Winning details

Margin: 4 len x len. **Time:** 1:59.25 6 started

Breeding: Night Raid – Entreaty – Winkie (ch g 4) **Owner:** H. R. Telford

Winner's Colors: Red, black and white hooped sleeves, red cap

Winning Numbers: 3, 4, 2 **Barriers:** 3, 4, 1

ALSO RAN

Veilmond	E. Price	W. Cook	7.11	10/1
Donald	E. F. Smith	S. Davidson	9.1	50/1
Fulham	D. Parker	W. Duncan	7.8	50/1

All started

initial opinion about Phar Lap, based on his looks, could be right. He was unplaced in four runs before being heavily backed to win a Maiden at Rosehill to score his only two-year-old success. He took time to get going at the resumption of his three-year-old season being unplaced in four runs, but he then showed what was to come by finishing second to smart performer Mollison in the Chelmsford Stakes. Thereafter, he was unstoppable. He took the Rosehill Guineas; AJC Derby (beating the high-priced colt Carradale owned by VRC Chairman L. K. S. Mackinnon) and the Craven Plate. Brought to Melbourne he beat Carradale – again – in the Victoria Derby, which prompted Mackinnon to get geldings banned from the Classic. Now even money favorite for the Melbourne Cup, Phar Lap finished only third after he fought against jockey Bobbie Lewis, who tried to restrain him, for much of the race. In the Autumn of his three-year-old season he was unbeaten in nine runs after a first-up third. Victories included the VRC and AJC St Legers and an Australasian record for 2¼ miles (3600m) in winning the Randwick Plate by 10 lengths.

HARRY TELFORD ... a harsh taskmaster who got the best out of Phar Lap.

Starting his Spring campaign in 1930, Phar Lap was "badly underdone" when he resumed in the Warwick Stakes where he failed by half a head behind Amounis, who equalled the track record of 1.38 for the mile. (That narrow loss prevented Phar Lap from setting a record winning sequence which would still survive today. Up to that defeat, he had won nine on end and after the Warwick Stakes loss he won the next 14 on the trot.)

Brought to Melbourne in mid-October, having won five on end in Sydney after that initial loss, Telford was keeping to himself whether Phar Lap would start in the Caulfield Cup, for which he was the hottest pre-post favorite on record. Most punters expected Phar Lap to start, but behind the scenes a betting "sting" involving Cups doubles bets was being planned, with a small section of astute punters backing Amounis in the Caulfield Cup. On paper Amounis

could not have beaten Phar Lap, but after Telford shocked the racing public by announcing that Phar Lap would not contest the Caulfield Cup, Amounis was a clear favorite for the race. This meant doubles bookmakers would face massive payouts if Amounis and Phar Lap won the two Spring Cups – and their worst fears were realised when Amounis won the first leg. (It was two weeks after this victory that gangsters attempted to maim Phar Lap by taking shots at him to prevent him starting in the Melbourne Cup. Shielded by his faithful strapper Tommy Woodcock, Phar Lap survived the attempt.)

Before starting in the Melbourne Cup, Phar Lap had other engagements, including the Cox Plate. He was the centre of attention and success in the race was considered a foregone conclusion. The expectation was achieved when the public idol scored an effortless win. Starting at the extremely cramped odds of 1-7, Phar Lap was never extended to win by 4 lengths.

However, it hardly made headlines. Typically, newspapers of the day gave little

How much more relaxed can a horse look at the end of a race? It's Cox Plate win number two for Phar Lap, who strode up on the outside to hit the front to win as he liked. It brought up his sixth successive win for the season, but he was only to win twice more.

– Picture: Equus Marketing Pty Ltd

information about the race – Phar Lap was only news when he was beaten or was the subject of drama. On the race track, he was expected to win – and that was not news.

"The Herald" had this succinct report on his Cox Plate victory:

"Phar Lap had his first outing at Moonee Valley in the W. S. Cox Plate and the race proved a very easy task for him to win. The event was run over the new 9½ furlongs track which runs across the centre of the flat.

"Mollison was the first to begin and Phar Lap was fifth when they had settled down, but he was so eager to go, that before the junction of the courses was reached he was within half a length of Mollison who had the rails.

"Racing along the back there was nothing between Mollison and Phar Lap, but Phar Lap had no effort in going the strong pace set by Mollison and the pair made the race from a spectator point of view, as it was not until the home turn that Pike let Phar Lap assert himself. This the champion did so readily that soon after the straight was entered he opened up a gap of five lengths and won very comfortably from the Melbourne Cup candidate Tregilla, who finished very well to gain second place, while the Derby favorite Veilmond did not finish on as well as expected, but possibly, racing the reverse way did not suit him. He looked very well and should do better next Saturday at Flemington. (Ironically Jim Pike rode Balloon King in the Derby to beat Veilmond again.)

TOMMY WOODCOCK ... devoted to Phar Lap.

"Phar Lap increased his stakes earnings today to £24,405."

And Phar Lap just kept increasing his earnings. He not only survived the shooting attempt on Derby Day, 1930, he went on to race on each of the four days of the Flemington Carnival and to win on each occasion. He took the Mackinnon Stakes (2000m) on the Saturday; the Melbourne Cup (3200m) on the Tuesday; the Linlithgow Stakes (1600m) on the Thursday and finally, over the 2400m of the C.B. Fisher Plate on the Final Saturday.

1931
(Saturday, October 24. Attendance: 20,880)

£650 plus £100 trophy Weight for Age 9½ furlongs

1.	PHAR LAP	H. R. Telford	9.4	J. Pike	1/14f
2.	Chatham	L. Foulsham	7.11	H. Morris	7/2
3.	Johnnie Jason	C. Unwin	7.11	J. Pratt	7/2

Winning details

Margin: 2½ len x 2 len. **Time:** 2:01.5 7 started.

Breeding: Night Raid – Entreaty – Winkie (ch g 5) **Owner:** D. J. Davis & H. R. Telford

Winner's Colors: Red, red and green hooped sleeves, black cap

Winning Numbers: 1, 8, 6 **Barriers:** 5, 7, 1

ALSO RAN

Le Region	J. W. Cook	J. Simpson	7.11	12/1
Veilmond	G. Price	J. Munro	9.0	6/4
Carry On	G. Price	M. McCarten	8.9	6/1
Cimbrian	L. Robertson	O. Phillips	9.4	7/2

Scratched: Loquacious, Ammon Ra

The pattern remained the same in the Autumn (four wins and a second in five starts) before he began his five-year-old season.

He came into the Cox Plate of 1931 with six wins in as many starts and became the shortest priced favorite (again) in the history of the race, at 1/14.

Once again, *"The Herald"* report was brief and to the point:

"Phar Lap, favorite for the Melbourne Cup, made his reappearance in Melbourne following his Sydney trip for the Cox Plate, in which he had six opponents. Phar Lap looked in magnificent condition. There was a great volume of betting done on a one-two basis. Veilmond was in most demand in combination with the champion.

"An odd bookmaker or two operated straight out on Phar Lap, and at barrier rise it was possible in a few isolated instances to lay £100 to £7 on. One backer laid £200 to £16 on and another punter laid £100 to £8 on. During the progress of the race a former bookmaker laid £100 to £4 on the champion.

"Phar Lap got away slowly. He was last for the first half furlong then Pike allowed him to stride out on the outside of the field. His gigantic strides quickly carried him to the front. From then the race was simply a procession. Phar Lap was always travelling leisurely in front.

"His performance was reassuring to his legion of admirers for the Melbourne Cup. It is evident that Phar Lap has never been in better condition at any stage of his career. Veilmond was last for most of the race, but finished on well. Chatham, a Derby and Cup candidate, showed his best form to date by running second.

"This was Chatham's fourth start. He has apparently done well since he arrived in Melbourne. Johnnie Jason looked brighter than he did in Sydney. He did well to gain third place.

"Totalisator supporters of Phar Lap again discovered the futility of backing him on the machine as in both the Win and Place pools they received only their money back. In the Win section he carried £395/10/- out of a pool of £418 and in the place £572 out of £1200/10/-.

"Phar Lap's stake earnings now amount to £55,935. This was his sixth successive victory this season."

He was to win only twice more. He struggled to win the Melbourne (Mackinnon) Stakes the following week and two days later was asked to lump 10st 10lb (70.5kg) over the two miles of the Melbourne Cup. Even Pike knew he had the job in front of him and he advised Phar Lap's faithful strapper Tommy Woodcock that he would not knock Phar Lap about if it looked beyond him. On this occasion the Handicapper won, as Phar Lap could finish only eighth.

"Big Red" then went to America to contest a 2000m race at Agua Caliente in Mexico, which against all odds – including a bad stone bruise leading up to the race – Phar Lap won in record time. Six days later he was dead, in circumstances which are still a mystery. Debate continues today about whether he was accidentally or deliberately poisoned. The most accepted theory is that he died from the effects of an accidental overdose of arsenic, which had been sprayed on trees at Menlo Park stables, where he was resting, and some of the poison had dripped onto the grass he was eating.

But there was one matter over which there is no debate. "Big Red" stands tall as Australia's greatest equine hero – on and off the track – and is the most famous winner of the Cox Plate.

1932, 1934 — CHATHAM WAS A DURABLE PLATE STAR

Great horses are defined by a number of things, not the least of them being the ability to perform successfully over a variety of distances, and in all types of going.

Top class stayers, for instance, will often win over sprint distances fresh, with a good example being the 1950 Melbourne Cup winner Comic Court, who at his next start three months later won the 1200m William Reid Stakes at Moonee Valley in record time.

In the early 1930's, Chatham, a son of the 1925 Melbourne Cup winner Windbag, was considered the finest "miler" of his generation, winning two Epsom Handicaps and a Doncaster Handicap.

But he can also lay claim to being the best middle-distance horse in an era which boasted some outstanding gallopers including the likes of Hall Mark and Rogilla.

Chatham contested the Cox Plate in four successive years, from 1930 to 1934. He finished second to none other than Phar Lap at his first appearance, won the following year, was a close-up fourth in 1933, then produced probably his best effort to win in 1934.

Confirming his effectiveness at 2000m he also won the Craven Plate at Randwick on three successive occasions between 1932 and 1934, on the final occasion defeating the dual Melbourne Cup winner Peter Pan.

Quite often horses of stature have something other than sheer ability that sets them apart from the opposition. Tulloch had a sway back; Dulcify a parrot-mouth. Chatham made a strange noise. When galloping, he produced a kind of "whistle" normally associated with a wind infirmity. In fact, it was related to a weakness in his bloodstream, and did not affect his ability to gallop.

His win in the 1932 Cox Plate was expected, and not just because of his excellent showing the previous year behind the horse already accorded legendary status. Although Chatham was to record one of his greatest victories – the 1934 Doncaster Handicap – in the Autumn, essentially he was a Spring horse. Certainly this proved the case in the Spring of 1932, for in the lead-up to the Cox

Chatham contested the Cox Plate in four successive years, from 1930 to 1934. He finished second to none other than Phar Lap on his first appearance, won the following year, was a close-up fourth in 1933, then produced probably his best effort to win in 1934.

Confirming his liking for 2000m he also won the Craven Plate at Randwick on three successive occasions between 1932 and 1934, on the final occasion defeating the dual Melbourne Cup winner Peter Pan.

1932

(Saturday, October 22. Attendance: 23,020)

£750 plus £100 trophy Weight for Age 9½ furlongs

1.	CHATHAM	F. Williams	9.0	*J. Munro*	10/9f
2.	Viol D'Amour	E. J. O'Dwyer	9.0	*H. Badger*	7/1
3.	Johnnie Jason	C. Unwin	9.0	*P. Reynolds*	20/1

Winning details

Margin: ¾ len x 2 len. **Time:** 2:02.75 10 started.

Breeding: Windbag – Myosotis – The Welkin (b h 4) **Owner:** A. E. Blair

Winner's Colors: Pink, pale blue sleeves & cap

Winning Numbers: 6, 4, 5 **Barriers:** 8, 6, 10

ALSO RAN

Denis Boy	F. McGrath	A. Reed	9.4	10/1
Oratory	L. Robertson	W. Duncan	7.11	12/1
Oro	J. King	F. Dempsey	7.11	33/1
K. Cid	H. W. Gabell	J. O'Brien	7.11	33/1
Chetowaik	F. Robinson	A. Wilson	7.11	10/1
Glenanton	J. Bott	M. McCarten	9.4	50/1
Cimbrian	L. Robertson	E. Baxter	9.4	25/1

All Started

CHATHAM ... a dual Cox Plate winner whose followers were prepared to overlook his flop in the race of 1933 when they backed him into favoritism in 1934. – Picture: HWT

As a six-year-old in the Spring of 1934, Chatham's extraordinary ability showed no sign of being on the wane, although he found the task of carrying 67.5kg to a third Epsom Handicap victory beyond him. But he engaged in some terrific weight-for-age duels with some truly outstanding horses, the likes of 1932 Melbourne Cup winner Peter Pan, the 1933 Victoria Derby and Melbourne Cup winner Hall Mark, not to mention his old adversary, Rogilla.

Plate the four-year-old remained unbeaten in four races, albeit including a dead-heat with Rogilla in the Tramway Handicap at Randwick.

Returning to Randwick three weeks later, Chatham started favorite in the Epsom Handicap and this time proved much too good for Rogilla, with high class sprinter Winooka leading but weakening into third place.

It was quite obvious that, going into the 1932 Cox Plate, Chatham had improved immensely upon his form of the previous year, and therefore was deemed the logical winner. In his lead-up run, he won the 2000m Craven Plate, defeating two very fine horses in Veilmond, a genuine and very versatile galloper, and Gaine Carrington, who the following year won the Caulfield Cup. His opposition at Moonee Valley lacked that kind of class, and with Jim Munro barely asking him for an effort he coasted home to the easiest of wins.

Chatham came to the 1933 race with an even better record than he'd achieved in 1932. He won six races in succession, among them the Epsom Handicap with 61.5kg, the Craven Plate and the Caulfield Stakes. Not surprisingly, he started a red-hot favorite at 15-8 on. Totally unexpected was his inability to finish in the placings. Ridden close to the lead by Jim Pike, Chatham appeared to travel easily in the run, and went to the front nearing the turn ahead of Waltzing Lily and Dermid.

On straightening up though, the favorite was the first horse beaten, and it was left to the Melbourne Cup favorite Rogilla to storm home and win comfortably, with Chatham weakening into fourth place.

His connections could offer no excuses. Chatham ate up that night and the morning after was, according to newspaper reports, "as bright as a button". Twelve days later he proved his well-being with a strong win in the Linlithgow Stakes.

Despite Chatham being a stallion, no thought was given to retiring him to stud, and the following Autumn he recorded what many believe was his greatest victory, in the AJC Doncaster Handicap. Ridden by Jim Pike and carrying 65.5kg Chatham missed the start several lengths but displayed great courage on a bog track to beat a high class field that included Rogilla.

As a six-year-old in the Spring of 1934, Chatham's extraordinary ability showed no sign of being on the wane, although he found the task of carrying 67.5kg to a third Epsom Handicap victory beyond him. But he engaged in some terrific weight-for-age duels with some truly outstanding horses the likes of 1932 Melbourne Cup winner Peter Pan, the 1933 Victoria Derby and Melbourne Cup winner Hall Mark, not to mention his old adversary, Rogilla. He beat Peter Pan and Rogilla to win his third successive Craven Stakes, then went down by a head to Hall Mark, with Rogilla third, in the Caulfield Stakes.

Two weeks later, the placegetters at Caulfield resumed battle at Moonee Valley in the 1934 Cox Plate, and of course they dominated the betting market. Hall Mark, by virtue of a narrow win at Caulfield, was the opening favorite but Chatham's backers, obviously prepared to overlook his out-of-character run the previous year, rallied to him and at post time he once again was the favored runner.

In the old days of the strand barrier, luck at the start was always important. On this occasion luck deserted Rogilla, who wheeled away from the line at the moment of barrier rise, and lost all of 10 lengths. At the same time, jockey Stan Davidson, who'd partnered Chatham throughout the Spring, sent his mount into the lead and immediately set about dictating the pace. He slowed the field right up in the run down to the 1400m turn, and went around to the 1000m mark in complete control of the race.

At this stage, Frank Dempsey on Hall Mark realised he needed to be closer to the leader but as he pushed up Davidson suddenly accelerated on Chatham and shot away with a break of four or five lengths.

Naturally, it was impossible to give a horse of Chatham's ability that kind of start, particularly in light of the fact he'd done virtually no work in the early stages. Davidson had a peep under his arm upon straightening up, saw he had the race well in his keeping, and let his horse coast home to an easy win. The effort of chasing saw Hall Mark struggling over the final 100m but the little horse was nothing if not game, and he managed to hold off the fast finishing Rogilla to claim second place.

Given the amount of ground Rogilla lost at the start, it could be assumed that had he jumped cleanly he would have troubled the winner, but it's unlikely he would have pressured Chatham for the early lead.

A week later, Chatham ran unplaced behind Peter Pan in the Melbourne Stakes and was retired. He was a success at stud, siring among others the Sydney Cup winner Craigie, and Stradbroke Handicap winner High Rank.

But it is as a racehorse he will be remembered, and he deserves to be ranked among the greats.

> In the old days of the strand barrier, luck at the start was always important. On this occasion, luck deserted Rogilla, who wheeled away from the line at the moment of barrier rise and lost all of 10 lengths. At the same time jockey Stan Davidson, who'd partnered Chatham throughout the Spring, sent his mount into the lead and immediately set about dictating the pace.

1934
(Saturday, October 27. Attendance: 18,910)

£900 plus £100 trophy Weight for Age 9½ furlongs

1.	CHATHAM	F. Williams	9.4	S. Davidson	2/1f
2.	Hall Mark	J. Holt	9.0	F. Dempsey	9/4
3.	Rogilla	L. Haigh	9.4	D. Munro	3/1

Winning details

Margin: 2½ len x ½ len. Time: 2:03 6 started.

Breeding: Windbag – Myosotis- The Welkin (b h 6) Owner: A. E. Blair

Winner's Colors: Pink, pale blue sleeves & cap

Winning Numbers: 4, 5, 3 Barriers: 6, 2, 4

ALSO RAN

Silver Ring	R. W. King	M. McCarten	9.4	25/1
Aztec	F. Foulsham	H. Morris	7.11	20/1
Curator (lost rider)	I. Foulsham	R. Bailey	7.11	100/1

Scratched: Closing Time

1933 — ROGILLA ALWAYS PUT UP A FIGHT

When the Depression temporarily halted picnic racing, Rogilla was leased to Newcastle trainer Les Haigh, who turned the unfashionably bred gelding into a giant-killer.

Among the scalps claimed by Rogilla in a career spanning five seasons were the champion Peter Pan, who finished fourth behind him in the 1932 Caulfield Cup, and Chatham, who was unplaced behind him in the 1933 Cox Plate.

But for the winner, the Flying Handicap at Newcastle in early August, 1933, would have been just another nondescript entry in the result book,

No doubt the appearance of a horse who the previous year had won the Caulfield Cup would have created plenty of interest among Newcastle race fans, and they would have applauded his winning the 1200m dash carrying a hefty 67.5kg.

In winning that late Winter race at Newcastle, Rogilla achieved something which, while not in the same league, is mindful of Comic Court's Melbourne Cup – William Reid Stakes double in 1950-51.

At Newcastle, Rogilla was resuming from a four month spell. In his previous two runs, he had won the Sydney Cup over 3200m, and at his last run before being turned out had ran fourth over 3600m. So to return from such a long break and win a sprint was an exceptional effort.

Indeed it was the mark of a horse who was competitive in the extreme. Rogilla rarely failed to put up a fight, shown by the fact that in the course of 26 career wins he dead-heated for first on five occasions.

Not bad for a horse who was so ungainly as a juvenile he was seen as being fit for racing only around the picnic circuit in the southern Riverina. When the Depression temporarily halted picnic racing, Rogilla was leased to Newcastle trainer Les Haigh, who turned the unfashionably bred gelding into a giant-killer. Among the scalps claimed by Rogilla in a career spanning five seasons were the champion Peter Pan, who finished fourth behind him in the 1932 Caulfield Cup, and Chatham, who was unplaced behind him in the 1933 Cox Plate.

There is little doubt Rogilla's Spring preparation in 1933 was aimed at having him at his peak on Melbourne Cup day. His lead-up campaign, which took in most of the Sydney Carnival, saw him stepped up in distance in all but one of six starts after his initial win over 1200m at Newcastle. He finished third, more than five lengths behind Chatham in the Warwick Stakes over 1600m, then carried 61kg to win the Chelmsford Stakes over 1800m at Randwick.

Rogilla again ran into Chatham in the Hill Stakes over 1600m at Rosehill in mid-September, and finished fourth, about 3½ lengths in arrears of the great miler. Now his Cup

1933
(Saturday, October 28. Attendance: 21,610)

£900 plus £100 trophy Weight for Age 9½ furlongs

1.	**ROGILLA**	L. Haigh	9.4	D. Munro	10/1
2.	**Dermid**	J. A. Donohue	9.4	W. Cook	12/1
3.	**Waltzing Lily**	S. Smith	8.9	E. Baxter	10/1

Winning details

Margin: ½ len x ¾ len. **Time:** 1:58.5 7 started.

Breeding: Roger De Busli – Speargila – Brakespeare (ch g 6) **Owner:** L. Haigh

Winner's Colors: Black, red armbands & cap

Winning Numbers: 1, 2, 5 **Barriers:** 1, 3, 4

ALSO RAN

Chatham	F. Williams	J. Pike	9.4	8/15f
Break Up	H. R. Telford	E. Preston	7.11	10/1
Topical	W. Kelso	M. McCarten	9.4	25/1
Gothic Gem	E. J. O'Dwyer	H. Badger	7.11	33/1

Scratched: Limarch

ROGILLA crosses the line first from Dermid to win the 1933 Cox Plate and race into favor for the Melbourne Cup, but he couldn't repeat the effort at Flemington. – Picture: HWT

campaign began in earnest. On Epsom Handicap day at Randwick he stepped out over 2400m in the Spring Plate and showed his liking for the extended trip by scoring an emphatic win. Two days later Rogilla was back at Randwick to contest the 2800m Metropolitan Handicap, in which he carried topweight of 61kg.

It was a big ask of the gelding given the track was very heavy, and those who looked at the race objectively were hardly surprised when the six-year-old was beaten into sixth place.

Writing in the Melbourne *Herald "Orleigh"* described how Rogilla "came through a severe test unscathed, and showed no outward signs of distress after having ploughed through heavy ground…" In fact the correspondent was of the opinion Rogilla would be all the better for the race. "There is not a fitter horse in Australia," he wrote, "and Victorians will see a Rogilla vastly improved on the one that won the Caulfield Cup."

It was an astute observation, but made no doubt with an eye to the Melbourne Cup, and not the Cox Plate. That Rogilla was set firmly on a Melbourne Cup path was confirmed when, just five days after the Metropolitan, he tackled and won the 3200m Randwick Plate and consolidated his position at the head of the Cup betting charts.

As the Spring focus switched to Melbourne, it was Chatham who dominated discussion in the lead-up to the Cox Plate. He arrived having won all of his five starts in Sydney, and promptly chalked up win number six, in the Caulfield Stakes.

Cox Plate day dawned fine and sunny, and punters flocked to Moonee Valley in the expectation of seeing a champion galloper once again confirm his greatness. Even the experts felt Chatham was all but over the line. That doyen of racing writers, Bert Wolfe *(Cardigan)*, declared Chatham the "undisputed king of the short distance weight-for-age division".

"Is he likely to meet defeat in the Cox Plate?" he wrote, then answered his own question. "It is hardly likely."

Rogilla, wrote *Cardigan,* was expected to run a good race but it was too much to expect even such a great horse to beat Chatham at the distance. Also his speed was expected to be dulled, given he'd been racing over much longer distances. Intrepid punters were happy to take odds-on about Chatham winning, and when the tapes went up he'd firmed to start at 15-8 on. Rogilla drifted at one stage to be a 12-1 chance, but late support saw him start at 10-1.

The speed was good from barrier rise and, although Chatham was tardy at the start, Pike rode him along to be up sharing the lead soon after. Rogilla, to the surprise of many, including no doubt *Cardigan*, began quickly and was no more than five lengths off the lead as the field swung down the back of the course.

So well was he going at this point that jockey Darby Munro gave him a little rein and in a flash the gelding strode forward. Munro, delighted no doubt with the response, took a hold again and was content to wait until the turn before unleashing his run. At this stage Chatham, to the dismay of most, began to labor and first Waltzing Lily, then Dermid reached the lead. But halfway up the straight Rogilla pounced, and raced away to an easy win.

It was a truly outstanding effort, and consolidated his position as the Melbourne Cup favorite.

One person very impressed with the win was Wolfe, for the following Monday he asked yet another question. "Has the mantle of Phar Lap fallen on Rogilla?" Many were inclined to think that it might have, but it descended into reality 10 days later when he ran unplaced in the Melbourne Cup.

No, he was never as good as Phar Lap, but Rogilla was indeed a great horse, and another classy winner of the Cox Plate.

1935 – OH! HE WAS A SURPRISE!

Defying his previous runs, Garrio confounded his critics by strolling home by a length from the favorite Hall Mark, with Feldspar third.

Instead of coming back to scale to the usual cheers, Voitre and Garrio were subjected to "a hostile demonstration from all parts of the course, racegoers evidently remembering his flop when favorite at Caulfield".

*O*rleigh of *The* (Melbourne) *Herald* considered the Cox Plate of 1935 "looks on paper, as being the race of the Spring".

He wrote that even the absence of the brilliant Peter Pan, winner of the 1934 Melbourne Cup, "cannot detract from the interest. On the contrary his absence will add to it", (obviously because Peter Pan would have dominated betting).

The field included the brilliant Hall Mark who had returned to form with a win in the Memsie Stakes and proven weight-for-age winner Sylvandale who had won the Chelmsford Stakes. However, it was the group of classy three-year-olds that caused most debate. These included Caulfield Guineas winner Young Idea and the runner-up Garrio; the classy Feldspar (Garrio's stablemate) who had bypassed the Guineas to win the Caulfield Stakes; AJC Derby dead-heater Allunga; and Valiant Chief, who even though he had blotted his copybook when unplaced in the Guineas, had won three on end beforehand.

While Hall Mark was a clear cut favorite, Young Idea was the form runner of the younger brigade, particularly after his ¾ length victory in the Caulfield Guineas after heading Garrio inside the 100m. It was another blow for Garrio, who up to that stage had raced five times as a three-year-old for four seconds (including a dead heat) and a third.

His chance to make amends appeared on Caulfield Cup day when he carried 54kg (.5kg more than weight-for-age) in the Windsor Handicap. Garrio started 9/4 favorite on his Guineas performance, but once again he had his colors lowered when he could finish only sixth after weakening over the concluding stages.

Little wonder then that, come Cox Plate day, Garrio, ridden by Keith Voitre, was unfancied at 14/1 to score his first win for the season; his stablemate Feldspar was more popular at 10/1. Defying his previous efforts, Garrio confounded his critics by strolling home by a length from the favorite Hall Mark, with Feldspar third.

Instead of coming back to scale to the usual cheers, Voitre and Garrio were

1935
(Saturday, October 26. Attendance: 20,860)

£900 plus £100 trophy Weight for Age 9½ furlongs

1.	GARRIO	L. Robertson	7.11	K. Voitre	14/1
2.	Hall Mark	J. Holt	9.4	H. Skidmore	2/1f
3.	Feldspar	L. Robertson	7.11	H. Badger	10/1

Winning details

Margin: 1 len x 1½ len. **Time:** 1:58.5 14 started.

Breeding: Chivalrous – Garrulity – Magpie (b c 3) **Owner:** A. T. Creswick

Winner's Colors: Black, blue sash, white armbands & cap

Winning Numbers: 14, 2, 13 **Barriers:** 13, 3, 7

ALSO RAN

Sylvandale	F. Williams	J. Pratt	9.0	7/1
Young Idea	F. Foulsham	A. Reed	7.11	5/1
Valiant Chief	F. W. Hoysted	S. Tomison	7.11	8/1
Sporting Blood	A. McIntosh	A. Breasley	9.0	100/1
Gay Lover	S. Murphy	H. Morris	7.11	20/1
Loud Applause	G. Price	H. Olsen	7.11	20/1
Gay Sheik	E. Pope	N. Percival	7.11	100/1
Allunga	J. F. Munro	R. Parsons	7.11	25/1
High Cross	T. Clune	J. O'Sullivan	9.4	100/1
Berestoi	J. King	D. Munro	9.1	12/1
Buzzard King	P. J. Healy	W. Elliot	7.11	25/1

All started

subjected to "a hostile demonstration from all parts of the course, racegoers evidently remembering his flop when favorite at Caulfield".

Perfectly ridden by Voitre who saved every inch of ground, Garrio shot to the lead entering the straight. Hall Mark (Harold Skidmore) gave chase and had every chance to overtake him, but Garrio found more in the run home and finished better than any other runner.

"Cardigan" wrote in *The Herald* that it was "an amazing reversal of form" considering the rise in class to his previous start. The task of Hall Mark, who had to concede 9.5kg to the winner, was not made easier by the fact that he had been galloped on during the race. However, his injury was only superficial, with Hall Mark taking his place in the Mackinnon Stakes the following Saturday, in which he finished third.

The favored three-year-old, Young Idea, finished fifth. He ran up to within two lengths of the leaders coming to the turn, but then began to weaken at the point at which he was expected to go on. The betting (Young Idea started 5/1 second favorite) and the form suggested that Young Idea would have no trouble accounting for Garrio at least, but it was Garrio who found the stamina instead.

The prediction about the depth of class in the 1935 Cox Plate field was borne out with subsequent results. The three-year-old form in particular proved very strong, as the placings in the Derby the following Saturday were made up of Cox Plate runners.

The Derby victor was Feldspar, runner-up was Allunga (11th in the Cox Plate), while Garrio finished third in the Classic. Sylvandale, who finished fourth at the Valley, won the Mackinnon Stakes (in which Hall Mark was third) and was then third in the Melbourne Cup.

And what of Young Idea?

He was to stamp himself as one of Australia's oustanding horses, winning or being placed in numerous weight-for-age races. His turn in the Cox Plate came in 1936 when he won it on the first of two occasions before finishing third to Ajax in 1938.

While Garrio is not in the same league as many other great horses in our past, there is no doubt that on that day in 1935 he accounted for some of our very best.

1936-37 — A PLATE DOUBLE IS A GREAT IDEA!

As a two-year-old Young Idea scored in the Champagne Stakes and the AJC Sires as well as the VRC version of the latter. The following year he took the Caulfield Guineas, before starting second favorite when unplaced in the Cox Plate. While it was undeniable that he had plenty of ability, up to that stage, Young Idea had yet to cement his name in the *real* big time.

In an era when great horses abounded, Young Idea was to etch his own name among them in the late 1930's.

As a two-year-old he scored in the Champagne Stakes and the AJC Sires as well as the VRC version of the latter. The following year he took the Caulfield Guineas, before starting second favorite when unplaced in the Cox Plate. While it was undeniable that he had plenty of ability, Young Idea had yet to cement his name in the *real* big time … until 1936.

He first came to prominence in the Spring of that year, when he ran a course record of 1:50½ in winning the Caulfield Stakes after sitting behind the leaders to the turn. That race was his prelude to the W. S. Cox Plate – but like the previous year when he was touted a big chance as a three-year-old – Young Idea was facing some formidable challengers of that age.

They were the New Zealanders, Silver Ring and Mala. Silver Ring was considered one of the best stayers in Australia at the time. Since arriving from the Dominion he had chalked up three wins – including victories over the classy Lough Neagh over 2400m and 3200m at Randwick. He was also considered unlucky not to have won the Craven Plate at Randwick, in which he finished third, after he tried to lead throughout, leaving himself a sitting duck for those finishing on over the final 200m. Mala also had great form, which included seconds in the Chelmsford Stakes and behind Talking in the AJC Derby.

On race day, punters made Mala favorite at 3/1, but were unable to split Silver Ring and Young Idea who were equal second picks at 4/1. Ridden by Billy Cook, Mala went to the front from barrier rise though he did not set a fast pace, and it appeared that he was waiting for another runner to take the lead from him. Silver Ring settled fourth while Young Idea was being patiently ridden by Harold Skidmore one place further back.

Not happy with the muddling pace, two other runners, Ramdin and Sarcherie tried to pinch a break, which forced Cook on Mala to quicken the tempo to keep the lead 1000m from home. Coming to the turn, Mala was still travelling comfortably in front; Silver Ring was struggling and Young Idea was making ground out wide.

In the stretch, Young

1936
(Saturday, October 24. Attendance: 24,680)

£900 plus £100 trophy Weight for Age 9½ furlongs

1.	**YOUNG IDEA**	J. Holt	9.0	*H. Skidmore*	4/1
2.	**Mala**	H. E. Russell	7.11	*W. Cook*	3/1f
3.	**Shakespeare**	G. P. Nailon	7.11	*R. Parsons*	6/1

Winning details

Margin: Hd x ½ hd. **Time:** 2:01 11 started.

Breeding: Constant Son (GB) – Persuasion – The Welkin (br h 4) **Owner:** P. Miller

Winner's Colors: Brown & pink halves, pink cap

Winning Numbers: 2, 8, 11 **Barriers:** 3, 4, 7

ALSO RAN

Sarcherie	M. Webster	D. Munro	8.13	8/1
Match King	G. Tantram	S. Tomison	7.11	20/1
Ramdin	C. P. Brown	A. Knox	7.11	25/1
Silver Ring	J. Stewart	A. Ellis	9.4	4/1
Arabian Knight	R. Horne	R. Cann	7.11	33/1
Conandale	E. Temby	N. Percival	7.11	50/1
Wotan	J. Fryer	N. Creighton	9.0	100/1
Buzbury	T. Bradfield	H. Bagder	7.11	100/1

All started

VALLEY OF THE KINGS

Idea quickly swept to the front and the race was over more than 50m out. The three-year-old Shakespeare also finished hard for third after being hampered when attempting a run on the inside of Mala.

The victory was Cox Plate success number four for trainer Jack Holt following on from the feats of Easingwold, Heroic and Highland but was to be the only Plate win for Skidmore who was on runner-up Hall Mark a year earlier.

One week later, Young Idea finished third in the Mackinnon Stakes and Mala again had to be content with another Classic second behind Talking in the Victoria Derby. The biggest subsequent winner however was the horse Wotan, who beat only one runner home in the Cox Plate. On that performance, Wotan was sent out a forlorn hope by punters at 100/1 in the Melbourne Cup – to become one of only three horses at that price to win the race.

The following year Young Idea was set to repeat Phar Lap's feat – to that stage Phar Lap had been the only horse to win successive Cox Plates (1930-31), while Chatham had a year between his two wins in 1932 and 1934.

The task for Young Idea was made easier when the connections of Mala opted to run in the Moonee Valley Cup (for another Valley second!). With Darby Munro atop, Young Idea was the popular elect with punters. He had won the Underwood Stakes at Williamstown; was second in the Memsie Stakes; and after an ordinary fifth in the Caulfield Stakes he was a fast finishing third over an unsuitable short trip at Caulfield on the Wednesday before the Cox Plate.

Also in Cox Plate contention were Charles Fox, winner of the Caulfield Stakes, and the three-year-olds Courtcraft, who followed a fourth in the AJC Derby with an easy win over 1600m at Randwick, and Lochlee, a last start winner of the Moonee Valley Stakes.

Sent out 2/1 favorite after easing from 7/4, it took all of Munro's considerable talent to land Young Idea by a head over the heavily backed Courtcraft (6/1 to 7/2) with Charles Fox a length away. For a time, it seemed as if the heavy support for Courtcraft, who took the early lead, would pay off. Approaching the 800m, Young Idea made a fast move from near the rear to go up to the leaders, which by now also included Charles Fox and Lochlee.

Taking an inside run, Munro slipped past Lochlee in pursuit of Charles Fox and Courtcraft and, on the turn, he was forced three wide to join the pair. Inside the 100m Young Idea got the upper hand on Charles Fox, but Courtcraft refused to give in as the pair went head up and down to the line, with Munro's mount just lasting. Though he was certainly not in the same class, Young Idea had emulated Phar Lap's feat.

Young Idea continued to perform with distinction, finishing third in the race the following year behind the brilliant Ajax and Royal Chief and winning the 1937 St George Stakes (when the winner weighed in light). He was also placed in the Futurity Stakes and again in the St George Stakes.

On reviewing his record, there is no doubt that he was right up among the best in that golden decade of racing.

1937
(Saturday, October 23. Attendance: 29,300)

£900 plus £100 trophy Weight for Age 9½ furlongs

1.	YOUNG IDEA	J. Holt	9.4	*D. Munro*	2/1f
2.	Courtcraft	F. Davis	7.11	*P. Atkins*	7/2
3.	Charles Fox	D. J. Price	9.4	*T. Webster*	9/2

Winning details

Margin: Hd x len. **Time:** 1:58.5 11 started.

Breeding: Constant Son (GB) – Persuasion – The Welkin (br h 5) **Owner:** P. Miller

Winner's Colors: Dark blue, light blue diamonds, red cap

Winning Numbers: 6, 12, 3 **Barriers:** 7, 3, 6

ALSO RAN

Bellevue	H. Hilton	J. O'Brien	7.12	50/1
Allunga	E. Hunter Bowman	E. Bartle	9.4	12/1
Bristol	W. Kelso	J. O'Sullivan	7.11	100/1
Gay Knight	D. Lewis	H. Badger	9.4	100/1
Sarcherie	M. Webster	A. Sibbritt	8.13	15/1
Prince Sion	H. Cousens	A. Reed	9.4	66/1
Lochlee	H. Wolters	J. Barry	7.11	20/1
Black Mac	E. McNaughton	R. Wilson	9.4	7/1

Scratched: Mala

1938 – AJAX LIVED UP TO HIS NAME AS A WARRIOR

It is cruel, considering his amazing career, that Ajax is most remembered for a defeat in the Rawson Stakes of 1939.

At the price of 40-1 on, Heroic's son became the shortest priced beaten favorite in Australian racing history. Even today he is still part of the Australian idiom, for when someone talks about something being a foregone conclusion, old-timers may chide: "Don't forget what happened to Ajax".

Like the Greek hero of the Trojan war, after whom he was named, Ajax was indeed a racing warrior.

The finest son of Heroic, Ajax was unplaced only once in 46 starts which yielded an amazing 36 wins – including 18 on end – with him either breaking or equalling six Australian records.

It is cruel then, considering his amazing career, that the race for which Ajax is most remembered is a defeat. The occasion was the Rawson Stakes (1800m) at Rosehill on March 25, 1939, when the chestnut was aiming for win number 19 on end, to equal the winning sequence record shared by Gloaming and Desert Gold. Ridden by regular jockey Harold Badger, Ajax had only two opponents, Spear Chief (Maurice McCarten) and Allunga (Darby Munro), after another acceptor, the aptly-named Defaulter, was scratched.

In such devastating form, Ajax was considered a certainty – but bookmakers still plied their trade, offering 1/40 about Ajax winning. (One punter was obviously thrilled about the prosect of earning an easy £35 as he outlayed £1155 to win that amount, taking the "good" odds of 1/33.)

Munro on Allunga kept the pressure on Ajax from the outset, but on reaching the turn Ajax had Munro's mount covered, only to see McCarten finish in fine style on Spear Chief to win by a ½ length.

At the price of 40/1 on, Ajax had become the shortest priced beaten favorite in Australian history. It is an occasion which has stuck – as even today when someone talks about something being a foregone conclusion, old-timers may chide: "Don't forget what happened to Ajax".

That blemish aside, Ajax was unplaced only once – in his third start as a two-year-old when favorite for the VRC Sires'. And after his Rawson Stakes defeat, he did make amends two starts later by equalling the Australasian record in the AJC Sires' when he scored by five lengths!

At three, he raced 11 times winning them all bar two, when he was second in both the Victoria and AJC Derbys. He ran records in both the Rosehill and Caulfield Guineas; took the

1938
(Saturday, October 22. Attendance: 28,580)

£900 plus £100 trophy Weight for Age 9½ furlongs

1.	AJAX	F. Musgrave	9.0	H. Badger	1/2f
2.	Royal Chief	F. Jones	9.0	E. Bartle	4/1
3.	Young Idea	J. Holt	9.4	D. Munro	10/1

Winning details

Margin: 2 len x hd. **Time:** 1:56.75 *(Australasian record)* 11 started.

Breeding: Heroic – Medmenham – Prince Galahad (ch h 4) **Owner:** E. L. Baillieu, A. Thompson

Winner's Colors: White, red seams and cap

Winning Numbers: 4, 7, 1 **Barriers:** 7, 2, 6

ALSO RAN

L'Aiglon	D. Lewis	H. Skidmore	9.0	200/1
Adios	G. Price	J. O'Sullivan	7.11	20/1
Catalogue	A. W. McDonald	H. Mornement	9.4	200/1
Bourbon	W. J. McLachlan jr	R. Parsons	9.0	200/1
Spear Chief	G. Price	M. McCarten	9.0	200/1
Aelous	P. Riddle	A. Dewhurst	7.11	100/1
The Trump	S. W. Reid	A. Reed	9.4	20/1
Amigo	L. Paul	O. Phillips	7.11	20/1

All started

first of three consecutive Futurity Stakes; and with 57kg, carried 3.5kg more than weight-for-age in winning the Newmarket Handicap.

Spelled in the Autumn of 1938, having won six races on the trot, Ajax was devastating as a four -year- old.

He resumed by winning the Underwood Stakes in August 1938 (another race he won three times in a row) and then took the Memsie Stakes at Caulfield over 1800m before closely winning the Melbourne Stakes over 1600m at Flemington. On cue for the Cox Plate, he also won the Caulfield Stakes, but he showed a tendency to race very erratically that day, veering to the outside rail and almost touching it, once he was in the straight. As it was, he lasted by only a neck. However, had jockey Badger been able to ride him right out, he would have saluted by a much bigger margin.

Having never raced at Moonee Valley, it was a big relief for trainer Frank Musgrave and Badger that Ajax galloped well at the track and handled the circuit without any signs of waywardness en-route to the Plate. Despite his amazing record, some astute judges considered Ajax a risk, as handling the Valley turns under race conditions was different from a track gallop and who could tell if he was over his inclination to hang out, as he had done at Caulfield?

As a result, Ajax started at the relatively good odds of 1/2 but, in hindsight, it should have been 1/20. He scampered around the tight circuit without a worry, running the 1900m in a record 1:56.75, slicing .25 seconds off the time set by Manfred in 1925.

Ajax went to the front 1600m from home and turned the 1200m corner well clear. Young Idea made a forward move at that stage, but so easily was Ajax going that Badger gave him a slight breather allowing the rest of the field to gain ground. Coming to the turn Ajax was given more rein, with the result that the race looked over at that point. The New Zealander Royal Chief continued with a sustained forward run to grab Young Idea close to the line for second place, but neither placegetter was ever going to catch Ajax at any stage in the run home.

Badger brought the entire back to a rousing reception, particularly when it was revealed he had run a new Australasian record time for 1900m.

Having won 11 races on end, Ajax continued in the same vein the following week at Flemington where he won the Mackinnon Stakes (2000m) on Derby Day, the Linlithgow Stakes (1600m) on Oaks Day and the C. B. Fisher Plate (2400m) on the Saturday, taking his successive winning sequence to 15 before being spelled.

On resuming, he won his three Victorian starts before his defeat in the Rawson Stakes – only to win his next two runs at the end of his four-year-old career. He continued to race in great heart as a five-year-old including wins in the Underwood and Memsie Stakes, but he did not compete in the Spring of that year after going amiss following the Memsie success.

During the Autumn of 1940, his wins included the King's Plate at Flemington and the All Aged Plate at Randwick. As a six-year-old he won his first three starts in the Spring, was second in the Caulfield Stakes and then had another crack at the Cox Plate. He had tough opposition in the Plate of 1940 facing Beau Vite (who had won the AJC Metropolitan and the Craven Plate at his preceding starts) and Beaulivre, who had won the Caulfield Cup the previous week. The gallant Ajax failed by only a half neck behind Beau Vite, in what was to be his farewell race, but this was not revealed at the time.

Retired to stud, Ajax's best progeny was Magnificent, winner of the AJC and Victoria Derbys. He was later sold to the United States as a replacement for legendary American sire Sea Biscuit, but he failed to live up to expectations.

On the racetrack however, it had been a completely different story.

1939 — MOSAIC DIDN'T FIT PLATE PATTERN

Considered only a stayer – Mosaic won the 1939 AJC St Leger and the Sydney Cups in 1939-40 – the 9½ furlongs of the Cox Plate looked to be far too short for him. Confirming this theory, his lead-up form included a dead-heat for first over 2400m before a second over 2 miles in the Randwick Plate.

If only racing were that simple!

The Cox Plate of 1939, which promised so much, resulted in more surprises than anyone could have predicted.

First, the price about the winner, Sydney stayer Mosaic, was a "blowout" for punters, being 50/1. On top of that, he ran the distance in the record time of 1:56.5 – a quarter of second better than that run by the illustrious Ajax the previous year. Adding more to the intrigue was the inglorious effort of odds-on favorite High Caste; Beau Vite losing his rider; and the disappointing finish of three-year-old Gold Salute, whose owner had backed him to win £100,000 in a Spring treble, of which the Cox Plate was the first leg.

Mosaic, who was having his first start in the anti-clockwise Melbourne direction of racing, had been sent to Victoria with the Melbourne Cup as his mission.

Considered only a stayer – he won the 1939 AJC St Leger and the Sydney Cups in 1939-40 – the 1900m of the Cox Plate looked to be far too short for him. Confirming this theory, his lead-up form included a dead-heat for first with Royal Chief over the 2400m of the weight-for-age Colin Stephen Handicap before a second (being beaten by only a long head) over 3200m in the Randwick Plate. If only racing were that simple!

Mosaic was neglected in the betting, not only on that form, but also because of the class of a quartet of three-year-olds who were up against him. Heading the list was the former New Zealander High Caste, known as the "Strawberry Bull" because of his powerful physique and his white-flecked coat. Coming into the Plate he had won the Rosehill Guineas, was a close second in the AJC Derby and then won another four on end, including the Caulfield Guineas and Caulfield Stakes. With that form behind him, it was no surprise that he was pre-post favorite.

Then there was Gold Salute whose owner, Mr Alan Cooper, declared would win the Cox Plate, Victoria Derby and Melbourne Cup. Moreover, he had backed

1939

(Saturday, October 28. Attendance: 27,130)

£900 plus £100 trophy Weight for Age 9½ furlongs

1.	MOSAIC	J. H. Abbs	9.0	D. Munro	50/1
2.	Gold Salute	W. J. Shean	7.11	F. Shean	3/1
3.	Reading	J. T. Cush	7.11	A. Knox	33/1

Winning details

Margin: Len x 2½ len. **Time:** 1:56.5 (Course record) 12 started.

Breeding: Posterity – Inlaid – Invincible (b h 4) **Owner:** J. H. Abbs

Winner's Colors: Black, orange Maltese cross and cap

Winning Numbers: 3, 9, 11 **Barriers:** 8, 3, 2

ALSO RAN

Landlaw	L. Robertson	O. Phillips	8.11	20/1
High Caste	J. T. Jamieson	E. Bartle	7.12	9/10f
Buzalong	A. Leftwich	H. Skidmore	9.4	50/1
Cooranga	S. R. Lomond jr	A. Reed	8.13	100/1
Billposter	D. Lewis	J. Conguest	7.11	50/1
Catalogue	A. W. McDonald	M. McCarten	9.4	50/1
The Progeny	W. Duncan	H. Badger	7.11	200/1
Cavallo	J. Parkinson	J. O'Sullivan	7.13	200/1
Beau Vite (L.R.)	T. R. George	W. Cook	7.11	5/1

All started

his assertion to win £100,000 for an outlay of £1,000. An easy last start Caulfield winner, Gold Salute had skipped around Moonee Valley in great style in his final gallop, and had to be restrained to stay back with another classy three-year-old, Reading, who had won the AJC Derby and been placed in the Caulfield Guineas and Stakes and was being set for the Victoria Derby.

Another runner with a big reputation was the Kiwi, Beau Vite, who had won the Canterbury Stakes and Clarendon Stakes at Hawkesbury and finished second in the Chelmsford Stakes and Craven Plate, being beaten by the classy High Caste in the latter.

Come Plate day, stable backers invested heavily on High Caste with bets totalling £2000, as a result of which his price firmed from 10/9 to 9/10. Mr Cooper, the owner of Gold Salute, was content to let his treble bet be sufficient so Gold Salute eased from 9/4 to 3/1. Beau Vite was also well in the market at 9/2, while Mosaic was considered to have no chance at 50/1.

At the start, Reading showed the way from Beau Vite and Gold Salute, with High Caste being prominent. Reading continued to set a fast pace to the 1200m where Gold Salute moved up to his girth. At that point, Beau Vite was fourth and High Caste was three lengths away. Gold Salute took the upper hand soon after, with Beau Vite's rider angling for a run in fourth place. Near the 800m Beau Vite clipped the heels of Reading and buckled, throwing his rider Billy Cook.

By now, Mr Cooper was on very good terms with himself, as Gold Salute had shot well clear coming to the turn and looked to have the race won from Reading. High Caste who had been slightly affected by the interference to Beau Vite had lost a little ground and Mosaic was finishing hard on his outside.

On straightening, Gold Salute was more than two lengths in front and being shaken up to increase his lead when Mosaic swept up to him to go on and score by a length. Amazingly, he had clipped a quarter of a second off Ajax's record.

While Gold Salute was disappointing, having relinquished such a good lead, he had fared the best of the three-year-olds, beating Reading by 2½ lengths. High Caste finished fifth.

After the Cox Plate, Reading took the Classic double when he beat High Caste in the Victoria Derby; beat him again in the VRC St Leger and won the AJC St Leger; Beau Vite finished 8th to Rivette in the Melbourne Cup; Mosaic, who started 6/1 second favorite in the Melbourne Cup, could finish only 10th but took the Sydney Cup for the second time the next year.

1940-41 — BEAU VITE — ONE OF THE PLATE'S ELITE

In his five-year career Beau Vite won more than half of his 60 starts in New Zealand and Australia against some of the very best. Purchased as a yearling for 900 gns, he earned almost £30,000 between 1938 and 1942 and joined the elite band who won successive W. S. Cox Plates.

Away from the track he was a sour-tempered stallion – but on it, Beau Vite had a much better reputation.

In his five-year career, he won more than half of his 60 starts in New Zealand and Australia against some of the very best. Purchased as a yearling for 900 gns, he earned almost £30,000 between 1938-42 and joined that elite band who won successive W. S. Cox Plates.

By the imported Beau Pere, who stood three seasons in new Zealand, Beau Vite was a slow starter being unplaced at his first four runs in the Dominion. At his first start he was unplaced behind Beaulivre, another son of Beau Pere, in a 800m race at Marton. His first glimpse of form was when third – again Beaulivre was the victor – in a Wellington two-year-old in January, 1939. The pair, who were both to find fame on the racetrack, were to clash on many occasions at the highest level.

Spelled in the Autumn of 1939 with a record of three wins and four placings in 11 starts (including one win over Beaulivre) Beau Vite was sent to Australia for the Spring. At his first run here he was unplaced behind High Caste before winning over 1200m at Canterbury and 1800m at Hawkesbury.

He was then stepped right up in class to compete in events such as the Caulfield Stakes, W. S. Cox Plate (when he lost his rider), the Victoria Derby and the Melbourne Cup, but was unplaced in them all.

Returning home, Beau Vite resumed in a 1600m weight-for-age race against old foe Beaulivre (who had won 10 on end) in late December, failing by less than a length when second. That run showed, however, that Beau Vite was back to his near best – and he proved that in convincing style from then on, winning 26 of his next 38 starts, and being placed seven times.

He avenged his defeat by Beaulivre when he ran a race record in the Great Northern Derby, and Beaulivre was again second to him in the 2000m Clifford Plate, after which Beaulivre's connections decided to send their colt to Australia, where he was placed in the Doncaster and the All-Aged Stakes and included among his wins the Doomben Cup.

BEAU VITE ... broke records, even in training gallops. – Picture: HWT

1940
(Saturday, October 26. Attendance: 26,680)

£900 plus £100 trophy Weight for Age 9½ furlongs

1.	**BEAU VITE**	F. McGrath	9.0	*E. McMenamin*	7/4f
2.	**Ajax**	F. Musgrave	9.4	*H. Badger*	2/1
3.	**Beau Livre**	G. Price	9.0	*A. Dewhurst*	9/4

Winning details

Margin: ½ nk x ½ hd. **Time:** 1:57.75 6 started.

Breeding: Beau Pere – Dominant – Martian (br h 4) **Owner:** R. Stewart

Winner's Colors: Red, yellow spots

Winning Numbers: 2, 1, 3 **Barriers:** 7, 1, 4

ALSO RAN

Rivette	H. Bamber	H. Mornement	8.13	100/1
Scientist	C. A. Russell	A. Breasley	7.11	50/1
The Adjutant	A. Murray	E. Preston	7.11	50/1

Scratched: Positron

Staying home, Beau Vite won a further six races as a three-year-old before embarking on another Australian campaign in the Spring of 1940. Beaulivre again had his measure over shorter distances at his first two runs here, before Beau Vite hit form – and how.

He beat High Caste in the Hill Stakes; set a record in the 2400m Colin Stephen Stakes and then established an Australasian record in winning the Metropolitan Handicap two days later. Proving his stamina, he stepped out again two days later and ran a course record, beating the time set by Phar Lap, in winning the Craven Plate.

Next stop was the Cox Plate, and if his devastating form wasn't enough to make people take notice, his final pre-race gallop at Caulfield was. Beau Vite was still breaking records – even in gallops – with *The Sun News Pictorial* head-lining Beau Vite running the best time ever recorded for 1600m on the course proper in his final hit-out, being timed to run the distance in 1:39½.

Even though he was up against Ajax (2/1) and Beaulivre again – this time fresh from a win in the Caulfield Cup – punters sent Beau Vite out 7/4 favorite, and the finish was as close as the betting suggested.

Ted McMenamin dashed to the front on Beau Vite ahead of Ajax with 1200m to go and, rather than waiting for a last run, pinched a two length break from Ajax with Beaulivre in third place. Little had changed to the turn, where Beau Vite was still travelling easily, with Ajax in hot pursuit. At that stage Arthur Dewhurst went for a rails run on Beaulivre but was baulked for room. With Beaulivre unable to get the run when Dewhurst wanted, Beau Vite continued on strongly to hold off Ajax by a half neck with Beaulivre finishing strongly only a half head away.

Now a hot favorite for the Melbourne Cup, criminals attempted to prevent Beau Vite from running in the race, for which he had been heavily backed. A hole was drilled into a stall at his Caulfield stables and shots were fired at a horse – but it was another brown horse, El Golea – and not Beau Vite – who was in the stall. (El Golea survived and went on to win big races including the Williamstown Cup and Eclipse Stakes, and was second to Beau Vite in the Mackinnon Stakes the year after he was shot.)

After the attempted maiming, Beau Vite went on to win the Mackinnon Stakes and was fourth when only 7/4 favorite in the Melbourne Cup. Returned home, he won the Auckland Cup prior to another successful Autumn in Sydney.

He spent the Winter in Australia before embarking on another campaign in the Spring of 1941. En -route to Melbourne he broke his own mark in setting a new Australasian record for 2000m in the Craven Plate and was then near last in the Caulfield Cup with 62.5kg

Much better suited by the weight-for-age conditions of the Cox Plate, Beau Vite started at the prohibitive odds of 1/3 in beating glamor mare Tranquil Star by 1½ lengths, with Laureate third.

Ridden by Darby Munro, who had been on him in all his starts as a five-year-old, Beau Vite was again ridden for the lead as he had been the previous year. At the 800m Tranquil Star momentarily got to the lead, but Munro gave his mount a dig to retain the rails position. It soon became obvious that the mare could not sustain her run and Munro drew away riding hands and heels to score as comfortably as the odds indicated.

Now in elite company having won two Cox Plates, Beau Vite scored again in the Mackinnon Stakes a week later before finishing third behind three-year-old Skipton in the Melbourne Cup.

He had only two more runs in Sydney the following Autumn and bowed out with a third in the Sydney Cup. On his return to New Zealand for stud duties, he stood alongside his regular rival, Beaulivre.

1941

(Saturday, October 25. Attendance: 29,910)

£1,000 plus £50 trophy Weight for Age 9½ furlongs

1.	**BEAU VITE**	F. McGrath	9.4	*D. Munro*	1/3f
2.	**Tranquil Star**	R. Cameron	8.9	*F. Shean*	6/1
3.	**Laureate**	H. Freedman	7.11	*H. Badger*	10/1

Winning details

Margin: 1½ len x ¾ len. **Time:** 1:58.25 9 started.

Breeding: Beau Pere – Dominant – Martian (br h 5) **Owner:** R. Stewart

Winner's Colors: Red, yellow spots

Winning Numbers: 1, 3, 4 **Barriers:** 1, 8, 7

ALSO RAN

It's Funny	J. W. Cook	J. Conguest	7/11	50/1
Vermont	P. B. Quinlan	J. Purtell	7/11	50/1
Gay Revelry	H. W. Gabell	S. Ralph	7/11	25/1
Galliard	J. T. Cush	N. Sellwood	7/11	100/1
Chatoona	S. R. Lamond jr	M. McCarten	9.0	100/1
Lugano	M. Crossey	H. Olsen	7/11	100/1

All started

1942, 1944 — SHE WAS A STAR, BUT SHE WASN'T TRANQUIL

Tranquil Star was hailed as being a world-beater one day – and as a duffer the next.

In all, she won 23 times and was placed on 32 occasions. While accepting it was not possible for Tranquil Star to keep winning and winning, in many of the 56 instances she was unplaced, there seemed no reason at all for failure.

Victorian mare Tranquil Star had an iron constitution, competing at the highest level for seven years.

She was also quirky. She was hailed as being a world-beater one day – and as a duffer the next. Proof of her durability is the fact that she started 111 times. In all she won 23 times and was placed on 32 occasions. While accepting it was not possible for Tranquil Star to keep winning and winning, in many of the 56 instances she was unplaced, there seemed no reason at all for failure.

Racegoers have to be a forgiving lot so, despite this trait, Tranquil Star remained a very popular mare to the end because of her durability and some of the feats she achieved. These included two W. S. Cox Plate wins and a Caulfield Cup success with 56.5kg, which is still the record winning weight for a mare.

Her record in these two races provides further proof of her amazing durability as she competed in both of them for five years straight against some of the best horses of the era. Her best year was as a five-year-old in 1942 when she took the Caulfield Cup and the Cox Plate.

Tranquil Star showed signs of things to come – in both ability and waywardness – from the outset. At the end of her two-year-old days she had started 13 times for two wins and four seconds. At three she won the Manifold Stakes at her second run in and then was runner up in the Victoria Derby (behind Lucrative, subsequent winner of the Sydney Cup) and astern of Session in a record-breaking VRC Oaks.

Resuming in the Autumn, she beat the top-liner High Caste over 1800m in the St George Stakes at Caulfield; was unplaced next outing in the Futurity, and then romped home in the VRC St Leger, leaving Lucrative five lengths in her wake over the 2800m. Two runs later, she again triumphed over High

1942
(Saturday, October 24. Attendance: 30,410)

£1,000 plus £50 trophy Weight for Age 9½ furlongs

1.	TRANQUIL STAR	R. Cameron	8.13	K. Smith	7/2
2.	Pandect	F. Musgrave	9.4	H. Badger	15/1
3.	Leahero	P. Burke	7.12	E. Preston	20/1

Winning details

Margin: 5 len x ½ hd. **Time:** 2:00.75 19 started.

Breeding: Gay Lothario – Lone Star – Great Star (ch m 5) **Owner:** T. G. Jones & R. Cobden

Winner's Colors: Mauve, cream band, sleeves & cap

Winning Numbers: 6, 1, 15 **Barriers:** 19, 9, 5

ALSO RAN

High Road	L. Robertson	A. Breasley	9.0	7/1
Grain Trader	S. B. Ferguson	J. Neale	7.11	20/1
Burrabil	W. O'Dwyer	O. Phillips	9.4	12/1
Tea Cake	P. B. Quinlan	J. Purtell	9.0	12/1
Home James	P. B. Quinlan	H. McLoud	7.11	33/1
Haros	V. Ryan	R. Heather	7.11	33/1
Philander	V. Ryan	J. Gilmore	7.6	50/1
Attorney	L. J. McCann	T. Unkovich	7.11	50/1
Noble John	T. J. Dunlop	E. Badger	7.11	100/1
Great Britain	H. Freedman	H. Morris	7.11	9/4f
Parida	W. N. Brodie	S. Ralph	7.11	50/1
Clayton	R. Roach	H. Olsen	7.11	50/1
Illyrian	W. Short	H. Mornement	7.13	33/1
Register	H. Hilton	W. Box	7.11	25/1
Gay Roi	R. J. Shaw	W. Beresford	7.11	100/1
Microphone	M. Crossey	C. Hughes	9.4	50/1

All started

TRANQUIL STAR ... when she was good she was very, very good ... and she was just that on two occasions in the W. S. Cox Plate. – Picture: HWT

Caste (with Beau Vite third) in race record time in the Chipping Norton Stakes. Appearing a certainty in the AJC St Leger the following week, she finished last behind Lucrative, only to come out four days later over the same distance in the Cumberland Plate to beat Lucrative by eight lengths! Three days later over the 3600m of the AJC Plate at the same track she finished last. At least she was consistently inconsistent!

Tranquil Star had 21 starts for two wins as a four-year-old but was placed in top company, which included seconds in the Caulfield Stakes (behind Lucrative) and to Beau Vite in the Cox Plate at her first run in the race.

Even though she won at Moonee Valley and in the Caulfield Stakes in the Spring of 1942 en route to the Caulfield Cup (run at Flemington) she was not given much chance in the Cup because of her wide barrier of 21; the massive weight she had to carry; and her inconsistency, which was always a consideration. However, nursed by Scobie Breasley, she lasted by a neck, despite conceding 4.5kg to the runner-up, Heart's Desire.

The Cox Plate the following week was rated a match between Caulfield Guineas winner Great Britain, 9/4 favorite, and Tranquil Star at 7/2. Tranquil Star was on her best behaviour for the third time running and made a one-act affair of the Plate, scoring by five lengths in a field of 19. She raced to the front in the first 400m and was never headed thereafter. She came back to the weigh-in enclosure to a huge reception. She was back in favor again.

The next week, Tranquil Star made it four wins on end when she took the Mackinnon Stakes, but the dream run finished when she was well down the track in the Melbourne Cup, unsuited by the rain affected track.

At her next campaign she won only once – beating Amana in the St George Stakes. However, Amana certainly had the measure of Tranquil Star in other races beating her in the Melbourne, Caulfield and Mackinnon Stakes. Amana also won the 1943 Cox Plate in which Tranquil Star finished fourth in a field of 8, taking her Cox Plate record to a win, a second and a fourth in three attempts.

Even at the age of seven Tranquil Star was not finished – though it had looked like it after she fell in what was to be her last race for the 1944 season, in the Glenara Handicap at Moonee Valley.

Tranquil Star injured her jaw so badly in a fall at Moonee Valley that it had to be wired, but she was back five months later. She resumed with three placings on end, and after being near last at 100/1 in the Caulfield Cup, won by Counsel from Lawrence and Tea Cake finishing third, the hardy mare tackled Cox Plate number four.

Even at the age of seven Tranquil Star was not finished – though it had looked like it after she fell in what was to be her last race for the 1944 season in the Glenara Handicap at Moonee Valley. Tranquil Star injured her jaw so badly that it had to be wired, but she was back five months later. She resumed with three placings on end, and after being near last at 100/1 in the Caulfield Cup, won by Counsel from Lawrence and Tea Cake, the hardy mare tackled Cox Pate number four.

Lawrence, who had been withdrawn from the Cox Plate the year before under extraordinary circumstances when he straddled a hurdle placed at the start to divide the field into two sections, was odds-on favorite for the 1944 Plate after it was announced that Counsel would not run. Despite her age, Tranquil Star was much better suited under the weight-for-age conditions than she was in the Caulfield Cup, and she was 7/2 second favorite.

Once again Tranquil Star won in a cakewalk, scoring by 2½ lengths from Lawrence, with Tea Cake again third. Unlike in her previous Plate win, Tranquil Star settled just off the pace, moving up to fourth, with Lawrence fifth, 800m from home to be within four lengths of the leader Three O Three.

Scobie Breasley then shot Tranquil Star around the leaders to hit the front on the turn from Tea Cake and Three O Three, with Sirius and Lawrence behind them. Lawrence then began chase but Breasley cleared out on Tranquil Star to win easily, with the mare being pulled up on the line.

There were excuses for Lawrence failing to run on as expected, as he was lame after the race and was forced to miss the Melbourne Cup because of the injury. It was the second year in a row he had been hurt in the Cox Plate – and the race hoodoo continued the following year when he started odds-on but could finish only fourth after having every chance.

In what was to be her final year, as an eight-year-old, Tranquil finished fifth in the Cox Plate behind the brilliant Flight, but she still recorded three wins for the season, including the Mackinnon Stakes. Fittingly, her last victory was in the William Reid Stakes at the Valley.

Then came six unplaced runs. In March 1946, Tranquil Star bowed out her own way – being unplaced at the Valley – but along the way she had earned a well deserved reputation as Australia's toughest mare, albeit also the most unpredictable.

1944

(Saturday, October 28. Attendance: 32,330)

£1,500 Weight for Age 1¼ miles

1.	TRANQUIL STAR	R. Cameron	8.13	A. Breasley	7/1
2.	Lawrence	L. Robertson	9.0	W. Williamson	1/2f
3.	Tea Cake	P. B. Quinlan	9.4	V. Hartney	25/1

Winning details

Margin: 2½ len x 2 len. **Time:** 2:06.75 9 started.

Breeding: Gay Lothario – Lone Star – Great Star (ch m 7) **Owner:** T. G. Jones & R. Cobden

Winner's Colors: Mauve, cream band, sleeves & cap

Winning Numbers: 6, 3, 1 **Barriers:** 3, 4, 6

ALSO RAN

Sirius	E. Fisher	R. Finger	9.0	15/1
Bootle	E. J. Willmott	H. Morris	7.11	12/1
New Yorker	F. Godby	H. McLoud	7.11	33/1
Three o Three	R. J. Shaw	A. Dewhurst	7.12	14/1
Lilette	H. Wolters	R. Heather	8.13	33/1
Frill King	F. Manning jr	O. Phillips	9.4	200/1

All started

1943 – AMANA BRIEFLY LIVED UP TO HIS NAME

Amana was bred to be a star. His father was the VRC and AJC Derby winner, Talking, while his dam was Epsom Handicap winner, Capris.

Amana's time came in the Spring of 1943, when he was hailed the weight-for-age star of the Melbourne Carnival. His success meant disappointment for the owners of brilliant mare Tranquil Star who ran an exasperating string of seconds behind Amana.

The sequence began in the Melbourne Stakes (1600m) in October 1943, when Tranquil Star finished three-quarters of a length astern of the Roy Shaw-trained galloper, and was repeated the following week in the Caulfield Stakes.

In a slowly run race that day, Arthur Dewhurst on Amana went to the front when the pace was too slow early, and did all the hard work, but was still able to stall off Tranquil Star's challenge. No doubt the connections of the mare were pleased the following week, when the Caulfield Cup was divided, that Tranquil Star had not drawn Amana's division!

Amana had drawn what was considered the tougher division of the Cup and put up a strong performance in finishing second behind Skipton, who had taken the Derby-Melbourne Cup double as a three-year-old two years earlier. Amana slipped away on the turn but was gathered in by Scobie Breasley on Skipton who went on to win by 1½ lengths after hitting the front halfway down the straight.

In the other division, Tranquil Star showed customary speed from the barrier and was still in front coming to the turn, after which she faded to beat only one runner home.

Considering his good showing – and his earlier weight-for-age form – Amana was entitled to be early favorite for the Cox Plate the following week. His effort in the Caulfield Cup showed that he could handle a distance, which in the case of the '43 Cox Plate, was increased by 100m to 2000m. The key was to have Amana sharp enough to come back from the 2400m of the Caulfield Cup.

The race began on a sensational note when, after the horses had been called into line, Caulfield Guineas winner Lawrence – a Derby

Amana was entitled to be early favorite for the Cox Plate the following week. His effort in the Caulfield Cup showed that he could handle a distance, which in the case of the '43 Cox Plate, was increased by 100m to 2000m.

1943
(Saturday, October 23. Attendance: 33,250)

£1,000 Weight for Age 1¼ miles

1.	AMANA	R. J. Shaw	9.0	A. Dewhurst	5/2f
2.	Sun Valley	F. W. Hoysted	9.4	J. Purtell	7/1
3.	Precept	J. Pengilly	7.11	E. Preston	6/1

Winning details

Margin: 2 len x hd. **Time:** 2:03.75 8 started.

Breeding: Talking – Capris – Captain Bunsby (ch h 4) **Owner:** W. Fink

Winner's Colors: Green, white sleeves, red armbands & cap

Winning Numbers: 7, 5, 10 **Barriers:** 7, 2, 4

ALSO RAN

Tranquil Star	R. Cameron	J. O'Brien	8.13	3/1
Gay Revelry	H. W. Gabell	O. Phillips	9.4	50/1
Phocion	L. Robertson	A. Breasley	9.4	33/1
Reception	P. B. Quinlan	H. Morris	9.4	20/1
Peter	J. O'Dwyer	W. Williamson	9.4	100/1

Scratched: Counsel, Lawrence (late scratching)

candidate – had to be withdrawn after injuring himself. He had straddled a hurdle placed at the start to divide the field. (Under the rules in those days, all bets on Lawrence were lost, as he was deemed to have been in the hands of the starter.)

Soon after this drama there was some slight interference at the start, which slightly hampered Amana, among others. It was evident that this could have occurred, as after Lawrence's withdrawal other runners were fractious, wheeling and turning waiting to be called up by the starter.

Gay Revelry led the field from barrier rise with Tranquil Star settling third, while Amana and the three-year-old Precept were at the tail of the field. Coming to the 1200m Tranquil Star hit the front and Amana was making his run from the rear of the field. With 1000m to go Amana was two lengths behind, but slowly making ground.

Approaching the turn, Precept moved up to the two older horses, with Amana on his heels. It was soon obvious that Amana had the measure of Tranquil Star yet again, as she was fading (eventually finishing fourth). Sun Valley flashed home over the final stages cutting Precept out of second place after he looked the certain runner-up.

The following week, Amana clashed with Tranquil Star again – and once more he was the victor – in the Mackinnon Stakes, beating the mare by 2½ lengths. The pair had met on four occasions in a matter of weeks and every time Amana had her measure.

Moonee Valley was soundly criticised over the mishap which caused the withdrawal of Lawrence, with *Lochiel* reporting:

"While barriers to divide fields serve a useful purpose, one was hurdly necessary in the Cox Plate with only nine starters. In any case, the barriers should be at least another foot high, and should be padded."

As it transpired, Lawrence was fit enough to take his place in the Derby field, finishing third to Precept who then ran a sound fourth to Dark Felt in the Melbourne Cup.

The following year Amana was second in the St George Stakes and won the Underwood Stakes, but never again found the same form he showed when he was the weight-for-age star of 1943.

1945-46 – STAR FILLY PUT HER OPPONENTS TO FLIGHT

She was tiny in stature and in price – but the Royal Step filly, Flight, made a huge impact on the racetrack.

Bought for a paltry 60 gns by subsequent AJC Chairman, Sir Brian Crowley, Flight showed from the outset that her ability far outweighed her cost. She began her career on a winning note in a Nursery Handicap and at the end of her first year her record stood at five wins, a second and a third in eight starts. One of the victories was in the Champagne Stakes after being beaten by only a head the previous week in the AJC Sires.

Resuming the following year, she was aimed immediately at the big-time – her wins included the Hobartville Stakes, Craven Plate and the Adrian Knox Stakes, while she was runner-up behind Moorland in the AJC Derby. Another valiant second placing was in the Doncaster Handicap when she carried 57kg only to be run down in the last stride and be beaten by a half head by Goose Boy, who was carrying 5.5kg less. Two days later, she closed her three-year-old year with another second in the All Aged stakes.

On paper, her four-year-old record looks a little disappointing with only two wins from 12 starts, but she did run placings in six of Sydney's best races. Her successes were in the Warwick Stakes and the Colin Stephen Handicap, while she was placed in races such as the Craven Plate and the Metropolitan. Weighted with the huge impost of 57kg in the Sydney Cup, the plucky mare finished third, within a length of Craigie and subsequent Melbourne Cup winner Russia. This was despite the fact that her saddle slipped soon after the start of the race and that she was conceding 4.5kg to the other two horses.

The 1945-46 season was to be her best. After three placings on resuming as a five-year-old (including a second behind the brilliant Shannon), she broke through for her first win that campaign when she avenged the defeat by Shannon in the Craven Plate. She then strolled home in the 2400m AJC Phar Lap Handicap as her prelude to her first trip to Melbourne and the Cox Plate.

Although she had been racing at top level in NSW, she was facing some stiff

> Weighted with the huge impost of 57kg in the Sydney Cup, the plucky mare finished third, within a length of Craigie and Russia who was to go on and win the Melbourne Cup.
>
> This was despite the fact that her saddle slipped soon after the start of the race and that she was conceding 4.5kg to the other two horses.

1945
(Saturday, October 27. Attendance: 31,060)

£1,500 Weight for Age 1¼ miles

1.	**FLIGHT**	F. Nowland	8.13	J. O'Sullivan	11/2
2.	**Don Pedro**	E. J. Willmott	7.11	W. Cook	9/2
3.	**Russia**	E. Hush	9.4	J. Duncan	25/1

Winning details

Margin: ½ hd x 3 len. **Time:** 2:08.75 8 started.

Breeding: Royal Step – Lambent – Tractor (b m 5) **Owner:** B. H. Crowley

Winner's Colors: Dark blue, orange diamond, sleeves & cap

Winning Numbers: 4, 6, 3 **Barriers:** 7, 6, 4

ALSO RAN

Lawrence	L. Robertson	A. Breasley	9.4	9/10f
Tranquil Star	R. Cameron	V. Hartney	8.13	7/1
Nestor	B. Price	J. Crilley	7.11	100/1
Hoyle	W. O'Dwyer	W. Williamson	8.0	100/1
Magnificent	A. S. Croall	N. Powell	7.11	33/1

Scratched: Blankenburg

competition in Melbourne, with the form of Lawrence being particularly strong. Coming into the Plate, Lawrence had won over the Plate distance in a Quality handicap at Moonee Valley; had beaten Derby favorite Don Pedro in the weight-for-age Melbourne Stakes and followed that with a close win over St Fairy in the Caulfield Stakes. Considering St Fairy had gone on to win the Caulfield Cup, it was hard to go past Lawrence, whose Cox Plate form to that stage was: scratched at barrier (1943); and pulled up sore after finishing second in 1944.

Once again the Cox Plate proved to be a "hoodoo" race for Lawrence, who finished fourth when odds-on, with the gutsy little Flight leading, defying the rest of the field to run her down after going to the front 1600m from home. Because she was having her first run here, Flight was inclined to hang on a couple of the turns, but also hung on gamely, to win by a half head over Don Pedro with Russia three lengths away.

While Flight bowled along in front from Magnificent and Tranquil Star, Lawrence, who was last early, began a forward move 1000m from home, but was still giving Flight a five lengths start. Even that far from home, bookmakers were yelling out that Lawrence was a 2/1 against chance – not the odds on he had been before the race. Flight was being ridden hard from the 400m, and despite the fact she did not corner smoothly, she refused to be run down.

Following that success she finished second to Tranquil Star in the Mackinnon Stakes and was then well back in the Melbourne Cup.

1946 (1st division)
(Saturday, October 26. Attendance: 30,850)

£1,150 plus £100 Cup Weight for Age 1¼ miles

1.	FLIGHT	F. Nowland	8.13	J. O'Sullivan	3/1
2.	Star Act	P. B. Quinlan	7.11	H. Badger	6/1
3.	Magnificent	A. S. Croall	9.0	V. Hartney	7/1

Winning details

Margin: 3½ len x hd. Time: 2:05.00 11 started.

Breeding: Royal Step – Lambent – Tractor (b m 6) Owner: B. H. Crowley

Winner's Colors: Dark blue, orange diamond, sleeves and cap

Winning Numbers: 8, 13, 6 Barriers: 11, 5, 8

ALSO RAN

Prince Standard	D. Lewis	W. Briscoe	7.11	7/1
Flying Duke	M. McCarten	W. Cook	7.11	5/2f
Russia	E. Hush	D. Munro	9.4	20/1
Concerto	D. Lewis	G. Moore	7.11	20/1
Earl Mond	P. Burke	G. Bougoure	9.4	100/1
Cherie Marie	W. Duncan	A. Breasley	8.9	50/1
Carlton	E. H. Nichols	R. Heather	9.4	100/1
Rimfire	S. Boyden	H. McFarlane	9.0	250/1

Scratched: Spam, Four Freedoms

Spelled in Victoria, Flight won four on end in the Autumn of 1946 in the Orr, St George, Essendon and Lloyd Stakes. Switched back to Sydney, she was shaded by only a head by the mighty Bernborough in the Chipping Norton Stakes, with a further 10 lengths to the third placegetter.

In preparing for her next Cox Plate campaign, Shannon ran an Australasian record to beat her in the George Main Stakes. Unplaced in the Caulfield Cup at her first run in Melbourne that Spring, her toughest opponent in the first division of the 1946 Plate (there were two divisions that year) looked to be the Sydney three-year-old Flying Duke, who had been unlucky when runner up in the Rosehill Guineas and the AJC Derby.

However, she had no opposition. After going out to a clear lead early Flight had 3 lengths to spare at the finish. At one stage she was five lengths in front, when she was given a breather. Coming to the turn she was still three lengths clear and no other runner could get near her in the run home. The record books show she won the Mackinnon Stakes by six lengths the following Saturday, though it was a hollow victory. The mighty Bernborough looked to have the race at his mercy – he certainly had Flight covered – until he broke down, never to race again, but was fortunately saved for stud duties.

Flight too, retired at the end of that season with 24 wins and 28 placings in 65 starts, for earnings of more than £31,000 – a huge return on her purchase price. Sent to stud, Flight's foals flopped, but her daughter, Flight's Daughter, produced the champion Sky High and Golden Slipper-AJC Derby winner, Skyline.

LEONARD STUNS WITH SURPRISE WIN

LEONARD caused the surprise of the Carnival in winning the seond division of the Cox Plate later that afternoon.

An inglorious last in the Caulfield Cup, Leonard was a 50/1 chance, the same quote as he had been in the Caulfield Cup.

Ridden by Queensland jockey Billy Briscoe, it was the first time this campaign that Leonard – who was third in the Melbourne Cup the previous year – had shown any good form. He went to the front soon after the start and still maintained that position with 600m to go.

Favorite, St Fairy – who was the medium of heavy backing – moved up at this point with the three-year-old Bold Beau, from Cotham and Monmouth.

On entering the straight it became clear that Leonard was travelling comfortably in comparison with the others around him and he went on to score by a half length.

Punters were blown away and much preferred to reminisce about Flight's Cox Plate that day.

1946 (2ⁿᵈ division)
(Saturday, October 26. Attendance: 30,850)

£1,150 plus £100 Cup Weight for Age 1 ¼ miles

1.	LEONARD	L. Robertson	9.0	W. Briscoe	50/1
2.	Monmouth	M. McCarten	9.0	H. Badger	12/1
3.	Cotham	T. Lewis	7.11	J. Gilmore	12/1

Winning details

Margin: ½ len x ¾ len. **Time:** 2:06 10 started.

Breeding: Dhoti – Jeanne Hachette – Heroic (ch h 4) **Owner:** A. H. Griffiths

Winner's Colors: Light blue, pink sleeves and cap

Winning Numbers: 5, 6, 9 **Barriers:** 9, 1, 3

ALSO RAN

Don Pedro	E. J. Willmott	R. Heather	9.0	7/2
Bold Beau	D. Judd	G. Moore	7.11	3/1
On Target	L. Robertson	A. Breasley	9.4	33/1
St. Fairy	T. Lewis	H. Bastion	9.4	2/1f
Knockarlow	T. Woodcock	J. Purtell	8.13	100/1
Laudate	J. Fryer	P. Simonds	7.11	200/1
Rotten Row	T. J. Smith	H. McLoud	7.11	100/1

Scratched: Cordale, Sir Actor

1947 – CHANAK MAKES IT PLATE No. 6 FOR HOLT

The colt Chanak made plenty of news – for right and wrong reasons – in the Spring of 1947.

The winner of the Moonee Valley Stakes, which took his record to seven wins and three placings in 13 starts, he was in the stable of top trainer Jack Holt. Coming into the Caulfield Guineas, Holt declared Chanak even fitter than he had been when he won at the Valley.

On that form, he was a clear 5/4 favorite for the Caulfield race before tackling the Cox Plate and the Victoria Derby.

His supporters were smiling over the concluding stages of the Guineas when Scobie Breasley dashed him to the front past the leader Denhoti with just over 200m to go. Such was his acceleration, he quickly shot about three lengths clear.

So confident was Breasley that he appeared to ease up over the last few bounds, when the 66/1 outsider Hororata swept up to Chanak. The judge called for a photo and the print showed that Chanak had been beaten. Punters had gone from holding pound notes to cardboard in the space of seconds.

Herald racing chief *"Cardigan"* summed up the controversial ride this way:

"There is little doubt that Chanak should have won but Breasley, although he had picked up the whip and was showing it to Chanak without using it, did not make haste for home, no doubt believing the race was safe."

While Breasley had nothing to say after the race, Billy Briscoe on Hororata admitted he was surprised.

"Halfway down the straight I didn't think I had any chance," he said. Stewards had the final say, suspending Breasley for failing to ride his mount out.

Next stop for Chanak was the Cox Plate, where the classy Royal Gem was considered the one to beat, starting 7/4 favorite on the strength of his good third in the Caulfield Stakes, with punters preferring to overlook his failure in the Caulfield Cup.

Chanak – with Harold Badger now in the saddle –

1947
(Saturday, October 25. Attendance: 45,860)

£1,500 plus £150 Cup Weight for Age 1¼ miles

1.	CHANAK	J. Holt	7.12	H. Badger	9/2
2.	Attley	W. Cutler	9.4	J. Purtell	9/2
3.	Sweet Chime	M. McCarten	8.9	N. Sellwood	12/1

Winning details

Margin: ½ hd x 1¾ len. **Time:** 2:05 11 started.

Breeding: Hellespont – Studio – Manfred (br c 3) **Owner:** K. M. Niall

Winner's Colors: White, dark blue spots & cap

Winning Numbers: 8, 1, 7 **Barriers:** 6, 7, 5

ALSO RAN

Royal Gem	G. R. Jesser	W. Williamson	9.4	7/4f
Murray Stream	G. Brown	D. Munro	9.4	14/1
Vrondi	E. J. Willmott	R. Heather	7.13	100/1
Hororata	E. J. Willmott	W. Briscoe	7.11	10/1
Anthelion	G. A. Alessio	G. Moore	7.11	50/1
Conductor	J. W. Cook	W. Cook	7.12	20/1
Buonarroti Boy	V. Piggins	G. Bougoure	9.4	100/1
Glamis Star	D. Judd	S. Ralph	9.4	100/1

Scratched: Don Pedro, Dumfries

was rated a 9/2 chance, while showing that his previous win was indeed fortunate to say the least, the Briscoe-Hororata combination was sent out at 100/1.

Badger took Chanak to the lead going past the stand, followed by Royal Gem, Attley, Murray Stream and Sweet Chime. At the 1600m, Attley went around Chanak and quickened the pace, to lead by two lengths with 1200m left to run. Sweet Chime came into contention when she made a forward move as the field approached the turn, but she was forced four wide as Chanak and Royal Gem also moved up.

Ironically, on this occasion, Chanak was the "chaser" in the run home – unlike in the Guineas – as entering the straight it looked as if topweight Attley would be the certain winner, having kicked two lengths clear. However, with Badger riding furiously, Chanak gradually got the upper hand in the last bounds to win by a half head, with Sweet Chime third. Royal Gem, who was beaten a long way from home, faded for fourth.

It was Cox Plate number six – and the last – for trainer Jack Holt who had previously prepared Easingwold, Heroic, Highland and Young Idea (twice). Badger, who had been booed when beaten in the previous race, came back to cheers, with the crowd remembering Chanak's ill luck at his previous start.

Coming through the race in fine style, Chanak was now 5/4 favorite for the Victoria Derby, in which he clashed with the smart South Australian Beau Gem, who had won a Caulfield three-year-old as his lead-up to the Derby. On form, Chanak looked superior, but on the day Beau Gem triumphed.

The pair were locked in battle for more than 200m with Beau Gem getting the verdict by an official half head – the camera was used for the Derby for the first time to split the pair – and had to run a record time to score.

1948 – A COPYBOOK RIDE BY BADGER

Carbon Copy was soon to show exceptional ability against his own age, at weight-for-age and against older horses in his Classic season, which saw him win nine races and be placed in five others in 18 starts. His earnings for the 1948-49 season were about £28,000, which was a record for his age group.

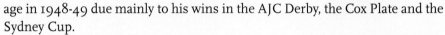

A slow starter, the big chestnut, Carbon Copy, became the best three-year-old of his year – which is a big accolade, considering his peers included the brilliant Comic Court, Bernbrook and Vagabond.

Comic Court and Carbon Copy were to stage many an enthralling contest, making it a vintage season for three-year-olds. Carbon Copy became the biggest stakeswinner for his age in 1948-49 due mainly to his wins in the AJC Derby, the Cox Plate and the Sydney Cup.

In his first season, his initial glimpse of form was when he was second over the 1400m of the Gibson-Carmichael Stakes at Flemington, before winning there over the same distance in March 1948. At the end of his two-year-old year Carbon Copy had the moderate record of a win and a second in eight starts – which was hardly a strong pointer of what was to come.

However, he was soon to show exceptional ability against his own age, at weight-for-age and against older horses in his Classic season, which saw him win nine races and be placed in five others in 18 starts. His earnings for the 1948-49 season were about £28,000, a record for his age group.

The winning sequence started when he won the 1600m Chatsworth Plate. Taken to Sydney, he finished second in the Chelmsford Stakes, had his colors lowered when a dismal 11th in the Rosehill Guineas, but then found top form. Ridden by Scobie Breasley, he scored a Classic success in beating Vagabond and Foxzami in a thrilling AJC Derby, with only a nose and a neck separating the trio.

The next obvious stop, for any three-year-old who could stay, was the Cox Plate, in which his chief opposition looked to be Caulfield Guineas winner Phoibos and the previous year's Derby winner Beau Gem. They were the first three in the betting and that's how the race panned out – but not in the order on the bookmakers' boards where Phoibos was a pronounced favorite at 6/4; Beau Gem at 4/1 and Carbon Copy at 5/1.

A perfect ride by Harold Badger saw Carbon Copy continue his winning way – due in no small part to Badger taking a "needle eye" opening at the top of the straight to put Carbon Copy in a winning position. The race had not been run

1948

(Saturday, October 23. Attendance: 47,570)

£1,550 plus £150 Cup Weight for Age 1¼ miles

1.	**CARBON COPY**	D. McCormick	7.12	*H. Badger*	5/1
2.	**Phoibos**	P. B. Quinlan	7.13	*W. Williamson*	6/4f
3.	**Beau Gem**	G. R. Jesser	9.0	*R. Heather*	4/1

Winning details

Margin: Nk x ¾ len. **Time:** 2:04.25 9 started.

Breeding: Helios(GB) – Havers – Windbag (ch c 3) **Owner:** A. G. Silk & H. J. Ascot

Winner's Colors: Green, white band & cap (carried all white colors of Club)

Winning Numbers: 9, 8, 2 **Barriers:** 2, 7, 6

ALSO RAN

Comic Court	J. M. Cummings	R. Hutchinson	7.11	20/1
Clement	H. Wolters	N. Sellwood	7.11	33/1
Columnist	C. Cullen	J. Thompson	9.4	11/2
Stamen	T. Woodcock	J. Tully	9.0	100/1
Anthelion	G. A. Alessio	W. Cook	9.0	12/1
High Tar	H. Wolters	G. Bougoure	7.11	50/1

Scratched: Hororata

to suit him, with a slow early pace and a sprint from the 1200m when Beau Gem dashed to the lead from Phoibos and Comic Court.

At the turn Beau Gem still led from the other pair with Carbon Copy making steady ground, when Beau Gem suddenly dropped back. Seizing the opportunity, Badger went for a "microscopic" inside run when he saw Beau Gem falter, rather than have the horse come back on him. Despite the narrow gap, Carbon Copy went straight through to grab the lead and simply outstayed the others. Phoibos, who had every opportunity, did not run out the journey strongly, finishing a neck behind Carbon Copy with Beau Gem sticking on for the minor placing.

(The same afternoon Badger was also seen at his best winning the Moonee Valley Cup on the New Zealander Howe, who was backed from 3/1 to 9/4. Badger accepted the ride on the horse in the Melbourne Cup, in which he started 7/4 favorite but could finish only fifth.)

Kept going, Carbon Copy attempted the Derby Double, tackling the VRC version in which he started 7/4 favorite, but could manage only third behind subsequent Melbourne Cup winners Comic Court and Foxzami. At his final start before a spell Carbon Copy finished a credible 8th in the Melbourne Cup, in which Comic Court was fourth.

Come Autumn, nothing changed as the pair continued their duels. Carbon Copy had the edge when he beat his foe by a short half head in the St George Stakes, but the tables were reversed at their next clash when Comic Court had a 3½ lengths margin in the VRC St Leger.

After winning the Kings Plate at Flemington, Carbon Copy continued his three-year-old season in Sydney. It was there that he cemented his title as the best of his age when he won four on end. He took the Chipping Norton Stakes; gave Comic Court a four lengths beating in the AJC St Leger ; beat Vagabond in the Sydney Cup (with Comic Court unplaced) and then thrashed 1946 Melbourne Cup winner Russia by an astounding 10 lengths over 3600m in the AJC Plate.

Carbon Copy won four races the following season including the Craven and Randwick plates and the Chipping Norton Stakes, was third in the Moonee Valley Cup, and twice placed at weight-for-age behind his familiar rival Comic Court to cement his place as one of Australia's best horses.

Retired to Glen Devon stud where he was born, Carbon Copy's best son was Grand Print, who emulated his father by winning the Sydney Cup in 1962.

1949 – RICHES FLOW FROM DELTA

Starting favorite in the Derby, Delta had to again be content with second placing – this time behind a horse called Playboy – after being held up for a run in a scrimmage in the mid stages. The two "novices" connected with Playboy had scored their first Derby success – being T. J. Smith, who was to go on and win the blue riband event a record number of times, and George Moore, who was to become one of the most skilled riders in the history of Australian racing.

Sydney jeweller Adolph Basser bought a "turf diamond" when he paid 2,600 gns for a brown colt by Midstream, the obvious influence in naming the colt Delta.

Giving him time to mature, trainer Maurice McCarten did not start him until the Autumn of his first season, which yielded two wins and two placings in as many starts. One of the wins was over 1400m and a placing over 1600m, so Mr Basser held high hopes for the colt in his Classic year, as it seemed clear he would handle a distance.

At his second run as a three-year-old in the 1949-50 season, it looked as if his expectations were going to become a reality. His chunky colt looked impressive in winning the 1800m Canterbury Guineas en route to the AJC Derby. Then disappointment, when Delta failed by a length behind Thracian Lad in the Rosehill Guineas. However, hopes for victory in the Derby were still high when it was revealed that the Rosehill winner was ineligible for the Classic.

Starting favorite in the Derby, Delta had to again be content with second placing – this time behind a horse called Playboy – after being held up for a run in a scrimmage in the mid stages. The two "novices" connected with Playboy had scored their first Derby success – being T. J. Smith, who was to go on and win the blue riband event a record number of times, and George Moore, who was to become one of the most skilled riders in the history of Australian racing.

Still convinced that the colt had the makings to win a major race, McCarten sent Delta to Melbourne with the aim of another treble – the Cox Plate, Victoria Derby and Melbourne Cup. While Delta had been campaigning in Sydney, a four-year-old who was to become one of Australia's greatest gallopers, was quickly adding to his already considerable reputation in Melbourne. Comic Court had won the Memsie, Craiglee and Turnbull Stakes and was then a close third behind Lincoln in sloppy conditions in the Caulfield Cup.

Here *was* a rival for Delta!

1949
(Saturday, October 22. Attendance: 40,600)

£1,550 plus £150 Cup Weight for Age 1¼ miles

1.	DELTA	M. McCarten	7.11	*N. Sellwood*	20/1
2.	Comic Court	J.M.Cummings	9.0	*J. Purtell*	5/4
3.	Persist	W. Kelso	8.9	*R.. Hutchinson*	10/1

Winning details

Margin: ½ len x 3 len. **Time:** 2:04.75 13 started.

Breeding: Midstream – Gazza – Magpie (br c 3) **Owner:** A. Basser

Winner's Colors: Brown & blue hoops, red cap

Winning Numbers: 12, 6, 9 **Barriers:** 10, 4, 12

ALSO RAN

Iron Duke	L. Robertson	W. Williamson	7.13	4/1
Glenvue	A. MacDonald	T. Unkovich	7.11	250/1
Playboy	T. J. Smith	W. Briscoe	7.11	50/1
Foxami	D. Lewis	W. Fellows	9.0	50/1
Cragwil	H. Wolters	N. Powell	7.11	25/1
Vagabond	D. Lewis	A. Ward	9.0	4/1
St. Comedy	J. M. Cummings	L. Lott	7.11	33/1
Thracian Lad	D. Lewis	B. Moon	7.11	50/1
Sanctus	T. Lewis	V. Hartney	9.4	100/1
Ellerslie	K. Hilton	S. Ralph	9.0	12/1

Scratched: Hurry Up, Chanak

DELTA ... he was holding Comic Court at bay on the line in the Cox Plate and the following week realised his owner's dream by winning a Derby. – Picture: HWT

To make the competition even tougher, others in the Cox Plate were Iron Duke, winner of the Caulfield Guineas and Caulfield Stakes and Ellerslie and Vagabond, who were placed in the Caulfield Stakes.

Neville Sellwood had the opporunity of riding Vagabond – at that stage Melbourne Cup favorite – or Delta, who was having his first run in Melbourne. Sellwood's judgment proved spot on in staying with Delta, who at the luxury odds of 20/1 defeated Comic Court by a half length with Persist three lengths back. As the field settled, Foxzami took the front running, Delta was travelling comfortably in third place while Comic Court was fifth. With 500m to go Foxzami still led from Persist, with Delta making a quick forward move from Iron Duke. At that point Comic Court was hemmed in and unable to gain a run.

Hitting the front on the turn Delta headed for home when Jack Purtell on Comic Court also stormed out of the pack. For a stride or two it looked as if Comic Court would prevail but on the line Delta was holding him at bay.

While the Cox Plate win had undoubtedly stamped him as being a horse of class, a Classic win still eluded him, so Delta was set for the second leg of his Melbourne treble, the Victoria Derby. Starting a hot favorite at 6/4 Delta realised Mr Basser's long held wish when he beat the dead-heaters Dickens and King's Coin by 1½ lengths. Now a hot favorite in the Melbourne Cup, he finished fifth behind Foxzami.

Delta won on two more occasions as a three-year-old – in the VRC St Leger and King's Plate.

At four, he earned a trip to Melbourne after winning the 3200m weight-for-age Randwick Plate, following earlier victories in the Chelmsford and Colin Stephen Stakes. His starting point was again the Cox Plate, for which he was a clear favorite at 11/8 on the strength of his trio of Sydney successes.

Unfortunately however, he had a luckless run being checked on two occasions – the first at the 1600m mark and again when he was making a forward move when Dark Marne came back on him at the 600m. Although he finished strongly in the straight the mishaps had cost him dearly, with the result he could finish only fifth behind Alister.

Delta's backers were let down again the following week when he was unplaced behind Comic Court in the Mackinnon Stakes, but rounded off the Melbourne Carnival on a better note when second to Playboy in the C. B. Fisher Plate.

Given a nine month break, Delta had his best year at five, with 11 wins and a second in 14 starts, with the highlight being victory in the Melbourne Cup – reputably earning jockey Neville Sellwood a "sling" of a Rolls Royce from an overjoyed Mr Basser.

Still a force at six, Delta ran an Australasian record in winning the Chelmsford Stakes (1800m) beating Hydrogen by four lengths – after which it was discovered he had chipped a sesamoid. Retired to stud he was a very disappointing sire, but he is still remembered as one of Australia's all-time great post-war stayers.

1950 — NEVER A TRUER WORD SAID IN JEST!

Slow to develop, Alister was placed only once in six starts as a two-year-old, but became an undisputed champion three-year-old.

After taking the AJC Derby he snared the Cox Plate before also scoring in the Victoria Derby.

Mr Bill Balloch, owner of Alister, jokingly predicted the outcome of the 1950 Cox Plate when a friend pointed out the trophy which was on display in a glass case on the Members' Lawn.

"There it is Bill. You'd better go and have a look at it," the friend said.

Half in jest, Mr Balloch replied: "It'll look fine on my mantlepiece. In fact I can already see it there."

Some minutes later, Mr Balloch did indeed have the Cox Plate trophy (which was a Cup) in his possession and no doubt destined for his mantlepiece. In winning the Cox Plate, Alister confirmed his reputation as the country's best three-year old, having taken the AJC Derby earlier in the season. This standing was undisputed after he also won the Victoria Derby following his Cox Plate success.

Slow to develop, Alister was placed only once in six starts as a two-year-old, and the following year he won a 1600m three-year-old at Caulfield, before shooting to prominence by winning the AJC Derby. Thereafter he finished second to Merry Scout in the Caulfield Guineas. Considering that race was over 1600m – combined with the fact that he had proven himself over a distance – it was felt that he would be well suited in the Cox Plate. The 2000m journey would suit him better than that of the Guineas and, as a three-year-old, he was favorably weighted against the older horses.

There was one negative however, in the form of a four-year-old stallion called Delta. The winner of the race the previous year, Delta was in peak form with three weight-for-age wins in the Chelsmford Stakes (1800m); Colin Stephen Stakes (2400m) and the 3200m Randwick Plate. Delta was a clear 11/8 favorite, with Iron Duke (a weight-for-age winner who was a last start fourth in the Caulfield Cup) second pick at 7/2 just ahead of Alister at 4/1.

But while the betting centred around Delta the race revolved around the two who were vying for second favoritism, with

1950
(Saturday, October 28. Attendance: 41,620)

£1,550 plus £150 Cup Weight for Age 1¼ miles

1.	ALISTER	H. Wolters	7.11	J. Purtell	4/1
2.	Iron Duke	L. Robertson	9.0	W. Williamson	7/2
3.	Bhutan	W. McEwan	9.0	S. Marvin	100/1

Winning details

Margin: Nk x 2 len. **Time:** 2:06.25 12 started.

Breeding: Whirlaway – New Flower – Nuffield (ch c 3) **Owner:** W. Balloch

Winner's Colors: Black & white stripes, red sash, sleeves & cap

Winning Numbers: 11, 6, 8 **Barriers:** 7, 2, 1

ALSO RAN

Rumyle	H. Darwon	E. Kremmer	7.13	100/1
Delta	M. McCarten	N. Sellwood	9.0	11/8f
Dark Marne	E. F. Silcock	R. Heather	9.4	25/1
Toastmaster	N. J. Plews	S. Dodd	7.12	33/1
Ellerslie	K. Hilton	S. Ralph	9.4	13/2
Prince Hussar	J. Finlayson	N. Powell	7.11	100/1
Morse Code	L. Robertson	R. Hutchinson	9.0	40/1
Sir Falcon	J. Mitchell	J. Thompson	9.4	33/1
Silver Buzz	J. Miller	A. Ward	9.4	200/1

All started

Alister lasting by a neck over Iron Duke. The chances of the hot favorite were dented slightly when he received a couple of checks, the first at the 1600m when Dark Marne came back onto him. Even though it was only slight and he was quickly back in stride, he was baulked for a run again near the 700m, with the result that he could finish only fifth.

In a slowly run race, the stayer Silver Buzz led with 800m to go, with Iron Duke perfectly placed third, Delta fifth and Alister two positions further back. Near the 600m, Iron Duke took over the lead, with Alister moving into fourth place. At this stage Delta had lost ground after being checked for the second time.

On straightening, Iron Duke kicked clear and looked the likely winner, until Jack Purtell started getting stuck into Alister who was coming on strongly out wide. With about 100m to go, Purtell's vigorous efforts resulted in Alister getting to Iron Duke to post only his third win in 13 starts, but it was a performance that left no doubt he would be a hot favorite for the Derby, and repeat his effort in the Sydney version of the Classic.

In the interim, *"Cardigan"* made a pertinent comment in *The Herald* about the Cox Plate that day when he wrote:

"The Cox Plate is a great contest, as looking through the list of winners, not one poor horse has ever scored in the race."

After the Cox Plate, Alister did as expected in the Derby, when starting 4/7 favorite, he spreadeagled the field to score by three lengths. Two days later, he started 3/1 favorite in the Melbourne Cup, in which his Cox Plate jockey Jack Purtell rode him, after tossing up whether to rider Comic Court. Purtell chose incorrectly on this occasion, as Alister was only 8th behind the other horse Purtell could have ridden.

Alister never regained his brilliant form of that Spring. He won two other races; finished second behind Midway (who he beat in the Derby) in the VRC St Leger; and was third in the AJC St Leger, after which he was sent to stud.

However, no-one can deny his star status in the Melbourne Spring of 1950.

1951 – PURTELL WAS A STAR "SCHOOL" PUPIL

The western boundary of Moonee Ponds Central School lines up with the 600m marker at the track.

It has become a significant landmark for jockeys.

It is the place where horses have to be making their runs to be in a prominent position before rounding the home turn for the short run home.

Moonee Ponds Central School – opposite Moonee Valley racetrack – has been a source of education for pupils and jockeys alike.

Situated in Wilson Street, it is the landmark referred to in countless thousands of race broadcasts when commentators refer to horses as being "at the school". The western boundary of the school lines up with the 600m marker at the track, but in truth horses can be referred to as being "at the school" anywhere from 600m to 450m from the finish line, depending on which school boundary they are passing.

It has become a significant landmark for jockeys. It is the place where horses have to be making their runs to be in a prominent position before rounding the home turn for the short run home.

Old time jockeys such as Billy Duncan and Harold Badger were outstanding "School graduates", as they would always ensure they were in a forward position at that point. Then, depending on how their mount was travelling, they would attempt to steal the race by accelerating from thereon, or make sure their mount was winding up then to be in a position to swoop on the leaders on the turn.

Years later, Jack Purtell became recognised as a Moonee Valley specialist by adopting similar tactics. He practised it to perfection in the Cox Plate of 1951 to land the prize on 25/1 chance Bronton, "stealing" the race from hot favorite Hydrogen (5/4), ridden by Neville Sellwood who, hailing from Sydney, had not been instructed on the association between the Moonee Valley circuit and the "school".

Two factors contributed to Bronton's win: Purtell's tearaway tactics, which caught Sellwood napping, and the fact that Hydrogen had raced ungenerously, "crabbing" around a couple of turns, and racing in under pressure in the straight. As it was, Hydrogen, who was fourth at the turn, flew home once he got clear in the straight and was quickly pegging back Bronton, but failed by a neck.

1951

(Saturday, October 27. Attendance: 45,670)

£2,000 plus £200 Cup Weight for Age 1¼ miles

1.	BRONTON	R. Sinclair	7.11	J. Purtell	25/1
2.	Hydrogen	E. Hush	7.11	N. Sellwood	5/4f
3.	Iron Duke	L. Robertson	9.4	A. Ward	4/1

Winning details

Margin: Nk x ½ len. **Time:** 2:05.5 11 started.

Breeding: Helios – Battle Royal – The Night Patrol (ch c 3) **Owner:** E. A. Underwood

Winner's Colors: Red, white diamonds, red sleeves and cap

Winning Numbers: 9, 6, 1

ALSO RAN

Akbar	K. J. Heaton	H. Wiggins	9.4	12/1
Morse Code	L. Robertson	W. Williamson	9.4	9/1
Friar's Hope	H. Wolters	N. Powell	7.11	25/1
Montana	M. McCarten	W. Cook	7.12	12/1
Aristocrat	T. Sweeney	D. Munro	9.0	12/1
Channel Rise	W. Chaffe jr	B. Smith	7.11	20/1
Sky Streamer	J. Ryan	D. Cann	9.4	200/1
Beau Cavalier	G. Sholl	N. McGrowdie	7.11	66/1

All started

Bronton, owned by Mr E. A. Underwood, became the fifth successive three-year-old to win the Cox Plate. Originally trained in Sydney, Bronton was sent to Melbourne because he could not become accustomed to the American-style starting stalls which, to that stage, had not been introduced here. Trained by Bob Sinclair, Bronton's lead-up form had hardly been inspiring, hence he started at the big odds of 25/1. He had won a three-year-old over 2000m at Flemington but was then unplaced over the shorter distance of the Caulfield Guineas, won in almost contemptuous style by Hydrogen.

In the Cox Plate, the whole field got away cleanly and Bronton settled midfield behind the early leader, Iron Duke, who had been heavily backed from 7/1 to 4/1. Hydrogen was further astern with Aristocrat and Channel Rise.

Coming to the 800m mark, Sellwood was giving Hydrogen more rein to go forward, but he scrambled around the back turn approaching the "school" where Iron Duke still led from Friar's Hope and Beau Cavalier. Bronton was just behind them on the rails with Purtell ready to pounce. By this time, Hydrogen had found his footing and was also making a fast move to stay with the leaders.

Soon after nearing the 600m mark, Purtell made a fast forward move. He quickly raced up to the leader Iron Duke, leaving Hydrogen in fourth position. Purtell's tactics had paid off as Bronton kicked clear around the turn and into the straight – in what proved to be a winning break. Sellwood, realising the situation, quickly shot forward and Hydrogen started to gather in Bronton in the straight, but was inclined to dive toward the inside rail under pressure.

While the honors on the day were with Bronton and Purtell's first class ride, punters already knew which horse they wanted to be on in the Derby the following week. Better suited by the long stretches at Flemington, punters sent out Hydrogen a skinny 9/4 favorite in the Victoria Derby, and their opinion was justified when he won the Classic by 1½ lengths from Shoreham, with Bronton again putting up a good display to finish third.

The Derby result was simply further proof that Purtell's tactics at the Valley the week earlier were a major factor in Bronton's Plate success. This opinion was proved beyond doubt in following years when Hydrogen's subsequent successes included successive Cox Plate victories in 1952-53.

While the honors on the day were with Bronton and Purtell's first class ride, punters already knew which horse they wanted to be on in the Derby the following week. Better suited by the long stretches at Flemington, punters sent out Hydrogen a skinny 9/4 favorite in the Victoria Derby and their opinion was justified when he won the Classic by 1½ lengths.

1952-53 — HYDROGEN ALMOST MADE IT THREE

Brought to Melbourne, Hydrogen stormed home from well back to romp in the Caulfield Guineas by three lengths, a performance which assured him of favoritism in the Cox Plate. Sent out at the skinny odds of 5/4, this was the Cox Plate which got away from Hydrogen – or, more precisely, from Neville Sellwood.

One of an elite group to have won dual Cox Plates, Hydrogen is unlucky not to have won it three times.

He failed by only a neck at his first attempt in the race as a three-year-old in 1951, when his rider Neville Sellwood was outridden by Jack Purtell who scored on Bronton. Hydrogen made amends the following two years, but should have the same standing as Kingston Town as a three-time victor.

After a late starting two-year-old career which yielded two wins and two seconds, Hydrogen's wins in the new season included the Rosehill Guineas (1600m) before an inexplicable flop in the AJC Derby (2400m) which raised doubts in some quarters about his ability to stay. Back to the 2000m of the Craven Plate, he strolled home by 2½ lengths – much to the annoyance of sections of the crowd who were still smarting over his Derby flop.

Brought to Melbourne, he flashed home from well back to canter in the Caulfield Guineas by three lengths, a performance which assured him of favoritism in the Cox Plate. Sent out at the short odds of 5/4, this was the Cox Plate which got away from Hydrogen – or, more precisely, from Neville Sellwood.

This was brought about by Jack Purtell's familiarity with the Valley circuit and lessons he had learned from jockeys such as Harold Badger and Bill Duncan who would win races at the track by making their runs at the "school" well before the home turn. Purtell did just this on Bronton, to steal a winning break, holding off Hydrogen who made up tremendous ground from fourth place, only to fail by a neck. Without doubt, had Purtell not cleared out when he did, Hydrogen would have won. His chances were also marred by the fact that he did not negotiate the tight turns smoothly and that he raced in under pressure in the straight.

That run overlooked, the colt buttered up for the Victoria Derby the following Saturday and after being near the rear for the major

1952
(Saturday, October 25. Attendance: 42,890)

£2,100 plus £100 Trophy		Weight for Age			1¼ miles	
1.	HYDROGEN	E. Hush	9.0	D. Munro	11/8f
2.	Ellerslie	K. Hilton	9.4	S. Ralph	6/1
3.	Advocate	F. Allotta	7.11	N. McGrowdie	25/1

Winning details

Margin: 1½ len x 2 len. **Time:** 2:04.5 13 started.

Breeding: Delville Wood – Sweet Sound – Magpie (bl h 4) **Owner:** E. R. Williams

Winner's Colors: Black and white stripes, red cap

Winning Numbers: 4, 2, 9 **Barriers:** 4, 5, 9

ALSO RAN

Morse Code	L. Robertson	R. Hutchinson	9.4	14/1
Wodalla	R. Sinclair	J. Purtell	7.11	12/1
Gallant Archer	A. Bellingham	A. Ward	7.12	25/1
Welloch	J. M. Cummings	D. Cowie	7.11	20/1
Deep River	M. McCarten	N. Sellwood	7.11	6/1
Top Level	C. Cullen	P. Burkhardt	7.11	100/1
Zealant	H. R. Bird	K. Mitchell	7.12	50/1
Reformed (NZ)	A. J. Brown	E. Low	9.4	20/1
Flywood	P. J. Murray	T. Unkovich	7.11	40/1
Idlewild	T. J. Smith	G. Moore	7.12	20/1

All started

HYDROGEN ... he was unlucky when second in his first Cox Plate but made amends in this easy fashion in 1952, repeating the effort the following year as well. – Picture: HWT

part of the race, the 9/4 favorite picked up the leaders in the straight to win by 1½ lengths. So much for the theory that he couldn't stay! Three days later he finished fifth in the first of the three Melbourne Cups in which he ran – without ever running a place.

In Melbourne for the Autumn, he was a five length winner of the St Leger (2800m) and rounded off his three-year-old season with wins in the Rosehill Cup and AJC St Leger, but again failed over the 3200m journey of the Sydney Cup. Bought for 3200 gns by Mr Ernie Williams, one of the founders of the Australian Woolworth's store chain, Hydrogen had earned more than £22,000 at the conclusion of his Classic season.

Resuming his four-year-old season with wins in the Hill Stakes and the Craven Plate (2000m) he was brought to Melbourne

1953
(Saturday, October 24. Attendance: 46,800)

£4,000 plus £200 Trophy Weight for Age 1¼ miles

1.	**HYDROGEN**	E. Hush	9.4	W. Williamson	3/1
2.	**Prince Morvi**	E. J. Fellows	7.11	N. Sellwood	9/1
3.	**Cromis**	R. Sinclair	7.11	J. Purtell	9/1

Winning details

Margin: 1 len x 1½ len. **Time:** 2:05.25 15 started.

Breeding: Delville Wood – Sweet Sound – Magpie (bl h 5) **Owner:** E. R. Williams

Winner's Colors: Black and white stripes, red cap

Winning Numbers: 2, 11, 12 **Barriers:** 3, 14, 10

ALSO RAN

Morse Code	L. Robertson	V. Hartney	9.4	33/1
Carioca	P. C. Hoysted	W. Cook	9.4	9/4f
My Hero	O. F. Watson	N. Eastwood	9.4	20/1
Aldershot	D. Judd	B. Shaw	9.4	20/1
Callide River	C. C. Sinclair	D. Coleman	7.11	80/1
Silver Phantom	J. Green	J. O'Sullivan	9.0	10/1
Welloch	J. M. Cummings	P. Glennon	9.0	40/1
Silver Hawk	H. R. Telford	R. Hutchinson	7.11	50/1
Walu	A. Lopes	J. Gilmore	7.11	16/1
Friendly Feeling	R. F. Ferris	T. Mullane	8.13	200/1
Reformed	A. J. Brown	E. Sellers	9.4	200/1
Flying Halo	O. N. Marshall	R. Heather	9.4	12/1

All started

for another crack at the Cox Plate. Obviously his connections had learned a valuable lesson from the previous year!

One of the last four with 800m to go, his rider Darby Munro raced up to the leaders before the turn – in much the same manner as Bronton had done the previous year – to win by 1½ lengths. After being in a prominent position early, Munro eased his mount before commencing his forward move. He began to gather in the leaders before entering the straight and it appeared obvious that even at that stage he had their measure. Unplaced in the Melbourne Cup, Hydrogen also won the C. B. Fisher Plate on the final day of the VRC Carnival.

After a spell, Hydrogen wintered in Brisbane winning the O'Shea Stakes, and finally proved he *could* run 3200m when he scored in the Brisbane Cup.

Proving he had an iron constitution – he had been up since February – Hydrogen was kept going in Queensland at the start of the new season and came back to Sydney in the Spring where he won three of four races, including the Colin Stephen Stakes and the Randwick Plate (2800m). One of his defeats, however, had been in the Metropolitan at the hands of the brilliant Carioca, who had lumped 60.5kg, (conceding 2kg to Hydrogen) to score by a long head. Carioca, the 1953 Sydney Cup winner, had also won the Theo Marks Quality in the Spring of 1953 as a prelude to the Cox Plate.

Still without a let up, Hydrogen continued onto Melbourne – for Cox Plate number three. Unlike the previous two years when he had been favorite, this time he was second fancy, with Carioca being sensationally backed from 4/1 to 9/4. Also in commission was AJC Derby winner Prince Morvi and Cromis who, at his only start for the Spring, had been runner-up in the Caulfield Guineas.

However, as distinct from the betting activity, the activity on the track belonged solely to Hydrogen, who won by more than a length from Prince Morvi. Carioca finished fifth and observers described him as "not the same Carioca who had carried all before him in Sydney". The consensus was that he did not stretch out as well as usual because of the Valley circuit.

As *"Heroic"* commented:

"Many a class galloper has failed to show his true form first time around the Valley. As the Cox Plate was run, the slow early pace did not in any way affect Carioca's chance."

At the 800m, Bill Williamson began a forward move on Hydrogen, whereas Billy Cook was content to wait until he hit the top of the straight before commencing his run on Carioca, who made a short dash but never looked like overhauling the placegetters.

A week later, Hydrogen took the Mackinnon Stakes, but it was not third time lucky in the Melbourne Cup where, as 4/1 favorite, he finished sixth. He rounded off the Carnival winning the Fisher Plate and then went for a well earned rest, after racing continually for 10 months.

In the Autumn, he suffered two bleeding attacks, but was allowed to race in Melbourne, because there was no uniformity of rules in those days, where he won the Queens Plate in March 1954. The old campaigner still had more life left in him. In the Spring, he finished third to Rising Fast in the Caulfield Stakes and had yet another tilt at the Cox Plate, when starting 4/1 second favorite he finished midfield behind Rising Fast. After start number 60 when unplaced in Rising Fast's Mackinnon Stakes, Hydrogen went to the paddock.

Rising Fast was the new star – but Hydrogen had sniffed the air there, too.

Rising Fast .... his very name conjures up images of speed.

This New Zealand hero of the 50's has a special place in Australian racing history, by coming within an ace of being the only horse to win the Melbourne Spring Carnival "double Double" – that is winning the Caulfield and Melbourne cups two years running.

He took both races as a five-year-old in 1954, won the Caulfield Cup the next year and finished a controversial second in the '55 Melbourne Cup, behind Toporoa – to whom he was conceding 15kg – being beaten by three-quarters of a length. Toporoa appeared to bore out under pressure over the final stages, but Rising Fast's jockey, Bill Williamson, did not lodge a protest. However, stewards subsequently suspended Toporoa's rider Neville Sellwood, for two months, for causing interference to Rising Fast. People still conjecture what might have been had Williamson protested.

Bought for a mere 325 gns by Whakatane accountant Leicester Spring, and initially trained by Jack Winder, Rising Fast managed only one placing in five runs as a two-year-old in 1951-52. He began to show form the following season with five wins and four seconds in 10 runs, which showed he was well above average, but he had yet to win races of any class.

After winning at his third run in his four-year-old season over 1600m at Waikato, he was expected to run well in the 2000m Te Awamutu Cup staged by the Waipa Racing Club on December 12. He flopped, beating only five home in a field of 18; but it was the reason why he flopped that concerned stewards. After an inquiry, they suspended Winder and apprentice jockey R. Salisbury for one month. (On appeal, Winder's sentence was *increased* by first to one year and then to five years!)

After that poor performance, Rising Fast won a 2000m weight-for-age race at Paeroa. When Winder appealed his initial term of suspension, Rising Fast, too, became embroiled in proceedings with stewards also disqualifying the horse, before lifting the penalty on appeal. However, it meant that Rising Fast

In a ceremony at Moonee Valley before returning to his home country, Rising Fast was paraded in front of an emotional crowd who farewelled one of the greatest horses New Zealand has produced and Australia has seen.

1954
(Saturday, October 23. Attendance: 39,430)

£4,000 plus £250 Trophy Weight for Age 1¼ miles

1.	**RISING FAST**	I. J. Tucker	9.4	*J. Purtell*	11/8f
2.	**Prince Delville**	S. R. Lamond	7.11	*R. Selkrig*	13/2
3.	**Pride Of Egypt**	E. Hush	7.11	*N. McGrowdie*	20/1

Winning details

Margin: 4 len x 1½ len. **Time:** 2:03.8 16 started.

Breeding: Alonzo – Faster – Mr Steadfast (b or br g 5) **Owner:** L. R. Spring

Winner's Colors: Blue, black sleeves, gold armbands & cap

Winning Numbers: 2, 16, 15 **Barriers:** 10, 2, 15

ALSO RAN

Sunium	T. Lewis	R. Hutchinson	7.11	66/1
Master Proven	T. J. Smith	A. Burton	9.4	66/1
Prince Courtald	M. McCarten	A. Ward	9.0	5/1
Telyar	M. McCarten	J. Gilmore	7.11	100/1
Baroda Beam	W. J. Allan	B. Wilson	7.11	66/1
Hydrogen	E. Hush	W. Camer	9.4	4/1
Nealing	W. McKay	K. Ford	9.0	100/1
Pandie Star	C. S. Hayes	T. Newcombe	7.11	50/1
Spearfolio	D. Judd	R. Faux	9.4	200/1
King Amana	J. M. Cummings	R. Were	9.4	80/1
Tradfield	O. M. Lynch	N. Allen	7.12	66/1
Aldershot	W. Smart	D. Munro	9.4	33/1
King Boru	A. Lopes	S. Cassidy	7.11	10/1

All started

RISING FAST ... one of the greatest horses to have raced in Australia, found the Cox Plate a cakewalk. – Picture: HWT

missed big New Zealand races until the appeal was upheld. Annoyed by the whole process, Mr Spring decided to take his bay to Australia – Rising Fast was never to race in New Zealand again.

Campaigning in Brisbane, now under the care of Ivan Tucker in the Winter of 1954, Rising Fast was twice placed, in a Doomben Flying and in the Doomben Cup. The new season was only weeks away and what a season it was!

After winning over 2000m at weight-for-age in Brisbane, he had his first run in Melbourne in the Memsie Stakes, when fourth behind Coppice. Connections engaged Bill Williamson as his new rider after that run and the pair combined first-up to win the Feehan Stakes at Moonee Valley, beating the classy galloper Cromis. Wins followed in the Turnbull and Caulfield Stakes, ensuring he was a short priced favorite for the Caulfield Cup, which he won with last minute replacement rider Arthur Ward, after Williamson was hurt in a race preceding the Cup.

The Cox Plate looked like it would be a stroll in the park. And it was! Ridden by Jack Purtell for the first time, Rising Fast streaked away from the turn to win by four lengths from Prince Delville. Restrained in the early stages, Purtell moved up quickly to the leaders before the turn and had a winning advantage on entering the straight, where Rising Fast stretched right out. (This was in contrast to the performance of second favorite Hydrogen. Having his fourth Cox Plate start, the old campaigner made a forward move at the 800m, being forced wide, but could not sustain his normal dash over the remainder of the trip.)

By now the talk of the town, Rising Fast did as everyone expected in winning the Melbourne Cup and the Fisher Plate, making it seven wins on end.

Spelled, Rising Fast had another change of trainer – Fred "Father" Hoysted – after Ivan Tucker was disqualified when another of his horses returned a positive swab. Three placings and a win, in the Spring of 1955, ensured Rising Fast was Caulfield Cup favorite again. Williamson got his revenge for missing out on the winning mount the previous year when he had an armchair ride to win the Cup by three lengths from Ray Ribbon.

He could not, however, repeat the previous year's effort in the Cox Plate and emulate the feats of Young Idea, Beau Vite, Flight and Hydrogen. Rising Fast showed none of his usual dash and was a beaten horse with 600m to go, which was in complete contrast to his sustained run to win the Caulfield Cup the previous week.

Despite predictions to the contrary, because of his Cox Plate flop, Rising Fast was again favorite for the Melbourne Cup, in which he just failed behind Toporoa. He rounded off the Melbourne Carnival by winning the C. B. Fisher Plate on the final day.

Back for another campaign at seven, there was still fire in the old warrior, who won the Memsie Stakes and was second in the Caulfield Stakes. For the third year running, he started favorite in the Cox Plate, and ran gallantly to be a very close runner-up behind Ray Ribbon. He also had another crack at the Melbourne Cup, finishing a game fifth.

In a ceremony at Moonee Valley before returning to his home country, he was paraded in front of an emotional crowd who farewelled one of the greatest horses New Zealand has produced and Australia has seen.

1955 – BOOKMAKERS CHEERS FOR KINGSTER

Sydney colt, Kingster, dented the reputations of some of Australia's all-time great horses when he scored a surprise win in the 1955 Cox Plate.

By Star Kingdom, Australia's most influential sire, Kingster surprised even his trainer Jack Green, who was despairing about the colt winning a race over a distance. With three-year-olds filling all the placings, Kingster became one of the longest priced winners of the race at 33/1 in beating the good stayer Caranna and Bendigo's subsequent international star, Sailor's Guide.

Also in his wake were horses the calibre of Rising Fast, Redcraze and Cromis. It was the shock result of the Spring, as the form around other runners was far superior to that of the winner.

Rising Fast (6/4 favorite), who had won the race the previous year was coming off wins in the Herbert Power Handicap and Caulfield Cup; Caranna, hot favorite for the Victoria Derby, had won three on end including the AJC Derby and Caulfield Guineas; and Cromis had won three of his five starts for the season and was a last start third in the Caulfield Stakes.

And the form of Kingster? It looked as if Caranna easily had his measure going on previous history.

As a two-year-old, Kingster showed promise with wins in the Randwick Breeders Plate and the AJC Sires; was second in the Champagne Stakes and during the Autumn won the Merson Cooper Stakes at Caulfield. At three, he won the Hobartville Stakes and, after a second to Somerset Fair in the Hill Stakes, found Caranna too strong. That horse beat him again in the Rosehill Guineas; and then Kingster was unplaced behind Caranna in the AJC Derby and in the Caulfield Guineas.

Trainer Jack Green gave jockey Bill Camer simple instructions for the Cox Plate – go to the front and try to steal the race with his light weight.

Camer carried out the instructions perfectly, with Kingster being only momentarily headed once in the race, and at the finish he was able to hold off a late challenge by the more fancied Caranna, to last by half a neck.

Camer kicked Kingster to the front on leaving

> Kingster surprised even his trainer Jack Green, who was despairing about the colt winning a race over a distance. With three-year-olds filling all the placings in the 1955 Cox Plate, Kingster became one of the longest priced winners of the race at 33/1 in beating the good stayer Caranna and Bendigo's subsequent international star, Sailor's Guide.

1955
(Saturday, October 22. Attendance: 40,750)

£4,000 plus £250 Trophy Weight for Age 1¼ miles

1.	KINGSTER	J. Green	7.11	W. Camer	33/1
2.	Caranna	E. Hush	7.11	A. Mulley	13/8
3.	Sailor's Guide	G. Daniel	7.11	N. Sellwood	20/1

Winning details

Margin: ½ nk x 2 len. **Time:** 2:04.4 8 started.

Breeding: Star Kingdom – Canvas Black – William of Valence (br c 3) **Owner:** L. C. Gibson

Winner's Colors: Yellow, tartan sash & cap

Winning Numbers: 9, 8, 7 **Barriers:** 6, 7, 4

ALSO RAN

Cromis	R. Sinclair	J. Purtell	9.4	9/2
Redcraze	S. A. Brown	V. J. Sellars	9.4	20/1
Rising Fast	F. W. Hoysted	W. Williamson	9.0	6/4f
Prince Dante	E. J. Fellows	J. O'Sullivan	7.11	33/1
Beaupa	F. C. Allsop	R. Hutchinson	9.0	66/1

Scratched: Plato

the barriers and with 1600m to go he just led from fellow 33/1 chance Prince Dante. Caranna and Sailor's Guide were three lengths behind at this stage, with Rising Fast close up two horses back. Coming to the 800m Kingster had shaken off Prince Dante, and at this point Caranna had moved up to second, being tracked by Rising Fast, with Sailor's Guide last.

At the 600m Athol Mulley on Caranna was content to sit behind and make Kingster do all the bullocking and Bill Williamson ranged up out wide on Rising Fast. In an instant, however, it became obvious that Rising Fast could not win as he failed to make any impression on the leaders once he had got to them. (From then on he wilted and beat only two home.)

Turning for home, Mulley realised he had a race on his hands with Kingster, who, to his surprise, did not look like surrendering the lead. Mulley was forced to use all his vigour to get to the leader, but once there, he could not get past. Sailor's Guide continued to make ground to be two lengths away in third place.

A thrilled Jack Green now knew that he had a horse who could stay and he immediately announced Derby plans for the colt. Despite the victory, Caranna started favorite in the Classic, but finished third after having a chequered run, which resulted in Kingster's jockey Bill Camer being suspended for causing interference to Caranna on two occasions.

The Derby winner was the brilliant Sailor's Guide, who went on to excel at top level here and overseas where he won the Washington DC International (on protest) and won another four races there in 1959-60.

Kingster too, continued to race with distinction, if not in the same class as Sailor's Guide. Showing his versatility, he took the Newmarket Handicap (1200m) at Flemington, the C. M. Lloyd Stakes and the George Main Stakes in 1956. He reappeared in the Cox Plate two years later but beat only one runner home in the race won by Ray Ribbon. In his final season, he won the 1957 Stradbroke Handicap in record time, carrying the steadier of 59kg.

While his Cox Plate victory seemed a fluke over the much more fancied runners those years earlier, there is no doubt that Kingster rightly enhanced the reputation of Star Kingdom's first crop.

1956 – PURTELL TIES UP No. 4 WITH RAY RIBBON

The 1956 Cox Plate carried record prizemoney of £5,250, making it the most valuable weight-for-age race of the Spring.

Significantly, it was now worth £1,000 more than the Moonee Valley Cup, which hitherto had been the focal point of the Club's main race day. However, earlier that year, the MVRC Committee showed just how serious it was about the future of the Cox Plate by announcing a long range plan to make the Plate a £10,000 race. The first step was the £1,000 boost to the 1956 event.

In keeping with the record prizemoney on offer was a "field of gold", with the 10 runners between them having won almost £205,000. Leading the charge was Rising Fast, with earnings of £65,765. Then followed Sailor's Guide ($32,144); Fair Chance and Caranna, each with just over £25,000; the previous year's winner Kingster with £21,104; while Ray Ribbon, had won almost £18,000.

For the third year running, the betting revolved around Rising Fast who had won when 11/8 favorite two years earlier but beat only two home when 6/4 favorite in 1955. (Such was the hype about Rising Fast, it was reported that the Governor, Sir Dallas Brooks, "was one of the many thousands who supported Rising Fast, having a modest bet with bookmaker Ray Williams".)

Leading up to the race of 1956, he had won the Memsie Stakes at Caulfield and, at his final run before the Plate, was second behind Redcraze in the Caulfield Stakes. While he was 7/4 favorite, there were a few other runners in the market. These included Ray Ribbon (4/1), Sailor's Guide (9/2) and the 1955 race winner Kingster at 8/1.

The New Zealander, Ray Ribbon, was a deserved second pick. The previous Spring, he was second to Rising Fast in the Caulfield Cup and the Mackinnon Stakes before winning the Williamstown (now Sandown) Cup. In the Spring of 1956, he quickly got back into the swing of things. In only three runs from a spell, he

> Such was the hype about Rising Fast for the 1956 Cox Plate, it was reported that the Governor, Sir Dallas Brooks, "was one of the many thousands who supported Rising Fast, having a modest bet with rails bookmaker Ray Williams".

1956
(Saturday, October 27. Attendance: 38,350)

£5,000 plus £250 Trophy Weight for Age 1¼ miles

1.	**RAY RIBBON**	G. S. Barr	9.4	*J. Purtell*	4/1
2.	**Rising Fast**	F. W. Hoysted	9.4	*W. Williamson*	7/4f
3.	**Caranna**	E. Hush	9.0	*A. Ward*	12/1

Winning details

Margin: Sht ½ hd x 3 len. **Time:** 2:04.9 10 started.

Breeding: Perilous (GB) – Lady Yelverton – Revelation (b h 5) **Owner:** C. R. Newman & C. Pateman

Winner's Colors: Green, gold check, black armbands & cap

Winning Numbers: 2, 1, 6 **Barriers:** 7, 6, 8

ALSO RAN

Auteuil	J. M. Cummings	G. Lane	7.11	33/1
Tricky Lad	J. E. Bond	I. Saunders	7.11	50/1
Fair Chance	A. D. Webster	R. Hutchinson	9.4	25/1
Sailor's Guide	G. Daniel	N. Sellwood	9.0	9/2
Ark Royal	A. L. Powell	R. Skelton	9.0	10/1
Kingster	J. Green	A. Mulley	9.0	8/1
Arab's Choice	C. Wilson	J. O'Sullivan	7.11	12/1

All started

RAY RIBBON ... in 1956 he provided Cox Plate win number four for Jack Purtell in a close contest with Rising Fast (outside), which was rated the best race that Spring.

– Picture: HWT

beat Sailor's Guide in the Underwood Stakes; was fourth to Redcraze in the Caulfield Stakes and was then a good fifth from a wide barrier to the same horse in the Caulfield Cup. Sailor's Guide, who was third in the Cox Plate the previous year, had since raced twice at the Valley without success.

Leading up to the Plate he won the Craiglee Stakes and was second in the Memsie and Underwood Stakes before fifth in the Caulfield Stakes. Kingster had finished ninth in that race after previously scoring in the George Main Stakes.

In what was to be Jack Purtell's last winning ride in the race – making it success number four – Ray Ribbon lasted by the barest of margins from Rising Fast – who Purtell had partnered to victory two years earlier.

It was to be the best weight-for-age race for the Spring, with Rising Fast finishing with a withering run from well back. So close was the finish that neither Purtell nor Rising Fast's jockey Bill Williamson gave any indication as to whether they had won as they trotted back to the enclosure while waiting for the result of the photo. Caranna, runner-up when favorite a year earlier, also finished strongly for third, three lengths from the other pair, after being last at the 600m mark.

Ray Ribbon and Rising Fast were giving the leaders Arab's Choice and Kingster a long start with 1200m to run, but as usual Purtell began his run near the "School" to be in touch with the lead on the turn. As soon as he began his forward move, Williamson followed.

On the turn however, Ray Ribbon momentarily kicked clear. Rising Fast was immediately in pursuit and was gradually gaining on Purtell's mount in the short run home, only to fail by the barest of margins. Once again, Purtell had timed his run to perfection as it appeared that had the race been any longer the finishing positions would have been reversed.

The following week, Ray Ribbon finished third behind the bolter Sir William in the Mackinnon Stakes before finishing midfield in the Melbourne Cup.

After suffering a bleeding attack, he won the Caulfield Stakes the following year, which convinced connections he should run in the Cox Plate again. Starting 11/4 second favorite, and with Neville Sellwood atop, Ray Ribbon pulled hard early in the race and had nothing left at the finish, beating only one runner.

But he had had his moment of glory 12 months earlier in what was quickly becoming recognised as one of Australia's best races.

1957 – PROMISE PAYS WITH REDCRAZE

While a Melbourne Cup win will certainly bring lasting fame, Redcraze is proof that even a three-time loser of the race can still make an indelible mark on turf history.

While Redcraze did not win a Melbourne Cup at three attempts, he is not remembered for that – rather, memories are of his gutsy victories in a glamor era of racing, when he slugged it out with champions such as Rising Fast and Sailor's Guide – and more often than not, finished ahead on points.

A rich chestnut, Redcraze scored 32 wins and 20 placings in 85 starts setting weight and time records against the cream of Australia's gallopers.

Unraced at two, when under the care of Syd Brown, he spent his three and four-year-old seasons in the Dominion. With a moderate record of two wins and four placings at three, he started to show what was in store as a four-year-old. He won 11 races that season, albeit many were restricted events. However, after winning races such as the Wanganui and Awapuni Cups and rounding off the season with three wins on end, including the Hawkes Bay Cup (2000m), he was aimed at Australia.

And was he set an ambitious program! In all, Redcraze had 14 starts in three months. Placed in the Feehan and Craiglee Stakes in the Spring of 1955, he scored his first Australian victory in the Turnbull Stakes, beating Rising Fast by a length. Thereafter followed three unplaced runs, including fifth behind Kingster in the Cox Plate. Despite being sent over 2000m in a gallop on the morning of the Melbourne Cup, Redcraze still performed brilliantly when he overcame a buffeting to finish fourth behind Rising Fast.

Returned to New Zealand, he won three good Handicap races, by which time Sydney trainer Tommy Smith convinced Mrs Ada Bradley, the widow of the owner, to transfer the horse to him.

The new partnership started in brilliant fashion with wins in the O'Shea Stakes and the Brisbane Cup. Smith was looking forward to a great Spring Carnival!

Redcraze was unplaced in the Chelmsford Stakes when he resumed his six-year-old season but then struck a purple patch, winning five on end. The successes included an Australasian record for 1700m in the Hill stakes; a close victory over Rising Fast in the Caulfield Stakes and he lumped a record

1957
(Saturday, October 26. Attendance: 40,870)

£5,250 plus £250 Trophy Weight for Age 1¼ miles

1.	**REDCRAZE**	T. J. Smith	9.4	G. Moore	4/1
2.	**Prince Darius**	J. W. Cook	7.11	A. Ward	10/9f
3.	**Pandie Sun**	C. S. Hayes	9.4	R. Hutchinson	7/1

Winning details

Margin: ½ hd x 2 len. **Time:** 2:05.6 9 started.

Breeding: Red Mars – Myarion – Myosotis (ch g 7) **Owner:** Mrs A. B. Bradley

Winner's Colors: Gold, black sleeves, blue cap

Winning Numbers: 1, 8, 5 **Barriers:** 8, 3, 9

ALSO RAN

Timor	C. Munro	P. Maddock	9.4	20/1
Straight Draw	J. M. Mitchell	N. McGrowdie	9.4	66/1
Sir William	I. Pearson	W. Williamson	9.4	16/1
Gay Saba	H. Wolters	A. Burton	7.11	16/1
Ray Ribbon	N. D. Hoysted	N. Sellwood	9.4	11/4
Ruthless Don	C. Cullen	D. Coleman	9.0	200/1

All started

63kg to win the Caulfield Cup by four lengths. Re-handicapped for the Melbourne Cup he had to carry 10st 3lb (65kg) and failed by only a half neck behind Evening Peal, to whom he conceded 14kg. Tommy Smith's promise to Mrs Bradley that the horse would win big races and prizemoney in Australia had certainly been correct – and there was a lot more to come.

In the Autumn, Redcraze won six of nine starts – with Sailor's Guide being runner-up four times in the St George Stakes, the Queen's Plate, the Queen Elizabeth Stakes and the Autumn Stakes.

Still with one more campaign in his legs, as a seven-year-old he won the Hill Stakes over 1800m and, after placings in the Colin Stephen Stakes and the Craven Plate, was sent to Victoria for what was to be his last hurrah – the Cox Plate and the Melbourne Cup.

It was the Cox Plate which got away from Redcraze's regular rider Arthur Ward – who was never to win the race – and a lucky pick-up ride for George Moore. The circumstances were that Ward, who had ridden Redcraze in every win since he had been with Smith, had committed himself to ride the smart three-year-old Prince Darius in the Victoria Derby. Ward had also been on the colt in the AJC Derby when he finished a distant second behind Tulloch and had agreed then to be on Prince Darius in his Derby lead-up races in Melbourne. Another bonus was that Prince Darius was favorite. He had finished second in the Caulfield Stakes and his placings behind Tulloch in the Rosehill Guineas and AJC Derby were proof of his class. It was to be Moore's only ride on Redcraze, who resoundingly answered the critics who said he was over the hill, by narrowly scoring from Prince Darius, with Pandie Sun third.

Even though he was forced wide at the mid stages, Moore did not attempt to force a passage through the field. He was still wide at the turn where Prince Darius had shot a length clear. Ward was first to go for the whip and for a stride it seemed as if the colt would hold off the older horse but, under heavy riding by Moore, Redcraze gathered in the leader in the straight to score by a half head.

The win was the first in the event for Tommy Smith, who was to become the most successful trainer in the history of the race, with seven winners and two third-placed runners from 37 starters.

After the Cox Plate, Prince Darius finished eight lengths astern of Tulloch in the Derby (which occurred seven times, earning Prince Darius the nickname of "Tulloch's Shadow").

When the controversial decision was made not to start Tulloch in the Melbourne Cup, connections decided to run Prince Darius, who was again pitted against Redcraze, with Ward back in the saddle. Once again Ward's luck was out, as Prince Darius, ridden by Athol Mulley, finished second, while Redcraze was eighth.

The Plate form held up well, as Straight Draw, who had flashed home to finish fifth the previous week, won the Cup, while Pandie Sun, third in the Cox Plate, filled the same placing in the Melbourne Cup.

The Melbourne Cup was the swansong for Redcraze who was sent back to New Zealand to graze out his days, having earned a reputation as one of the greatest horses to have raced in Australia.

1958 — FAVOR REPAID — WITH INTEREST!

Jockey Larry Wiggins never forgot how fellow hoop Les Whittle looked after him in India in the mid 1930's .... and he repaid the favor by giving Whittle a winning Cox Plate ride 25 years later.

The story surrounding the return of the favor involved Wiggins' trip to the sub-continent decades earlier in an endeavour to secure some rides. A very experienced rider, Wiggins had been associated with some of the best horses New Zealand has ever produced – including Kindergarten. At the time of Wiggins' arrival, Whittle had been in India for some time and knew his way around.

"Larry had come over without a retainer, so I knew he was wasting his time," Whittle recalled.

"I told him he wouldn't get any work being a freelance but that if he wanted to have a break he was welcome to stay with us. He stayed for a couple of weeks and I showed him around a bit. When he left he said that he'd never forget what I'd done and that one day he'd repay the favor."

That payback occurred in late October, 1958, three days before the running of the Cox Plate – and a quarter of a century after Wiggins' Indian sojourn.

"The phone rang and blow me down if it wasn't Larry, who was now a trainer," Whittle said. "He said that he hadn't forgotten the favor he owed me and that he had a runner in the Cox Plate. What's more, he said it would win and he would like me to ride it."

Racegoers would love to have been "in" on the information Wiggins relayed, as his horse, Yeman won the Cox Plate at the handsome odds of 33/1.

"Many people would look at that and say it was a fluke win. But it wasn't. He was a very good horse and there were specific reasons why he won that day after failing at his previous start," Whittle said.

"He had been ridden out hard from the barrier in the earlier run and was then eased. Wiggins said that was not the way to ride him. He said that Yeman was the sort of horse who liked to make his own pace. He said you had to let him go out of the barrier as he liked, let him settle, and then find his own pace. Once he'd done that, he would respond as you wanted. It's just that he had a mind of his own early."

Because these instructions were not followed at the earlier run,

> The payback occurred in late October, 1958, three days before the running of the Cox Plate.
>
> "The phone rang and blow me down if it wasn't Larry, who was now a trainer," Whittle said. "He said that he hadn't forgotten the favor he owed me and that he had a runner in the Cox Plate. What's more, he said it would win and he would like me to ride it."

1958
(Saturday, October 25. Attendance: 37,380)

£5,200 plus £300 Trophy Weight for Age 1¼ miles

1.	YEMAN	H. N. Wiggins	9.4	L. Whittle	33/1
2.	Stormy Passage	J. B. Cummings	7.12	G. Aistrope	25/1
3.	Master Rane	F. W. Hosyted	7.11	A. Yoemans	8/1

Winning details

Margin: ¾ len x 3 len. **Time:** 2:16.4 10 started.

Breeding: Sabean – Wardress – Lord Warden (ch g 6) **Owner:** S. N. Sparks & H. Korman

Winner's Colors: Red, grey Maltese cross

Winning Numbers: 2, 11, 9 **Barriers:** 1, 5, 6

ALSO RAN

Prince Darius	J. W. Cook	G. Moore	9.0	2/1f
Webster	T. Woodcock	R. Hutchinson	7.11	9/2
Gay Saba	H. Wolters	R. Heather	9.0	20/1
San Remo	D. A. Osborne	B. V. Hall	7.13	8/1
White Hills	E. F. Silcock	N. McGrowdie	9.4	12/1
Jordan	T. A. Jenner	N. Sellwood	7.11	3/1
High Value	P. Homann	P. Glennon	9.4	100/1

Scratched: Caranna, Dawdie

Yeman had been the centre of a demonstration by punters who heckled him when he finished third at 11/8 favorite, 14 lengths from the winner in a race at Randwick. On that form, however, Yeman was hardly a Cox Plate chance, particularly up against the likes of George Moore's mount Prince Darius or the crack South Australian colt Jordan, being ridden by Neville Sellwood.

Prince Darius, who was runner-up the previous year, was racing in great heart with two wins and two seconds in four starts from a spell. At his first run in Melbourne from Sydney, he was a great second behind Lord in the Caulfield Stakes. Jordan had won two races in good style and was then an unlucky second in the South Australian Derby. Another in contention was Webster, who had won six on end in the Winter and had flown home for second behind Wiggle (so called because her owner considered her rear gait was akin to Marilyn Munroe's wiggle) in the Caulfield Guineas.

There was also little incentive to back Yeman in the Cox Plate, on what Wiggins told the Press in the lead-up to the race. He said on the Tuesday before the Plate: "Just wait for Melbourne Cup day, particularly if the track is heavy. But he's not a weight-for-age horse."

Against this background, it was no surprise that Yeman started at 33/1 in what would have been a bonanza result for bookmakers, with the runner-up Stormy Passage at 25/1 and Master Rane third at 8/1. Favorite Prince Darius finished fourth, while Jordan (3/1) beat only one home.

Yeman had been the medium of very heavy betting on the day – from a Melbourne Cup perspective – before he won the Plate. The gelding had been backed into second favoritism for the Melbourne Cup at Moonee Valley – but these same punters neglected him in the Cox Plate to be run later in the afternoon.

Run in heavy conditions – which were to Yeman's liking – the gelding was out last from the barrier, with Whittle following instructions to the letter.

Whittle said that he was unconcerned because he had been told by Wiggins that the horse would gradually pick up in his own time.

"It happened approaching the 1000m," Whittle said. "Yeman was getting right into his stride and I was moving into third place behind George Moore on Prince Darius, who had Sellwood's mount Jordan on his outside. Wanting to make Jordan cover more ground, Moore moved out a bit from the rail.

"I saw the gap and went for it. Yeman was travelling beautifully, he picked up the bit immediately and we just slipped straight through on the inside. Moore got the shock of his life. He was concentrating on how Jordan was going and wasn't expecting me to be there on his inside.

"I'll never forget what Moore said to Sellwood when I went through. He yelled: 'Gawd strewth. Look at Whit'."

And Moore could only keep looking from thereon, as Yeman just keept going.

"I went past them as if they were standing still, and even though it was a long way from home, I knew at that stage that he was going like a winner," Whittle said.

Under a long-standing agreement, Sellwood was on Yeman in the Melbourne Cup, when he started a very short-priced favorite at 9-4, and finished fourth to Baystone.

Whittle however, was still savouring the previous week, when he won the Plate at the age of 46 in his first and only ride in the race. Courtesy of a long-standing favor between two mates.

1959 — OH BROTHER, NOHOLME WAS ALSO A STAR

The Star Kingdom-Oceania colt, Noholme, certainly had something to live up to when he stepped out onto the track for the first time.

His brother was the freakish sprinter Todman, an eight length winner of the inaugural Golden Slipper Stakes two years earlier. At his first start, Todman had run an Australian record of 57.8 seconds for five furlongs in the AJC December Juvenile Handicap at Randwick in 1956, when he beat Prince Darius by 10 lengths.

So there was more than a touch of dejavu at Noholme's first start for trainer Maurice McCarten, who also prepared Todman. Here was Todman's brother having his first race start, competing in the same race at Randwick as Todman had contested at his debut.

The result was the same too – only nowhere near in the same style, with Noholme scoring by less than a length and running the distance more than four seconds slower than his brother. But, there was no doubt that here was a horse with potential.

Noholme followed his brother's path in his first season, and though unplaced in the Golden Slipper, like Todman (who beat Tulloch in his year), Noholme too, won the Champagne Stakes.

As a three-year-old, Todman was an amazing eight lengths winner of the Canterbury Guineas, a race in which Noholme was unplaced. At his first start against older horses in the Hill Stakes, Todman broke down badly and was off the scene for two years. Following the same pattern, Noholme also contested the race two years later, and won it by five lengths. That race was a turning point for Noholme – he had come out of Todman's "shadow" at last!

Kept going against the more seasoned campaigners, Noholme then took the Epsom Handicap, running the mile in a slashing 1:34.9, the fastest time for a three-year-old for the distance. McCarten then set his sights on the Melbourne Spring, where the colt was beaten in a photo in the Caulfield Guineas after being four wide for some time. Next start was the Cox Plate.

However, it wasn't Noholme who was making news on the eve of the race, rather it was the owners of five-year-old gelding, Mac, who couldn't agree about a Spring program for their good stayer.

There was more than a touch of dejavu at Noholme's first start for his trainer Maurice McCarten, who also prepared Todman.

Here was Todman's full brother having his first race start, competing in the same race at Randwick as Todman had contested at his debut .... a race Todman had won by eight lengths.

1959
(Saturday, October 24. Attendance: 39,980)

£5,200 plus £300 Trophy Weight for Age 1¼ miles

1.	NOHOLME	M. McCarten	7.11	N. Sellwood	4/1
2.	Grand Garry	G. Ray	9.0	J. Purtell	16/1
3.	Prince Lea	B. Conaghan	7.11	A. Burton	10/1

Winning details

Margin: 4 len x ½ len. **Time:** 2:02.7 (race record) 10 started.

Breeding: Star Kingdom – Oceana – Colombo (ch c 3) **Owner:** S. Wootton

Winner's Colors: Red, yellow sleeves, pale blue cap

Winning Numbers: 10, 6, 8 **Barriers:** 9, 4, 6

ALSO RAN

Mac (=4)	A. Munro	F. Green	9.4	11/2
Moon Bridge (=4)	H. G. Heagney	G. Lane	9.0	50/1
Travel Boy	T. J. Smith	R. Hutchinson	7.11	5/2f
Yeman	I. J. Tucker	W. D. Skelton	9.4	20/1
Baystone	J. Green	R. Williams	9.4	50/1
Trellios	J. B. Cummings	B. MacDonald	9.4	10/1
Webster	C. A. Wilson	W. Williamson	9.0	9/2

All started

Mr J. H. Eden and Mr I. D. Kitto were known as "The Battling Owners"- because it appeared there was little they could agree about when it came to their horse. Things had got so bad that when Mr Eden had nominated Mac for the Caulfield Cup, Mr Kitto had scratched the gelding because he didn't want Mac to incur a penalty for the Melbourne Cup.

Mr Eden said after the scratching that he would have the final say on a run at Flemington – and the gelding's run in the Cox Plate would have a big bearing on what would happen. Punters were in a quandary, as Mac was favorite for the Melbourne Cup having won the Turnbull Stakes and the Herbert Power Handicap in his two previous starts.

While they were bickering, trainer Tommy Smith was talking up the Cox Plate prospects of his colt Travel Boy, who he raced with publishing magnate, Sir Frank Packer. A runner-up in the Rosehill Guineas and the AJC Derby, he had been an effortless winner of the Craven Plate, and the Cox Plate was his big test.

Noholme was also attracting his share of supporters, with the pair vying for favoritism. Interestingly, Neville Sellwood, who was the regular rider of Travel Boy, was on Noholme, while Ron Hutchinson was aboard Smith's colt, who was to start favorite.

Riding to plan, Sellwood led all the way to win by four lengths in race record time, from Jack Purtell's mount Grand Garry (16/1) with 10/1 chance Prince Lea third. While many believed that Noholme would be suspect over the 2000m journey, he was in front from the outset and was never headed, putting the pressure on all other runners throughout. Travel Boy made his bid when he went to within a half length of him at the 600m, but he could not sustain that effort and faded from thereon to finish sixth. Mac also made a forward move at the 600m being forced three wide as he attempted to hit the front, but he stuck on to finish equal fourth.

Noholme had beaten off all challengers on the turn and kicked three lengths clear in the straight, and while Grand Garry made up ground, he was never going to overhaul the leader.

After the race, McCarten said he did not want to run the colt in the Derby – an opinion supported by Sellwood. Instead he was reserved for the Linlithgow Stakes, which he won by four lengths. He then won the 2400m C. B. Fisher Plate on the final day of the Carnival, in which he started at the good odds of 7/4 because many doubted he would run out the trip.

Back in the Autumn, Noholme won the All Aged Stakes at Randwick after being placed in two of three other starts. By now Todman was back in work and, at the age of five, had won three on end, including the Futurity Stakes, after which he was sent to Widden stud in NSW. Noholme went further afield, to race in America where he won only two races and was placed seven times, after which he also went to stud.

The brothers, who were both outstanding racehorses, also became outstanding sires. Todman's progeny included the Golden Slipper winners Eskimo Prince and Sweet Embrace, but it was Noholme who really excelled in America, starting his own breeding dynasty. He produced a world record of 24 individual two-year-old winners in his second crop. His best son was Nodouble, who was twice voted the North American Handicap Horse of the Year, and is now a valuable sire in his own right.

And what of Mac? The owners agreed to start him in the Cup in which he started 5/1 favorite, but finished near last. Ironically the winner was Macdougal!

However, Mac made amends by winning the Adelaide Cup in the Autumn. The following year he was third in the Caulfield Cup, won the Moonee Valley Cup and was fifth in the Melbourne Cup. Surely Messrs Eden and Kitto had settled their differences after that!

1960 — SIMPLY, HE WAS T.J.'s BEST

The Trifecta of the best horses to race in Australia is a cinch – if you list them in the order of their birth. Carbine, Phar Lap and Tulloch.

It's when you try to put them in finishing order that arguments can arise. Suffice to say that, of the thousands of horses Tommy Smith had through his stables, he rated Tulloch the best – triple Cox Plate winner Kingston Town included.

In a 53 start career, he won 36 times and was placed in every other race bar one. But what makes his record more amazing is that he did not race for two years because of a life-threatening stomach illness. What he could have achieved bar that illness, in what should have been his peak years, is anyone's guess. It would only have added more confusion to the order of the Big Three.

A seven time winner in 13 starts at two, his victories included the VRC, AJC and QTC Sires. In the Sydney running, he beat the brilliant Todman, an eight length winner of the Golden Slipper. (Smith had bypassed the Slipper with Tulloch because he believed he was not suited by the shorter distance.)

At three, he was near invincible, with 14 wins and two placings in as many runs. He broke Phar Lap's long-standing record in the AJC Derby; took the Caulfield Guineas by eight lengths and became the shortest priced runner in the history of the Caulfield Cup (4/6) which he won in Australasian record time. Re-handicapped by the maximum 10lb (4.5kg) to carry 8.4 (52.5kg) in the Melbourne Cup – which would have been a weight-carrying record for his age – in a controversial decision, Tulloch's owner, Mr E. A. Haley, opted not to run the colt. Instead he took the Victoria Derby and continued his winning way in events such as the QTC Derby; VRC and AJC St Legers and the All Aged and Queen Elizabeth Stakes in Sydney.

Spelled, Mr Haley received huge American offers to buy his horse, who looked to have the big events at his mercy when he resumed as a four-year-old. Tragically however, this never eventuated, with Tulloch suffering from a life-threatening mystery stomach illness, which resulted in an enforced 23 month lay-off.

On March 12, 1960, he made his much heralded

What the oustanding Tulloch could have achieved bar an illness, in what should have been his peak years, is anyone's guess. It would only have added more confusion to the order of the best three horses to have raced in Australia.

1960
(Saturday, October 22. Attendance: 50,670)

£5,200 plus £300 Trophy Weight for Age 1¼ miles

1.	**TULLOCH**	T. J. Smith	9.4	N. Sellwood	2/1f
2.	**Dhaulagari**	B. Courtney	9.0	G. Lane	3/1
3.	**Persian Lyric**	J. W. Cook	7.11	R. Hutchinson	14/1

Winning details

Margin: ½ len x 3 len. **Time:** 2:01.1 (Aust. & MV record) 15 started.

Breeding: Khorrassan – Florida – Salmagundi (b h 6) **Owner:** E. A. Haley

Winner's Colors: Red & white stripes, black sleeves & cap

Winning Numbers: 1, 7, 15 **Barriers:** 15, 1, 5

ALSO RAN

Howsie	P. Burgess	W. Williamson	9.0	20/1
Ma Cherie	A. R. Beale	D. Weir	8.13	8/1
Sky High	J. Green	W. Camer	7.11	9/2
Le Storm	J. Davis	G. Podmore	7.11	33/1
Nilacrco	R. G. Chapman	J. Purtell	9.0	12/1
Valerius	F. J. Dalton	J. Thompson	9.4	33/1
Grand Garry	T. J. Smith	P. Glennon	9.4	20/1
Samson	A. Lopes	A. Burton	7.12	33/1
On Line	F. McGrath	B. Howlett	9.4	100/1
Red Wind	R. G. Mills	R. Higgins	9.4	100/1
Demeter	R. Dini	J. Johnson	8.13	200/1
Liqueur	B. Courtney	W. A. Smith	7.11	25/1

All started

TULLOCH ... Tommy Smith's champ shows his fighting qualities to hold off Dhaulagiri. – Picture: HWT

return, in which he narrowly defeated the Melbourne favorite Lord in the weight-for-age Queens Plate over 2000m. He had another four starts that campaign, winning them all. It appeared he was back to his best! Resuming in the Spring of 1960, he was set for the Cox Plate after winning the Craven plate at Randwick. It was to be one of the most memorable Cox Plates of all!

His main opposition looked to be Dhaulagiri, who had dead-heated for first in the Caulfield Stakes before finishing second to Illumquh in the Caulfield Cup. The other main contender was the brilliant youngster Sky High who had been placed in the Rosehill Guineas, AJC Derby and the Caulfield Guineas.

Such was the interest in the race that the betting ring was almost empty five minutes before the start as people rushed to gain a good vantage point. In the ring, Tulloch was 2/1 favorite, shading Dhaulagiri at 3/1, with Sky High at 9/2.

Once again, Tulloch broke their hearts. In a thrilling finish, going head and head to the line with Dhaulagiri, Tulloch lasted by a half length, running half a second faster than the Australian record. The crowd began cheering at the 600m mark as it appeared as if Tulloch would win – and the cheering continued unabated until he was led away after the weigh-in. Such was the din that the course broadcast could not be heard over the cheers.

Jockey Neville Sellwood said on dismounting that he had gone out with a set plan. He let Tulloch go along quietly early even though Sky High and Samson set a brisk early pace. Sellwood began his forward move 1000m from home, quickly going around the field, catching the rest of the jockeys unaware. Tulloch was in front at the 600m with Dhaulagiri making ground. That pair and Sky High turned for home together. The fast early pace set by Sky high soon told, leaving Tulloch locked in battle with Dhaulagiri. Both riders were throwing everything at their mounts, and Tulloch slowly inched to the front with every stride to just land the money.

The Valley had not seen such scenes of public adulation as Sellwood bought his charge back to scale.

An effervescent Smith did not let Tulloch rest on his laurels. Next stop was the Mackinnon Stakes, in which he again beat Lord. Despite having to lump 10.1 (64kg), Tulloch started in the Melbourne Cup and, after being well back, could not make up ground with the crushing weight. He finished 7th behind outsider Hi Jinx.

On the final day of the Carnival, he returned to his winning ways, beating Dhaulagiri in the C.B. Fisher Plate.

His finale came the following Autumn. After winning in Adelaide, he went to Brisbane where he was a six length winner of the O'Shea Stakes in his prelude for the Brisbane Cup, which was to be his last race. Despite having to carry 62.5kg, he went out in winning style. In scenes similar to those after the Cox Plate, the crowd went wild.

That was the day that Smith paid Tulloch his greatest tribute. The boy who left home in his early teens to become a man; who survived on his wits to triumph over all the hardships that racing could throw up; who journeyed from an outback humpy to become a multi-millionaire; coped with the emotion like others who had not experienced anything like his tough upbringing.

Tommy Smith cried.

1961 – DHAULAGIRI CONQUERS HIS "EVEREST"

In an era of class horses such as Tulloch, Sky High, Aquanita and Lord, Dhaulagiri more than held his own.

Named after a Himalayan peak (his sire was Hyperion's son Mountain Peak), Dhaulagiri continually competed at top level. His 17 victories included wins over Tulloch and Derby winners Sky High and New Statesman; he was twice placed in the Caulfield Cup; third and fourth in the Melbourne Cup and had a win and a close second (behind Tulloch) in the Cox Plate.

While wins such as these stamped his class, but for a string of close seconds, Dhaulagiri would be considered among Australia's greatest horses.

He was runner up on 18 occasions, more often than not finishing within a length of the winner. His second placings include the VRC's Queen Elizabeth Stakes (short half head); Sandown Cup (three-quarters of a length); the 1960 Caulfield Cup and Cox Plate when he failed by a half length; the Underwood, Turnbull and Mackinnon Stakes. So the list goes on.

Trained by Brian Courtney, Dhaulagiri was a dual winner at two and won only two races the following season. His placings in that year, however, were a lot better pointer to his potential. He won minor prizemoney in races such as the Alister Clarke Stakes, Stanley Plate, VRC St Leger and the Sandown Cup.

At four, he started to realise what he had shown the previous season. He dead-heated with Lord to take the Caulfield Stakes and was then second to Illumquh in the Caulfield Cup.

At his next start, he stretched the neck of Tulloch in the Cox Plate. Dhaulagiri finished only a half length astern of the champion, who had to run an Australian record to score. Next stop for Dhaulagiri was the Melbourne Cup in which he was a close up fourth.

Back the following Autumn, Dhaulagiri won the Blamey, Alister Clark and St George Stakes (in which Tulloch was third).

Resuming as a five-year-old in the Spring of 1961, he was again dogged by placings, culminating with a third in the Caulfield Cup behind Summer Fair. His biggest win was only a week away, but it looked a

> But for a string of close seconds, Dhaulagiri would be considered among Australia's greatest horses.
> He was runner up on 18 occasions, more often than not finishing within a length of the winner. His seconds include the VRC's Queen Elizabeth Stakes; Sandown Cup; the 1960 Caulfield Cup and Cox Plate; the Underwood, Turnbull and Mackinnon Stakes. So the list goes on .....

1961
(Saturday, October 28. Attendance: 40,280)

£6,000 plus £250 Trophy Weight for Age 1¼ miles

1.	DHAULAGIRI	B. Courtney	9.4	G. Lane	9/2
2.	New Statesman	B. Courtney	7.11	J. Purtell	14/1
3.	Sky High	J. Green	9.0	G. Moore	4/9f

Winning details

Margin: Nk x nk. **Time:** 2:04.8 8 started.

Breeding: High Peak – Solar Circle – Solar Bear (b h 5) **Owner:** J. P. O'Connor

Winner's Colors: Green, purple stripes, white sleeves

Winning Numbers: 1, 8, 5 **Barriers:** 1, 6, 5

ALSO RAN

Blue Lodge	D. N. McInnes	C. McLaughlan	9.0	25/1
Aquanita	R. J. Shaw	A. Burton	9.4	10/1
Bargoed	G. G. Cameron	E. Sellers	9.0	33/1
Far Away Places	W. Tait	D. Coleman	9.4	200/1
Sharply	W. J. Elliott	P. Glennon	9.4	20/1

All started

formidable task on paper against the Sydney star Sky High, ridden by George Moore.

While Dhaulagiri had run only placings in the lead up to the Plate, Sky High's form was all picket fences. In five runs from a spell he'd won the lot, including the Epsom Handicap and the Caulfield Stakes.

No wonder Moore sounded confident on race eve when he said he had no set plan on how to ride the champ, who was to start at the prohibitive odds of 4/9, with Dhaulagiri second pick at 9/2.

Already a conqueror of Tulloch, Sky High was another champ to fall to Dhaulagiri, ridden by pin-up jockey Geoff Lane. In a hectic finish, Dhaulagiri picked up the field with a paralysing run over the last 100m to win by a neck from his stablemate (and subsequent Victoria Derby winner) New Statesman, with the hot favorite third. It was the first home town success in the race for 10 years.

In some ways it was a lucky victory – not because of the way Dhaulagiri raced – but the fact that he was even in the field. After his Caulfield Cup placing Courtney had doubts about starting Dhaulagiri, and only changed his mind after the entire put in a stunning gallop at trackwork two days before the race.

Courtney's "second string", New Statesman, ridden by Jack Purtell, led early and slowed the field once he got out of the straight. This pace did not suit Sky High who was reefing for his head, so with 1000m to go, Moore took Sky high up to New Statesman. At this point Purtell was happy to keep apace with Moore. Approaching the 600m, Moore appeared to be getting anxious to get more from his mount, whereas Purtell was sitting quietly. When Moore went for the whip, Purtell went for home, but halfway down the straight, Lane and Dhaulagiri loomed up to go on and grab the race in the last bounds.

Courtney said later that he had given neither jockey instructions – emphasising that he had not told Purtell to go to the front and make the pace for his stablemate. As it was, Purtell almost won the race by using such tactics.

Sky High, who had wanted to hang out when he went up to New Statesman, got his revenge the following week. He equalled the Australasian record over the 2000m of the Mackinnon Stakes – and Dhaulagiri was runner-up, within a length of him.

Thereafter, Dhaulagiri was third behind Lord Fury in the Melbourne Cup and rounded off the Flemington Carnival by winning the Fisher Plate.

Other big wins continued to evade him the following Winter when, during a Queensland campaign, he was placed in the Ipswich Cup, O'Shea Stakes and the Brisbane Cup before he broke through to win the Tattersall's Cup at Eagle Farm.

After four runs in the Spring of 1962, yielding a win and two seconds, Dhaulagiri was bought for stud duties by a French syndicate. His main success as a sire was in producing French St Leger winner Dhauvedi, but he was eventually put down in 1968 because of poor fertility.

1962 – THE STAR FROM THE WEST

In only its second year, the Cox Plate was won by a horse from Western Australia, but it took one short of a further 40 years for another galloper from across the Nullarbor to lay claim to the weight-for-age championship. And if ever a horse deserved to win it, a striking black stallion by the name of Aquanita surely did.

Stretched over four seasons, Aquanita contested the best races the length and breadth of the country, over distances ranging from 1200m to 3200m, and rarely performed with anything other than distinction.

As previously mentioned, the very early 1960's were halcyon days for racing, fairly littered with weight-for-age stars and outstanding handicappers. Aquanita took on all of them, and, as often as not, was able to beat them.

He was a six-year-old when he won the Cox Plate, having finished fifth the previous year behind Dhaulagiri, and he won at Group 1 level in each of four seasons, from 1959 to 1962, at weight-for-age and under handicap conditions.

Aquanita emerged as a serious contender as a four-year-old in the Spring of 1960, coming out of the West in possession of a three-year-old CV that included success against the older horses in races such as the Railway Stakes, the Lee Steere Stakes and the Easter Quality. His first major success in the Eastern States came in the 1960 George Adams Handicap (now Emirates Stakes) over 1600m at Flemington on the final day of the Melbourne Cup Carnival. In the placings behind him were the 1959 Golden Slipper winner Sky High, and South Australia's outstanding sprinter-miler Mardene.

The following Autumn, he was placed in weight-for-age races in Melbourne and Sydney, but found his real form in Brisbane, winning the Healy Stakes and Doomben 10,000, as well as being placed in the Stradbroke Handicap.

From then on Aquanita was rarely out of work, but thrived on racing, and it seemed there wasn't a finish in which his by now familiar green and gold colors didn't feature. He won the Underwood Stakes beating Dhaulagiri; was second to Sky High in the Caulfield Stakes, and ran an even race to finish just behind the placegetters in the 1961 Cox Plate won by Dhaulagiri. At the Melbourne Cup Carnival he demonstrated his versatility by running well for third to Sky High over 2000m in the Mackinnon; was just beaten over

> Stretched over four seasons, Aquanita contested the best in races the length and breadth of the country, over distances ranging from 1200m to 3200m, and rarely performed with anything other than distinction.
>
> The very early 1960's were halcyon days as far as racing is concerned, fairly littered with weight-for-age stars and top handicappers the likes of Sky High, Dhaulagiri, New Statesman, Lord, Mardene and Weonoa Girl, to name just a few. Aquanita took on all of them, and, as often as not, was able to beat them.

1962
(Saturday, October 27. Attendance: 40,490)

£6,000 plus £250 Trophy Weight for Age 1¼ miles

1.	**AQUANITA**	R. J. Shaw	9.4	F. Moore	4/5f
2.	**Grand Print**	J. Besanko	9.4	R. Higgins	12/1
3.	**New Statesman**	B. Courtney	9.0	G. Lane	11/4

Winning details

Margin: 1½ len x ¾ len. **Time:** 2:04.3 6 started.

Breeding: Wateringbury – Reinita – Panto (br h 6) **Owner:** J. J. Thomas & W. Thomas

Winner's Colors: Green, yellow stripes, red cap

Winning Numbers: 3, 1, 5 **Barriers:** 6, 3, 2

ALSO RAN

Royal Belltor	E. Broadhurst	P. Wallen	9.0	33/1
Le Storm	A. V. Evans	J. Purtell	9.4	12/1
Tara's Pride	R. A. Tudor	W. A. Smith	7.11	6/1

All started

1600m by Anonyme in the Linlithgow Stakes five days later; and two days on produced a brilliant finish to win his second successive George Adams Handicap carrying 59.5kg.

Spelled for a couple of months, he came back to beat all but the speedy Wenona Girl over the 1000m of the Lightning Stakes at Flemington in February, and later that month won the Futurity. He was beaten less than two lengths when running fourth in the Newmarket Handicap behind Victorious, then two weeks later went out and beat fellow West Australian, On Guard, in the Alister Clark Stakes over 2000m.

Aquanita again campaigned in Queensland during the Winter of '62 but finished mid-field in both the Stradbroke and the Doomben 10,000. Still, when he embarked upon his Melbourne Spring campaign, Aquanita was considered one of the measuring sticks, as evidenced by his weight of 59kg in the Melbourne Cup.

He began with a pipe-opening fourth in the Memsie Stakes at Caulfield but, a little over three weeks later, returned to the track on Show Day and, with regular rider Frank "Tiger" Moore up, scored a convincing win in the Underwood Stakes over 2000m.

For Aquanita's next assignment, trainer Roy Shaw chose Flemington's Turnbull Stakes, then run over 2400m. The race conditions meant the six-year-old would be required to carry 63kg, so there were some doubts about him, particularly as he had not won in three starts beyond 2000m. Shaw, though, was confident. "He's never been better," he said. Aquanita proved that two days before the Turnbull, when he ran a trackwork record for 1000m, galloping 10m out on the course proper.

The black horse took his trackwork form to the races and was untroubled to beat the likes of Grand Print and Lord, thus putting paid to any lingering doubts about his ability to stay. Promoted to equal Caulfield Cup favoritism, Aquanita had his final lead-up race in the Caulfield Stakes, which back then was run on the Wednesday before the Cup.

It would be safe to say the horse was given a hit-out and nothing more. As Sky High bowled along in front, Moore had Aquanita back last, some 20 lengths from the lead, with 1000m to go. Given his head at the 400m mark, Aquanita charged home at a terrific rate and only just missed a place. "He would have been placed if Anonyme hadn't broken down in front of me," a po-faced Moore said later.

Punters flocked to back Aquanita pre-post for the Caulfield Cup, but in the end they did their money cold. A heavy track on race morning convinced Shaw to scratch the favorite, but whether he could have beaten the eventual winner, the freak New Zealand stayer Even Stevens, is open to conjecture.

The Cox Plate a week later attracted a disappointing field of only six runners, of which only two, Aquanita and New Statesman, were given any real chance of winning.

It would have been twice as good a contest had Sky High run, but his trainer Jack Green decided against a start after walking the Moonee Valley track late on Wednesday afternoon. Ironically, the track on raceday was rated good, which would have suited the front-running Sydney star to a tee. As it was, Aquanita overcame what one racing scribe termed "suicidal tactics" on the part of "Tiger" Moore to record an emphatic victory.

In the small field, Aquanita was never better than four wide for most of the race, and Moore had no hesitation in kicking him into a clear lead 800m from home.

By rights, this should have given New Statesman and Grand Print the opportunity to run him down, but neither they, nor any other runner, was capable of it. Fleetingly, at the top of the straight, Grand Print appeared set to gather him in, but Moore gave Aquanita a good kick in the ribs and his mount found another gear to coast home an easy winner by 1½ lengths.

Describing the run as "sensational", Moore said he'd had no doubts about letting Aquanita bowl along out wide and taking the lead when he did, as opposed to wrestling him in behind the pace.

Now the horse was being talked about as a possible Melbourne Cup winner, despite the fact Even Stevens would be getting 6kg from him over Flemington's stamina-sapping 3200m. Still, it was hard to argue against Aquanita being capable of anything when, just seven days after the Cox Plate, he handed odds-on favorite Sky High a two length thrashing in the Mackinnon Stakes.

That he was able to finish a gallant third behind Even Stevens and Comicquita in the Melbourne Cup is a measure of just how great a horse Aquanita was. Quite clearly, he didn't really stay the distance, but his extraordinary will to win enabled him to keep going up the long straight when others had called it quits.

The following Autumn, Aquanita had just four starts and won three of them – the Orr Stakes, the Duke Of Edinburgh Stakes and the St. George Stakes. He was back in the Spring of '63 but, after three unplaced runs, it was decided he had earned retirement.

1963 — NO DOUBT, HE WAS UP TO WFA CLASS

The Cox Plate, now billed as the "Weight-for-age Championship of Australasia", has always been one of the toughest of racing tests.

So imagine the task for New Zealand gelding Summer Regent, who was taking his place in the field even though he had never started in a weight-for-age race.

But, as they say, they breed them tough in New Zealand, and he defied very tough odds to record his biggest win. Like the favorite, Sometime, Summer Regent was by Summertime.

Summer Regent's form leading up to the Plate had been sound – but it was the fact that he had never stepped out in such class which was the concern. He had won over 2200m in New Zealand and, sent to Australia, lined up in the Caulfield Cup in which he was a great fourth to Sometime.

However, he was up against some classy performers the following week. These were headed by the Caulfield Cup winner Sometime, who had also won the Feehan, Turnbull and Caulfield Stakes in his earlier runs. Connections of Sometime were following the same trail – though more in hope than conviction – of the champion New Zealander, Rising Fast, who had won the same races in 1954 before taking the Cox Plate, Mackinnon Stakes and the Melbourne Cup.

Then there was Nicopolis. He had won the Liston Stakes, finished midfield in the Underwood but bounced back to take the Toorak Handicap by three lengths. Another contender was Tatua who had been third in the Turnbull before finishing fifth in the Caulfield Stakes. Importantly, these horses had proven themselves in racing's top class.

Sent out a 10/1 chance, Summer Regent convincingly proved he was up to weight-for-age when he led for the final 1400m holding off all challengers to beat Tatua by a length with hot favorite Sometime (5/4) third. The tearaway tactics used by his rider, John

> They breed them tough in New Zealand and Summer Regent defied very tough odds to record his biggest win.
>
> Summer Regent's form leading up to the Plate had been sound – but it was the fact that he had never started at weight-for-age which was the concern.

1963
(Saturday, October 26. Attendance: 33,570)

£6,000 plus £250 Trophy Weight for Age 1¼ miles

1.	SUMMER REGENT	R. T. Cotter	9.4	J. Riordan	10/1
2.	Tatua	W. J. Pratt	9.0	G. Edge	11/2
3.	Sometime	L. J. Patterson	9.4	W. Pyers	5/4f

Winning details

Margin: Len x len. **Time:** 2:06.2 10 started.

Breeding: Summertime – Mayina – Instinct (br g 5) **Owner:** R. B. Walker

Winner's Colors: Orange, blue braces, brown sleeves, blue cap

Winning Numbers: 2, 4, 1 **Barriers:** 7, 1, 3

ALSO RAN

Nicopolis	D. Judd	B. Gilders	9.0	9/4
Ilumquh	E. Ropiha	R. Skelton	9.4	25/1
Contempler	L. Armfield	D. Coleman	7.11	15/1
Sir Dane	R. J. Shaw	W. A. Smith	7.11	14/1
Proteus	B. Courtney	J. Purtell	7.12	33/1
Brandan	W. J. Murrell	P. Wallen	7.11	50/1
Lady Oro	W. J. Allitt	B. MacDonald	8.13	200/1

All started

SUMMER REGENT .... he won the Cox Plate at his first weight-for-age start, beating Tatua and Sometime. – Picture: HWT

Riordan, meant that Summer Regent avoided some of the bustling that inconvenienced the second and third placegetters.

Riordan settled his mount midfield and, after going wide at the first turn, quickly moved up to the lead to dictate terms. At the 800m, Summer Regent was travelling comfortably in the lead from Lady Oro and Nicopolis, with Sometime travelling wide. Soon after, Bill Pyers decided to move forward on Sometime to gain a clear passage and avoid some scrimmaging.

However, no matter how hard he tried to urge Sometime on, his mount was not responding in the manner expected, and even at that point, favorite backers suspected they would not be in the collect queue.

Coming to the turn, Summer Regent still held sway when Tatua and Nicopolis put in their challenges. Unflustered, Riordan did not go for the whip and vigorously rode hands and heels to the line.

After his Cox Plate victory, Summer Regent started 9/4 favorite in the Melbourne Cup, but he beat only four home, with one of them being Tatua, who had been runner-up in the Cox Plate. Illumquh, who was fourth in the Cox Plate, showed his appreciation of Handicap conditions when he finished second in the Cup, one length behind Gatum Gatum.

HOOFNOTE: On Cox Plate day, the New Zealand mare Lei, who had been second in the Caulfield Stakes, won the Phoenix Handicap. Ironically, she too was by Summertime, the sire of the first and third horses in the Cox Plate. Years later Lei was to make a much bigger name for herself, being the mother of Leilani (by Oncidium). Leilani was to become one of Australia's greatest staying mares, including in her wins races such as the Caulfield Cup, Mackinnon Stakes, Australian Cup and AJC Oaks. She was also runner-up to Think Big in the 1974 Melbourne Cup.

1964 – IT SHAW WAS GOOD ADVICE!

The owners of classy New Zealander Sir Dane were grateful they heeded the advice of trainer Roy Shaw before the 1963 Victoria Derby.

They had been offered £15,000 for the colt, but Shaw told them not to sell. It was a very tempting offer as, to that stage, Sir Dane had won only about £2,000, although he had shown potential, particularly when runner-up behind Proteus in the Moonee Valley Stakes. Even though Sir Dane didn't win the Classic – he finished second, robbing Geoff Lane of three wins straight – he was to provide his owners, Mr H. Rees and Mr D. Cameron, with great enjoyment and thousands of pounds in prizemoney in years to come.

After his Derby run, Sir Dane had to contend with second placing again in a major race in the Autumn, this time behind Better Lad in the VRC St Leger. However, things changed for the better in the Spring. He won the Craiglee and Turnbull Stakes and was placed in good races such as the Underwood and Caulfield Stakes. Such was his form that he was sent out 4/1 favorite for the Caulfield Cup, in which he finished ninth.

His jockey that day, Roy Higgins, said that he blamed himself to an extent for the defeat. He had to ride him along early to make him hold his position from the number 4 barrier, but when the field slowed, Sir Dane began to pull, which affected his chances in the run home. He made only a short dash at the leaders in the straight before weakening.

Higgins also believed that Sir Dane was a much better horse under weight-for-age conditions than he was in handicaps and so it was proven a week after his Caulfield Cup failure when he won the Cox Plate.

In what looked to be an even field, Sir Dane started fourth pick in the betting at 11/2, drifting alarmingly from an opening quote of 3/1. Favorite was the Sydney three-year-old Strauss, a winner of the Canterbury Guineas before finishing second in the Rosehill Guineas and the AJC Derby. Second fancy was the Adelaide four-year-old Contempler, who had beaten Sir Dane in the Caulfield Stakes and had been fourth in the Caulfield Cup. Another danger looked to be Toorak Handicap victor Nicopolis.

> Roy Higgins believed that Sir Dane was a much better horse under weight-for-age conditions than he was in handicaps and so it was proven a week after his Caulfield Cup failure when he won the Cox Plate.

1964
(Saturday, October 24. Attendance: 39,490)

£10,000 plus £300 Trophy Weight for Age 1¼ miles

1.	**SIR DANE**	R. J. Shaw	9.0	R. Higgins	11/2
2.	**Contempler**	L. M. Armfield	9.0	J. Johnson	4/1
3.	**Nicopolis**	D. Judd	9.4	B. Gilders	5/1

Winning details

Margin: 4 len x 2½ len. **Time:** 2:03.9 11 started.

Breeding: Summertime – Casa – Treasure Hunt (br h 4) **Owner:** H. Rees & D. Cameron

Winner's Colors: White, black spots, red armbands, red & white cap

Winning Numbers: 8, 9, 2 **Barriers:** 5, 4, 7

ALSO RAN

Our Fun	W. Accola	E. Sellers	8.9	7/1
Strauss	J. Green	D. Lake	7.11	5/2f
Sometime	L. J. Patterson	P. Wallen	9.4	20/1
Count Radiant	T. J. Smith	P. Hyland	9.4	16/1
Reveille	J. Green	W. A. Smith	7.6	10/1
Pablo Star	A. Lopes	J. Stocker	7.11	50/1
Gatum Gatum	H. G. Heagney	N. Mifflin	9.4	66/1
Blue Lodge	D. McInnes	C. MacLaughlan	9.4	80/1

Scratched: Bon Filou, Summer Regent

SIR DANE .... he made amends for his Caulfield Cup failure with the easiest of wins a week later in the Cox Plate.
– Picture: HWT

Higgins rode a copybook Moonee Valley race – settling back early and moving up to the lead near the 600m – to win by four lengths. He said later that he knew he had it won 800m from home.

The race was made for him due to the early pace made by the Sydney filly Reveille, with Sir Dane sitting off the pace waiting to strike. When Higgins shook him up, Sir Dane quickly went to the lead followed by Contempler, with Nicopolis in third place on the turn. However, it was clear at that point that Higgins was travelling easily and had the rest of the field covered – including Strauss, who struggled home for fifth.

The win took to more than £24,000 the amount Sir Dane had won since his owners refused the offer prior to the Derby the previous year. It was also a coup for the sire, Summertime, with one of his progeny winning the race for the second year in a row.

After the Cox Plate, the connections were looking forward to significantly adding to that amount, planning runs in the Mackinnon Stakes and the Melbourne Cup. After taking the Mackinnon, Sir Dane was a cramped 3/1 favorite for the Cup.

On learning that he had drawn the outside barrier, Higgins still showed his confidence by declaring "It doesn't matter. He could win from out in the carpark."

The Cup was run on a hard track, which showed another side to Sir Dane. He had shallow feet and could jar up when there was no "give" in the surface. His legs reacted badly to the track in the Cup, with the result that he beat only two home and came back very sore.

The following Autumn he won the Blamey and Futurity Stakes.

Of the beaten brigade in the Plate of 1964, Strauss failed by a neck to win the Victoria Derby, but he did strike an exceptional youngster in Royal Sovereign, who had also beaten Strauss in the AJC Derby. To cap off his Derby skills, Royal Sovereign later made it three Classic successes when he also took the Queensland version – by 10 lengths.

1965 – ANGUS UNEARTHS A PLATE STAR

Angus Armanasco is usually remembered for his amazing success with two-year-olds, so it is often forgotten he trained the winner of a Cox Plate.

Not just any old winner either, rather a young horse that in the Spring of 1965 proved himself the equal of some truly great horses, not the least of them being Tobin Bronze.

Star Affair wasn't the first outstanding horse to carry the pale blue, dark blue and yellow colors of Alan Dibb and his son Keith. Some 10 years earlier, they were associated with Sailor's Guide, who won the Victoria Derby and was placed in both the Cox Plate and the Caulfield Cup.

Sailor's Guide was an outstanding weight-for-age performer, but is perhaps best known for winning the Washington International at Laurel in the USA in 1957. Certainly Star Affair does not possess a record as impressive as Sailor's Guide's, but who knows what he might have achieved had he not been retired to stud at the end of his three-year-old career?

A sturdy, bay colt by Star Kingdom out of the Comic Court mare Royal Lark, Star Affair was a quality two-year-old. He won the Merson Cooper Stakes at Caulfield and the Ascot Vale Stakes, now a race for three-year-olds but then an Autumn two-year-old feature, at Flemington.

That the colt might possess real class was more than glimpsed in Sydney a couple of weeks later when he ran home strongly to beat all but the speedy filly Riesling in the 1965 Golden Slipper Stakes at Rosehill.

It was highly promising form, yet when Star Affair began his Spring campaign in early September his connections had no clear picture as to what sort of races he might contest. His breeding suggested he would be suited in staying races such as the Caulfield Cup and the Victoria Derby, but in the back of his mind Armanasco harbored some doubts as to whether the colt was capable of getting those distances.

Also, Star Affair proved somewhat difficult to train in the early stages of his Spring preparation, his inconsistent trackwork making it hard to gauge his level of fitness. Still, when he made his seasonal debut in the Whittier Handicap over 1200m at Caulfield on September 4 there was enough confidence in his ability to warrant backing him from 12-1 to start at 8-1.

Star Affair wasn't the first outstanding horse to carry the pale blue, dark blue and yellow colors of Alan Dibb and his son Keith. Some 10 years earlier, they were associated with Sailor's Guide, who won the Victoria Derby and was placed in both the Cox Plate and the Caulfield Cup.

Sailor's Guide was an outstanding weight-for-age performer, but is perhaps best known for winning the Washington International at Laurel in the USA in 1957.

1965
(Saturday, October 23. Attendance: 36,760)

£10,000 plus £300 Trophy Weight for Age 1¼ miles

1.	STAR AFFAIR	A. Armanasco	7.11	P. Hyland	3/1
2.	Winfruex	C. A. Wilson	9.0	J. Johnson	11/8f
3.	Yangtze	R. Dini	9.0	R. Higgins	9/2

Winning details

Margin: Hd x 3 len. **Time:** 2:02 11 started.

Breeding: Star Kingdom – Royal Lark – Comic Court (b c 3) **Owner:** A.C. & K. Dibb

Winner's Colors: Pale blue, dark blue band, yellow cap

Winning Numbers: 11, 6, 7 **Barriers:** 7, 2, 1

ALSO RAN

Royal Duty	S. McGreal	L. McCutcheon	9.4	25/1
Sail Away	S. A. Brown	W. D. Skelton	9.4	66/1
Bore Head	R. Dillon	F. Clarke	9.4	25/1
Ripa	B. Conaghan	D. Lake	8.13	7/1
Kiltaza	L. O'Sullivan	W. A. Smith	7.11	25/1
Pyramus	T. J. Smith	H. White	7.11	40/1
The Dip	J. B. Cummings	C. Winslett	9.4	125/1
Empyreus	K. Quinlivan	R. Taylor	9.0	14/1

All started

Another galloper, No Shenanegans, was also backed from 12's to 8-1, and it was he who landed the money. Star Affair finished a creditable second, and gave the distinct impression he would be much improved by the run.

Three weeks elapsed before Star Affair's next outing, this time against his own age in the Moonee Valley Stakes. Not only was he being asked to step up from 1200m to 1600m, a difficult task at the best of times, he was also pitted against a highly talented South Australian by the name of Tobin Bronze.

The visitor started favorite, and might have won but for the inspired riding of Roy Higgins aboard Star Affair, who held Tobin Bronze in a pocket rounding the home turn then stole a winning break in the run to the line.

"It meant Star Affair going earlier than I wanted, but it was worth it," Higgins said later.

Talking of future plans for Star Affair, Armansco made no mention of the Cox Plate, instead citing the Caulfield Cup and the Victoria Derby as possible targets.

A second confrontation between the two high class colts came just two weeks later, in the Caulfield Guineas, again over 1600m. Added spice came in the form of classy Sydneysider Fair Summer, considered a tough nut to crack despite running unplaced when odds-on favorite in the AJC Derby at his previous start.

Punters sent out the Sydney colt favorite at 11-8, with Star Affair a 5-2 chance, and Tobin Bronze the outsider of the trio at 13-4. Brilliantly ridden by Higgins, Star Affair was always handy to the lead in a rough-run race and comfortably held off Tobin Bronze to win by a length. Fair Summer was never on the track, but still showed little zip and beat only two home.

Once the decision was made to bypass the Caulfield Cup with Star Affair, it stood to reason he would be a leading contender for Cox Plate honors. Good three-year-olds had rarely failed to run well in the race, and it's fair to say the Dibbs' colt was a few shades better than just good. Not that winning the championship was going to be easy. General feeling was that Star Affair was one of the main chances, but that the four-year-old Winfreux was the one to beat.

As it transpired, this exceptional galloper was in the first year of what was to be an outstanding career, both at weight-for-age and in major handicaps. The Mick Wilson-trained gelding won a Maiden at Bendigo in March, 1965, but so meteoric was his rise up the equine success ladder that within the space of four months he could also lay claim to the Stradbroke Handicap – Doomben 10,000 double. In the early Spring, Winfreux began to assert himself as an outstanding weight-for-age prospect, and in fact went into the Cox Plate having at his previous start broken the Australasian record for 1800m in winning the Caulfield Stakes.

Included in the Cox Plate line-up were the Caulfield Cup winner Bore Head, New Zealand's weight-for-age champion Empyreus, along with Yangtze and the Tommy Smith-trained three-year-old Pyramus. Star Affair also had to contend with a new rider. The sparse but long-framed Higgins was never a chance to ride the colt at 49.5kg, and so the mount was taken by talented rival Pat Hyland.

Almost from start to finish, the Cox Plate was a three-horse race. Yangtze led, Winfreux sat on his tail, and Hyland on Star Affair trailed the pair of them. The rest toiled along behind but made little or no impression when it counted.

At the 800m, Yangtze skipped away with a four-length break, but neither Jim Johnson on Winfreux nor Hyland was panicked into going too early. As expected, Yangtze came back to the pair on the turn, where Star Affair took up the running with Winfreux poised to have the last crack at him.

It could be Winfreux actually headed his younger rival in the straight, but Hyland told pressmen later he was never worried. "Even when Winfreux challenged in the straight, I had him covered and as soon as I cracked Star Affair with the whip he bounded away."

Well, not quite "bounded away". Although the margin was clear in Star Affair's favor, he beat Winfreux by only a head, but his time of 2 min. 2 sec. was the second fastest – only Tulloch's was better – in 20 years.

It was enough to promote Star Affair to the head of the betting for the following Saturday's Victoria Derby, but in that race Armanasco's doubts about the colt's true staying ability were confirmed. Star Affair as usual ran gamely, but his was a laboring sixth as his old rival Tobin Bronze, relishing the 2400m trip, skittled his rivals to win with total authority.

Star Affair quickly demonstrated both his mettle and his versatility by coming out five days later and easily beating the classy sprinter-miler Nicopolis over 1600m in the weight-for-age Linlithgow Stakes.

The following Autumn, the colt won the William Reid Stakes first-up, and later won the Futurity Stakes. Clearly though, he was not running to his Spring form and, when he finished second last in the Alister Clark Stakes at Moonee Valley in March, the decision was made to retire him.

Star Affair proved a reliable, if not outstanding, sire with his progeny being solid performers, rather than showing the class of their sire.

1966-67 – "BRONZE" WAS A GOLD MEDAL CHAMP

It is doubtful there has ever been a more emotion-charged Cox Plate win than that of Tobin Bronze in 1967.

Not only was he a magnificent individual, his gleaming, bronze-like chestnut coat highlighting a near perfect conformation, but his explosive ability made him one of the best racehorses ever to have raced in Australia.

He came to the Cox Plate that day already a winner of the coveted weight-for-age championship – he won it in 1966 – and having a week earlier scored a truly memorable win in the Caulfield Cup. Above all though, it was to be the last appearance in Australia of the mighty horse whose deeds over three seasons captured the imagination of the racing public, and indeed the public at large.

Tobin Bronze was bred to be a good horse, being by the imported stallion Arctic Explorer, from the VRC Oaks winning mare Amarco. And under the experienced eye of Adelaide trainer Grahame Heagney he quickly made his mark.

As a two-year-old, he won four from seven races, showing enough brilliance to win the Breeders' Stakes at Morphetville, and developing stamina to land the Gibson Carmichael Stakes at Flemington. His staying ability came to the fore the following Spring with victory in the Victoria Derby, and in the Autumn his class shone through with a weight-for-age win in the Blamey Stakes.

And so, at the age of four, Tobin Bronze was set to establish himself among the top echelon of weight-for-age gallopers and he did just that, winning four set weight races on end, a highlight being his defeat of the champion mare Light Fingers in the Underwood Stakes at Caulfield.

A subsequent win in the Turnbull Stakes, then run over 2400m, saw Tobin Bronze at almost unbackable odds in the Caulfield Cup, for which he started at 8-11.

Punters are always in dangerous territory when forced to lay odds, and Caulfield Cup day, 1966, proved no exception. Tobin Bronze jumped in the air at the start, had to be hunted up, then grabbed the bit and refused to settle. He was in front before the

And so, at the age of four, Tobin Bronze was set to make a name for himself among the top echelon of the weight-for-age gallopers and he did just that, winning four set weight races on end, a highlight being his defeat of the champion mare Light Fingers in the Underwood Stakes at Caulfield.

1966
(Saturday, October 22. Attendance: 37,200)

$20,000 plus $600 Trophy Weight for Age 1¼ miles

1.	TOBIN BRONZE	H. G. Heagney	9.0	J. Johnson	9/10f
2.	Winfruex	C. A. Wilson	9.4	I. Saunders	5/1
3.	Light Fingers	J. B. Cummings	8.13	G. Hughes	3/1

Winning details

Margin: 2½ len x 2 len. **Time:** 2:07.2 8 started.

Breeding: Arctic Explorer – Amarco – Masthead (ch h 4) **Owner:** A.D.C. & W. E. Brown

Winner's Colors: Purple, white spots & cap

Winning Numbers: 5, 3, 6 **Barriers:** 3, 4, 2

ALSO RAN

Prince Grant	T. J. Smith	G. Moore	9.0	6/1
Samson	N. Creighton	R. J. Hall	9.4	50/1
Sunhaven	B. Courtney	H. White	7.11	25/1
Castle Command	J. Moloney	P. Hyland	7.11	25/1
Trevors	A. C. Shepherd	P. Gumbleton	9.4	50/1

All started

TOBIN BRONZE .... his victory in 1967 had thousands of racegoers in raptures, calling for more. – Picture: HWT

turn but was swamped in the straight and finished sixth, the race being won in whirlwind fashion by the Bart Cummings-trained Galilee.

Disappointed though they might have been, Tobin Bronze's legion of fans descended upon Moonee Valley a week later confident their idol – for in every sense that is what he was – would redeem himself.

Somehow, more than 37,000 crammed into Melbourne's smallest venue to see Tobin Bronze take on the likes of Light Fingers, the undisputed Queen of the Turf, the AJC Derby winner Prince Grant and the highly talented Winfreux, runner-up to Star Affair the previous year.

This time there was to be no mucking around. Tobin Bronze settled just off the pace, and when jockey Jim Johnson unleashed him approaching the turn the chestnut surged clear and cruised down to the line the easiest of winners. He returned to a hero's reception. To imagine a bigger one was impossible, yet a year later it was dwarfed by the response of a similar sized crowd.

Through season 1966-67, Tobin Bronze clearly stamped himself the best weight-for-age galloper in Australia. It was expected he would be a major force in the Spring of 1967, but few could have imagined the sheer magnitude of the public adulation that swept the nation in the weeks leading up to the Cox Plate.

Partly, this was due to extraordinary events that happened away from the track, which had their beginnings in an invitation for Tobin Bronze to start in the Laurel International, run at Maryland in the US in late November. The impetus for such an invitation came from his Autumn form, which saw him win at both weight-for-age and under handicap conditions: he was lumped with 59.5kg to win the Doncaster Handicap at Randwick in a truly memorable performance.

Tobin Bronze's owners, Adelaide scrap-metal dealers Alf , Walter and

1967
(Saturday, October 28. Attendance: 36,890)

$20,000 plus $600 Trophy Weight for Age 1¼ miles

1.	**TOBIN BRONZE**	H. G. Heagney	9.4	*J. Johnson*	1/6f
2.	**Terrific**	M. Ritchie	9.4	*G. Hughes*	7/1
3.	**Cratfsman**	A. R. White	9.4	*P. Hyland*	25/1

Winning details

Margin: 1½ len x 2½ len. **Time:** 2:04.8 7 started.

Breeding: Arctic Explorer – Amarco – Masthead (ch h 5) **Owner:** W. Breliant, I. M. Litz

Winner's Colors: Purple, white spots & cap

Winning Numbers: 1, 2, 3 **Barriers:** 5, 4, 2

ALSO RAN

Meriweather	C. Cerchi	W. A. Smith	7.11	80/1
Bellition	G. M. Hanlon	H. White	8.13	12/1
Karloon Pride	R. W. Roden	P. Alderman	7.11	40/1
Swift General	J. B. Cummings	J. Miller	9.0	100/1

Scratched: Stellar Belle, Regal Rhythm

Donald Brown, were keen for their champion to take on the best in the US, but when no financial assistance to get him there was forthcoming they decided against the trip.

With another Cox Plate in his sights, Tobin Bronze embarked upon a Spring preparation but early on contracted a virus, the effects of which delayed his racetrack return until late September.

He resumed in the Nulla Nulla Handicap at Moonee Valley on September 30, just 28 days before the Cox Plate, carried 63kg, started odds-on, and won as he liked. Two weeks later, he went out to contest the Toorak Handicap with 62.5kg and, after racing handy to the lead, shot away in the straight to win by two lengths from the Cummings-trained stayer Red Handed.

Barely had the dust settled than rumours about the impending sale of Tobin Bronze began to circulate, and they became a reality when the Browns announced the five-year-old had been sold to US businessmen William Breliant and Irving Litz.

A condition of the sale was for Tobin Bronze to start in the Caulfield Cup, for which he was favorite. That he did and, carrying his original colors of purple and white spots, plus a hefty 61.5kg, he staged a game performance to hold off the fast finishing Red Handed to win by a half length.

By now, public adulation for the horse was running at fever-pitch, and rose to even greater heights when it was announced his attempt to win a second Cox Plate would be his final race in Australia. No one, not even the bookmakers, doubted he would win. Unbackable at 1-6, only the New Zealander Terrific, a 7-1 chance, was at single figure odds to beat him.

Again a huge crowd of around 37,000 turned out to farewell their hero and, when he drew clear of Terrific soon after straightening, a mighty wave of sound surged with him to the line.

For many, there were tears of joy mingled with tears of regret. Heagney wept unashamedly. "That is how I wanted him to go out. What a champion!"

Ovation followed ovation as jockey Jim Johnson paraded Tobin Bronze down the straight. The bronze champion kept nodding his head, as if in acknowledgment. When he disappeared under the stand on his way back to his stall the crowd called for more. "Toby, Toby, we want Toby," they cried.

Exactly a week later, Tobin Bronze was flown to the US where, on an interrupted preparation, he finished a game third in the Laurel International.

1968 – PURCHASE PRICE REPAID IN FULL!

A win in the Cox Plate – then worth a total of $25,000 – would take Rajah Sahib's earnings since being puchased by the Stanleys to £31,300, within cooee of the $40,000 they had paid for him. Thereafter, the Derby prizemoney, and whatever else came his way, was cream.

The "knockers" were out in force when former New Zealander Rajah Sahib began racing in Sydney as a three-year-old in the Spring of 1968.

Sydney trainer Tommy Hill had paid $40,000 for the Pakistan II colt for his long-time friends, Mr and Mrs Bill Stanley, with the intention of winning the AJC Derby. Hill had negotiated the purchase after Rajah Sahib had won three two-year-old races at Ellerslie in the Dominion when under the care of trainer Eric Ropiha. Ropiha was well known to Australian racegoers having prepared Ilumquh, who won the 1960 Caulfield Cup and was placed in the Melbourne Cups of that year and 1963.

However, in his early races in NSW, Rajah Sahib failed to reproduce the same form he had shown as a two-year-old, and people were doubting Hill's judgment. Their attitude was soon to change as the colt gradually began improving. First, it was a second in the Rosehill Guineas and thereafter he was fourth in the AJC Derby won by Wilton Park. Even though Rajah Sahib had not lived up to Hill's early predictions, at last the colt was showing something like his best. And the Melbourne Spring Carnival provided ample opportunities to make amends, with the Victoria Derby being a prime goal following his failure in the AJC version.

Rajah Sahib was right back to his best at his first Victorian start when he beat smart performers Crewman and Goree King in the Caulfield Guineas after which Hill set him on the trail of the Cox Plate and the Victoria Derby.

A win in the Cox Plate – then worth a total of $25,000 – would take Rajah Sahib's earnings since being puchased by the Stanleys to £31,300, within cooee of the $40,000 they had paid for him. Thereafter the Derby prizemoney, and whatever else came his way, was cream.

With the colt back in form, punters warmed to his chances even more when star Sydney jockey George Moore announced that he would waste to take the ride in the Cox Plate. Other good chances included Shorengro, who had won the Feehan Stakes and finished second in the

1968
(Saturday, October 26. Attendance: 28,750)

$25,000 plus $600 Trophy Weight for Age 1¼ miles

1.	RAJAH SAHIB	T. W. Hill	7.11	G. Moore	7/4f
2.	Fileur	C. S. Hayes	9.0	J. Stocker	6/1
3.	Crewman	A. Armanasco	7.11	J. Johnson	12/1

Winning details

Margin: 2½ len x 2½ len. **Time:** 2:04.8 13 started.

Breeding: Pakistan II – Gay Princess – Sabaean (br c 3) **Owner:** Mr & Mrs W. G. Stanley

Winner's Colors: Yellow, black armbands, green cap.

Winning Numbers: 13, 5, 11 **Barriers:** 2, 9, 3

ALSO RAN

Shorengro	M. Willmott	P. Hyland	9.0	3/1
Speed of Sound	T. J. Smith	G. Lane	9.1	25/1
Prince Grant	T. J. Smith	R. Higgins	9.4	20/1
Vanishing	R. J. Hutchins	F. Reys	7.11	40/1
Cedar King	B. Courtney	P. Jarman	7.11	25/1
Wilton Park	M. F. Anderson	J. Courtney	7.11	40/1
Goree King	J. B. Cummings	R. Mallyon	7.11	9/1
Dhama Star	H. Wilson	P. Gumbleton	8.9	100/1
Alcatraz	N. D. Hoysted	A. McLean	9.4	9/1
Regal Rhythm	T. J. Smith	K. Mitchell	9.0	16/1

Scratched: Tried And True, Tizio

Caulfield Stakes before fourth to Bunratty Castle in the Caulfield Cup. Also in contention were Goree King (3rd in the Caulfield Guineas) and Adelaide four-year-old Fileur, who had been fourth behind top-liners Lowland, Rain Lover and Galilee in the Craiglee Stakes.

The Rajah Sahib – Moore partnership proved the clearest choice by far for punters on race day, who backed the combination from 11/4 into 7/4. Just as they had dominated the betting, so they dominated the race. Perfectly ridden, Rajah Sahib was always travelling easily and had 2½ lengths to spare from Fileur at the finish with Crewman the same margin further back for third.

After leading out of the barrier, Moore let his mount settle in second place, getting a cover behind Speed Of Sound. Moore was content to hold his position at the 800m, being trailed by Fileur who was moving up to his outside with Shorengro fourth.

Coming to the turn, Moore shot Rajah Sahib to the lead with John Stocker also moving up on Fileur. For a few strides, it appeared as if Fileur was going to fight it out to the line, but once Moore released the reins, Rajah Sahib quickly put a space between himself and the rest of the field.

On that performance, Rajah Sahib was considered a first-rate chance of winning the Victoria Derby the following week. His main rival was the Charlie Waymouth-trained Always There, who had been third in the AJC Derby. The pair started 9/4 equal favorites, but it was the backers of Always There who were on the money, while the co-favorite finished fourth after injuring himself in the run.

While Rajah Sahib was forced to miss the Melbourne Cup because of his injury, Fileur, who had finished second to him in the Cox Plate, finished in the same position behind Rain Lover in the Cup. Third placegetter in the Cup was Fans, trained by Eric Ropiha, who no doubt took the opportunity on Derby Day to see how his former top two-year-old had developed since leaving him some 12 months earlier.

Although Rajah Sahib had failed narrowly to recoup his purchase price for his new owners in his three-year-old season, he was to repay them with interest. He went on to win the 1971 Doncaster and Stradbroke Handicaps, while placings included the 1969 and 1970 Doomben Cups and the 1971 Australian Cup.

1969 — HE WAS REALLY ROBERT'S JOY!

Daryl's Joy had only a brief but all-conquering seven week stint in Australia which saw him beat the seemingly invincible Vain; win the Cox Plate and bid farewell with a tearaway win in the Victoria Derby.

New Zealand-bred Daryl's Joy was a "bargain-basement" champion. Bought by Singapore hotelier Mr Robert Goh for only $1,100 Daryl's Joy – named after Mr Goh's son – won in top company in three countries. He had only a brief, but all-conquering, seven week stint in Australia which saw him beat the seemingly invincible Vain; win the Cox Plate and bid farewell with a tearaway win in the Victoria Derby.

After winning some $74,000 in that sojourn he went to America where he was a six-time winner for a further $US190,000.

Despite the fact that he bought Daryl's Joy cheaply, Mr Goh was even luckier to have retained sole ownership of the entire for his two biggest Australian wins. He had entered negotiations to sell Daryl's Joy to America for $225,000 before his Cox Plate success, but the sale fell through when the three-year-old failed a veterinary test because of what was perceived to be a problem with one of his knees. This in fact was the legacy of an incident a year earlier when he had knocked the knee against the starting stalls. Even though it affected his performance that day, it had no lasting ill-effect, as shown by his subsequent form.

After being placed in his first four starts, Daryl's Joy won twice over 1000m at Canterbury (NZ) before finishing second over 1100m at Wanganui on December 11, 1968. It was in this race that he knocked his leg coming out of the stalls. Proof that no damage was done came two starts later when he equalled the race record in winning the Auckland Eclipse Stakes. The nuggety brown entire then found rare form to complete four wins on end at the conclusion of his first season, including the Manawatu Sires', the Great Northern Champagne Stakes and the Ellerslie Champion Stakes. In 14 starts in his debut season he had won seven times and been seven times placed, for earnings of almost $22,000. Trainer Sid Brown knew the colt's next assignment was the big-time of Australia and big-stakes of the Melbourne Spring.

At his first outing here in the Ascot Vale Stakes, Daryl's Joy was pitted against the all-conquering Vain, who numbered the Golden Slipper and the Champagne Stakes in his six wins in seven starts the previous season. Though beaten by five lengths, it was a fair effort from the

1969

(Saturday, October 25. Attendance: 36,610)

$30,000 plus $600 Trophy Weight for Age 1¼ miles

1.	DARYL'S JOY	S. A. Brown	7.11	*W. Skelton*	7/2
2.	Ben Lomond	J. W. Winder	9.4	*R. Lang*	7/4f
3.	Fileur	C. S. Hayes	9.4	*J. Stocker*	3/1

Winning details

Margin: 2½ len x 2 len. **Time:** 2:05.4 10 started.

Breeding: Stunning – Ruthla – Ruthless (br c 3) **Owner:** R. K. C. Goh

Winner's Colors: Red, white stars, blue armbands & cap

Winning Numbers: 8, 1, 2 **Barriers:** 2, 4, 1

ALSO RAN

Nausori	A. Ward	D. Lake	9.4	8/1
Crewman	A. Armanasco	R. Higgins	9.0	16/1
Divide And Rule	N. Begg	R. Setches	7.11	20/1
Tails	P. J. Murray	R. Mallyon	9.0	15/1
Future	K. Hilton	R. Dawkins	9.4	33/1
Golden Sound	J. B. Page	W. A. Smith	7.11	50/1
Cardiff Prince	N. J. Forbes	J. J. Miller	9.0	200/1

All started

Shaky Isles' contender, considering Vain's awesome reputation.

At his next start, Daryl's Joy produced the shock of the season when he beat Vain (4-9 fav) over the 1600m of the Moonee Valley Stakes. Vain led clearly into the straight but Daryl's Joy was able to peg him back in the short run home to score by three-quarters of a length. The pair clashed again two weeks later, this time in the Caulfield Guineas, when Vain was back to his brilliant best. He restored his reputation in slashing style by running a race record to hammer Daryl's Joy by three lengths, with the third runner a further six lengths astern.

At the same time, another New Zealander was making a big reputation. The proven stayer Ben Lomond – he was to run third in the Melbourne Cup that year – had run a slashing third in the Caulfield Stakes at his first run for nine months. With that run under his belt it was considered that he would test Daryl's Joy in the Cox Plate.

However, there was no danger to Daryl's Joy (7/2) who won as he liked by 2½ lengths from Ben Lomond (7/4 fav) with Fileur, who had been second in the Cox Plate the previous year, filling the minor placing.

Ridden by Bill Skelton, Daryl's Joy piloted the field from soon after the start and was never headed. Even when pressure was applied by other runners at various stages, Skelton just kept giving his mount more rein. On reaching the turn, he allowed Daryl's Joy to skip more than a length clear and then go on to win as he wished.

Next stop for Daryl's Joy was the Victoria Derby. There was drama on the morning of the race when he appeared lame as a result of a nail being driven into the quick of one of his feet when he had been shod. Despite this setback, Daryl's Joy was still able to take his place in the Classic and spreadeagled the field to beat Top Flat by three lengths with Gallicus a further four lengths behind.

Still wanting to give Daryl's Joy a chance in America, Mr Goh sent him to famed trainer Charles Whittingham in California. He raced there with distinction, numbering among his wins the $50,000 Del Mar Handicap (11 furlongs) in which he set a course record when ridden by John Sellars, who had also ridden him during a stint in Australia. His other major success there was in the $100,000 Oak Tree Stakes at Santa Anita.

Now proven in three countries, Daryl's Joy was retired to stud, having made a name for himself in two hemispheres.

HOOFNOTE: Mr Goh and trainer Brown unearthed another extra smart galloper two years later in Classic Mission, who won the AJC-Victoria Derby double and finished 7th in the 1971 Cox Plate.

1970 — OH FOR A CHAMPION!

While the Cox Plate had built up a reputation for class winners over the years, the race of 1970 was lacking by comparison.

The headline in *The Herald* on the eve of the race, said it all. "OH, FOR A CHAMPION!" it thundered.

Chief Racing Writer Jack Elliott pulled no punches either. "Australia's richest weight-for-age race, the $30,000 W. S. Cox Plate to be run at Moonee Valley tomorrow, has attracted its BIGGEST and WORST field for years," was his opening salvo.

"With 16 runners, the race has its safety limit and the same size field that Rising Fast beat in 1954. But I cannot remember a worse lot of horses to contest the race in the past 30 years," Elliott continued.

"Since the race was first run in 1922, it has been won by such champions as Manfred, Heroic, Amounis, Highland, Nightmarch, Phar Lap (2), Chatham, Rogilla, Flight (2), Carbon Copy, Delta, Alister, Hydrogen (2), Rising Fast, Redcraze, Noholme, Tulloch, Tobin Bronze (2) and Daryl's Joy.

"Any one of those horses would be a greater crowd-pleaser than tomorrow's 16 starters put together.

"It must be very disappointing to the Moonee Valley Racing Club, the richest racing Club in Australia, to have such a poor calibre field racing in its feature event of the year.

"Missing from the race is the Melbourne Cup favorite Voleur, the third favorite Arctic Symbol, equal third favorite Regal Jane, the Caulfield Cup winner Beer Street, the New Zealander Baghdad Note and the Sydneysider Gallicus."

Also absent were the class three-year-olds Silver Sharpe (AJC Derby) and Royal Show who had finished fourth in the AJC Derby and was equal third in the Caulfield Cup.

Despite the lack of depth in the field, some 34,000 racegoers were undeterred, and had no trouble in the betting ring to nominate the likely winner, the Bart Cummings-trained mare, Gay Poss. She had been in topsy-turvy form in her lead-up, winning the Craiglee Stakes and then finishing only eighth when favorite in the Invitation Stakes at

1970
(Saturday, October 24. Attendance: 34,340)

$30,000 plus $600 Trophy Weight for Age 1¼ miles

1.	ABDUL	G. T. Murphy	7.12	*P. Jarman*	33/1
2.	Tails	P. J. Murray	9.4	*G. Lane*	15/1
3.	Rough 'N Tumble	T. J. Smith	7.11	*R. Setches*	20/1

Winning details

Margin: 3 len x nk. **Time:** 2:05.5 16 started.

Breeding: Sovereign Edition – Fyfe – Gabador (gr c 3) **Owner:** R. Wilson

Winner's Colors: Cerise, green rings & cap

Winning Numbers: 10, 5, 14 **Barriers:** 1, 12, 2

ALSO RAN

Swift And Sure	B. Courtney	B. Gilders	9.0	66/1
Fileur	C. S. Hayes	J. Johnson	9.4	12/1
Gay Poss	J. B. Cummings	R. Higgins	8.9	7/4f
Gunsynd	H. R. Wehlow	J. Thompson	7.11	15/1
Sir Trutone	J. Winder	R. Lang	9.4	25/1
Rajah Sahib	T. J. Hughes	R. Mallyon	9.4	10/1
Royal Guardsman	G. T. Murphy	A. Trevena	7.11	25/1
Sky Call	J. W. Pengilly	W. A. Smith	7.6	12/1
Gay Icarus	C. L. Beechey	H. White	7.12	8/1
Shorengro	M. L. Willmott	P. Hyland	9.4	7/1
Index	C. A. Wilson	A. McLean	9.0	66/1
Tavel	J. B. Cummings	R. Ball	9.0	66/1
Eastern Court	M. D. Appleton	J. Stocker	7.11	9/1

All started

ABDUL .... he might have beaten only the "B-Grade" team, but Paul Jarman makes sure he had no let up as he rides him out strongly to the line. – Picture: HWT

Caulfield. Subsequent to that, she dead-heated for first with Arctic Symbol in the Caulfield Stakes and was then a disappointing eighth in the Caulfield Cup.

Punters were prepared to take her on trust once more, making her a firm 7/4 favorite, with the next in favor being Gay Icarus, who had finished second in the Moonee Valley Stakes before winning the 1800m Burwood Handicap at Caulfield. At that stage, Gay Icarus was simply a three-year-old with staying potential – which was realised the following season when his wins included the Caulfield Cup, Caulfield Stakes and Underwood Stakes. The only other runner under double figures with bookmakers was the Adelaide three-year-old Eastern Court, who had beaten Gay Icarus in the Moonee Valley Stakes and was then second behind Dual Choice in the Caulfield Guineas.

Completely overlooked in the betting was one of the most consistent runners, albeit his form was in weaker races. Three-year-old colt Abdul, prepared by Geoff Murphy, had scored three wins on end against his own age. The victories included one over 1400m at Caulfield and another over the same trip at Sandown before he was fourth in the Caulfield Guineas. Quite apart from the rise in class, the distance was also a big query. As a result, Abdul was "friendless" in the betting, drifting from an opening quote of 20/1 to 33/1.

While punters at large ignored Abdul's chances, Murphy was not shocked when the gelding ran the race of his life to score in Australia's greatest weight-for-age race by three lengths from the veteran Tails, with outsider Rough 'N Tumble third.

Ridden a heady race by Paul Jarman, Abdul was taken to the front 500m from home and shot clear while other jockeys were waiting for breaks which were not forthcoming. Caught napping, other riders had no chance of making up the leeway, and it was a procession for the outsider over the final 200m.

Tails, who had finished only 15th in the Caulfield Cup, made up good ground, gaining an inside run over the final stages, while Rough 'N Tumble also finished stoutly, his chances being hampered after he received a check at the 1000m.

As predicted, some of the best horses missed the Cox Plate that year, as was proven during the VRC Carnival. Silver Sharpe, who had been reserved for the Victoria Derby instead of the Plate, won the Classic; Baghdad Note who was home in his stall on Plate day took the Melbourne Cup; and Voleur won the Mackinnon Stakes to start favorite (but finish sixth) in the Melbourne Cup.

1971 — 'BUSHIE' SHOWS THE CITY SLICKERS

To live the dream is what inspires people to go racing and, as they drove back down the Glenelg Highway to Dunkeld, nestling in the southernmost shadow of the Grampians about 260 km west of Melbourne, trainer Bob Agnew and Tauto's owner Eric Remfry reckoned only the sky was the limit.

Bob Agnew only ever trained one good horse, but it was good enough to write him into the record books and put the tiny Victorian Western District town of Dunkeld on the map.

Tauto was one of those horses that fuels the dreams of anyone and everyone who has ever had anything to do with a thoroughbred. Nothing to look at, no breeding to speak of, trained in the bush by a little-known trainer, Tauto was barely sighted as a young horse. His first win came in a Maiden at Bendigo, and he didn't emerge as a horse of any consequence until he was five years old.

But, over four seasons, this son of Good Brandy proved more than competitive in the best of company from 1400m to 2000m, at a time when some very smart horses graced the Australian turf. Tauto quickly graduated into city company and, in the 1970 Newmarket Handicap at Flemington, indicated he might be something better than just ordinary, by finishing a gallant second behind brilliant Sydney sprinter Black Onyx.

To live the dream is what inspires people to go racing and, as they drove back down the Glenelg Highway to Dunkeld, nestling in the southernmost shadow of the Grampians about 260 km west of Melbourne, Agnew and Tauto's owner Eric Remfry reckoned only the sky was the limit.

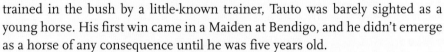

They waited only a few short months to find out that indeed it was. Tauto drew the services of Mick Mallyon in the 1970 Invitation Stakes (now Vic Health Cup) at Caulfield, and flew home to beat Regal Vista. Less than three weeks later he returned to Caulfield and proved he was no Group 1 flash-in-the-pan, by winning the Toorak Handicap.

Tauto won only one more race that season, but it was a significant one. Having his first real test beyond 1600m, Tauto tackled the Cox Plate distance (2040m) in the Alister Clark Stakes at Moonee Valley late in March, 1971, and beat a high class field that included the previous year's Cox Plate winner, three-year-old colt Abdul, who finished third.

1971
(Saturday, October 23. Attendance: 37,450)

· $30,000 plus $600 Trophy Weight for Age 1¼ miles

1.	TAUTO	R. M. Agnew	9.4	*L. Hill*	12/1
2.	Igloo	A. E. Didham	9.0	*E. Didham*	11/4f
3.	Beau Sovereign	G. T. Murphy	7.11	*A. Trevena*	8/1

Winning details

Margin: ½ len x 1¾ len. Time: 2:03.9 13 started.

Breeding: Good Brandy – San Patricia – Dacian (b or br g 6) Owner: E. Remfry

Winner's Colors: Grey, red & blue diamond

Winning Numbers: 8, 10, 12 Barriers: 4, 5, 11

ALSO RAN

Gunsynd	T. J. Smith	R. Higgins	9.0	5/1
Rajah Sahib	P. J. Hayes	R. Mallyon	9.4	9/2
Tails	P. J. Murray	G. Howard	9.4	15/1
Classic Mission	S. A. Brown	R. Quinton	7.11	9/2
Silver Knight	S. A. Brown	H. White	9.0	16/1
Crown Law	S. A. Brown	B. Gilders	9.4	33/1
Royal Shah	T. J. Smith	R. Setches	9.4	66/1
Haarle	G. M. Hanlon	S. Aitken	7.11	16/1
Not Again	M. E. Ritchie	F. Reys	9.4	33/1
Gallic Temple	A. Ward	R. J. Hall	9.4	200/1

Scratched: Big Philou

That win sowed in Agnew's mind the seeds of a Spring campaign that would centre around the Cox Plate. Tauto made his seasonal debut at Sandown in late August, in the 1400m Liston Stakes. His performance signalled that, if anything, the now six-year-old was better than ever.

He powered home to win, in the process beating Tolerance, the Blue Diamond Stakes winner from the previous season. Tauto's next trip to town was for the Craiglee Stakes at Flemington, and a clash with Caulfield Cup favorite Gay Icarus, and the outstanding mare Dual Choice.

Those who happened to see Tauto unloaded from Agnew's two-horse float might have wondered at his travelling companion, a pony called Patch. Agnew explained how Patch played a big part in keeping Tauto calm both during the long float trip and at the course.

Calm or not, Tauto was no match for Dual Choice. The mare produced a quite extraordinary display of sustained speed to lead throughout in a time that was within a second of the Flemington (and Australian) record for 1600m. Tauto tried valiantly to get on terms with Dual Choice at the 400m but could not reel her in, although he finished clear second, more than two lengths ahead of Gay Icarus.

The form from the Craiglee proved decisive at the Caulfield Show Day meeting and, when Gay Icarus won the Underwood Stakes, it could have been expected Tauto would be a short-priced favorite to win his second successive Invitation Stakes. Quite likely his weight of 62kg proved something of a deterrent, and he went to the post a 4-1 chance, with the South Australian mare Tango Miss the 11-4 favorite.

Those who stuck with the Dunkeld champ reaped a fine reward when he unwound a powerful run from the 400m mark to win clearly. That back-to-back success completed, Tauto then attempted to emulate his 1970 success in the Toorak Handicap. He ran a game race under another big weight, 61kg, but found a couple too good for him. The winner was Gunsynd, the "Goondiwindi Grey", who the previous Saturday had won the Epsom Handicap at Randwick.

The field for the 1971 Cox plate lacked neither for quality nor quantity. Kiwi galloper Igloo was the favorite on the strength of wins in both the Turnbull Stakes and the Coongy Handicap, and a last start second in the Caulfield Cup.

Cup winner Gay Icarus was there, along with Gunsynd and, heading a strong three-year-old contingent, the Caulfield Guineas winner, Beau Sovereign. Also in the field were the subsequent Melbourne Cup winner Silver Knight, and Classic Mission, who was to win the Victoria Derby a week later.

Tauto was to be ridden by Pat Hyland, no stranger to big-race riding given he'd been associated with the champion sprinter-miler Vain a couple of years earlier. As fate would have it, Hyland suffered a fall in the first race on the Cox Plate program, and was lying in hospital with a broken left foot when the Cox Plate was run.

Queensland jockey Len Hill, trying his luck in Melbourne but ironically sidelined soon after he arrived with a broken foot, gained the last minute ride on Tauto and rode a gem of a race.

Agnew reasoned there was every chance Tauto would pull hard if restrained early, so he instructed Hill to lead if nothing else wanted to.

Outsider Crown Law led from the barrier, but Tauto was soon pulling Hill's arms from their sockets, so he let the gelding stride into the lead. To lead and win a Cox Plate is difficult; to pull hard as well, makes it almost impossible – which is why Tauto's win was very special.

The pace was strong, which should have set the race up for something to come late. Surprisingly though, the only real challenge came from Igloo, who, after enjoying a perfect run on the rails, moved out to pressure Tauto strongly from the 400m mark. He was entitled to run past him, but every time he raised the bar, so did Tauto, to the extent the three-quarter length margin at the finish would have been no less even had the race been a bit further. Hill was so exhausted afterwards he couldn't unsaddle the winner. Agnew was only too happy to do the honors.

The battler from the bush had prevailed over the cream of Australian racing; it was a moment to savor.

1972 — GUNSYND WAS ALWAYS CROWD FAVORITE

In his time, the greatest stakes-winner in Australian racing history, Gunsynd won from 1200m to 2500m, ran third in a Melbourne Cup and third in a Caulfield Cup, and had more than 41,000 racegoers agog with joy – some were literally crying – the day he won the 1972 Cox Plate.

A horse who has a song written about him, a four metre high statue dedicated to him and upon his death provoked hundreds of bereavement cards, must have been some horse.

Not since Phar Lap has a thoroughbred so fired the imagination of the Australian racing public as did Gunsynd, the "Goondiwindi Grey", in the early 1970's.

A handsome grey, he captured the hearts of racegoers with his amazing will to win, and almost human personality. His owners bought him for just $1,300 and by the time he was retired to stud Gunsynd had earned them more than $500,000 in stakemoney and stud sale fees.

He was by the moderately successful sire Sunset Hue, out of a mare named Woodie Wonder, a twin, who as a racehorse was described by her owner as "the slowest mare I have ever seen".

So much for breeding!

In his time, the greatest stakes-winner in Australian racing history, Gunsynd won from 1200m to 2500m, ran third in a Melbourne Cup and third in a Caulfield Cup, and had more than 41,000 racegoers agog with joy – some were literally crying – the day he won the 1972 Cox Plate.

And boy, did he love a crowd. Jockey Roy Higgins remains adamant Gunsynd knew exactly what was going on, and who was the star of the show.

"The year he won the Cox Plate, when he went on to the track the public address system wasn't working," Higgins recalled.

"He went five yards, stopped, and looked up into the grandstand. I couldn't get him moving.

"Then the announcer came on and mentioned 'the great Gunsynd', and the applause started. He gave an almighty flourish and off he trotted," Higgins said. "He knew, alright."

Owned by a publican, a newsagent, a retired bookie and a grazier, all from the NSW town of Goondiwindi, Gunsynd was originally trained in Brisbane by Bill Wehlow, who broke him in and won 10 races with him.

His wins included the 1970 Chelmsford Stakes

1972
(Saturday, October 28. Attendance: 41,720)

$45,000 plus $600 Trophy Weight for Age 2,000 metres

1.	**GUNSYND**	T. J. Smith	59kg	*R. Higgins*	6/4f
2.	**All Shot**	I. Saunders	57kg	*E. Sellars*	4/1
3.	**Magnifique**	E. Temperton	54.5kg	*R. B. Marsh*	33/1

Winning details

Margin: ¾ len x len. **Time:** 2:01.9 14 started.

Breeding: Sunset Hue – Woodie Wonder – Newton Wonder (gr h 5)
Owner: A. Bishop, G. McMicking, A. Pippos & J. Coorey

Winner's Colors: Purple and white halves, purple cap

Winning Numbers: 1, 7, 10 **Barriers:** 13, 8, 7

ALSO RAN

Longfella	G. T. Murphy	A. Trevena	49.5	3/1
Altai Khan	T. J. Hughes	R. Mallyon	57	50/1
Gay Icarus	C. L. Beechey	J. Miller	59	8/1
The Fixer	T. J. Smith	T. Fraser	49.5	80/1
Gold Brick	T. A. Kennedy	S. Aitken	49.5	20/1
Tauto	R. M. Agnew	P. Jarman	59	33/1
Jan's Beau	T. J. Hughes	G. Edge	59	33/1
Triton	S. A. Brown	H. White	59	16/1
Abdul	A. Armansco	P. Hyland	59	66/1
Oncide	H. G. Heagney	L. Hill	49.5	100/1
Turbino	P. G. Wadham	E. Didham	57	100/1

All started

GUNSYND ... the popular "showpony" who eclipsed Tulloch's stakes record in winning the Cox Plate. – Picture: HWT

and the 1971 Rawson Stakes, and he also contested class races such as the Golden Slipper Stakes (6th behind Baguette in 1970), the AJC Derby (3rd to Silver Sharpe in 1970) and the Victoria Derby (unplaced behind Silver Sharpe in 1970).

But in September, 1971, Gunsynd was transferred into the all-conquering stables of Tommy Smith, and subsequently became a legend. Versatile as he was, the 1600m journey was his specialty. Possessed of an electric finishing burst, he mowed down and beat quality opposition in Australia's biggest "mile" handicaps – in 1971 the Epsom, Toorak and George Adams, and in 1972 the Doncaster.

Ironically, when Gunsynd lined up a week later for the 1972 Cox Plate, success in the race for the grey meant he would usurp the great Tulloch as Australia's greatest stakeswinner.

In the week leading up to the race all of the publicity centred upon the "Goondiwindi Grey", to such an extent even Higgins, the ultimate professional, began to feel the pressure.

"I felt a tremendous sense of responsibility," he said, "knowing what it would mean to that great horse's career if I did something wrong."

But even when he wasn't winning, he was forever giving his all, and it was this never-say-die attitude, often under huge weights, that added to his extraordinary aura.

For instance, in the Spring of 1971, he followed his Epsom Handicap win with starts over a variety of distances that included a fourth in the 2400m Caulfield Cup behind Gay Icarus, seventh in the 2040m Cox Plate behind Tauto, and a scintillating win in the 1600m George Adams.

As if to prove he could do anything that was asked of him, the extraordinary galloper came out a week later and won the 2400m Sandown Cup.

Before going to Sydney to win the 1972 Doncaster, Gunsynd won the Queen's Plate over 2000m and the Queen Elizabeth Stakes over 2400m, both at Flemington. Then, straight after the Doncaster, he was far from disgraced in finishing fifth in the Sydney Cup.

Such was the power of his racecourse performances, Gunsynd, although unfashionably bred, was considered hot property from a breeding angle and late in September he was sold for more than $270,000 to a syndicate of breeders to stand the 1973 season at Kia Ora Stud in the Hunter Valley. A condition of the sale was that he continue to race in his original ownership until after the 1973 Sydney Autumn Carnival.

Gunsynd's quest for the Cox Plate began as a three-year-old in 1970, when he ran seventh behind Abdul, to be followed by his fourth in the 1971 renewal of the championship.

In his lead-up to the 1972 Cox Plate, Gunsynd indicated that while his days as Australia's best "miler" were perhaps numbered – his colors were lowered by Triton in the Epsom – his ability to stay, perhaps had strengthened. He beat Triton in the Hill Stakes at Rosehill over 1750m just before the Epsom, and immediately after won the Colin Stephen Stakes over 2400m at Randwick.

Roy Higgins, who'd passed up the opportunity to ride Gunsynd in his Sydney campaign, was reunited with his old mate in the Caulfield Stakes, which he duly won. That same day an outstanding three-year-old, Sobar, trounced his rivals in the Caulfield Guineas.

The following week the pair met in the Caulfield Cup. Gunsynd, with 62kg, was always going to struggle to give a 14kg start to a brilliant colt such as Sobar – he had only 48kg – but, as the younger horse charged home an easy winner, the gallant grey never stopped trying back in third place.

Ironically, when Gunsynd lined up a week later for the 1972 Cox Plate, success in the race for the grey meant he would go past Tommy Smith's favorite, Tulloch, as Australia's greatest stakeswinner. And whoever won would create their own slice of history, for it was to be the first time the Cox Plate was run over the metric distance of 2040m.

The field of 14 included two former Cox Plate winners, Tauto and Abdul, but it was felt Gunsynd's main opposition would come from All Shot, a strong-finishing galloper trained by Ian Saunders; the previous year's Caulfield Cup winner Gay Icarus; and the classy three-year-old Longfella, trained by Geoff Murphy.

Not that there was ever any doubt Gunsynd would start favorite, which he did at 6-4 despite drawing barrier 13, one from the outside. Rather than risk being caught wide, jockey Roy Higgins elected to restrain the grey from barrier rise, and crossed over to be in about 10th place running down the hill towards the 1400m. New Zealand visitor Turbino led at this stage from Tauto, with Longfella tucked away on the fence, Gay Icarus mid-field, and All Shot back behind Gunsynd near the tail of the field.

Coming off the turn at the 800m, Higgins found an opening and set Gunsynd alight, getting him to the outside to begin a long, sweeping run towards the leaders. Past the 500m, by the famous landmark "the school," Longfella had dashed through to lead but Gunsynd was closing fast on the outside, and shadowing him was All Shot.

Gunsynd headed Longfella turning into the straight but he was under the whip, and for a few strides it seemed inevitable the powerful finish of All Shot would overwhelm the favorite. But as always, Gunsynd was not only grey, he was also great, and when Higgins asked him to dig deep, he responded as only champions do. At the post he was safely holding All Shot, with the New Zealand staying mare Magnifique running on into the minor placing.

All Shot's rider Ernie Sellers best summed it up when he said: "I thought I had him turning for home, but he just kept finding more and more. He is one of the all-time greats."

Ten days later Gunsynd stepped out in the Melbourne Cup. He didn't win it but as always he gave it his best shot, defying his breeding in that long slog up the Flemington straight to cling onto third place behind the Tasmanian-owned outsider Piping Lane and the favorite Magnifique.

Gunsynd bowed out of racing the following Autumn, but not before winning weight-for-age races in both Melbourne and Sydney.

Thousands flocked to Flemington in mid-March to farewell him and he didn't let them down, winning the Queen Elizabeth Stakes then acting the showman as speeches made in his honor compared him to the idols of old – Carbine, Phar Lap and Tulloch.

In his final appearance, he finished a gallant second behind New Zealand star Apollo Eleven in the Queen Elizabeth Stakes over 2400m at Randwick in April.

Even then his adoring public could not let go of him. More than 5,000 turned up to see him paraded on the racetrack at Goondiwindi, which for days was bedecked in his familiar purple and white colors.

Soon after his arrival at Kia Ora Stud, people came in droves, uninvited, just to stare at him over the fence. Eventually they had to erect a sign, *"Strictly No Visitors"*, just to get some work done.

Gunsynd was only of moderate success at stud, before having to be put down in 1983. But it mattered not to the legend. "The Goondiwindi Grey" will be remembered forever in racing's history books, and in the minds of those fortunate enough to see him.

1973 — BART BREAKS HIS PLATE "DUCK"

In the week leading up to the 1973 Cox Plate, it became apparent that the main thrust would come from the strong three-year-old entry, headed by Caulfield Guineas winner Grand Cidium.

A three-year-old won it, but it wasn't Grand Cidium. He in fact was a surprise scratching on the morning of the race. The winner was a colt who later in 1973 was described by no lesser authority than the racing correspondent of *The Times* in England as the greatest three-year-old in the world.

A bold statement to be sure, but, when Taj Rossi, trained by Bart Cummings, defeated Caulfield Cup winner Swell Time in a Cox Plate to remember, he began a stretch of wins that demonstrated a versatility only great horses possess.

He was tough too, for he raced without a proper break from early June until mid-November, and won over distances ranging from 1200 to 2500m. Owned by Mr. and Mrs. Vic Peters, Taj Rossi was by one of Australia's best sprinting sires Matrice, out of the Star Kingdom mare Dark Queen, a bloodline that helps explain his versatility.

Cummings bought the colt "on spec" at the 1971 Adelaide yearling sales but it wasn't until three months later he found an owner for him, after a chance meeting with Peters on a Melbourne to Adelaide flight. A similar chance meeting with Cummings 11 years earlier led to Peters racing Fulmen, who won both the Adelaide and Brisbane Cups.

Taj Rossi made a winning debut at Flemington in June, 1973, scoring by a short half head over 1000m, and followed up less than two weeks later with a very easy win over 1400m at Sandown, significantly perhaps on a heavy track.

After a short let-up, Taj Rossi resumed in a three-year-old race over 1200m at Moonee Valley on Freeway Stakes day, and ran home strongly into third place, but three weeks later started at 12-1 in the first of the Spring's top three-year-old races, the Ascot Vale Stakes. He gave a start and a beating to the two favorites, New Gleam and Sincere Pride, and two weeks later was kept up to the mark with a run over 1400m at Caulfield, and won carrying 61kg.

On the same day at Rosehill in Sydney, Grand Cidium won the Hill Stakes, and Analie won the STC Cup. Both those

> **BART CUMMINGS ...** bought Taj Rossi "on spec" at the 1971 Adelaide yearling sales but it wasn't until three months later he found an owner for him, after a chance meeting with Vic Peters on a Melbourne to Adelaide flight. A similar chance meeting with Cummings 11 years earlier led to Peters racing Fulmen, who won both the Adelaide and Brisbane Cups.

1973
(Saturday, October 27. Attendance: 35,300)

$75,000 plus $600 Trophy Weight for Age About 2,000 metres

1.	**TAJ ROSSI**	J. B. Cummings	49.5kg	*S. Aitken*	7/1
2.	**Swell Time**	W. C. Winder	54.5kg	*D. Peake*	16/1
3.	**Zambari**	T. J. Smith	59kg	*R. McCarthy*	8/1

Winning details

Margin: Hd x 5 len. **Time:** 2:08.3 12 started.

Breeding: Matrice – Dark Queen – Coronation Boy (b c 3) **Owner:** Mr & Mrs V. Peters

Winner's Colors: White, brown rings

Winning Numbers: 13, 9, 3 **Barriers:** 2, 8, 5

ALSO RAN

Glengowan	J. W. Harris	N. Harris	59	9/2
Craig Win	S. A. Brown	J. Stocker	49.5	25/1
All Shot	I. Saunders	R. Higgins	59	10/1
Young Ida	E. Temperton	H. Rauhihi	56.5	4/1f
Strike Again	W. Winder	R. Skelton	59	7/1
Leica Lover	J. B. Cummings	F. Reys	49.5	12/1
Millefleurs	D. Judd	B. Gilders	54.5	50.1
Magnifique	E. Temperton	B. F. Andrews	56.5	12/1
Analie	T. J. Smith	H. White	54.5	10/1

Scratched: Sobar

SWELL TIME

TAJ ROSSI

horses at that stage were on a collision course with Taj Rossi for the Cox Plate. The following weekend the three-year-olds were again on centre stage, both in Melbourne and in Sydney.

In his sixth start since his winning debut in June, Taj Rossi was decisive in beating Purple Patch over the 1600m of the Moonee Valley Stakes. Just a few minutes earlier, at Randwick, a spine-tingling finish to the AJC Derby saw Imagele just beat Leica Lover and Grand Cidium in a three-way photo, with star New Zealand colt Craig Win not far behind them.

Two weeks before the Cox Plate, on Caulfield Guineas day, racegoers in essence were treated to a couple of Cox Plate previews, in the Guineas itself and also in the Caulfield Stakes. An injured Leica Lover was absent from the Guineas, but the AJC Derby form held up when Grand Cidium gained his revenge over Imagele in no uncertain manner. Beaten into fourth place was Taj Rossi, leaving many with the belief that, good as he might be, the Cumming's trained colt wasn't quite up to the class of the first two.

Some 40 minutes earlier, top New Zealand stayer Glengowan beat All Shot by a half head in the Caulfield Stakes, with Sobar and Magnifique following them home. Among those unplaced was the Kiwi mare Swell Time, but a week later she came out on a bog track to beat Gala Supreme in the Caulfield Cup. She was well backed in that race, not just because of her ability to handle the wet, but also because she'd finally recovered from a deep seated stone bruise, a condition which hadn't been made public.

A series of events leading up to the Cox Plate certainly helped make Taj Rossi's winning task easier, not the least being the shock scratching of Grand Cidium on race morning, the earlier withdrawal of Sobar, and the overnight rain that gave the Cummings colt conditions he revelled in.

The ride was taken by leading apprentice Stan Aitken, who was instructed by Cummings to let the colt settle back in the field, tactics which flew in the face of doubts Taj Rossi would not stay the 2000m plus trip.

The possibility of him getting a soft run was erased shortly after the start when stablemate Leica Lover surged to the front and proceeded to set a strong gallop. At one stage, he had the Cox Plate field strung out over 20 lengths or more, and with less than 600m to travel still held a five length margin over his rivals.

His race was run at the top of the straight as Swell Time swept past him, but at the same time Aitken brought Taj Rossi up to challenge the Caulfield Cup winner. The pair settled down to a slogging dual, first one then the other appearing to have the upper hand. In the final strides though Taj Rossi, aided by a 5kg pull in the weights, gained the ascendancy to win by a head.

As good a win as it was, some still held doubts as to Taj Rossi's true ability, but they began to fade a week later when he outstayed Leica Lover to win the Victoria Derby. They were erased completely a further week on, when the colt returned to Flemington, stepped back in distance and confronted some serious "milers" in the George Adams (now Salinger) Handicap over 1600m.

Seemingly giving his rivals an impossible start, with 400m to run Taj Rossi unleashed an awesome finishing burst to win running over the top of the likes of Millefleurs and Toltrice. Thus it was almost a formality when, a further seven days on, he stepped out in the Sandown Guineas. Almost a formality? He won in a canter by five lengths.

It's arguable, but the gentleman from *The Times* might have been right.

1974 – HE ALWAYS PUT UP A GOOD BATTLE

Gary Willetts cannot put an exact time on it, but he can still recall one day getting a phone call from close friend Tim Douglas asking him to come to his Waikato farm and ride a couple of horses.

Willetts, then one of New Zealand's leading riders, jumped up on a lovely, long-barrelled youngster just turned three. A nice horse, Willetts thought. As they were riding over the hills, Douglas turned to Willetts and said, "That's the best horse you'll ever throw a leg over."

As it turned out, Douglas, a former captain of New Zealand's polo team and one of the country's finest horsemen, was wrong, but only just.

In a career spanning more than 30 years, the best horse Willetts rode was champion sprinter Manikato. But, he says, a kind-natured, iron-willed gelding named Battle Heights comes a very close second.

Interestingly, both were geldings who enjoyed long racetrack careers that earned them the respect and the affection of the racing public. Also, they are particularly remembered for their Moonee Valley performances, Battle Heights for his win in the 1974 Cox Plate, and Manikato for a host of weight-for-age wins at the track, including five straight in the William Reid (now Australia) Stakes.

Tim Douglas, it seems, was destined to own and train Battle Heights. He bought Battle Heights' dam, Wuthering Heights, as a polo pony for less than $300 and later, when she'd already proven herself to be a successful producer, lent her to Matamata studmaster Bill Brown to be mated with Battle Waggon.

Douglas then turned around and bought the resulting foal at auction for little more than $200, and called him Battle Heights. It could be said the gelding came to greatness gradually. He won his first race, a Maiden at Rotorua, as a three-year-old, but as a rising six-year-old in July, 1973, his eight wins from 45 starts included nothing of note.

In September that year,

> Willetts, then one of New Zealand's leading riders, jumped up on a lovely, long-barrelled youngster just turned three. A nice horse, Willetts thought. As they were riding over the hills, trainer Tim Douglas turned to Willetts and said, "That's the best horse you'll ever throw a leg over."

1974
(Saturday, October 26. Attendance: 41,360)

$75,000 plus $600 Trophy Weight for Age 2,050m

1.	**BATTLE HEIGHTS**	R. Douglas	59kg	G. Willetts	7/1
2.	**Taras Bulba**	G. M. Hanlon	49.5kg	J. Stocker	5/2f
3.	**Bellota**	R. J. Campbell	54.5kg	S. Aitken	20/1

Winning details

Margin: 1½ len x hd. **Time:** 2:09.9 13 started.

Breeding: Battle Waggon – Wuthering Heights – Avocat General (br g 7)
Owner: Mr & Mrs R. Douglas

Winner's Colors: Purple, gold spots, red sleeves, gold cap

Winning Numbers: 1, 12, 10 **Barriers:** 5, 6, 3

ALSO RAN

Igloo	T. J. Smith	R. Dawkins	59	14/1
Kenmark	J. B. Cummings	H. White	49.5	6/1
Go Fun	P. J. Murray	G. Howard	59	25/1
Passetruel	T. J. Smith	K. Langby	59	25/1
Oopik	D. J. O'Sullivan	E. Didham	57	6/1
Chelsea Tower	E. Temperton	N. Harris	59	16/1
Pyramul	F. J. Penfold	B. Gilders	49.5	10/1
Gala Red	B. M. Ryan	M. Goreham	59	140/1
Plush	J. J. Moloney	P. Hyland	49.5	7/1
Citadel	N. Kelly	R. Setches	59	9/1

Scratched: Leica Lover

BATTLE HEIGHTS ... the $200 yearling became the weight-for-age champion of Australasia with this emphatic win in 1974. – Picture: HWT

he won the Spring Handicap over 2200m at Ellerslie but then was unplaced in eight starts before lining up in the Auckland Cup on New Years Day, 1974.

He didn't win it but his second to Rose Mellay, incidentally a runaway winner, seemed to awaken the ability that had been slumbering, and two starts later Battle Heights secured his first Group 1 success, in the 3200m Wellington Cup.

The six year old survived a protest, but his rider Alvin Tweedie was less fortunate. His riding of the winner earned him a suspension, and prompted Douglas to approach Willetts with a view to riding Battle Heights in future engagements.

At his very next start, with Willetts up, Battle Heights notched his first weight-for-age victory, in the Trentham Stakes. It was the beginning of a long and highly successful partnership. Taken to Sydney for the Autumn Carnival, Battle Heights immediately came down with a heel infection and ran moderately at his first Australian start, in the Autumn Stakes won by Igloo.

Douglas worked night and day to get the gelding right for the Sydney Cup, but as the rain tumbled down at Randwick on Cup day his only instructions to Willetts were, "don't kill him". He didn't have to. So confident was Willetts, that early in the straight he allowed Grand Scale to run a half length past him topping the rise before giving Battle Heights full rein and urging him to a convincing win. If that wasn't enough to convince racegoers of his ability, Battle Heights returned to Randwick two weeks later for the postponed running of the Queen Elizabeth Stakes, and put paid to the likes of Dayana and Igloo.

After a well-earned rest back home in New Zealand, Battle Heights returned to Sydney to begin what proved to be a gruelling Spring campaign. His immediate mission was the Metropolitan Handicap at Randwick but, after performing well in two lead-up races, the gelding was never sighted in the Group 1 staying test and finished 13th. "It was a shocker," says Willetts. "He never felt right at any stage, yet afterwards we could find nothing wrong with him."

Five days later, Battle Heights redeemed himself to some extent by finishing second to Leica Lover in the 2000m Craven Plate, at least giving Douglas and Willetts some cause for hope in the Cox Plate two weeks hence.

Battle Heights in fact enjoyed a problem-free lead up to the race, and taken to

> Misfortune of a different kind struck the following day. Riding at Geelong, Willetts fell from Kiwi stayer Marinoto in the Geelong Cup, suffering facial cuts and, more seriously, a wrist injury. Only Willetts knew the extent of the injury but he managed to play it down and was able to pass a fitness test on the eve of the Cox Plate, despite being in constant pain.

Moonee Valley on the Tuesday before the race produced a solid gallop that thrilled his connections. Misfortune of a different kind struck the following day. Riding at Geelong, Willetts fell from Kiwi stayer Marinoto in the Geelong Cup, suffering facial cuts and, more seriously, a wrist injury.

Only Willetts knew the extent of the injury but he managed to play it down and was able to pass a fitness test on the eve of the Cox Plate, despite being in constant pain.

Not so lucky was Battle Heights' conqueror in the Craven Plate, Leica Lover, who was scratched on race morning having failed to recover from a minor hoof injury. It robbed the race of a genuine chance, but still the opposition was formidable. Proven weight-for-age performer Igloo was there, along with Metropolitan Handicap winner Passetreul, plus a couple more high-class gallopers from New Zealand, Oopik and Chelsea Tower.

Heading the three-year-old challenge was the Rosehill Guineas and AJC Derby winner Taras Bulba, along with Caulfield Guineas hero Kenmark and Moonee Valley Stakes winner Plush.

Although the track on raceday was rated slow, the going was probably closer to dead (a track description that did not exist then) which probably explains why Taras Bulba, a notable failure on soft tracks, started favorite at 5-2. It may also explain why there was a sizeable plunge on the Cummings-trained Kenmark, another with a preference for firm ground.

Despite the fact he was having his first ride at Moonee Valley – in fact it was his first ride in Melbourne – Willetts was confident about the prospects of Battle Heights, and his determination to win on the gelding doubled after the running of the race prior to the Cox Plate, the Moonee Valley Cup won by Lord Metric.

He'd ridden that horse in the Caulfield Cup and could have ridden him again but, because of the injury to his wrist, he had knocked back all rides on the day other than Battle Heights.

Determined to be patient and be guided by the pace of the race, Willetts found himself back near last as the field raced away from the stands, led by Plush but with several others pushing towards the front. Epsom Handicap winner Citadel went up to challenge Plush at the halfway mark to keep the pace on, and 400m later, despite still being near the back of the field, Willetts was growing in confidence.

"He was going so well. I knew if I could get on the back of something to take me into the race he would finish all over them," he said.

That "something" proved to be Taras Bulba. As he rushed towards the leaders approaching the turn, Willetts and Battle Heights were right on Taras Bulba's back. There were horses right across the track as the field straightened, with Kenmark just in front but under pressure, Igloo pushing up along the inside, and Taras Bulba claiming them out wide.

In the moment the Derby-winning three-year-old was being acclaimed the winner, Battle Heights pounced upon him, and with Willetts riding confidently, drew clear to win by 1½ lengths. "He won quite easily in the finish. It really was a fantastic performance," Willetts said.

A week later, Battle Heights beat all but the Caulfield Cup-winning mare Leilani in the Mackinnon Stakes, but on the following Tuesday finished down the track in the Melbourne Cup after leading half-way up the straight. Willetts believes the gelding should have won, but blames himself and his injured wrist for Battle heights being beaten. "I just couldn't hold him when I went to go forward before the turn," is his honest assessment.

Battle Heights continued to race in the best company for the next three years, and struck another purple patch in the Spring of 1976, winning the Metropolitan and the Craven Plate, and finishing second to How Now in the Caulfield Cup.

As perhaps a final demonstration of both his durability and his versatility, the gelding won first up over 1100m at Taumarunini just two days short of his 10th birthday. Four months later he broke down during the running of the 1978 Mackinnon Stakes and was retired to Douglas' farm in New Zealand. There he remained a pampered pet for the best part of 21 years, outliving his owner-trainer before being put down just a few months after the death of Douglas in March, 1999.

Manikato might have been the best galloper Willetts rode but, justifiably, there is a special place in his heart for the great Battle Heights.

1975 — HE WENT LIKE FURY IN THE MUD

As much interest as there was in the horse, equally the choice of rider for Fury's Order's Australian campaign was a source of fascination. Baby-faced Brent Thomson was barely 17 when he packed his bags and, in the company of his 6'7" (200cm) mate Paul Harris, headed off to Melbourne to ride in the two biggest races of his fledgling career.

When Fury's Order arrived in Australia from New Zealand in early October, 1975, not a thought was given to him winning the Cox Plate – not even by his trainer.

The rather flashy but still magnificent chestnut had the Melbourne Cup virtually as his one and only mission. A run in the Cox Plate was only to serve the purpose of having him at peak fitness on the first Tuesday in November. He was top-weight in the Cup with 59.5kg, a rating his admirers believed to be recognition of his claim to be the best racehorse in Australasia.

Opinion as to the capabilities of Fury's Order was divided. Writing in *The Australian*, Tony Arrold said there were those who believed the stallion to be the ultimate racing machine. Others, he said, felt he was simply over-rated.

Certainly the five-year-old's record was that of a good, rather than an outstanding horse. The best of his 15 wins was the 1974 New Zealand Cup, a good staying handicap but rated below the Auckland and Wellington Cups, in both of which he was unplaced in early 1975.

As a two-year-old, he won four races in succession and the following year he headed the New Zealand Free handicap for three-year-olds despite being beaten in the Classics. For all of that, he did look an ideal Melbourne Cup horse, which is why, on the eve of him departing for Melbourne, his owner, dairy farmer Les Bridgeman, knocked back a purchase offer of $175,000 made on behalf of a Sydney syndicate.

Fury's Order was trained in partnership by veteran horseman Wally McEwan and former jockey Charlie Gestro. McEwan won the 1954 Brisbane Cup with a horse called Lancaster, "the best horse I ever trained," he said, – although it is likely he changed his mind after the Cox Plate.

As much interest as there was in the horse, equally the choice of rider for Fury's Order's Australian campaign was a source of fascination. Baby-faced Brent Thomson was barely 17 when he packed his bags and, in the company of his 6'7" (200cm) mate Paul Harris, headed off to Melbourne to ride in the two biggest races of his fledgling career.

In New Zealand, the fact he'd already booted home 150 winners led to him being dubbed the "Wanganui Whiz Kid". But

1975

(Saturday, October 25. Attendance: 28,760)

$125,000 plus $600 Trophy Weight for Age 2,050m

1.	FURY'S ORDER	W. McEwan	59kg	B. Thomson	7/1
2.	Kiwi Can	F. R. Beguely	59kg	R. Lang	25/1
3.	Analight	C. L. Beechey	54.5kg	P. Trotter	7/1

Winning details

Margin: ¾ len x 8 len. **Time:** 2:20.4 13 started.

Breeding: Indian Order – Our Fury – Le Filou (ch h 5) **Owner:** L. H. Bridgeman

Winner's Colors: Pale blue, black band, gold cap

Winning Numbers: 1, 2, 8

ALSO RAN

Taras Bulba	G. M. Hanlon	G. Willetts	57	10/1
Wave King	J. H. Hely	M. Baker	59	6/1f
Dalrello	J. J. Atkins	L. Olsen	59	9/1
Our Cavalier	E. A. Bell	D. Messingham	49.5	20/1
Denise's Joy	T. J. Smith	K. Langby	47	12/1
Caboul	A. Lopes	E. Didham	49.5	8/1
Prince Of All	J. B. Cummings	J. Duggan	49.5	20/1
Rafique	J. B. Cummings	H. White	49.5	7/1
Zambari	T. J. Smith	J. Stocker	59	7/1
Plush (pulled up)	J. J. Moloney	P. Hyland	57	8/1

All started

FURY'S ORDER ... his rider Brent Thomson proved his mettle in the mud and the big-time at his Australian debut. – Picture: HWT

hard-nosed Australian racing men still wondered whether a boy had been sent across the Tasman on a man's errand.

Given Fury's Order was stabled at Mornington with ex-Kiwi trainer Theo Howe, McEwan didn't bother taking the horse to trial at Moonee Valley on the Tuesday before the Cox Plate. "Too much traffic," he said.

Thomson of course had never ridden there, so it was a case of first time for both horse and rider when they stepped out onto the track on raceday. And what a day it was. It began raining in the early hours of the morning, and never let up. As the meeting unfolded the track became progressively worse, and by the time of the Cox Plate, was a quagmire.

The previous race, the Moonee Valley Cup, was won by Bart Cummings' young stayer Holiday Waggon, whose time of 3min 04secs, was about 15 seconds slower than the average.

Many jockeys felt the meeting should be called off, but the stewards seemed determined to keep going. At least, it was argued, nothing was in danger of falling over, for the horses were going into the ground almost up to their fetlocks. Visibility though, was practically non-existent.

A field of 13 lined up for the feature race, among the runners the Caulfield Cup winner Analight, Doncaster Handicap winner Dalrello, classy weight-for-age performer Taras Bulba, and another high class New Zealander, Kiwi Can.

Given his ability to handle wet tracks, Fury's Order had plenty of supporters at 7-1. The 6-1 favorite in a wide-open betting race was Liston Stakes winner Wave King, more by virtue of his superior wet track form than for his overall ability.

It was a slog from start to finish. Down the back of the course the runners were barely visible, as Plush led Zambari and Wave King, with Fury's Order, Taras Bulba and Kiwi Can all racing forward.

Plush had had more than enough at the 600m mark and in fact was pulled up. Taras Bulba had gone for home but tracking him were the two Kiwi gallopers, with Kiwi Can looking the stronger of the pair.

At the top of the straight, Kiwi Can headed a struggling Taras Bulba, with Fury's Order out in the middle of the track, and a long gap to Analight. It was then Thomson belied his supposed lack of experience and made a move that won him the race. He angled the big-striding Fury's Order back towards the fence, and halfway up the straight drew level with Kiwi Can. The pair of them slugged it out to the line, but in what was probably slightly better going, Fury's Order forged clear to win by three-quarters of a length. The runners returned to scale, weary and covered in mud.

Dalrello's jockey Larry Olsen had to be assisted to the first aid room, his eyes full of mud. Other riders told of how they had no idea where they were in the race. "I could have been in front, for all I knew," a rider of one of the tailenders commented.

The presentation was a farce. Guest of honor was Princess Margaret, but a red carpet laid out for her to crosss the track to a presentation dais all but disappeared into the mire.

To the surprise of no-one, 15 minutes after the running of the Cox Plate, the remainder of the meeting was cancelled. Top racing scribe, Jack Elliott, made the observation that had it not been Cox Plate day the program would have been ditched after the third race.

The events of the day tended to overshadow what in fact was an immense performance by both Fury's Order and his teenage jockey. It was a moment that called for strength and courage, and the pair were not found wanting in either department.

A shifting track was blamed for the lacklustre form of Fury's Order in the Melbourne Cup, but one suspects he was left with nothing to give after such a torrid run in the Plate.

Fury's Order eventually retired, and in 1977 was bought to stand at Yallambee Stud in Western Victoria. His success as a sire was moderate, to say the least.

1976 – FILLY WAS SURROUNDED WITH TALENT

Good breeding is no guarantee of success on the harsh, no quarter-given confines of the racetrack, but it seems in some bloodlines that success breeds success. On that score, Surround was destined for greatness, if only for the simple fact her family tree fairly groaned with proven performers.

Only three females have won the Cox Plate – and only one of those was a filly. This explains why Surround's win in 1976 holds a special place in the long history of the great race.

It was the crowning glory to a glittering racing career that ranks her firmly on a par with the other two female winners, legendary mares Tranquil Star and Flight. Her outstanding record as a three-year-old suggests there has not been a better filly to grace the Australian turf.

In the Spring of 1976, she remained unbeaten in seven races, beating all ages and all-comers over distances ranging from 1200m to 2500m.

Her three Group 1 successes during that period best illustrate the class of this compact grey filly. In the first of them, the Caulfield Guineas, she took on the best colts and geldings in Australia over 1600m and beat them comprehensively. Two weeks later, in the Cox Plate, Surround was confronted with an outstanding array of equine talent led by the Caulfield Cup winner How Now, but won almost as she liked, defeating fellow three-year-old Unaware by a commanding three lengths.

Surround was not entered for the Victoria Derby – unfortunately perhaps – given she had easily beaten subsequent Derby winner Unaware in the Cox Plate, but there was no betting on her winning the Oaks.

She started a long odds-on favorite for the Classic and was almost contemptuous of her rivals, strolling home to an easy win over her stablemate Savoir, no mean filly herself and the winner of the Thousand Guineas.

Good breeding is no guarantee of success on the harsh, no quarter-given confines of the racetrack, but it seems in some bloodlines success breeds success. On that score, Surround was destined for greatness, if only for the simple fact her family tree fairly groaned with proven performers.

Bred in New Zealand by Ralph Stuart and close friend and fellow breeder

1976

(Saturday, October 23. Attendance: 33,850)

$125,000 plus $2,500 trophies Weight for Age 2,050m

1.	**SURROUND**	G. T. Murphy	47kg	P. Cook	7/2
2.	**Unaware**	C. S. Hayes	49.5kg	E. Didham	16/1
3.	**Better Draw**	O. M. Lynch	54.5kg	G. A. Ryan	10/1

Winning details

Margin: 3 len x 1¼ len. **Time:** 2:04.3 (Course record) 14 started.

Breeding: Sovereign Edition – Micheline – Le Filou (gr f 3) **Owner:** G. T. Murphy, W. L. Betteson, R. Ansell & I. N. McCusker

Winner's Colors: Red, black & white striped sleeves, black cap

Winning Numbers: 14, 12, 10

ALSO RAN

How Now	C. S. Hayes	J. Stocker	54.5	7/4f
Purple Patch	J. Denham	A. Denham (a)	59	12/1
Kiwi Can	F. R. Beguely	R. Lang	59	25/1
Happy Union	W. C. Winder	G. Willetts	57	16/1
Van Der Hum	L. H. Robinson	R. Skelton	59	25/1
Battle Heights	R. Douglas	L. Olsen	59	14/1
Perhaps	C. M. Jillings	B. F. Andrews	56.5	25/1
Elton	G. T. Murphy	P. Trotter	49.5	100/1
Great Lover	T. J. Smith	J. Letts	49.5	10/1
Taras Bulba	T. J. Smith	R. Higgins	59	4/1
Northbridge Lad	A. G. Bentley	A. Matthews (a)	59	25/1

All started

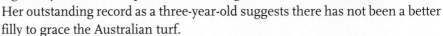

SURROUND ... She was bred to be a champion and here's the proof as she leads the field home in the Cox Plate.
– Picture: HWT

Patrick Hogan – Stuart owned the mare, Hogan the sire nomination -Surround's sire was the highly successful import Sovereign Edition. Her dam, Michelene, by Le Filou, was a daughter of that grand broodmare Dulcie.

To say she came from an outstanding family is an understatement.

Michelene was a sister to outstanding gallopers, Fileur, a classy weight-for-age performer and second to Rain Lover in the 1968 Melbourne Cup; Fulmen, winner of both the Adelaide and Brisbane Cups; and Toorak Handicap winner Gay Filou. Her half-brother, Balmerino, proved an outstanding weight-for-age horse in Australasia before racing in Europe and finishing second to the mighty Alleged in the 1977 Prix de l'Arc de Triomphe.

Given her broodmare potential, Surround was never for sale, but when leading Melbourne trainer Geoff Murphy visited Hogan's Cambridge Stud in late 1974 he was given the pick of any young horse in a paddock-full, and he chose Surround. The following year, Murphy arranged for the filly to be leased for two years to his wife Betty, Isobel McCusker and Ross Ansell, all from Melbourne, and Brisbane clothing manufacturer Lloyd Betteson.

Well-bred horses don't always run fast, but Surround did enough in her early work to suggest that she would be more than competitive, thus she started second favorite for her debut, in the Maribyrnong Trial at Flemington in early October, 1975. She finished a promising third, and three runs later won over 1000m at Caulfield on Boxing Day, then followed up with a win over 1000m at Sandown.

Surround was beaten at her next start, so Murphy, a keen student of the Sovereign Edition breed with which he had exceptional success, decided to bypass the Blue Diamond Stakes and instead gave her a short spell before sending her to Winter in Queensland.

In early June, Surround won a Nursery Handicap at Eagle Farm and was then stepped up into what was her first serious test, the 1600m Marlboro Stakes (now Group 1 Castlemaine Classic).

Given she was attempting 1600m for the first time, and was coming off a 1200m sprint run, she ran an excellent race, beating home all but two very smart colts in Romantic Dream, runner-up in the Golden Slipper Stakes and winner of the QTC Sires Produce, and Family Of Man.

Her connections were thrilled with the performance, but even they could not have envisaged that Surround would not be beaten again that year. Two more Queensland starts yielded wins at Eagle Farm and Doomben, then, after a short let-up, the filly was sent back south to begin her Spring preparation.

She made her Melbourne re-appearance over 1200m in the Ailsa Handicap at Moonee Valley on August 21, and signalled her arrival as a horse of real substance by winning with ridiculous ease.

Those who failed to heed the message had the point rammed home to them two weeks later, in the Group 2 Ascot Vale Stakes at Flemington. Bagalot was favorite but Surround blew him and the rest of the opposition away with a resounding win.

The win confirmed what Murphy at least had always thought, that the kindly grey filly was a horse right out of the top drawer.

Her next start came in the Moonee Valley Stakes, and a return bout with Family Of Man, who'd finished in front of her in the Marlboro Classic during the Winter. This time the colt couldn't get near her, and in fact was beaten for second by Surround's stablemate Savoir, a very good, very game filly who had the misfortune to be pitted against a superstar in her three-year-old year.

Having two such fillies in his stable could have left Murphy with something of a headache trying to keep them apart, and in the end he couldn't. But for the time being he had plenty of options. One of these was to enter Savoir for the Edward Manifold Stakes at Flemington, and keep Surround for the Caulfield Guineas a week later. Savoir made it to Flemington, but not to the race. She was listless on arrival at the track and was subsequently found to have been doped. A man was later charged with the offence and was warned off for life by the VRC.

The episode devastated those associated with the Murphy stable, and it was left to Surround to lift their spirits. A week later, the filly gave the best male three-year-olds in the land a thrashing in the Caulfield Guineas. Among the beaten brigade were Family Of Man and Romantic Dream, a disappointing favorite who was later found to have pulled muscles in his hindquarters.

Surround's win gave Murphy his biggest thrill in 16 years as a trainer, and his delight knew no bounds when, four days later, Savoir bounced back to win the 1000 Guineas. For almost all of her career, Surround had been ridden by Alan Trevena, who'd established a fine rapport with the grey filly. Sadly there was never any chance of him being able to make Surround's Cox Plate weight of 47kg, so lightweight Sydney jockey Peter Cook was called upon to pilot her.

Given her record, Surround would have been a worthy Cox Plate favorite. But the very classy mare How Now had staged a remarkable performance to win the Caulfield Cup the previous Saturday, and she started the popular elect at the somewhat cramped odds of 7-4.

Barrier 10 can sometimes be an awkward draw, particularly at the Valley's 2040m start, but Murphy and Trevena were convinced Surround should be racing right on the pace, and so Cook was instructed to push forward from barrier rise.

The tactic paid a handsome dividend for, at the turn out of the straight, Surround was sitting fourth on the fence behind the pacemaker, Unaware. Not so lucky was How Now, who knuckled over at the start and soon after was badly checked by horses crossing from the outside, to be near last as the field streamed down the hill towards the 1400m mark.

From that point on the only question was whether Surround was good enough to beat her fellow three-year-olds and the older horses in Australia's best weight-for-age test, for no horse had enjoyed a better run in the race. Unaware, ridden by Midge Didham, carried the field along at a good clip but while horses such as Taras Bulba and How Now were doing it hard, the grey filly coasted on the back of the leader. Cook's only anxious moment came near the 500m when for a few strides it seemed as though he might get caught in a pocket. But as Taras Bulba dropped off, the gap appeared and Surround quickly dashed through to go up and challenge Unaware at the entrance to the straight.

It was all over in a twinkling. Surround dashed away with a winning break, and nothing was good enough to challenge her. Unware fought bravely to hold second place ahead of Better Draw, and How Now ran on strongly and probably should have finished closer.

But nothing could be taken from the winner, who had become the first filly to win the Cox Plate, and had created a new race record to boot!

When she retired, just over a year later after injuring a tendon, Surround had firmly established herself as arguably Australia's best ever three-year-old filly. Twice she made history, first with her Cox Plate win, then by becoming the first filly to win the VRC, the AJC and the Queensland Oaks.

She won $347,040 in prize money, a then record for a mare in the Southern Hemisphere, and was judged Horse of the Year by both the VRC and the Australian Racing Writers.

The day Surround won the Cox Plate, a 21-year-old golfer described as "a Queensland surfie" was 10 shots clear of the field in a tournament in Adelaide and on the way to his first professional victory.

Greg Norman and Surround. Champions both.

1977 — KEEPING IT IN THE FAMILY

Out beyond the Back o'Burke they still talk about the one that got away – a yearling who was running around in a paddock close by the tiny NSW township of Nevertire, on the edge of the Great Beyond.

One day the youngster was trucked off to the south, bought for $4,000 as part of a package deal by a couple of chaps who had just purchased former US sire Lots Of Man and were scouting the land for his progeny.

The two men were business partners from Victoria, Ray Richards and John Cuthbertson. The horse they "found" went on to become one of the most durable gallopers in Australia, also one of the best. Family Of Man.

He won his first race as a two-year-old at Flemington in the late Spring of 1975 and won his final start, at Pinjarra in Western Australia, in the early Summer of 1980.

In between, he took on some of the best horses to have ever raced in Australia, sometimes beating them, quite often being beaten by them, but rarely giving of anything but his very best.

He was sold to Perth millionaire Robert Holmes a'Court for $300,000 early in 1979 to stand at his Heytesbury Stud south of Perth, but after one season returned to the racetrack amid some controversy.

Family Of Man raced a further 16 times for just one win, but still possessed the will to be competitive at the highest level. His trainer George Hanlon had no hesitation in declaring him the best horse he trained, an accolade that commands respect.

The first inkling Family Of Man might be anything more than a good, average galloper came in the Winter of 1976, in the two-year-old Marlboro Stakes over 1600m at Eagle Farm. Family Of Man finished second behind Romantic Dream, who'd previously been runner-up to Vivarchi in the Golden Slipper Stakes. Third in the Marlboro was a filly called Surround who, in the Spring, was to sweep all before her, Family Of Man included.

Family of Man was placed behind her in both

Family of Man took on some of the best horses to have ever raced in Australia, sometimes beating them, quite often being beaten by them, but rarely giving of anything but his very best.

1977
(Saturday, October 22. Attendance: 34,563)

$147,500 plus $2,500 trophies Weight for Age 2,050m

1.	**FAMILY OF MAN**	G. M. Hanlon	57kg	*B. Thomson*	10/1
2.	**Raffindale**	D. M. Whitney	59kg	*R. Higgins*	3/1
3.	**Vice Regal**	J. W. Campin	57kg	*G. Willetts*	40/1

Winning details

Margin: Long nk x 1 len. **Time:** 2:05.3 14 started.

Breeding: Lots Of Man – Colleen – Karendi (b h 4) **Owner:** R. C. Richards & J. H. Cuthbertson

Winner's Colors: Blue, yellow braces, red armands

Winning Numbers: 5, 1, 6

ALSO RAN

Marceau	T. J. Smith	S. Young (a)	48.5	100/1
Unaware	C. S. Hayes	J. Stocker	57	9/2
Stormy Rex	J. B. Cummings	S. Burridge	48.5	40/1
Belmura Lad	J. B. Cummings	P. Trotter	48.5	50/1
Sir Silver Lad	B. Petley	D. Wyatt	57	6/1
Luskin Star	M. G. Lees	J. Letts	48.5	7/4f
How Now	C. S. Hayes	R. Mallyon	56.5	25/1
Ming Dynasty	J. B. Cummings	H. White	57	20/1
Flirting Prince	T. J. Smith	R. Quinn (a)	48.5	160/1
Lefroy	G. T. Murphy	B. F. Andrews	48.5	50/1
Pelican Point	L. J. Irwin	G. Palmer (a)	48.5	50/1

All started

FAMILY OF MAN ... he toppled the best in the best class and such was the case when he comfortably beat Raffindale in the Cox Plate. – Picture: HWT

the Moonee Valley Stakes and the Caulfield Guineas, but the merit of that form was highlighted when Surround soundly defeated the cream of Australasia's weight-for-age stars in the Cox Plate.

Family Of Man ran third in the Victoria Derby behind Unaware, but taken to Perth in the Summer beat the older horses in the Marlboro Stakes over 1800m before winning the 2400m Australian Derby. And in the Autumn he managed to at least get onto level terms with Surround, dead heating with her in the Alister Clark Stakes.

As has been so often the case with other Cox Plate winners, the race, while on the Spring agenda for Family Of Man, was not his main mission. Winter was still very much in the air when Hanlon declared the Caulfield Cup to be the four-year-old's main Spring target.

His preparation began in early August and struck the right chord from the very beginning. A 12-1 chance for the 1000m Moondah Plate at Caulfield and ridden by Robert Heffernan, the powerful bay sprinted home over the top of his rivals to record an impressive win.

He followed up with a strong second placing in the Freeway Stakes at Moonee Valley, then was a shade disappointing when favorite and second to Wave King in the Memsie Stakes at Caulfield.

Hanlon was unperturbed, and in fact had some cause to celebrate when champion jockey Roy Higgins agreed to ride Family Of Man at his next start, in the Craiglee Stakes at Flemington.

Higgins had always had an option to ride the horse in his Spring campaign, and seemed quite happy with him, despite being beaten by Ming Dynasty. He wasn't quite as chirpy when Family Of Man failed to run a place in the Underwood Stakes at Caulfield behind Denise's Joy – and neither was Hanlon.

Just over two weeks later though, they were smiling again as Family Of Man stormed home to beat Unaware and New Zealand visitor Royal Cadenza in the Caulfield Stakes, the win more than good enough for Higgins to confirm the riding engagement for the Caulfield Cup. Family Of Man didn't run badly in the Cup. Far from it. He ran fourth, beaten perhaps by better stayers in the winner Ming Dynasty, and the placegetters Unaware and Salamander.

Higgins wasn't entirely disappointed, but faced with a choice of mounts in the Cox Plate, elected to ride the imported grey Raffindale, who'd produced an outstanding effort to lead all the way and win the Epsom Handicap in Sydney early in October. As a replacement rider, Hanlon looked no further than 20-year-old Brent

Thomson, who two years earlier, having his first ride in the Cox Plate, left a deep impression by winning the race on Fury's Order.

Neither Family Of Man nor Raffindale started favorite. That honor befell the outstanding colt Luskin Star, winner of the Golden Slipper the previous season and, just two weeks before the Cox Plate, the brilliant winner of the Caulfield Guineas.

The Tuesday before the race, the Luskin Star camp suffered a scare when he nicked a vein in his near foreleg, but this did not deter punters from wagering heavily upon him on race day and he firmed from 9-4 to start a solid 7-4 favorite.

In fact, only four horses in the 14-strong field started at single figure odds, the others being Raffindale at 3-1, Unaware 9-2 and the highly rated New Zealander, Sir Silver Lad, a 6-1 chance.

Family Of Man had good support at 10-1, but there was little money for anything else, including the Liston and Feehan Stakes winner, Vice Regal, who started at 40-1.

Thomson rode a beautiful race. Family Of Man sat fourth or fifth for most of the way, as Vice Regal made the running ahead of Raffindale and Unaware. Luskin Star was ridden out of his extreme outside barrier by John Letts but couldn't cross the field and was forced to settle off the pace.

When the moves came coming off the 800m turn it was Raffindale who was the first to be niggled at, and he looked beaten when Luskin Star raced around him to go after Vice Regal. Then Thomson unleashed Family Of Man, but, as he swept up to the leaders, Raffindale found his second wind and trailed him into the straight. Try as he might though, the grey never really looked likely to peg back Family Of Man.

"Once we were in the straight I knew it would take a top horse to run past him," Thomson commented later. "He really did travel beautifully throughout."

Higgins, while full of praise for the winner – "a super horse at 2000m" – said he felt Raffindale would have won on a bigger track.

"When they sprinted at the 600m it took him a while to wind up," he said.

Family Of Man ran unplaced in the Melbourne Cup at his next start, but after a spell resumed with an eye-catching win in the William Reid Stakes at Moonee Valley in January, 1978.

He beat Unaware in the Queen's Plate at Flemington later that Autumn, but the following Spring produced some truly outstanding form, winning the Craiglee Stakes, the Mackinnon Stakes and the George Adams Handicap (now Emirates Stakes) with 59kg. He was also a game second behind So Called in the Cox Plate.

The following Autumn he was placed third behind champions Dulcify and Manikato in the Australian Cup, and won the Alister Clark Stakes.

Sold to Holmes a'Court, he stood at Heytesbury Stud for the 1979 season, but the following year was put back into work and on a limited preparation produced an extraordinary effort to finish second to Hit It Benny in the Doomben 100,000. In the Spring he was placed in the Freeway, the Feehan and the Craiglee Stakes before being beaten a short half head by Belmura Lad in the Mackinnon Stakes.

Fittingly perhaps, Brent Thomson was reunited with Family Of Man for his last run, and he went out a winner in the Sunspeed Stakes at Pinjarra in December, 1980, beating Brechin Castle and subsequent Perth Cup winner Magistrate.

At stud in WA and later Victoria, Family Of Man experienced modest success, but is best remembered for his racing ability.

1978 — OWNERS CALLED IT RIGHT

So Called, owned by six war-time mates, didn't race until he was three, but within the space of just 13 months was being talked about in the same breath as one of the all-time greats of the Australian turf.

It seemed that as the 1970's drew to a close, the jockey who'd come to Australia a fresh-faced kid of 17 and won the Cox Plate at his first try, was determined to make the race his own.

Cox Plate wins on Fury's Order in 1975 and Family Of Man in 1977 certainly helped Brent Thomson secure the prized job as stable rider for the powerful Colin Hayes stable, replacing John Stocker.

As such, Thomson found himself associated with a horse that Hayes had no hesitation in describing as the best horse he'd trained, a horse he once said "could be the next Tulloch".

So Called, owned by six war-time mates, didn't race until he was three, but within the space of just 13 months was being talked about in the same breath as one of the all-time greats of the Australian turf.

Just how good So Called was we can never really know. At only his second start after brilliantly winning the 1978 Cox Plate he broke down irretrievably, and was retired to stud.

Peter Watson, a former Spitfire pilot, bred So Called from his mare Calling, who he sent to New Zealand to be mated with Sobig, in the hope of getting a good stayer. Calling won five races on Victorian provincial tracks but couldn't break through in the city. Watson raced her with three former RAAF men – Ray Riley, Dick Banks and Harry Vine – plus former Army men Noel Moore and Bill Chipindall, so it was a natural thing to do to reform the syndicate to race Calling's son by Sobig.

Left in New Zealand until well into his two-year-old year, So Called had plenty of time to develop, and this, according to Hayes, was the making of him.

"He is a strong, robust horse with a marvelous temperament," he commented prior to the then four-year-old's Spring campaign. The manner by which Hayes came to train So Called was somewhat unusual in that Watson, who'd never met the great trainer, wrote and asked him if he would consider taking the Sobig colt into his stable.

Almost from the outset, Hayes was confident So

1978
(Saturday, October 28. Attendance: 25,686)

$147,500 plus $2,500 trophies Weight for Age 2,050m

1.	**SO CALLED**	C. S. Hayes	57kg	B. Thomson	5/1
2.	**Family Of Man**	G. M. Hanlon	59kg	H. White	5/1
3.	**Karaman**	B. J. Ralph	48.5kg	G. Murphy (a)	9/2

Winning details

Margin: 1½ len x sht ½ hd. **Time:** 2:08.7 12 started.

Breeding: Sobig – Calling – Better Boy (b h 4) **Owner:** P. Watson, R. Riley, R. Banks & H. Vine

Winner's Colors: Red, orange sleeves & cap

Winning Numbers: 5, 1, 9

ALSO RAN

Panamint	J. B. Cummings	R. Higgins	59	15/1
Salamander	T. J. Hughes	G. Palmer (a)	59	8/1
La Mer	M. K. Smith	D. Harris	56.5	7/4f
Hauberk	R. E. Hoysted	J. Stocker	48.5	16/1
Just A Steal	T. J. Smith	W. Treloar	48.5	25/1
Marceau	T. J. Smith	J. Letts	57	50/1
Prunella	B. N. Freeman	M. Broadfoot (a)	46	50/1
Vice Regal	J. W. Campin	R. Lang	59	33/1
Fralo	T. M. Courtney	N. Barrett	48.5	33/1

Scratched: Lefroy

SO CALLED ... the best horse Colin Hayes trained was at his brilliant best in winning the 1978 Cox Plate. – Picture: HWT

Called would develop into a high class galloper, and the colt confirmed his trainer's faith when coming from near last to win the 1977 Sandown Guineas.

A planned trip to the Perth Carnival was abandoned when the colt was found to be suffering severe swelling in his joints, but he returned in the Autumn to finish an unlucky second to Lefroy in the Champion Stakes over 2000m at Randwick, before reversing the tables on that horse in no uncertain fashion in the VRC St. Leger.

Hayes commented then that he believed So Called could win the Caulfield Cup in the Spring, and this confidence was barely dented when the colt finished fourth in a slowly run Adelaide Cup at his last start before going for a spell.

When he returned to racing, on a heavy track in the Liston Stakes at Sandown, So Called made an immediate impact. Handy throughout he raced clear at the top of the straight and was untroubled to beat Hyperno by more than two lengths.

"I could have led all the way if I'd wanted to," Thomson said, and claimed him to be the best horse he'd ridden. "He has unlimited potential."

Three weeks later at Moonee Valley, Thomson proved his point by taking So Called straight to the front at the start of the Feehan Stakes, and leading all the way to record an easy win.

At his next start, in the Underwood Stakes at Caulfield, So Called was pitted against an old mate of Thomson's, the reigning Cox Plate champion Family Of Man. The champ ran well to finish third, but was absolutely no match for the new kid on the block, who powered home to another impressive win.

Talk was now of So Called making a clean sweep of the "big three" races, the two Cups and the Cox Plate, and even Hayes admitted it was possible.

It was back to reality though some 10 days later, when So Called was comprehensively beaten by Lefroy in the Turnbull Stakes at Flemington, albeit the result of a rare ill-judged ride by Thomson.

The jockey admitted he'd panicked when So Called missed the start slightly, and had booted him up to try and gain a forward position. The tactic resulted in him being caught three wide for most of the way, and earned for Thomson a "two out of 10" rating for his ride from an irate Hayes.

So Called and Lefroy met again two weeks later in the Caulfield Cup. Neither was placed and So Called, from

BRENT THOMSON ... three Cox Plate wins in as many rides.

an extreme outside barrier, was never able to get into the race and finished 14th, the Cup coming down to a two-horse war between two very good stayers, Taksan and Arwon, who fought out a nail-biting finish.

The two defeats in punters' minds seemed to cancel out So Called's quite brilliant early Spring form. If the Cox Plate had been run two weeks after the Underwood Stakes, So Called would have run a short-priced favorite.

As it was, not only did he not start favorite, he was in fact on the third line of betting at 5-1, along with Family Of Man. The New Zealand mare La Mer, coming off some good form in her own country, was a somewhat dubious favorite at an even more dubious price, 7-4. Second pick at 9-2 was the three-year-old Karaman, on the strength of a Moonee Valley Stakes win and a second placing, behind potential star Manikato, in a controversial Caulfield Guineas.

Thomson arrived at Moonee Valley not having ridden a winner for three weeks, and in his own words "only hoping" for a change of luck. But he was firm in his intention to ride a patient race on So Called in the Cox Plate.

A muddling pace early saw Vice Regal take up the running and he went out to lead long-shot Prunella, with La Mer nicely placed ahead of Karaman. Family Of Man lay mid-field and So Called was back near the rear with only the stayer Panamint behind him.

"I told Mr.Hayes it was my intention not to make a move until the 800m, and he agreed with me," Thomson explained later. This he did, and his confidence grew as the bay accelerated past other runners without any effort.

Approaching the turn, Vice Regal had dropped off and Prunella was leading on sufferance. Karaman was battling on but it was Family Of Man who looked the likely winner as he strode up purposefully on the outside.

But just when it appeared as though a second Cox Plate win was within the Hanlon-trained star's sights, Thomson drove So Called between him and Karaman, and in the space of just a few metres, the race was over.

"I only hit him with the stick for about 20 metres," Thomson said later, as he reflected on his brief Cox Plate career which from three rides had yielded three wins. "Unbelievable."

Once again, So Called was back in favor and 10 days later he started a 9-2 favorite for the Melbourne Cup and ran a game race to finish fifth behind Arwon. He had every chance, and it could be he just didn't quite stay the maximum distance.

The four-year-old was immediately spelled, his connections looking forward to some exciting times with him in the Autumn. Sadly they got to see him parade just once more, in the Orr Stakes at Sandown in early February, 1979.

As budding champion Manikato scorched to an easy win, So Called, who'd faltered badly at the 400m mark, was being led by a distressed Thomson back to the mounting yard, and it soon became clear his racing days might be over.

Vets diagnosed a strained tendon in his near foreleg, and less than two months later it was announced So Called would be retired to stud.

Sold for $400,000 he stood at Toolern Vale Stud in Victoria, but like so many Cox Plate winners before him achieved only moderate success as a stallion.

1979 – DULCIFY'S BRILLIANT CAREER CUT SHORT

The cheap yearling who blossomed into the brilliant Dulcify, was responsible for one of the most awesome wins in the record of the Cox Plate when he romped home by seven lengths in 1979.

It was a performance that stamped him as a champion. Tragically, less than two weeks later he was lost to racing because of an accident in the Melbourne Cup, at a stage when his rider, Brent Thomson, said he was travelling like a winner.

The conjecture about what "might have been" aside, no-one can dispute the absolute authority he showed when he unwound an electrifying sprint to storm to the front in the Cox Plate of 1979 to win as he wished. Nor will anyone who saw the awesome display forget it.

The previous season, as a three-year-old, Dulcify signalled his inherent greatness by winning the Victoria and AJC Derbys, and had been emphatic in defeating all-comers in the weight-for-age Australian Cup.

As a four-year-old, with much of his racing career still in front of him – both trainer Colin Hayes and jockey Brent Thomson believed he would be an even better horse in 1980 – it seemed only bad luck or injury could prevent him emulating, and possibly even surpassing, the deeds of many of Australia's greatest horses.

Which is why his death, just days after his magnificent Moonee Valley performance, remains one of racing's greatest tragedies.

After winning the Mackinnon Stakes on the Saturday after the Cox Plate, Dulcify was a 7/4 favorite for the Melbourne Cup, but was stricken after being galloped on mid-way through the race. Vain attempts were made to save him, but he was eventually put down some hours after the running of Flemington's great race.

If there is any consolation – and there is little – it is that his Cox Plate win will be remembered forever as a performance that will rank among the best whenever the conversation turns to great wins and great horses. And from

Jockey Brent Thomson, having ridden extensively around the world and, in particular, high-class gallopers in the UK, still nominates Dulcify the best horse he has ridden.

"If you wanted him to, he could sprint, two, even three times in a race. That is a rare thing."

1979
(Saturday, October 27. Attendance: 25,612)

$172,500 plus $2,500 trophies Weight for Age 2,050m

1.	**DULCIFY**	C. S. Hayes	57kg	*B. Thomson*	7/4f
2.	**Shivaree**	D. O'Sullivan	59kg	*R. Lang*	9/4
3.	**Lawman**	G. M. Hanlon	48.5kg	*B. Clements (a)*	5/1

Winning details

Margin: 7 len x 4 len. **Time:** 2:04.9 12 started.

Breeding: Deceis – Sweet Candy – Todman (b g 4) **Owner:** W. Rigg, A. Maller & Mrs B. D. Hayes

Winner's Colors: Black, blue sleeves & cap

Winning Numbers: 8, 1, 14

ALSO RAN

Arbre Chene	P. K. Cathro	R. Higgins	59	20/1
Salamander	T. J. Hughes	M. Broadfoot (a)	59	33/1
Karaman	B. J. Ralph	P. Trotter	57	15/1
Runaway Kid	K. J. Curtain	W. Treloar	48.5	33/1
Top Ware	C. Cerchi	D. Coleman	48.5	50/1
Gypsy Kingdom	J. B. Cummings	J. Miller	59	12/1
Imposing	T. J. Smith	M. Johnston	57	13/4
Ming Dynasty	J. B. Cummings	P. Cook	59	50/1
Quiet Snort	R. K. McMahon	A. Williams	59	66/1

Scratched: Happy Union, Golden Key

DULCIFY ... the cheap yearling who was responsible for one of the most awesome wins in the record of the Cox Plate when he romped home by seven lengths in 1979.

It was a performance that stamped him as a champion and, anyone who saw the display, will never forget it.

Tragically, less than two weeks later he was lost to racing because of an accident in the Melbourne Cup, at a stage when his rider, Brent Thomson, said he was travelling like a winner.

– Picture: HWT

such humble beginnings, too, for he cost Hayes just $NZ3,350 as a yearling, a price no doubt influenced by his parrot mouth (where the upper jaw protrudes significantly in front of the lower jaw), which Dulcify proved conclusively is only a cosmetic issue.

Although powerfully built, Dulcify was a plain type, of average height (about 15.3 hands) with nothing to distinguish him from a host of other reasonably well bred youngsters. He was by the staying sire Deceis, and those who looked past his immediate maternal family – his dam Sweet Candy was by Todman out of a Wilkes mare – found stamina in abundance. Not the least such influence was his fourth dam Sweet Nymph, who was the third dam of 1977 Melbourne Cup winner Gold And Black.

Dulcify's racecourse debut, in August 1978, was auspicious for two reasons. He won over 1200m at Morphettville, and started at a then record South Australian price of 330/1.

Not that Hayes was unaware of Dulcify's ability, far from it. He believed the horse to have enormous potential, but in light of the hype that surrounded his 1978 Cox Plate winner So Called, Hayes decided this time to let the horse do the talking.

Over the next eight months, the parrot-mouthed gelding positively shouted his ability. He proved himself the outstanding three-year-old that season in beating horses the calibre of Double Century, Turf Ruler and Karaman. Adding to his reputation was his defeat of two truly great horses, Manikato and Family Of Man – among others – in the 1979 Australian Cup. His only real blemish was to be beaten out of a place twice during the Perth Summer Carnival, but that was of minor concern in comparison to what occurred on the trip back east.

Dulcify, who hated flying, played up badly when being loaded upon a flight at Perth airport, to such an extent a float was hired to transport him back to Melbourne across the Nullabor. About 200km west of Ceduna the float broke down, leaving Australia's best three-year-old stranded in temperatures touching 40 degrees. Realising the gravity of the situation, strapper Terry Ryan hitched a lift into Ceduna, hired another float, and went back to rescue his precious charge.

There was a further wait of two days while the original float was repaired, and the ordeal left its mark upon the gelding. It took all of Hayes' experience and dedication to bring Dulcify back for what proved to be a highly successful Autumn campaign, culminating in his AJC Derby win – albeit on protest – from Double Century.

The Cox Plate was Dulcify's main Spring mission in 1979, yet Hayes did not rule out a start in the Melbourne Cup. The gelding began his Spring with an unplaced run over 1000m in Adelaide, but didn't take long to find top form. Opposed to a classy field in the Craiglee Stakes at Flemington – old rival Double Century and classy NZ weight-for-age galloper Arbre Chene were among his opponents – Dulcify gave them a start and a sound beating, coming from last at the top of the straight to win running away.

The gelding went to Caulfield for his next start, in the Underwood Stakes over 2000m, but failed to live up to expectations, going down to Valley Of Georgia and Double Century in a slowly run race on a shifting track.

Back to his favorite venue, Flemington, for his Cox Plate warm-up in the Turnbull Stakes, Dulcify made amends with a dominating win, and one that confirmed his favoritism for the weight-for-age championship at Moonee Valley. Given only three horses in the Cox Plate field were at less than double figure odds, it has been suggested the opposition fell short of top class. Nothing could be further from the truth.

COLIN HAYES ... Dulcify was "something special".

Second favorite Shivaree was a high-class galloper whose weight-for-age credentials were impeccable, confirmed the previous Autumn with Sydney wins in the Tancred Stakes (now Mercedes Classic) and the Queen Elizabeth Stakes.

Third favorite Imposing was coming off wins in the George Main Stakes and the Epsom Handicap, while the three-year-old contingent included Caulfield Guineas winner Runaway Kid and Lawman, who despite chronic leg problems, was later to develop into a highly talented weight-for-age galloper. Also there was Ming Dynasty, winner of the 1977 Caulfield Cup, and destined to win another in 1980.

In the words of Shivaree's highly respected trainer Dave O'Sullivan, Dulcify made those horses "look second rate", if only for the fact jockey Brent Thomson made what under normal circumstances would appear to have been a premature run on the favorite.

Thomson sent Dulcify racing around the field with all of 500m to go, saying later he saw some of his rivals under pressure at that point, "so I let go hoping to put them under greater pressure".

Thomson, having ridden extensively around the world, and in particular, high-class gallopers in the UK, still nominates Dulcify the best horse he has ridden.

"If you wanted him to, he could sprint, two, even three times in a race. That is a rare thing."

Hayes, in an illustrious career spanning 40 years and the preparation of many outstanding horses among his more than 5,300 winners, never wavered in his opinion of the plain, parrot-mouthed champion who sadly died at the peak of his career.

"He was something else," Hayes said.

1980-82 — HE WAS KING OF THE VALLEY AND BEYOND

The fans came to know him as "The King" – around the stable he was simply "Sam" – and on three occasions at Moonee Valley he showed why he deserved his regal title. First it was in the1980 Cox Plate, next in 1981, and finally, in 1982.

All this from a horse initially considered a "Sydney Wonder", a high class galloper there, but a lesser beast when racing in Melbourne.

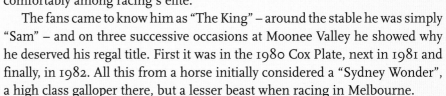

The history of the Cox Plate suggests it is very rarely won by anything other than a class horse and, down through the years, by some genuine champions.

How then do you rate a horse who won three Cox Plates, in fact the only horse to have achieved such a feat?

Champions, true champions that is, are few and far between. But there can be no doubt David Hains' big, black galloper Kingston Town stands more than comfortably among racing's elite.

The fans came to know him as "The King" – around the stable he was simply "Sam" – and on three successive occasions at Moonee Valley he showed why he deserved his regal title. First it was in the 1980 Cox Plate, next in 1981 and finally, in 1982. All this from a horse initially considered a "Sydney Wonder", a high class galloper there, but a lesser beast when racing in Melbourne.

Kingston Town was bred by Hains, a wealthy Melbourne financier who had ventured into thoroughbred breeding upon the urging of his close friend, legendary golfer and avid racing follower, Norman Von Nida. Sent to the yearling sales he failed to reach his reserve of $8,000, and after being given time to mature, went into training with Tommy Smith and had his first start in a two-year-old handicap at Canterbury in March, 1979.

Perhaps the gods knew what was in store for the son of Bletchingly and decided upon a spot of teasing, for Kingston Town ran last, beaten some 30 lengths. Immediately, a decision was made to geld him and it is arguable that this was the making of a champion. Had he remained a stallion, Kingston Town might not have reached such heights as a racehorse. And if he had, it is unlikely he would still have been racing at the age of five, when he won his third Cox Plate.

His inglorious debut was but a brief aberration. He won his next six starts, four as a three-year-old in the Spring of 1979, and it was with this record that he arrived in Melbourne to run in the Caulfield Guineas.

He started favorite at even money, was on the

1980

(Saturday, October 25. Attendance: 29,995)

$196,500 plus $3,500 trophies Weight for Age 2,050m

1.	**KINGSTON TOWN**	T. J. Smith	57kg	*M. Johnston*	6/4f
2.	**Prince Ruling**	J. J. Atkins	57kg	*R. Higgins*	40/1
3.	**Our Paddy Boy**	C. S. Hayes	48.5kg	*R. Skelton*	10/1

Winning details

Margin: 5 len x len. **Time:** 2:07.3 14 started.

Breeding: Bletchingly – Ada Hunter – Andrea Mantegna (bl g 4) **Owner:** Mr & Mrs D. H. Hains & Mr & Mrs G. Monsbourgh

Winner's Colors: Yellow, red striped sleeves & cap

Winning Numbers: 5, 6, 11

ALSO RAN

Waitangirua	T. L. Millard	P. Hyland	59	14/1
Yir Tiz	V. P. Sutherland	M. Riley (a)	46	33/1
Ming Dynasty	J. B. Cummings	E. Didham	59	20/1
Sovereign Red	G. T. Murphy	R. Quinton	48.5	3/1
Palaban	N. C. Begg	R. Heffernan	48.5	100/1
Tasman	B. J. Ralph	B. Clements (a)	48.5	200/1
Family Of Man	G. M. Hanlon	J. Miller	59	15/1
My Blue Denim	D. J. O'Sullivan	P. Cook	56.5	25/1
Glenson	W. C. Warke	G. Murphy	48.5	14/1
Torbek	W. H. Walters	M. Campbell	59	8/1
Tolhurst	J. R. Hawkes	J. Letts	57	33/1

All started

wrong leg throughout, and finished third behind Runaway Kid, who incidentally won the race on protest from Bold Diplomat. A week later, Kingston Town ran a game fourth in the Caulfield Cup, again not handling the track.

The Cup winner was his stablemate Mighty Kingdom, who two weeks later started favorite in the Victoria Derby but finished fourth. Kingston Town, who was ridden by Roy Higgins with Johnston being required for Mighty Kingdom, finished second in the Derby, being beaten by only a head behind Big Print.

Higgins is in no doubt Kingston Town should have won. The gelding suffered interference near the 800m, and began to race rather ungenerously. After the race, it was found his off-fore plate had became twisted.

"Another couple of strides and he would have won," Higgins said.

Nevertheless, the record stood at three Melbourne starts, no wins. So much for the Sydney "champ". Just under 12 months later Kingston Town returned to Melbourne, this time with even bigger wraps upon him in light of 11 wins straight, all but one at Group level, and including the AJC Derby and the Sydney Cup. It was a performance which deservedly earned him the title Australian Champion Racehorse of the Year, but still he had to prove himself in Melbourne.

He ran second in the Caulfield Stakes behind Hyperno, after which jockey Malcom Johnston declared him unable to handle Melbourne's left-handed way of going.

Smith disagreed, and a week later sent the black gelding out to finish third to Ming Dynasty in the Caulfield Cup. He ran well, for the first time appearing more comfortable racing anti-clockwise.

Two days before the Cox Plate, Kingston Town was given his first look at the tight Valley circuit. He worked there with stablemate Dynasty, who surprisingly galloped behind, rather than with him.

1981
(Saturday, October 24. Attendance: 28,300)

$196,500 plus $3,500 trophies Weight for Age 2,050m

1.	**KINGSTON TOWN**	T. J. Smith	59kg	R. Quinton	4/6f
2.	**Lawman**	G. M. Hanlon	59	R. Higgins	6/1
3.	**Binbinga**	F. R. Quan	48.5kg	P. Cook	3/1

Winning details

Margin: ¾ len x len. Time: 2:06.7 10 started.

Breeding: Bletchingly – Ada Hunter – Andrea Mantegna (bl g 5) Owner: Mr & Mrs D. H. Hains & G. A. Monsbourgh

Winner's Colors: Yellow, red striped sleeves & cap

Winning Numbers: 1, 3, 10

ALSO RAN

Silver Bounty	G. M. Carson	E. Didham	57	12/1
Sovereign Red	G. T. Murphy	M. Goreham	57	10/1
Deck The Halls	R. J. McGuinness	P. Clarke	54.5	25/1
Belmura Lad	J. B. Cummings	L. Olsen	59	33/1
Koiro Trellay	E. Temperton	M. Gillies	59	33/1
Fearless Pride	E. H. Broadhurst	P. Riley	48.5	16/1
Prince Ruling	J. J. Atkins	H. White	59	125/1

All started

Smith believed Kingston Town worked better when he had a horse chasing him, and when he sailed around the track almost effortlessly to run his last 400m in 25 seconds, no one could disagree.

For all his Melbourne defeats, the punters stayed loyal to "The King" and he went to the post a solid favorite at 6-4. This time he didn't let them down.

His opposition included Ming Dynasty, the Caulfield Guineas winner Sovereign Red, AJC Derby winner Our Paddy Boy, past Cox Plate champ Family Of Man, plus a couple of very snappy "milers" in Torbek and Yir Tiz. According to Johnston he had the race won well before the halfway mark.

In Graeme Kelly's excellent record of the champion, titled simply *"The King"*, Johnston says, "I knew at the 1600m he was going to win and by the 800m I was wondering by how far."

Approaching the turn, Kingston Town was poised behind the leaders, and when Johnston gave him his head, he burst to the front and streaked away to win by five lengths, to the deafening cheers of an admiring but also relieved crowd. Everyone loves a great horse, and at last Melbourne racegoers could acclaim Kingston Town as just that. Sadly, the big horse, upon cooling down, was found to be lame, later diagnosed as a strained suspensory ligament in his off-foreleg, an injury that was to plague him for the remainder of his career.

It not only kept him out of the 1980 Melbourne Cup, but also forced him to miss the entire Autumn and Winter Carnivals, delaying his re-appearance until August, 1981.

Kingston Town burst back into racing with a much talked about win in the Premier Stakes over 1200m at Rosehill. Johnston, trying to give "The King" a soft run, eased him up when in front near the line and was almost run down by a 160-1 shot.

Once again, Kingston Town embarked upon a Cox Plate program. In the lead-up he contested five weight-for-age Group races and won them all.

With no rides at Caulfield the following week, Johnston took mounts at Randwick, and subsequently found himself before the stewards charged with careless riding. He was suspended until Melbourne Cup eve, lost an appeal, and thus forfeited the Cox Plate ride on Kingston Town to Ron Quinton.

Having ridden the great horse in trackwork, Quinton was not unfamiliar with him, but alarm bells rang when Kingston Town drew barrier one in the weight-for-age championship. "He was a horse who needed room to gallop," Quinton said later.

In his favor, the 1981 Cox Plate field was short of top class. The only horses under double figure odds other than the favorite were Lawman, a highly talented but injury prone galloper, and the three-year-old Binbinga, who previously had won the Caulfield Guineas at 100-1.

In the race, Quinton's worst fears were realised when Kingston Town became pocketed coming down the side past the 500m mark. At this stage Binbinga had taken the lead from Lawman, with Silver Bounty rushing up on the outside of the champ.

Quinton said afterwards he knew he was going well enough to win if only he could gain a run, so when Silver Bounty wobbled slightly on the point of the bend Kingston Town shouldered him out of the

1982

(Saturday, October 23. Attendance: 25,804)

$271,0000 plus $4,000 trophies Weight for Age 2,050m

1.	**KINGSTON TOWN**	T. J. Smith	59kg	P. Cook	7/4f
2.	**Grosvenor**	G. T. Murphy	48.5kg	B. Clements	13/2
3.	**My Axeman**	T. K. Griffin	59kg	W. Robinson	6/1

Winning details

Margin: ¾ len x 1¼ len. **Time:** 2:05.5 14 started.

Breeding: Bletchingly – Ada Hunter – Andrea Mantegna (bl g 6)
Owner: Mr & Mrs D. H. Hains & G. A. Monsbourgh

Winner's Colors: Yellow, red striped sleeves & cap

Winning Numbers: 1, 13, 3

ALSO RAN

Fearless Pride	E. H. Broadhurst	B. Thomson	57	8/1
Allez Bijou	C. J. Honeychurch	G. Willetts	59	50/1
No Peer	J. B. Cummings	H. White	59	9/1
Gurner's Lane	G. T. Murphy	M. Goreham	57	33/1
Magari	R. S. McDonald	R. Heffernan	57	9/1
English Wonder	J. R. Hawkes	P. Shepherd	46	50/1
Lawman	G. M. Hanlon	R. Higgins	59	33/1
Silver Bounty	G. Carson	E. Didham	59	50/1
Debs Mate	H. S. Wadham	Deb Healey	59	25/1
Isle Of Man	G. M. Hanlon	R. Quinton	57	50/1
Rare Form	B. Mayfield-Smith	R. Hardwicke	57	25/1

All started

way and in the space of 50m the race was all over.

The big crowd accorded him a champion's welcome back to the winner's enclosure and soon after his mentor paid him the highest compliment.

"I never thought I would have another horse like Tulloch," Smith said.

"Now I have to say Kingston Town is his equal."

As good as they are, champion racehorses are not machines. A week later Kingston Town was beaten by the Bart Cummings-trained Belmura Lad in the Mackinnon Stakes, then only beat the scrubbers when finishing 20th in the Melbourne Cup.

Kingston Town's proposed Autumn campaign failed to eventuate. Five weeks into his preparation it became obvious his battle-worn forelegs needed a longer break, so he was sent back to the spelling paddock.

In the lead-up to the 1982 Cox Plate, Kingston Town enjoyed his share of success, but on two occasions had his colors lowered, once due to an ill-judged ride by Johnston, the other beaten fair and square by the three-year-old Cossack Prince.

A month before the Cox Plate, Kingston Town, with Johnston on board, won the George Main Stakes at Randwick. On the same day, Johnston incurred his 26th suspension for careless riding, was outed for almost five weeks and once again found himself watching the Cox Plate at home on TV.

This time Peter Cook was the fortunate one, and he made his first acquaintance with Kingston Town in the Caulfield Stakes, piloting him to an easy win.

The strength of the opposition in the Cox Plate lay mainly with the Geoff Murphy-trained Grosvenor, winner of the Caulfield Guineas, and the New Zealander My Axeman, a good but somewhat workmanlike weight-for-age galloper.

Calling the race both on and off the course that day was Bill Collins, nicknamed "The Accurate One" but also a commentator who was never afraid to call it as he saw it.

As the field streamed towards the home turn, Fearless Pride led My Axeman, with Grosvenor out wide making ground quickly and looking ominous. Where was Kingston Town?

For 100m or more Cook had had the black gelding under the whip for no noticeable improvement. Collins spotted this, and in an almost matter-of-fact tone commented, "Kingston Town can't win."

Champions though, can never be written off. No sooner had Grosvenor swept to the front, at the 200m mark, than Kingston Town began to reel him in. For a moment it seemed Grosvenor might hold on, but then "The King" put in three or four mighty bounds and put his third straight win beyond doubt.

The roar that erupted when Collins cried "and Kingston Town flashing.....he might win yet, the champ" gained in crescendo with every one of those huge strides, and when he hit the line it was ear splitting.

Three in a row! Not bad for a horse which, if the truth be known, didn't particularly like racing the Melbourne way of going.

Some 10 days later Kingston Town ran in the Melbourne Cup. Johnston, reunited with his favorite horse, clicked up to go around a horse passing the 500m but Kingston Town caught him by surprise and sprinted forward to be in front around the turn.

In the dying stages, he was run down by the Caulfield Cup winner Gurner's Lane, to whom he was giving 3kg. Johnston conceded later had he not gone so early then "The King" would have won.

No doubt about it though, he was the "King of the Valley" and beyond.

1983 — MANY TURNS IN ROAD TO FAME

Strawberry Road is a horse overlooked by many when thoughts on the best 10 horses since the War are being tossed around. Yet he is a horse that surely would be unlucky not to be included. He was a dominant three-year-old, he won the Cox Plate as a four-year-old, and as a five-year-old gained success at international level, something few Australasian champions can lay claim to.

It's a form of discussion that racing buffs never tire of: Who is the best horse of all time, the best horse since the war, the best sprinter, stayer, mare, filly, colt, mudlark, front-runner?

The best horse since the War, for example. Those who saw him would probably say Tulloch; others might settle on Kingston Town, while some younger fans might nominate Might And Power.

Strawberry Road cannot lay claim to the title, but he is a horse overlooked by many when thoughts on the best 10 horses since the War are being tossed around. Yet he is a horse that surely would be unlucky not to be included. He was a dominant three-year-old, he won the Cox Plate as a four-year-old, and as a five-year-old gained success at international level, something few Australasian champions can lay claim to.

His is a story with many twists and turns, so much so, he was rarely out of the sporting headlines, and in fact dominated at least the racing pages for almost all of 1983. Strawberry Road was bred by his part-owner, Canberra electrical contractor Jim Pantos, from a mare he'd bought for just $3,000 as a weanling. He was by the grandson of the great Northern Dancer, Whiskey Road, who at the time of the mating to Pantos' mare Giftisa was a sire of little note. But by the time Strawberry Road reached the racetrack, Whiskey Road's stocks had taken a sharp upward turn, courtesy of his son Just A Dash winning the 1981 Melbourne Cup.

Pantos in the meantime had brought his brother Arthur Pantos and friends George Georgopoulos and Mando Menegazza into a partnership to race Strawberry Road.

It was decided to race Strawberry Road in Queensland – one of the part-owners lived in Brisbane – and so he entered the stables of unheralded Brisbane trainer Doug Bougoure, a former jockey who'd trained some good horses but never one good enough to take interstate. Throughout his career, Strawberry Road often made headlines because of someone wanting to buy him. The first, an offer of $100,000 from a leading Australian trainer, came just days after he won his first race, a Maiden at Eagle Farm in August, 1982.

1983
(Saturday, October 22. Attendance: 27,385)

$271,0000 plus $4,000 trophies Weight for Age 2,050m

1.	STRAWBERRY ROAD	D. Bougoure	57kg	L. Dittman	11/2
2.	Kiwi Slave	C. S. Hayes	59kg	G. Hall	100/1
3.	Mr McGinty	C. M. Jillings	57kg	R. Vance	9/2

Winning details

Margin: 3½ len x 1½ len. **Time:** 2:09.1 13 started.

Breeding: Whiskey Road – Giftisa – Rich Gift (b h 4)
Owner: J. & A. Pantos, M. Menegazza & G. Georgopolous

Winner's Colors: Red, white band and armbands, black cap

Winning Numbers: 6, 4, 5

ALSO RAN

Handsome Seattle	J. Kennedy	B. Clements	48.5	33/1
Sir Dapper	L. J. Bridge	P. Cook	48.5	7/2ef
Debs Mate	H. S. Wadham	Deb Healey	59	33/1
Fine Offer	C. S. Hayes	M. Clarke (a)	48.5	8/1
Perfect Bliss	R. E. Laing	P. Alderman	46	20/1
Albany Bay	G. T. Murphy	D. Gauci	48.5	20/1
Allez Bijou	C. J. Honeychurch	P. Hyland	59	66/1
Emancipation	N. C. Begg	R. Quinton	54.5	7/2ef
Trissaro	J. B. Cummings	H. White	59	11/2
Come To London	C. S. Hayes	E. Didham	57	100/1

All started

Although it would have meant a healthy profit, Pantos and his friends turned it down. This decision was vindicated when Strawberry Road won his next four starts and further confirmed in the Autumn of 1983 when he won the Rosehill Guineas and the AJC Derby. Again an offer was made for the colt, this time of $1 million. Again it was refused.

Strawberry Road returned to Queensland to win three races including the Queensland Derby, prompting a bid of $2 million purportedly from New Zealand but, in fact, it was from well known US breeders and investors the Murty brothers. The Pantos syndicate considered selling but eventually negotiations fell through.

Strawberry Road began the new racing season with a reputation to live up to, courtesy of him being judged the Victoria Racing Club's Champion Australian Racehorse for 1982-83. It was a controversial decision, given he'd performed only in the latter half of the season, and was voted ahead of horses such as Caulfield and Melbourne Cup winner Gurner's Lane, and evergreen weight-for-age champion Kingston Town, who was judged the winner of the rival Australian Racing Writers' Racehorse of the Year.

Strawberry Road's Spring campaign centered upon the Caulfield Cup and the Cox Plate, and when he won the Freeway Stakes first up at Moonee Valley, finished second in the Memsie Stakes at Caulfield, then returned to Moonee Valley to win the Centennial Stakes, he was a hot favorite to win both targeted races.

He fell from favor though, when unplaced in the Underwood Stakes, and then in the Caufield Stakes. It was subsequently discovered Strawberry Road had contracted a virus, thus ruling out a start in the Caulfield Cup. The virus, which infected a lung and inflamed the throat, was quite serious, and Bougoure was to say later he doubted then whether Strawberry Road could have continued his Spring campaign. "But," he said, "if you put your heart and soul into a horse and take the best veterinary advice it is marvellous what you can come up with."

What they came up with on Cox Plate day was a horse able to record an emphatic victory. One perhaps helped by a track that definitely was on the worst side of dead, Strawberry Road's preferred going, but nonetheless very impressive. His rivals included the outstanding four-year-old mare Emancipation, the Champion Stakes winning three-year-old Sir Dapper, plus the Caulfield Stakes winner, classy New Zealand weight-for-age star Mr McGinty.

There were lots of excuses – according to their respective riders Sir Dapper was checked early; Mr. McGinty didn't handle the soft track; and Emancipation did not handle Moonee Valley's tight turns. But Strawberry Road won by more than three lengths, and from the top of the straight, where jockey Mick Dittman gave him one crack of the whip, he was never going to be beaten.

Dittman's ride was a beauty. He had no hesitation in bouncing his mount straight to the front, then eased him after 400m to find an ideal position just behind the leaders, before unleashing him just before the turn into the short straight.

Days after the race, attempts were again made to buy the horse. Robbie Porter, a popular Australian singer who'd become a successful record producer in the US, offered $2 million but couldn't get a satisfactory vet report.

The Pantos syndicate continued to race the horse, albeit with little success during the Sydney Autumn Carnival, but then well known advertising executive and radio personality John Singleton bought a half share for $1 million, and split that with friend Ray Stehr.

It was Stehr who had the notion to race Strawberry Road overseas. So, in July of 1984 the entire went into work with former Australian trainer John Nicholls at Chantilly in France, heading towards the Prix de l'Arc de Triomphe. On the way, he won a Group 3 race at Baden Baden in Germany (with Brent Thomson in the saddle), and partnered by English jockey Greville Starkey ran a very creditable fifth behind French ace Sagace in the Arc after leading around the home turn. Soon after, he ran in the Washington International, and the Japan Cup. He was nothing if not durable.

1984 — 'T.J' INHERITS A CHAMP

When champion three year old colt Red Anchor won the 1984 Cox Plate, he gave legendary trainer Tommy Smith his seventh win in the weight-for-age championship.

But had history taken a different turn then Sydney trainer Paul Sutherland might well have been the one receiving the accolades for Red Anchor's success. For it was Sutherland who originally bought Red Anchor as a yearling for just $11,000 and who trained him throughout his two-year-old career.

Early on, Sutherland sold Red Anchor to a group of Sydney businessmen headed by John Gigante, but retained a share of the colt. At his first start, the son of Sea Anchor out of a mare from the family of English Derby winner Mill Reef started at 400/1 and finished third in a race at Rosehill in November, 1983. For the remainder of his career, unfortunately a relatively short one, Red Anchor never finished further back than second.

The Cox Plate is a race that rarely, if ever, is not won by a class horse. Some winners, certainly not all, have been champions. Red Anchor was one of the latter. A deep-girthed, solidly built chestnut, his racing career barely covered 16 months, for, after suffering an injury to his off foreleg early in 1985, he was sold for $3 million and retired to stud. In all he raced 14 times for nine wins, four seconds and a third, and earned $779,970 in stakemoney, a then record for a three-year-old in Australia.

In the care of Sutherland, he won the AJC Champagne Stakes and the QTC Sires' Produce Stakes, but at the end of his two-year-old season a dispute arose between Sutherland and his other part-owners as to the colt's proposed Spring campaign. When it couldn't be resolved Gigante and his fellow owners bought Sutherland's share in the horse and transferred him to the stables of Tommy Smith.

It must have been a gut-wrenching decision for Sutherland, for he was well aware of Red Anchor's potential. Just before the colt's win in the Champagne Stakes in March, 1984, he was quoted as saying, "From the start of his career I

1984
(Saturday, October 22. Attendance: 23,413)

$394,0000 plus $6,000 trophies Weight for Age 2,050m

1.	**RED ANCHOR**	T. J. Smith	48.5kg	*L. Dittman*	8/11f
2.	**Street Café**	T. Green	48.5kg	*B. Clements*	33/1
3.	**King Delamere**	J. W. McGreal	57kg	*R. J. Skelton*	20/1

Winning details

Margin: ¾ len x 1¼ len. **Time:** 2:03.7 (Course record) 14 started.

Breeding: Sea Anchor – Decoy Girl – Decoy Boy (ch c 3)
Owner: Mr & Mrs J. Gigante, Mr & Mrs J. J. & J. A. Symond & A. R. Hely

Winner's Colors: Pale green, pale blue diagonal stripes & quartered cap

Winning Numbers: 11, 13, 8

ALSO RAN

Lord Of Camelot	R. J. McGuinness	D. Gauci (a)	48.5	10/1
Riverdale	N. R. Ward	N. Barker	57	8/1
King Phoenix	T. R. Howe	P. Hyland	57	25/1
Mr Ironclad	R. E. Hoysted	P. Jarman	57	25/1
Beechcraft	C. S. Hayes	B. Thomson	57	11/2
Librici	W. C. Winder	W. Robinson	57	14/1
Admiral Lincoln	G. T. Murphy	G. Willetts	59	250/1
Eastern Bay	N. C. Begg	G. Hall	54.5	200/1
Kiwi Slave	C. S. Hayes	M. Clarke	59	33/1
Al Dwain	T. G. Autridge	H. White	59	25/1
Oxberry Way	J. B. Cummings	R. Heffernan	48.5	200/1

All started

knew he would make a great three-year-old, but he's so good he's able to match it with the best now."

Prophetic words indeed, for by the time Red Anchor came to contest the Cox Plate he had already proved himself to be the best of his age in Australia. His first run for Smith came on September 1 at Randwick over 1200m in the Roman Consul Stakes. He totally eclipsed his rivals, after which he was sent to Melbourne to prepare for the major three-year-old races. At that stage a start in the Cox Plate was barely being considered, but the idea began to take substance when at his next start Red Anchor won the Moonee Valley Stakes over 1600m after racing on his wrong leg for most of the way.

In that race, he was ridden by Gary Willetts, who rated him the equal of Rose Of Kingston, upon whom Willetts won the AJC Derby and the VRC Oaks. "He is top class and will only improve on a bigger track," the jockey commented.

He wasn't the only one to think so. A few days later an offer of $3 million was made for Red Anchor, an enormous sum but one that didn't even tempt Gigante and his partners. "I want to win the Derby with him," Gigante was quoted as saying. "No offers will even be considered until after the Autumn."

This decision gained strength a week or so later when Red Anchor contested the Caulfield Guineas, again over 1600m, and, ridden by Mick Dittman, powered away from his rivals to win by more than three lengths. Afterwards Smith, in typical fashion, declared the colt had the potential to be as good as his thrice Cox Plate winner Kingston Town. On the Tuesday before the Cox Plate, Red Anchor was taken to Moonee Valley to gallop, a gallop which went within an ace of being a million-dollar tragedy.

Ridden by Dittman and galloping with stablemate Movie Maker, the colt was going effortlessly when he suddenly slipped and skidded near the 800m mark, almost coming down. "It was really scary," Dittman said later.

"He was completely off balance and headed for the ground."

Nothing was found to be amiss with Red Anchor after the workout, and on Cox Plate day he opened a rock solid favorite at 9/10, touching evens for a brief period before being backed heavily to start at 8/11.

Red Anchor won, and he won well. But inside the 500m his backers were entitled to be nervous, for it appeared the colt was not going anywhere. Dittman was forced to flick him with the whip several times to get him moving.

The jockey said later Red Anchor had been loafing, a trait not uncommon in class horses, but could it have been the colt's memory of the trackwork mishap that caused him to take things easy at that point in the race? Whatever, it made no difference. Livened up, Red Anchor swung into stride beautifully around the turn and quickly gathered in the 33/1 pacemaker Street Café. Dittman had to use the whip on his mount, and to his credit Street Café refused to give in, to be beaten only three-quarters of a length. But it really appeared as though Red Anchor did only as much as was required to win, although in a fast run race he clocked 2min 3.7secs, less than a second outside the then record of 2.3.0.

A week later, Red Anchor demoralised his opponents in the Victoria Derby in winning by four lengths, prompting Smith, now nursing a broken arm, to declare him the "new Tulloch". A big statement, yes, but Smith's great rival Colin Hayes, who trained Derby runner-up National Gallery, was moved to place Red Anchor among "the all-time greats".

Certainly he was a great horse. Sadly though, Red Anchor raced only once more, winning the Apollo Stakes at Randwick in March, 1985, before being injured.

Just how good he was, we'll never know.

1985 – 'BULLDOG' ATTACKS AT RIGHT TIME

Certainly the ability of Rising Prince pales into insignificance when matched against that of many other Cox Plate winners. But the "Bathurst Bulldog", as he was known, was a tough, durable galloper who, in essence, happened to be in the right place at the right time – and made the most of it.

It is easy to write the 1985 Cox Plate field off as being of less than the usual high standard, and Rising Prince was admittedly not the best performed runner in the race.

Certainly his ability pales into insignificance when matched against that of many other Cox Plate winners. But the "Bathurst Bulldog", as he was known, was a tough, durable galloper who, in essence, happened to be in the right place at the right time – and made the most of it.

And he created Cox Plate history by being the first winner trained by a woman, the unassuming but very highly respected mentor Deidre Stein. Stein's mother-in-law, Violet, bred Rising Prince, a striking chestnut with a distinct white blaze. As a three and early four-year-old he could still be seen racing in places such as Forbes, and on his home track at Bathurst.

But Stein predicted very early on the gelding would be a horse of some consequence, so it came as no surprise to her when, at the end of 1984, he captured the AJC's Group 3 Summer double, the Villiers Stakes over 1600m, and the Summer Cup over 2400m. That he became only the third horse in the space of 94 years to complete the double was a significant effort, even allowing for the likelihood of a limited number attempting it.

The following Autumn he confirmed not only his ability, but also his adaptability, by winning the Group 1 Queen Elizabeth Stakes over 2000m, after finishing sixth in the Doncaster Handicap, upon which his preparation had been based. Come the Spring, Stein mapped out an ambitious program for her charge, one which included Group 1 handicaps from 1600m to 3200m, plus weight-for-age assignments.

Rising Prince kicked off with a close second in the Warwick Stakes at Warwick Farm in late August, an excellent effort given he was notoriously slow to come to hand. Three more weight-for-age contests had Rising Prince primed to be very competitive in the Epsom Handicap, and he ran a great race to finish a close

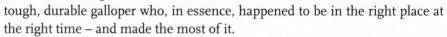

1985
(Saturday, October 26. Attendance: 24,852)

$494,0000 plus $6,000 trophies Weight for Age 2,050m

1.	**RISING PRINCE**	D. L. Stein	59kg	*K. Langby*	7/1
2.	**Roman Artist**	C. Newham	49kg	*M. Logue*	16/1
3.	**Drawn**	L. J. Bridge	48.5kg	*L. Cassidy*	7/2f

Winning details

Margin: 2½ len x ¾ len. **Time:** 2:05.3 14 started.

Breeding: Round Top – Bonlene – Capricorno (ch g 5) **Owner:** Exchange Racing Syndicate

Winner's Colors: Orange, black crossed sashes and sleeves, orange and black quartered cap

Winning Numbers: 3, 13, 12

ALSO RAN

The Filbert	D. N. Couchman	G. Phillips	59	7/1
King Phoenix	T. R. Howe	M. Goreham	59	9/2
Foxseal	R. Hore-Lacy	P. D. Johnson	59	10/1
Kingdom Bay	J. G. Taylor	N. Harris	57	20/1
Acumen	G. T. Murphy	M. Clarke	48.5	11/1
Riverdale	N. R. Ward	N. Barker	59	8/1
Centaurea	R. S. McDonald	W. Treloar	54.5	16/1
Delightful Belle	C. S. Hayes	D. Gauci	54.5	9/1
Spirit Of Kingston	R. E. Hoysted	G. Willetts	54.5	40/1
Hayai	G. R. Lee	M. Johnson	59	16/1
Importune (P.U.)	H. Hicking	G. Murphy	57	66/1

All started

fourth behind Magnitude after being with the pace throughout and reaching the lead half-way up the Randwick straight.

A week later he was floated to Melbourne in the care of Bill Aspros, a familiar figure in central New South Wales. His wife Leanne worked for Stein for six years, so Bill, a leading jockey in the district, volunteered to come to Melbourne to ride the horse work. In the week leading up to the Caulfield Cup, Rising Prince showed a clear dislike for galloping anti-clockwise, and proved more than a handful for Aspros. This was duly reported, and probably accounted for the fact Rising Prince was sent out a 25-1 chance at Caulfield.

Mindful of his mount jumping from 1600m to 2400m, jockey Kevin Langby didn't try to fight him when he rushed out of the gate, and it was the best part of 800m before he could get the gelding to come back onto the bridle.

Given he was taken on from about the 1200m and didn't really handle the track, it was a mighty effort for him to be still in front nearing the 200m mark, and even then he kept grinding away to finish fifth, less than four lengths from the winner Tristarc.

A week later, Rising Prince faced 13 opponents in the Cox Plate, the 2040m being a much more suitable distance for him. At odds of 7-1 he was considered by many to represent great value, particularly in view of the fact the two horses above him in the market had no better credentials.

Three-year-old Drawn, the heavily backed 7-2 favorite, had won the Caulfield Guineas but was untried at the distance, while King Phoenix, the winner of the Elders Mile two weeks earlier, was unplaced in his only two attempts beyond 1600m. For some unknown reason, horses trained the Sydney way of racing, when brought to Melbourne, invariably race better at Moonee Valley than they do at Caulfield.

One who didn't was the Sydney three-year-old Roman Artist, which indirectly set up the Cox Plate to be won by Rising Prince. Stein had some concerns about Rising Prince quite possibly having to make all of the running, which is always difficult, but much more so in a race such as the Cox Plate, where the pressure invariably comes on at about the 700m mark.

Langby was of a more open mind, but in the end the decision was made for him when Roman Artist hung badly around the turn out of the straight, leaving his young rider Maurice Logue no option but to let him stride. Langby slotted Rising Prince in behind him, to enjoy the perfect run. "I couldn't have asked for a better run," he said later.

Knowing the distance was not a problem for his horse, Langby sent Rising Prince after Roman Artist from the 600m mark and claimed him on the point of the turn. From there he never looked likely to be beaten. Two and a half lengths was the winning margin, and significantly perhaps, none of his rivals was able to get past Roman Artist, who battled on gamely to run second. The following week Rising Prince led throughout to win the Mackinnon Stakes at Flemington, and reappeared at Headquarters three days later to contest the Melbourne Cup.

As good as he was, the Cup distance quite simply proved beyond him, and after racing in second place to the turn he faded to finish back among the tailenders.

1986 — THE HYPE WAS RIGHT!

Approaching the 800 metre mark, Gary Stewart suddenly hooked Bonecrusher around the heels of his rival and set him alight. Lance O'Sullivan had no option but to go with him and the pair fairly rocketed up to the leaders.

Bill Collins' call, echoing across the intimate reaches of the amphitheatre that is Moonee Valley, even early on, contained a level of anticipated excitement, but as the two champs let go, so did (broadcaster) Bill Collins.

The Race of the Century! That is what it was billed as, and in direct defiance of the laws of probability, promoters got it right.

Although drained to the point of exhaustion, legendary racecaller Bill Collins – ".... and Bonecrusher races into equine immortality..." – somehow got it exactly right as the New Zealand chestnuts Bonecrusher and Our Waverley Star crossed the line in the 1986 Cox Plate.

Not just Bonecrusher though. A memorable contest requires a noble loser, and so Our Waverley Star is entitled to be accorded just as much of the race glory.

And the connections too, Bonecrusher's owner Peter Mitchell, trainer Frank Ritchie and his assistant, son Shaune. On the other side was the O'Sullivan clan, trainer Dave and his sons, Paul the assistant and Lance the jockey, and of course, Our Waverley Star's larger-than-life owner, the Queensland Racing Minister, Russ Hinze.

Their sportsmanship before, and particularly after the race, gave lie to the perception that racing as a sport is succumbing more and more to racing as a business.

Remarkably perhaps, the 1986 Cox Plate was talked about as being a two-horse race many, many weeks before it actually came to pass.

Bonecrusher had established his credentials in no uncertain fashion the previous season, to such an extent there were those who were talking about him in the same breath as the greatest New Zealand-bred of them all, Phar Lap. Already he'd acquired the same nickname, Big Red.

After winning the New Zealand Derby, he was sent across the Tasman to contest two Group 1 races at Sydney's 1983 Autumn Carnival. He arrived with a big reputation, and only proceeded to add to it.

First, he conquered the older horses at weight-for-age in the Tancred Stakes; then demolished his own age in the AJC Derby. On both occasions he gave his rivals a start and a beating, storming home after being near last on the home turn.

As he began his four-

1986
(Saturday, October 25. Attendance: 24,256)

$744,0000 plus $6,000 trophies Weight for Age 2,040m

1.	BONECRUSHER	F. T. Ritchie	57kg	G. M. Stewart	9/10f
2.	Our Waverley Star	D. O'Sullivan	57kg	L. O'Sullivan	3/1
3.	The Filbert	D. Couchman	59kg	G. Murphy	80/1

Winning details

Margin: Nk x 3 len. **Time:** 2:07.2 13 started.

Breeding: Pag-Asa – Imitation- Oakville (ch g 4) **Owner:** P. J. Mitchell

Winner's Colors: Cream, brown sash, striped sleeves & cap

Winning Numbers: 2, 3, 1

ALSO RAN

Dandy Andy	C. V. Cerchi	J. Marshall	49	50/1
Drought	J. F. Meagher	D. Gauci	48.5	10/1
Drawn	L. J. Bridge	P. Hyland	57	10/1
Dinky Flyer	K. J. Walker	G. Hall	56.5	66/1
Tristram	G. T. Murphy	G. Willetts	49.5	12/1
Ma Chiquita	N. Begg	R. S. Dye	54.5	33/1
Abaridy	S. Watkins	G. Doughty	48.5	50/1
Society Bay	G. Setchell	R. Stocker (a)	46	10/1
Roman Artist	N. Begg	M. Logue	57	125/1
Imprimatur	G. A. Chapman	P. Shepherd	48.5	1001

All started

BONECRUSHER ... he never knew when to give up and got the verdict by a whisker when he ranged up on the outside of Our Waverley Star in the last bound. – Picture: HWT

year-old year Bonecrusher was well on the way to earning $1 million in stakes. Our Waverley Star, on the other hand, began the new season with less than $100,000 against his name, by virtue of the fact he had not raced outside of New Zealand and his best win as a three-year-old came at Group 2 level.

He'd won six of his nine starts though, and if his ability to beat Bonecrusher was questioned early in the Spring of 1986, it was answered to some extent when he won the Admiralty Handicap over 1200m at Ellerslie on August 23, beating Bonecrusher into third place. From that point on both horses remained unbeaten in the lead-up to the Cox Plate.

Our Waverley Star stayed in New Zealand and won over 1400m before winning twice over 1600m, in Awapuni's Highview Metric Mile and in the Matamata Cup. Bonecrusher did his Cox Plate preparation in Melbourne against superior opposition, beating subsequent Melbourne Cup winner At Talaq in the Underwood Stakes at Caulfield, then blitzing a quality field in the Caulfield Stakes just over two weeks later.

In the fortnight leading up to the Cox Plate, the racing talk was of nothing other than the two New Zealand stars. Generally it was felt Bonecrusher had the edge, although most agreed a wet track on the day would certainly tip the scales in Our Waverley Star's favor.

On raceday there was money for both horses, with Bonecrusher opening at odds-on but easing for just a few moments to even money when heavy support for Our Waverley Star forced his price into 5/2.

At post time, Bonecrusher was the favorite at 9/10, with Our Waverley Star at 3/1 and the rest 8/1 or better. Given the impending clash between the two was a publicist's dream, and that the media had latched onto the prospect of a two-horse war with unmitigated fervor, it was therefore surprising, and no doubt disappointing, that a crowd of less than 25,000 came to watch. By the time the race was over many more thousands were wishing they'd made the effort to get there, and in later years if everyone claiming to have been there had been there, then to a man there must have been 50,000 at Moonee Valley that afternoon.

On a dry track, the leaders went off at a terrific rate, with Roman Artist making the running ahead of

Dandy Andy and Society Bay. At this stage, Bonecrusher and Our Waverley Star were within a length of one another, racing towards the rear of the field, although Our Waverley Star was caught three wide.

Then, approaching the 800m mark, Gary Stewart suddenly hooked Bonecrusher around the heels of his rival and set him alight. Lance O'Sullivan had no option but to go with him and the pair fairly rocketed up to the leaders.

Bill Collins' call, echoing across the intimate reaches of the amphitheatre that is Moonee Valley, even early on, contained a level of anticipated excitement, but as the two champs let go, so did Collins.

"Our Waverley Star will want to be Phar Lap (voice rises) but here's Bonecrusher, he's pulled him to the outside, shooting around them, and Our Waverley Star going with him ...."

There was a rumbling in the crowd as Collins switched back to the leaders, then seconds later a roar erupted as his voice again reached another octave.

"Here come the New Zealanders, Our Waverley Star and Bonecrusher, they've raced to the lead 600 out, have they gone too early?"

For a few strides it appeared they must have, but as they quickly moved away from the remaining runners it became apparent the predicted two horse war was to become a reality.

Or was it? Collins again. *"But Our Waverley Star, he's got a half length on Bonecrusher, he's gone for the whip on Bonecrusher."*

O'Sullivan admitted later he thought at this stage the race was his. "I was delighted," he commented. It was but a fleeting feeling.

"The two great New Zealanders have come away on the turn, Our Waverley Star a half length to Bonecrusher. Big Red won't give in."

Like the two horses, Collins' voice was now stretched to the limit. *"Bonecrusher responds to the whip, the roars of the crowd, he races up to Our Waverley Star."*

The last 200m almost defy description. Stride for stride the two horses went, their jockeys throwing everything at them. Collins' voice was all but strangled, but such was the frenzy of the crowd it's doubtful anyone on course heard him anyway.

Renowned racing scribe Les Carlyon, writing in *The Age* two days later, described it thus. "Two red horses blundering up the straight, caught in a hell of their own making. A place beyond pain, beyond exhaustion... beyond sense."

For one, just moment a deadheat was a possibility.

"One hundred metres out, Bonecrusher, Our Waverley Star, stride for stride, nothing in it, Our Waverley Star the rails, Bonecrusher the outside." Hoarse with emotion, Collins too was pulling out all the stops.

Then the race was over. *"And Bonecrusher races into equine immortality, one and a half million dollars as he photo finishes Our Waverley Star."*

Carried down from the stands on a sea of emotion, the connections of both horses had the look of men coming back from battle. Frank Ritchie and Dave O'Sullivan embraced; each shook the other's hand. They sensed it to be one of those rare occasions when the mere fact of winning or losing was but a minor issue.

They were not alone. Master trainer Bart Cummings, without a runner, rushed down from the grandstand to offer his congratulations.

"That's the best race I've ever seen, or ever hope to see," he said.

As usual he got it right.

HOOFNOTE: Bonecrusher was put down at the old age of 32 on the property of his owner Shirley Mitchell in New Zealand in June, 2015 after contracting the hoof disease, laminitis. The 18-time winner in 44 starts – 10 at Group 1 level – was buried at Auckland's Ellerslie racecourse where he won his first Group 1, the New Zealand Derby in 1985. Trainer Frank Ritchie said Bonecrusher's continued will to win at all costs had taken a physical toll on him later in his career.

1987 – HATS OFF TO HARRY

Two months before the 1987 Cox Plate, jockey Harry White drove to Moonee Valley one morning to ride the South Australian-trained Rubiton in a trial.

White was no stranger to the big brown, having won the Futurity Stakes on him at Caulfield the previous Autumn.

Back then, the quiet, unassuming White had declared Rubiton a "top class horse, a real good one." The Moonee Valley trial in September reinforced this opinion.

"He's big, he's well-built," White said after jumping off him. "He only has to relax a bit to get a middle distance." Then came prophetic words. "If he can do that then a race like the Cox Plate would be well within his scope."

Rubiton's trainer Pat Barnes would be the first to agree that had it not been for White, the exceptional ability possessed by Rubiton might never have been realised. He didn't race as a two- year-old, but won his first three races in the new season, the third of them being an emphatic five length win in the Group 3 Red Anchor Stakes over 1200m at Moonee Valley in early September.

He would have started one of the favorites for the Moonee Valley Stakes, but developed shin soreness and was sent home to Adelaide for a spell.

Back in training the big, strong colt proved more than a handful for those riding him, and after he'd run unplaced in the William Reid Stakes and refused to settle before finishing third in the Autumn Stakes at Sandown, Barnes knew something had to change.

In desperation he asked White, a master of the soft hands, if he could try to teach Rubiton to relax. Every day for three weeks, White rode the colt trackwork, not fighting him, instead sweet talking him out of his battle with the bit.

As White was to say some months later, "If you try to fight him with brute strength it's like having a rope on a lamp post – he'll break your back."

At the end of the second week, White rode Rubiton in the Oakleigh Plate, and managed to settle him before finishing strongly for third. A week later the pair tackled the Futurity. Rubiton led, but only at White's bidding, and when he booted away to win by two lengths Barnes knew he'd found the right combination.

A week later, the colt

> "He's big, he's well-built," White said after jumping off him. "He only has to relax a bit to get a middle distance." Then came prophetic words. "If he can do that then a race like the Cox Plate would be well within his scope." – *Harry White assessing Rubiton two months before the 1987 Cox Plate.*

1987
(Saturday, October 24. Attendance: 27,203)

$1,000,000 plus $25,000 trophies Weight for Age 2,040m

1.	**RUBITON**	P. C. Barns	57kg	H. White	7/4f
2.	**Our Poetic Prince**	J. R. Wheeler	48.5kg	G. A. Phillips	7/1
3.	**Fair Sir**	B. O'Malley	57kg	M. Sestich	7/1

Winning details

Margin: Long nk x len. **Time:** 2:02.9 (course record) 12 started.

Breeding: Century – Ruby – Seventh Hussar (br h 4)
Owner: D. L. & R. V. Bayliss & Trans Media Stud Syn

Winner's Colors: White & pink stripes, black cap

Winning Numbers: 2, 12, 5

ALSO RAN

Vo Rogue	V. R. Rail	G. Small	57	9/2
Beau Zam	J. B. Cummings	J. Marshall	48.5	5/1
Midnight Fever	C. S. Hayes	M. Carson	46	20/1
Marwong	G. T. Murphy	D. Murphy	48.5	50/1
Kaapstad	C. S. Hayes	M. Clarke	49	25/1
Tidal Light	J. A. Gibbs	G. Cooksley	54.5	16/1
Campaign King	J. B. Cummings	L. Dittman	59	20/1
High Regard	T. W. Harper	R. Bligh	49	50/1
Drought (PU)	J. F. Meagher	G. Hall	57	7/1

Scratched: Sky Chase, Tri Belle

ran a super race to finish third behind Placid Ark in the Newmarket Handicap, and when stepped up to 1500m for his final race of the season, Rubiton finished a promising second in the Phar Lap Stakes at Rosehill.

One person impressed with the son of Century was media personality Mike Willesee, owner of Trans Media Stud at Cootamundra. He negotiated with Rubiton's owners, David and Rod Bayliss, to buy a quarter share in the colt, with a view to standing him at Trans Media upon his retirement.

Back from a Winter spell, Rubiton looked magnificent. And four days after trialling at Moonee Valley he returned there for the real thing and demolished a good weight-for-age field in the 1200m Manikato Stakes, easing up to win by three lengths.

Once again, White waxed lyrical about the horse and his Spring chances. "He's 16.5 hands and it's all muscle and bone. I really believe he can win the Cox Plate," he said.

Only four horses opposed Rubiton at his next start, in the Memsie Stakes at Caulfield. The best of them were the Bart Cummings-trained four year old Broad Reach, winner of the Rothmans 100,000 at Doomben during the Winter, and New Zealand mare Society Bay, who'd won the Edward Manifold Stakes at Flemington the previous season.

> He could be the best horse in the world, jockey Harry White told a wide-eyed part-owner, Mike Willesee. A heat of the moment statement perhaps, but by the end of September the stallion had done nothing to change White's opinion. To the contrary, authoritative wins in the Feehan Stakes at Moonee Valley and in the Underwood Stakes at Caulfield only enhanced it.

It took all of Rubiton's ability to run down Society Bay, ridden cleverly in front by Pat Hyland, but afterwards White was positively ecstatic. He could be the best horse in the world, he told a wide-eyed Willesee.

A heat of the moment statement perhaps, but by the end of September the stallion had done nothing to change White's opinion. To the contrary, strong wins in the Feehan Stakes at Moonee Valley and in the Underwood Stakes at Caulfield only enhanced it.

In the Feehan, Rubiton disposed of the talented front-runner Vo Rogue, in the process equalling the track record for 1600m. He was even more impressive winning the Underwood, swooping from near last at the 800m to have the race within his keeping on the turn, leaving the likes of the Australian Guineas winner, Military Plume, among his vanquished rivals.

Before the Underwood, White was beginning to talk in terms of Rubiton perhaps being the best horse he'd ridden, better even than his Caulfield Guineas and Caulfield Cup winner Sobar, according to White the only champion horse he'd been associated with. After the Underwood he was in no doubt. "He's the best horse I've ever ridden," he said, then added, "I never thought the day would come when I would say a horse was better than Sobar. No way."

White was suspended for causing interference during the running of the Underwood, but because it was due to end the day before Rubiton's final Cox Plate lead-up race, the Caulfield Stakes, he was unfazed.

What did rankle him, and Barnes as well, were the jibes of some who reckoned they'd overrated the big horse. "Perhaps I'm not big enough for them," Barnes commented, in reference to a suggestion that if Rubiton was in the care of a big-name trainer, the impression would be different.

The Thursday before the Caulfield Stakes, Rubiton worked on the steeple grass at Flemington, but in Barnes' opinion didn't work hard enough. The following morning he had White gallop the four-year-old on the sand track. This time Rubiton really turned it on, almost pulling White out of the saddle as he worked over 1200m.

HARRY WHITE ... predicted early that Rubiton was Cox Plate material.

With hindsight, Barnes admits working the horse twice in two days was a mistake. To the dismay of punters who sent him to the post a 1-3 favorite for the Caulfield Stakes, Rubiton struggled into third place behind Drought and Fair Sir, two horses he'd given a thrashing in the Underwood Stakes.

With just two weeks up his sleeve, Barnes decided to send Rubiton to the bush for some rest and recuperation. Almost until the eve of the Cox Plate, the stallion trotted and cantered around the soft hills that characterize veteran trainer George Hanlon's training property at Leopold, just outside of Geelong.

Rubiton returned to Flemington a much more relaxed horse, but Barnes could only cross his fingers and hope it would be reflected in an improved performance on race day.

The Rubiton fan club, and it was a big one, had no doubts. They sent him out a firm favorite at 7-4 despite opposition the calibre of Turnbull Stakes winner Vo Rogue, high class New Zealand three year old Our Poetic Prince and AJC Derby winner Beau Zam, to name just a few.

With a bold front-runner such as Vo Rogue in the race, there was never any likelihood of the '87 Cox Plate being run at anything but a cracking pace, so White was unperturbed when Rubiton drew the extreme outside in barrier 12.

White had no hesitation in dropping the stallion out to last in the run down the straight the first time, as up front the New Zealand mare Tidal Light made a half-hearted attempt to lead Vo Rogue.

The Queensland champ was having none of it though, and after 600m jockey Cyril Small had him six lengths clear of Tidal Light, with the rest stringing out behind. This margin was increased to eight lengths at the 1000m mark, at which stage Rubiton was back third last and some 20 lengths from the tearaway leader.

As good as he was, Vo Rogue just had to come back to the field, and approaching the turn he was overhauled by Our Poetic Prince, with Fair Sir also making a bid.

White had set Rubiton alight at the 600m mark, and the big horse's immediate response struck a relieved chord in Barnes, watching anxiously from the stands. "I knew at least he was his old self," the trainer commented later.

There was work to do though, for Our Poetic Prince was going strongly at the 300m mark and Rubiton appeared to be flat out catching him. But as only great horses do, he lengthened his stride to join the battle, drawing level inside the 100m and forging clear to win by three-quarters of a length.

Our Poetic Prince was gallant in defeat, as was Fair Sir. And for Vo Rogue to hang on and run fourth indicated what over the next couple of seasons he proved to be – a champion.

White was subdued after the win, more in awe of Rubiton than anything else.

"His best win was the Underwood Stakes," he explained. "He just kept giving today, as good horses do, but he did not have the same dash."

For all of that, his connections decided to run Rubiton in the Mackinnon Stakes at Flemington a week later. He won, but had to dig deep to beat King Of Brooklyn and Military Plume.

There was much to look forward to in the Autumn, but sadly, Rubiton ruptured a tendon preparing for the William Reid Stakes in January and was immediately retired.

At the stud, Rubiton has been a success, having sired a number of high class gallopers, the best of them perhaps being the 1999 Stradbroke Handicap winner Adam, a fighter in the same mould as his dad.

1988 — PRINCE REIGNS AS PLATE KING

As a three-year-old Our Poetic Prince had campaigned quite extensively at the Carnivals in both Melbourne and in Brisbane, but success had eluded him. Not for want of trying nor, for that matter, a lack of class. He had seven starts at Group level and was runner-up in four of them.

When Our Poetic Prince arrived back in Australia from New Zealand in the Spring of 1988, he had some old scores to settle.

As a three-year-old he'd campaigned quite extensively at the Carnivals in both Melbourne and in Brisbane, but success had eluded him. Not for want of trying nor, for that matter, a lack of class. He had seven starts at Group level and was runner-up in four of them.

Of course there are those who still believe Our Poetic Prince should be in the record books as the winner of the 1987 Caulfield Guineas, in which he was first past the post but lost the race on protest to Marwong. It was a controversial decision, made even more so by the fact that two weeks later, Our Poetic Prince finished a game second – beaten a long neck – to Rubiton in the Cox Plate, with Marwong unplaced.

The Winter rains were still tumbling down when Our Poetic Prince began his 1988 Spring campaign, a campaign aimed specifically at the Cox Plate. That alone should have been enough to install the New Zealander as the early favorite, not only for trainer John Wheeler's belief his charge had something to prove, but also for his knack of setting goals and achieving them.

That his horse was on song, was evident at his first run back, when he had the likes of Bonecrusher and top mare Tri Belle behind him in winning the weight-for-age Foxbridge Plate over 1400m at Te Rapa on a heavy track. In another weight-for-age event at Hastings three weeks later, the bay was even more impressive, winning over 1400m with jockey Noel Harris easing him down over the last 100m.

Two starts for the season, two wins. On the strength of that it might have been expected Our Poetic Prince would start favorite at his seasonal debut in Australia, in the weight-for-age Feehan Stakes at Moonee Valley on Grand Final day. But with horses the calibre of Vo Rogue, Sky Chase and Flotilla in the field, the local punters let the Kiwi go around at 11-2. Nice odds indeed according to Wheeler. Even better when Our Poetic Prince, ridden off the cracking pace set by Vo Rogue, finished powerfully to beat Flotilla

1988
(Saturday, October 22. Attendance: 29,286)

$1,500,000 plus $25,000 trophies Weight for Age 2,040m

1.	**OUR POETIC PRINCE**	J. R. Wheeler	57kg	*N. Harris*	5/4f
2.	**Horlicks**	D. O'Sullivan	56.5kg	*L. O'Sullivan*	8/1
3.	**Bonecrusher**	F. T. Ritchie	59kg	*G. M. Stewart*	7/1

Winning details

Margin: 1¼ len x nk. **Time:** 2:06.9 11 started.

Breeding: Yeats – Finisterre – Biscay (b h 4) **Owner:** G. J. Pratt & W. L. Bolton

Winner's Colors: Maroon, gold diamonds, blue & gold armbands & quartered cap

Winning Numbers: 3, 7, 1

ALSO RAN

Run Straight Run	F. J. Wilson	D. Beadman	49	20/1
Almurtajaz	C. S. Hayes	M. Clarke	49	8/1
Flotilla	J. Denham	B. Thomson	57	6/1
Vitalic	A. E. Elkington	P. Cook	49	15/1
Planet Ruler	B. McLachlan	B. York	57	9/1
Imposera	R. S. McDonald	G. Hall	54.5	20/1
Glenview	J. B. Cummings	M. Heagney	46.5	50/1
High Regard	T. W. Harper	W. Treloar	57	40/1

Scratched: Vo Rogue

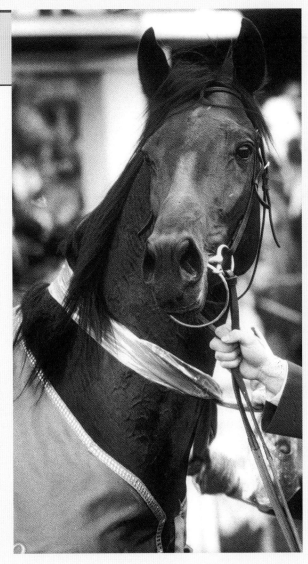

and Vo Rogue in Australian record time for 1600m of 1.33.10.

It seems the only one not impressed by the run was top trainer Bart Cummings, whose four-year-old Sky Chase wilted in the straight to finish fourth. Cummings claimed that the blistering early pace set the race up for the New Zealander, adding he expected his horse to set the record straight in the Caulfield Stakes a fortnight later. Sky Chase did. In a race which saw Our Poetic Prince unexpectedly make the pace from a wide barrier, the Cummings-trained entrant this time had the last crack and ran out an emphatic winner by two lengths.

Wheeler was far from disappointed, rightly so too, given Our Poetic Prince didn't flinch in the run up the straight despite his tough run in front. "He's right on target," the affable trainer commented. A week later Sky Chase ran 7-4 favorite in the Caulfield Cup and pulled up in 16th place, his action scratchier than an old 78 record. Three days later he was selected, along with Bonecrusher, to represent Australasia in the Japan Cup.

That decision did not go down well with Our Poetic Prince's supporters, but Wheeler just shrugged and got on with the business of having the horse at his peak for the Cox Plate. It seems reasons will always be found for good horses not to win good races. As the race drew near, some questioned the New Zealander's ability to run out a solid 2040m. Wheeler had a simple answer. "It took a damn good horse to beat him last year," he said. Indeed Our Poetic Prince was beaten a long neck by Rubiton, in course record time to boot.

Raceday dawned, and with it came a shock. The dead track rating convinced the connections of front-running star Vo Rogue to scratch him, and with him went the certainty of a truly run race. It was a controversial decision, made all the more so by claims that the Moonee Valley track had been over-watered despite forecasts for rain in the 24 hours leading up to the race.

Vo Rogue was considered one of the main chances, so his withdrawal put a sizeable hole in the betting market, at the same time enhancing the prospects of Our Poetic Prince. The majority of the 30,000 racegoers who flocked to the Valley on the day needed little convincing, and sent Our Poetic Prince off a hot 5-4 favorite ahead of horses such as Bonecrusher, the smart mare Horlicks, the 1988 Australian Guineas winner Flotilla, and the Caulfield Cup winner Imposera.

Jockey Noel Harris was able to steer Our Poetic Prince clear of early scrimmaging that did little for the chances of several runners, most notably Horlicks. A dawdling pace saw the favorite perfectly placed fourth on the rails, with Flotilla just ahead of him but with Bonecrusher and Horlicks behind him. The pace quickened from the 800m mark, but approaching the turn Harris hunted Our Poetic Prince around the leaders and sent him clear at the top of the straight.

From there, he never really looked like being beaten. First Bonecrusher tried to get on terms, then the unlucky Horlicks ran on late, but at the finish it was Our Poetic Prince by 1¼ lengths and doing it pretty easily.

A week later he ran unplaced in the Mackinnon Stakes at Flemington, but the following Autumn he confirmed his undoubted ability by winning two Group 1 contests in Sydney, the Tancred Stakes over 2400m, and the Queen Elizabeth Stakes over 2000m.

It is also worth noting, Horlicks won at Group 1 level in New Zealand the following Autumn and later in 1989 achieved a magnificent victory in the Japan Cup.

1989 — HAYES ON A WINNING SWANSONG

Almaarad raced only four times in Australia, but left an everlasting impression as a horse of great character, and one for whom defeat was never an option.

Yet, had it not been for a tendon injury suffered in the Autumn of 1989, it is highly likely Almaarad would have been back in England by the time Spring came around.

Injuries to racehorses are as frequent as they are feared, and all too often have ended prematurely, promising, or even illustrious careers.

Sometimes though, such an injury can have a positive outcome, providing the horse itself has the inner strength to overcome it.

One such horse was the imported stallion Almaarad, a coppery chestnut with a baldy face who pushed himself through the pain barrier to win a memorable Cox Plate in 1989.

Trained by Colin Hayes, he raced only four times in Australia, but left an everlasting impression as a horse of great character, and one for whom defeat was never an option.

Yet, had it not been for a tendon injury suffered in the Autumn of 1989, it is highly likely Almaarad would have been back in England by the time Spring came around. Originally trained there by John Dunlop he was owned by Sheik Hamden al Maktoum, whose blue and white colors were already a familiar sight on Australian tracks, and in fact were carried by At Talaq to win the 1986 Melbourne Cup.

Almaarad, a six-year-old at the beginning of 1989, was one of four overseas horses invited to Australia to contest the Tancred International at Rosehill in April. He was by far the best performed, making the frame each time in six starts the previous season, all of them over 2400m and all at Group level. He won three, including the Group 2 Hardwicke Stakes at Royal Ascot, and the Group 1 Aral-Pokal at Gelesenkirchen in Germany. He also finished a creditable fourth behind Mtoto in the King George and Queen Elizabeth Stakes, England's equivalent of the Cox Plate.

The day before the Tancred, Almaarad was found to have injured his off-fore tendon. Not only did it cause him to miss the race, but also prevented him from being flown back to England with the overseas contingent.

Immediate retirement to the stud was considered, but Sheik Hamdan decided the horse should be given one Australian preparation, essentially to help advertise his stallion properties. Hayes, as it transpired in his last year

1989
(Saturday, October 28. Attendance: 28,914)

$1,700,000 plus $6,500 trophies Weight for Age 2,040m

1.	ALMAARAD	C. S. Hayes	59kg	M. Clarke	11/4f
2.	Stylish Century	F. W. Mitchell	48.5kg	K. Moses	33/1
3.	Empire Rose	L. K. Laxon	56.5kg	T. K. Allen	15/1

Winning details

Margin: Hd x 5 len. **Time:** 2:03.2 14 started.

Breeding: Ela Mana Mou – Silk Blend – Busted (ch h 7)
Owner: Sheikh Hamdan Bin Rashid Al Maktoum

Winner's Colors: Royal blue, white epaulettes, striped cap

Winning Numbers: 1, 12, 8

ALSO RAN

Our Westminster	N. Fraser	P. Cook	59	25/1
Riverina Charm	B. Mayfield-Smith	K. Russell	54.5	33/1
King's High	C. S. Hayes	A. G. Clarke	57	25/1
Trsitanagh	J. B. Cummings	J. Marshall	46.5	9/2
Vitalic	A. E. Elkington	G. Duffy	57	9/1
Apollo Run	C. Alderson	D. Gauci	49	40/1
Courtza	R. S. McDonald	R. S. Dye	47	8/1
The Phantom	M. P. Baker	L. O'Sullivan	57	25/1
Procol Harum	V. Thomson	S. King	48.5	33/1
Vo Rogue	V. R. Rail	C. Small	59	5/1
Zabeel	C. S. Hayes	L. Dittman	49	9/1

Scratched: Cole Diesel, Horlicks

as a trainer, set about preparing Almaarad for a tilt at the Melbourne Cup, with the Caulfield Cup marked down as well. Initially the Cox Plate was not included in the horse's program. Gradually throughout the Winter Hayes worked the import up to race fitness on the forgiving Equitrack surface at his Lindsay Park complex, ever mindful of the need to protect the suspect tendon.

Also there was the problem of having to race Almaarad left-handed. Racing that way he'd shown a tendency to hang, and significantly all of his European wins were achieved on right-hand galloping tracks. The ever-resourceful Hayes fitted the horse with a one-eyed blinker; end of problem.

COLIN HAYES ... bowed out as a trainer on a winning note in the Cox Plate.

The Craiglee Stakes at Flemington in early September was chosen for Almaarad to make his Australian debut, although it was generally felt the 1600m would be a shade too short for him. It was, but only by a whisker, and only after he'd been momentarily held up for a couple of strides at a crucial stage of the race. Almaarad was beaten a short half head by Apollo Run, but according to his rider Gary Clarke would have won had not third-placed Super Impose crowded him for room half-way up the straight.

Some three weeks later, Almaarad gained his revenge when he came from second last before the turn to beat Apollo Run and The Phantom in the Group 1 Underwood Stakes. Two weeks later, he was promoted to favoritism for both the Caulfield and Melbourne Cups following another Group 1 weight-for-age victory, this time in the Caulfield Stakes, beating Vitalic and the bold, front-running Queenslander Vo Rogue.

Many labelled him unbeatable in the Caulfield Cup, but former top jockey Ron Hutchinson was not so sure. In a newspaper column Hutchinson noted Almaarad had rolled in and hit the running rail en route to winning at Caulfield. "This is not a good sign," wrote Hutchinson. "Something is amiss when a class horse behaves in this manner."

His thoughts were prescient. Almaarad was not among the final acceptors for the Caulfield Cup, with Hayes announcing a switch to the Cox Plate as part of the stallion's Melbourne Cup preparation.

Leg problems were not cited as the reason for this change of direction, but significantly perhaps Hayes sent Almaarad back to Lindsay Park and the Equitrack to continue his preparation. He did not return to Melbourne until two days before the Cox Plate, Hayes being unperturbed by the fact Almaarad would go to the Valley sight unseen. What he didn't count on, was the stallion tearing a shoe and part of his hoof off in the sandroll at Flemington shortly after his arrival from Lindsay Park.

At first stable farrier Ray Purdey doubted he could nail on another shoe, but then constructed a special shoe to support the horse's off fore foot. News of this drama did not come until after the race, and so the import was sent out favorite at 11-4, with money for the Bart Cummings-trained Tristanagh, Vo Rogue, of course, and another Hayes runner, the good three-year-old Zabeel.

Adding spice to the contest was Hayes' announcement two days before the Cox Plate that he would retire at the end of the season, and hand over to his youngest son, David.

Some titanic battles for the Cox Plate have been waged up the short Moonee Valley straight; this particular running provided one of the more memorable. Three-year-old colt Stylish Century always liked to run, and in this contest, run he did. From the barrier rise jockey Kevin Moses hunted him to the lead, at a pace not even the brilliant Vo Rogue could match. As the field strung out to the 1400m turn Stylish Century led by five lengths from Vo Rogue racing wide, with Almaarad back racing in sixth place on the rails.

Could Stylish Century maintain the pace? Racing towards the turn it became clear that he could, for several horses including Vo Rogue were struggling to stay in the contest.

Not Almaarad though. Clarke moved him up to challenge on the point of the turn, and with nothing else looking as strong, it seemed he must go on to a decisive win. Stylish Century, though, had other ideas, and flatly refused to give in. All of the way up the straight he came back at Almaarad, and it was only in the last few strides the baldy-faced favorite was able to gain the ascendancy and win by a head.

The previous year's Melbourne Cup winner Empire Rose finished third, but she was five lengths away in what essentially became a two-horse race.

Hayes, naturally, was overcome with emotion. "When you have been 40 years in the business, to win the premier race in the country in your last year as a trainer, it's very special. A great thrill," he said. Almaarad, now was a warm favorite for the Melbourne Cup, but sadly he never made it to Flemington. In fact he never raced again. The tendon, which always threatened to give way, finally did so, and prematurely ended the career of a great international trouper.

1990 — LIKE FATHER, LIKE SON

It is doubtful any trainer has begun his career under as much public scrutiny as did David Hayes when he inherited Australia's biggest training and breeding operation from his father Colin at the end of the 1989-90 racing season.

Hayes Snr. went out in a blaze of glory; a Cox Plate win with Almaarad, a record number of winners trained in Australia, world-wide respect for his training genius; the list of his achievements seemed endless.

Twenty-eight-year-old David was in simple terms on a hiding to nothing when, in August, 1990, horses from Lindsay Park began appearing as trained by " D. A. Hayes" as opposed to the familiar "C. S. Hayes". Within the space of a few short months it became clear David Hayes was not going to suffer a hiding. In fact, it was as though nothing had changed, and never more so than on Cox Plate day, when for the second year running the Classic fell to a Hayes-trained runner, a solidly built but hardly eye-catching grandson of Better Boy named Better Loosen Up.

He came into the care of Colin Hayes as a four-year-old prior to the Spring of 1989, after having been trained by, among others, Bart Cummings. Better Loosen Up was bred at Berrigan in NSW by Howard and Jan Martin. They sold three-quarters of him to local trainer Les Theodore, and soon after sold their remaining share to Albury motel owner Gabe Farrah.

Ironically Theodore, too, had sold out of the horse long before he became a superstar of the Australian turf, although he did prepare him to win a two-year-old race at Bendigo before taking a break from training and transferring the horse to Cummings.

As a late three-year-old, Better Loosen Up gave more than a hint of his potential by finishing second to the class filly Riverina Charm in the Canterbury Guineas before being transferred back to Theodore. A South Australian Derby campaign was contemplated but back problems forced the gelding into the spelling paddock and when returned to training he was sent to Lindsay Park.

To say Better Loosen Up improved as a four-year-old is a massive understatement. He in fact won four Group I races in three states, including the Honda Stakes at Flemington, and the

1990
(Saturday, October 27. Attendance: 28,074)

$1,700,000 plus $6,500 trophies Weight for Age 2,040m

1.	BETTER LOOSEN UP	D. A. Hayes	59 kg	M. Clarke	2/1f
2.	Sydeston	R. E. Hoysted	59 kg	L. Dittman	6/1
3.	Canny Lad	R. Hore-Lacy	48.5 kg	R. S. Dye	11/2

Winning details

Margin: ½ len x ½ len. **Time:** 2:01.5 (Eq. course record) 11 started.

Breeding: Loosen Up (USA) – Better Fantasy – Better Boy (b g 5)
Owner: L. Fink & Mesdames J. Y. & L. & Mr A. Farrah & L. Khoumi

Winner's Colors: White, green sash, black sleeves & cap

Winning Numbers: 2, 1, 8

ALSO RAN

The Phantom	M. P. Baker	G. Cooksley	59	16/1
Stylish Century	F. W. Mitchell	K. Moses	57	13/2
St. Jude	B. McLachlan	S. King	48.5	20/1
Shuzohra	E. B. Skelton	L. Olsen	56.5	25/1
Horlicks	D. O'Sullivan	L. O'Sullivan	56.5	4/1
Lord Revenir	B. J. Wallace	L. Cassidy	49.5	33/1
Integra	B. Mayfield-Smith	J. Marshall	48.5	16/1
King's High	D. A. Hayes	D. Gauci	59	40/1

All started

Segenhoe Stakes at Rosehill, beating the likes of Sydeston, Super Impose, Vo Rogue and the 1989 Japan Cup winner Horlicks.

Those were truly outstanding performances, but few if any could dispute the gelding proved an even better galloper as a five-year-old. Indeed, he was to become one of the best in the world. Some might say that in Better Loosen Up, David Hayes was handed the proverbial "silver spoon". Perhaps, but there is immense pressure training top horses, and Hayes handled it admirably. He announced at the beginning of the Spring that Better Loosen Up would be aimed specifically at the Cox Plate, with the Mackinnon Stakes a week later also on the agenda. And, Hayes said, the gelding would contest the Japan Cup if invited.

Better Loosen Up began his Spring campaign in the Liston Stakes at Sandown, and on a heavy track was beaten into fourth place, two lengths behind the winner, Sydeston. Hayes was unperturbed, as well he might have been, given the gelding had never performed at his best on rain-affected going. Perhaps because it had worked so well with Almaarad the previous season, Better Loosen Up was trained at Lindsay Park throughout his Spring campaign, being floated back to Melbourne a day or two before each engagement.

Three weeks after the Liston, Better Loosen Up was back in town to contest the Feehan Stakes at Moonee Valley, and proceeded to get right down to business. Settling back in the field he stormed home to beat the 1989 Victoria Derby winner Stylish Century in a photo, after giving that horse 10 lengths start from the 800m.

Jockey Michael Clarke was awed by the performance. "He has a tremendous will to win," Clarke said.

In the week before the Cox Plate, it was announced Better Loosen Up and Stylish Century would represent Oceania in the Japan Cup. "He'll do Australia justice," Hayes said. "He's ready to run the race of his life in the Cox Plate on Saturday." As it turned out Better Loosen Up needed to. Certainly his winning performance was the equal to that of any Cox Plate winner in modern times.

The favorite at 2-1, he gave away what 800m from home appeared to be an impossible start, yet won the race with authority. Given the free-running Stylish Century was the natural pacemaker, the 1990 Cox Plate was always going to be a fast-run race. Even so, few could have expected him to be leading by 10 lengths past the half-way mark. At that stage, Better Loosen Up was back second last in the 11 horse field – "going flat-out", Clarke said – a good 20 lengths from the tear-away leader. Hayes admitted later at that point he'd all but given up hope of winning.

What was it Clarke said about Better Loosen Up's tremendous will to win? That day, as the Cox Plate field charged toward the home turn, it became obvious Better Loosen Up's refusal to be beaten was going to be a crucial factor in the result.

Stylish Century had to come back to his rivals, and around the turn he was swamped by several of them, including the Caulfield Cup winner Sydeston. His rider, Mick Dittman, sensed victory. "I thought then nothing could come from behind and beat me," he said later. In any other circumstance, probably nothing could have. But Better Loosen Up was special. Somehow he kept digging deeper and deeper, all the time under the cool, hands and heels riding of Clarke.

A huge roar erupted as he swept up to win going away by a half length, soon followed by another when his time of 2.01.5 – equal to the course record – was posted.

The following week he won the Mackinnon Stakes, then made history by becoming the first Australian-trained horse to win the Japan Cup, again showing his trademark bloody-minded refusal to be beaten.

In the 1991 Autumn he won the Blamey Stakes first-up, then the Australian Cup, before injury forced him back into the spelling paddock. His record for the 1990-91 season stood at eight starts for seven wins straight, four of them Group 1, the others Group 2. Quite simply, Better Loosen Up was a champion.

1991 – PARADISE REGAINED FOR O'SULLIVANS

No-one could forget how gracious Dave O'Sullivan and his sons, Paul and Lance, were in defeat when Our Waverley Star was beaten a breath by Bonecrusher in the 1986 epic. And O'Sullivan could have made valid excuses, but didn't, when gallant mare Horlicks found trouble at every corner before being beaten by Our Poetic Prince in 1988.

As the 1980's drew to a close, New Zealand trainer Dave O'Sullivan, a horseman of consummate skill, began to despair of ever winning the Cox Plate.

Numerous attempts had failed, yet on several occasions he'd come tantalizingly close. There was perhaps no one more deserved of winning Australasia's weight-for-age championship.

No-one could forget how gracious O'Sullivan and his sons, Paul and Lance, were in defeat when Our Waverley Star was beaten a breath by Bonecrusher in the 1986 epic. And O'Sullivan could have made valid excuses, but didn't, when gallant mare Horlicks found trouble at every corner before being beaten by Our Poetic Prince in 1988.

Horlicks was a last minute scratching from the Cox Plate the following year, then finished unplaced behind Better Loosen Up in 1990. By then though, the O'Sullivan's had another star galloper looming on the horizon. Good horses so often have a way of finding themselves in the care of good trainers, and so it was with a weedy, unimposing Crested Wave yearling who was later given the somewhat exotic name of Surfers Paradise.

The colt was all but dismissed by O'Sullivan when he was invited to inspect him by his owners, but son Paul, his co-trainer, later caved in to repeated requests from one of them, New Zealand Sky Channel presenter Jim Smith, to give him a try.

A rather difficult horse to handle – he was eventually gelded – Surfers Paradise nevertheless went against O'Sullivan's expectations by winning two trials, then at his first race start ploughed through mud to win a two-year-old event at Pukekohe by four lengths. The following season Surfers Paradise was nigh on unbeatable, a fact which earned him New Zealand's Racehorse of the Year award.

He had nine starts at home for eight wins, including the New Zealand Two Thousand Guineas, the New Zealand Derby and the New Zealand Stakes, all Group I contests.

Taken across the Tasman for the Sydney

1991
(Saturday, October 26. Attendance: 29,311)

$1,700,000 plus $6,500 trophies Weight for Age 2,040m

1.	SURFERS PARADISE	D. O'Sullivan	57 kg	L. O'Sullivan	14/1
2.	Super Impose	D. Freedman	59 kg	D. Beadman	5/1
3.	Sydeston	R. E. Hoysted	59 kg	L. Dittman	7/1

Winning details

Margin: Len x 1¾ len. **Time:** 2:03.8 14 started.

Breeding: Crested Wave – Lady Aythorpe – Aythorpe (br h 4)
Owner: K. Chong, G. Fong, F. Cheung & J. D. Smith

Winner's Colors: Yellow, dark blue striped sleeves & quartered cap

Winning Numbers: 10, 2, 3

ALSO RAN

Prince Salieri	G. M. Hanlon	M. Clarke	59	30/1
Royal Creation	K. R. Verner	L. Cassidy	59	33/1
Ready to Explode	J. F. Meagher	S. King	48.5	12/1
Rough Habit	J. R. Wheeler	J. Cassidy	59	13/2
Dr. Grace	G. A. Chapman	R. S. Dye	59	20/1
Lord Revenir	B. J. Wallace	G. Cooksley	57	25/1
Stylish Century	R. N. Monaghan	D. Oliver (a)	59	66/1
Kinjite	N. J. Doyle	A. Cowie	49	14/1
Shaftesbury Avenue	J. B. Cummings	D. Gauci	59	6/4f
Stargazer	T. J. Smith	G. Hall	59	100/1
Chortle	B. J. McLachlan	P. Hutchinson	48.5	66/1

All started

Autumn Carnival he scored a brilliant win in the Rosehill Guineas before starting a solid favorite but managing to finish only sixth behind Durbridge in the AJC Derby.

That run was disappointing, but it did convince O'Sullivan the gelding was probably at his most effective over 2000m, and that the Cox Plate should be his Spring mission. Some horses handle wet tracks, others don't. Surfers Paradise was definitely in the latter category, thus a wet Spring in New Zealand played havoc with his preparation. O'Sullivan stuck with a plan to give the gelding all of his Cox Plate lead-up races in New Zealand. Four times he started and four times he was beaten, although twice finishing second, once behind Rough Habit, on the other occasion to Castletown.

Surfers Paradise's last race before heading to Melbourne came two weeks before the Cox Plate, in an open handicap at Ellerslie. Such was the state of the main track there, the races were switched to the tighter inside track, where the going was officially slow but, in the eyes of most, it was a mud-heap.

Surfers Paradise, a raging favorite on the Tote, was prominent early, but once let down was all at sea, and finished 10th of 11. Asked why he'd not ridden Surfers Paradise out in the straight jockey Lance O'Sullivan's answer was simple. "He'd have fallen over," he told the stewards.

The O'Sullivan clan arrived in Melbourne convinced their horse was fit, but with no real form line by which they could assess his Cox Plate chances. Neither could the punters, and so he drifted in to be a 14-1 chance on the day of the race.

On race morning, Dave O'Sullivan endeavored to calm his nerves by watching a video of past Cox Plates, but eventually switched it off half-way through the Bonecrusher – Our Waverley Star confrontation. However, he noted that in so many Cox Plates the pace was on from the outset, and that the winners came from behind, so he decided Surfers Paradise would be ridden from right off the speed, contrary to his normal pattern.

The 1991 Cox Plate was packed with Group 1 winners. To name just a few, the field included the mighty "miler" Super Impose, weight-for-age winners Dr. Grace and Shaftesbury Avenue, Caulfield Cup winner Sydeston, the evergreen great Rough Habit, plus a couple of very handy three-year-olds, Champion Stakes winner Kinjite, and Caulfield Guineas winner Chortle.

Chortle liked to be on the speed in his races, and so of course did another entrant, Stylish Century, who'd led the Cox Plate field a merry dance for 1600m the previous year. Speed in the race therefore was assured, although it might have come as a surprise to many to see Lance O'Sullivan position Surfers Paradise right back off it, to be a good 15 lengths from the leaders at the 1000m mark.

Earlier there was a sensation when Shaftesbury Avenue, the 6-4 favorite, slipped and almost fell on the turn out of the straight. He eventually finished near last and was later found to have suffered muscle damage.

Speed or no speed, the Cox Plate always seems to come alive around the 600m mark, and this year was no exception. Jim Cassidy set Rough Habit alight at this point and sent him around the field to lead on the turn, but almost immediately he came under pressure and was headed by Sydeston. His tenure in front was short-lived as well, for Super Impose surged past him and looked all over a winner inside the 200m mark.

It seemed Surfers Paradise came from nowhere. Just as the crowd began to rise in acclamation of the hometown favorite, the bright yellow colors of Surfers Paradise appeared almost under the roses, and he won by a length, drawing away.

The O'Sullivans were ecstatic. Already that day they'd won the Waterford Crystal Vase with Fine Commander, their first ever winner at Moonee Valley in more than 16 years of trying.

Now, less than an hour later, the Cox Plate was theirs too. Surfers Paradise won only one other race that season, and indeed never came close to reaching the dizzy heights achieved on that last Saturday in October, 1991.

1992 — A SUPER SECOND-STRINGER!

LEE FREEDMAN ... "just loved" Super Impose.

It is rare a winner of the Cox Plate should be in the race only as a stepping stone to a later contest, and be given little or no chance of winning by his connections.

Yet that was the prime reason one of Australia's greatest gallopers, Super Impose, ran in the 1992 Cox Plate, it being his final warm-up for the Melbourne Cup, in which he'd previously run twice for a second (in 1989) and a fourth (in 1991).

He wasn't altogether written off, for the previous year he'd run second in the race to Surfers Paradise, and more importantly had established himself as one of the all-time greats over 1600m, courtesy of dual wins in both the Doncaster and Epsom Handicaps. But those triumphs were behind him. In the Spring of 1992, the now eight-year-old Super Impose was finding the going a shade tough in top weight-for-age company, running a string of minor placings.

Attempting his third successive win in the Epsom Handicap in early October, he ran his heart out but anchored with 61.5kg had to be content with fourth place behind highly impressive four-year-old Kinjite. It was then trainer Lee Freedman decided to embark the veteran gelding upon his third Melbourne Cup campaign, and subsequently sent him off to the ACT for the Canberra Cup to get, as he put it, "the miles into his legs".

With a soft weight of 58kg against decidedly moderate opposition, Super Impose won easily. Mindful of the need to space the old-timer's runs, Freedman then nominated the Cox Plate as his final Cup trial, rather than leave it to the Mackinnon Stakes only three days before the staying test.

The 1992 Cox Plate field was no pushover. Quite to the contrary, for it included the best horses to have raced in Australia over three seasons, plus an excellent representation of the top three-year-olds.

At the head of the contest were Better Loosen Up and Let's Elope, respectively Horse of the Year winners in the seasons 1989-90 and 1990-91. Better Loosen Up, the 1990 Japan Cup hero, was struggling to regain form after injury, and therefore was a 50-1 chance, but Let's Elope was well in the market at 6-1.

Caulfield Cup winner Mannerism was there,

1992
(Saturday, October 24. Attendance: 33,028)

$1,700,000 plus $6,500 trophies Weight for Age 2,040m

1.	**SUPER IMPOSE**	D. L. Freedman	59 kg	G. Hall	16/1
2.	**Kinjite**	N. J. Doyle	57 kg	B. York	50/1
3.	**Slight Chance**	R. H. Thomsen	46.5 kg	R. S. Dye	20/1

Winning details

Margin: Hd x ½ len. **Time:** 2:05.5 14 started.

Breeding: Imposing – Pheroz Fancy – Taipan 11 (ch g 8)
Owner: C. Biggins, G. Longbottom, J. Journeaux, Mrs R. Moffat, J. Newton & K. Fawcett

Winner's Colors: Black, white sleeves, red cap

Winning Numbers: 2, 7, 14

ALSO RAN

Better Loosen Up	D. A. Hayes	S. D. Marshall	59	50/1
Let's Elope	J. B. Cummings	G. Childs	56.5	6/1
Prince Salieri	G. M. Hanlon	S. Scriven	59	50
Mannerism	D. L. Freedman	D. Oliver (a)	56.5	16/1
Coronation Day	M. G. Lees	L. Cassidy	48.5	6/1
Muirfield Village	J. B. Cummings	S. King	48.5	12/1
Burst	C. E. Connors	P. Payne (a)	46	50/1
Rought Habit	J. R. Wheeler	J. Cassidy	59	10/1
Sydeston (LR)	R. E. Hoysted	N. Wilson	59	200/1
Naturalism (LR)	D. Freedman	L. Dittman	57	Evensf
Palace Reign (fell)	D. A. Hayes	P. Hutchinson	48.5	50/1

All started

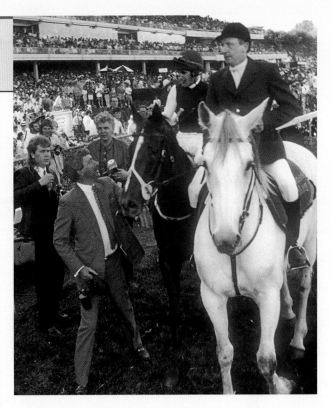

along with evergreen New Zealander Rough Habit, a crowd favorite who'd earned his share of applause on Caulfield Cup day by carrying 62.5kg on a soft track to win over 1400m. Epsom Handicap winner Kinjite was also there, albeit a 50-1 chance by virtue of his doubted ability to get the 2040 metre trip.

Three high-class colts, the Caulfield Guineas winner Palace Reign, the Spring Champion Stakes winner Coronation Day, and runner-up Muirfield Village headed a significant three-year-old contingent. Representing the fillies were Special Chance and Burst, who quinellaed the AJC Flight Stakes.

But the favorite, and a short-priced one at that, was another Lee Freedman-trained galloper, the highly talented four year old Naturalism. Unlucky to be beaten in the Victoria Derby, the colt emerged in the Autumn a very fine competitor indeed, and engaged in some memorable Group 1 battles with the outstanding New Zealand colt Veandercross, beating him in the Rosehill Guineas and the AJC Derby.

Following wins in all of his Cox Plate lead-up races – the Memsie, Feehan and Turnbull Stakes – Naturalism went to the post an even money favorite, in the capable hands of Mick Dittman.

Sometimes things are just not meant to be. Dittman is in no doubt Naturalism should have won; Freedman is inclined to believe him. Certainly with about 600m to go the horse was travelling beautifully and about to make his move. But in a split second he was out of the race. Up front Palace Reign, for no apparent reason, crossed his legs and fell. Others avoided him but Naturalism couldn't and fell over the top of him.

Sydeston too was interfered with, and suddenly as the field approached the turn the race had taken on a whole new complexion. Kinjite ran through to lead, but out wide Let's Elope and Better Loosen Up were coming with strong runs as Special Chance pushed up along the rail. Greg Hall was about three lengths off them on Super Impose, thanking his lucky stars for having pulled out wide coming off the turn at the 700m mark.

"If I hadn't, I would have gone straight over the top of the fallen horses," he said later.

In the short straight things really got tough. Let's Elope veered towards the inside under pressure, causing Better Loosen Up to almost run out of room and have to be severely checked. Let's Elope continued to grind towards the line and looked set to win until Hall, riding like a man possessed over the last 50m, booted Super Impose to the lead in the last bounds. Old Super had again dug deep and got there right on the line.

A clearly emotional Hall, standing high in the saddle waving his whip, said as he came back to scale: "To win a Cox Plate is fantastic, but to win on a great old horse like Super .... well .... that is something else."

Let's Elope was placed second – but not for long. The interference she caused to Better Loosen Up was severe enough to push him back into fifth place, so it was no surprise to see a protest was lodged, and even less that it was upheld. Thus the placings became Super Impose first; Kinjite second and Special Chance filling the minor placing.

For Freedman the win was bitter-sweet. Initially his concern for Naturalism overrode any joy at winning, but once he had established that horse had suffered no serious injury he was able to fully appreciate the extraordinary effort of his stable veteran.

A "super athlete" was how Freedman described Super Impose. "He covered a lot of ground with each stride and he had tremendous acceleration," Freedman said in Class Racehorses, 1992-93.

"I suppose his one failing, if he had one, was that he wasn't comfortable on rain-affected ground.

"I'd put that down to the fact he had such a long stride and that led him to becoming unbalanced when the ground was shifty.

"I was prepared to forgive him that .... because I loved the horse."

1993 – HE MADE THE MOST OF HIS CHANCE

Perhaps as a result of Vintage Crop's historic win in the Melbourne Cup, all else that happened in the Spring of 1993 seemed to pale into insignificance.

Some might even decry The Phantom Chance's win in the Cox Plate, but while the race itself was hardly memorable – in fact its prize level had dropped from $1.7 to $1.5 million – the chestnut gelding himself is entitled to be remembered as a very good racehorse.

Purchased as a yearling for $NZ57,270 by trainer Colin Jillings for Auckland owner, trucking magnate Wayne Ballin, The Phantom Chance didn't begin racing until well into his three-year-old year.

Jillings, one of New Zealand's greatest trainers, is a master of patience. And in Ballin he had an owner sensible enough to heed his advice. "A lot of trainers," Jillings said after the Cox Plate, "if they were left alone by their owners, would have a lot better horses."

The decision to give The Phantom Chance plenty of time to mature also might have been influenced by the fact his older brother, The Phantom, didn't begin racing until he was three. A durable performer over many seasons, The Phantom won the Memsie and Underwood Stakes before finishing second in the 1990 Melbourne Cup. He also twice finished third in the Caulfield Cup, in 1989 and 1993.

After being placed at his first two starts, The Phantom Chance strung together an amazing sequence of eight straight wins, beginning with a Maiden race at Ellerslie in November, 1992, and finishing with a win in the Group 1 International Stakes at Cambridge in mid-February.

Towards the end of that winning streak he triumphed in the Avondale Guineas, the New Zealand Derby and the Wellington Stakes. Jillings and his training partner Richard Yuill, both felt the gelding was probably most effective at 2000m, and so it was with the Cox Plate as his main mission that The Phantom Chance came to Melbourne in mid-September, 1993.

Already he'd raced twice over sprint distances in New Zealand but travelled badly and also suffered a hoof infection, causing him to miss a scheduled run in the Underwood Stakes at

1993
(Saturday, October 23. Attendance: 33,203)

$1,500,000 plus $6,500 trophies Weight for Age 2,040m

1.	THE PHANTOM CHANCE	M. Jillings	57kg	R. Vance	4/1
2.	Solvit	M. J. Murdoch	59kg	D. Walsh	10/1
3.	Golden Sword	J. F. Meagher	57kg	S. King	6/1

Winning details

Margin: 1 ½ len x 2 ¼ len. **Time:** 2:02.8 9 started.

Breeding: Noble Bijou – The Fantasy – Gate Keeper (ch g 4) **Owner:** W. Ballin

Winner's Colors: Orange, black sash and armbands

Winning Numbers: 9, 5, 8

ALSO RAN

Naturalism	D. L. Freedman	D. Oliver	59	2/1f
Kiwi Golfer	C. H. Faulkner	B. Compton	59	30/1
Veandercross	J. R. Wheeler	L. Dittman	59	4/1
Slight Chance	R. H. Thomsen	R. S. Dye	54.5	30/1
Never Undercharge	J. B. Cummings	G. Hall	57	12/1
Palace Reign	D. A. Hayes	M. Clarke	57	14/1

Scratched: Runyon

Caulfield. Despite having had a couple of solid runs over sprint distances in New Zealand it was felt he could only improve upon whatever he did in his first start here, the 2000m Turnbull Stakes at Flemington. Jillings said as much in a radio interview on race morning, then offered an apology when The Phantom Chance powered home to defeat local star Naturalism by a head in a slowly run race.

Although perhaps unexpected, the win provided a sorely needed tonic for owner Ballin, who on the eve of the race was admitted to Ballarat Hospital having suffered a mild heart attack.

Concerned The Phantom Chance might be lacking fitness, Jillings backed him up the following Saturday over 2000m in the Caulfield Stakes. He was once again opposed to Naturalism and also had his older brother The Phantom and outstanding weight-for-age star Veandercross to contend with. In fact, the race contained no less than 14 Group 1 winners, making it a very hot contest indeed.

In a race that befitted the quality of the field, halfway up the straight it seemed likely the two brothers would fight out the finish. The Phantom had reached the lead but was being strongly challenged on the outside by The Phantom Chance. Then, with less than 100m to run Naturalism burst between the pair to win by a neck. The Phantom Chance finished third, but the more astute took good note of rider Bobby Vance, who admitted to an "ordinary" ride. The following week The Phantom franked the fitness, if not the form, by finishing a game third in the Caulfield Cup behind the imported stayer Fraar.

Although a field of only nine contested the Cox Plate, all but one was a winner at Group 1 level. The race was robbed of some of its interest when Calm Harbour, a winner of 11 from 14 races in New Zealand, was injured and missed the final acceptance. In the week before the race, The Phantom Chance was taken to Moonee Valley for "Breakfast with the Stars", and confirmed he was right on target by defeating Veandercross and the Hayes-trained Maraakiz in a 1600m gallop.

Races are rarely run to script, but in the case of the 1993 Cox Plate it was – and it wasn't. Solvit, a tough, front-running customer from New Zealand who'd previously claimed the scalps of both The Phantom Chance and Veandercross, was expected to lead and did. The Phantom Chance settled midfield, with Naturalism and Veandercross behind him, all as anticipated.

Things began to go awry when at the halfway mark it became obvious the pace being set by Solvit was at the very best a gentle one. Vance, under the hammer for his Caulfield Stakes ride, realised then he had to make a move, and with 600m to run quickly moved up to sit just off Solvit's hindquarters approaching the home turn.

At the same time, both Naturalism and Veandercross were held up for runs, so Vance went for home, and in a twinkling The Phantom Chance raced to a clear lead. That was the end of it. Solvit battled on gamely for second, the Epsom and Toorak Handicaps winner Golden Sword ran on for third, but neither Naturalism nor Veandercross struck a blow.

Vance was in a state of disbelief for some time after the race. "I can't believe how easy it was," he said. "If he couldn't have won this he would never have won a good race."

For 63 year-old Jillings, it was the culmination of a lifetime spent with horses. He point blank refused to compare The Phantom Chance with another of his stars, McGinty, third in the 1983 Cox Plate. "I love all the horses," was his simple comment.

And what of the owner?

Ballin, wearing a giant Akubra, made it to the Valley from the hospital, mindful of a promise to break his habit of 60 smokes a day. "But I'll be having a drink tonight," he said, "a big drink."

Why wouldn't he?

1994 – THE DAY SIMPSON BECAME SAMSON

On the eve of the Karaka sales Moira Murdoch, her husband Michael, plus his sister and brother-in-law Adrienne and Doug Alderslade, put together a kitty with which to buy a horse "to have a bit of fun with".

Fun they got, in Spades.

As the New Zealand owners of 1993 Cox Plate winner The Phantom Chance celebrated in the next stall after the race, another Kiwi, trainer Moira Murdoch, gave her gallant runner-up Solvit an affectionate pat and made a silent vow, which was to come true 12 months later.

She would return to Moonee Valley and win the Cox Plate – a thought which would never have entered her mind a couple of years earlier.

Hobby trainers win races, but they rarely win big races. Quite simply, the odds about them ever getting a horse good enough are astronomical. Murdoch, wife of a New Zealand beef farmer and mother of two young children, certainly wasn't looking for a Cox Plate winner when she attended the Karaka secondary yearling sale in early 1990.

Smitten with ponies as a teenager, she'd turned to training "a couple" soon after leaving school and enjoyed enough success to keep at it. On the eve of the Karaka sales Moira, her husband Michael, plus his sister and brother-in-law Adrienne and Douglas Alderslade, put together a kitty with which to buy a horse "to have a bit of fun with".

Fun they got, in Spades. Fun to have paid just $4,500 for the bay son of little-known stallion Morcon; fun to discover the short-coupled, muscular youngster could run a bit; fun to eventually find out he could mix it with the best in Australasia.

The partners would have been happy to win one or two races with him, but in six starts as a two-year-old Solvit already had notched up two very smart wins. From the outset Solvit established himself as a free-wheeling galloper who loved nothing better than to set a good pace and defy his opponents to run him down. He had another trait too. Right-handed tracks he didn't like, and although he won racing clockwise he invariably finished closer to the outside than to the inside rail.

As a three-year-old his talent shone through when he defeated budding champion Veandercross by a head in the Wellington Guineas, and he followed

1994
(Saturday, October 22. Attendance: 33,855)

$1,500,000 plus $6,500 trophies Weight for Age 2,040m

1.	SOLVIT	M. J. Murdoch	59kg	*D. Walsh*	10/1
2.	Rought Habit	J. R. Wheeler	59kg	*R. Elliot*	50/1
3.	Redding	J. Kelly	59kg	*D. Brereton*	11/2

Winning details

Margin: ½ hd x ½ nk. **Time:** 2:02.6 14 started.

Breeding: Morcon – Yallah Sun – Yallah Native (b g 6)
Owner: D.S. & Mrs A.B. Alderslade & M.L. & Mrs M.J. Murdoch

Winner's Colors: Pale green, purple stripes & striped cap

Winning Numbers: 3, 1, 6

ALSO RAN

Alcove	T. J. Hughes jr	P. Payne	54.5	25/1
Danewin	R. H. Thomsen	J. Tse	48.5	25/1
Durbridge	D. L. Freedman	S. Marshall	59	7/1
Tristalove	J. B. Cummings	D. Oliver	54.5	7/1
St Covet	D. A. Hayes	A. Matthews	48.5	8/1
Tenor	J. R. Hawkes	G. Cooksley	57	33/1
Snap	D. O'Sullivan	L. O'Sullivan	54.5	9/1
River Verdon	D. M. Hill	J. Marshall	59	16/1
Soho Square	I. G. Saunders	G. Hall	59	80/1
Jeune	D. A. Hayes	R. Griffiths	59	3/1f
It's All In Fun	T. J. McDonald	S. King	59	66/1

Scratched: Ball Park

up with a win in the Waikato Guineas. A lightning foray across the Tasman late in 1992 came to nothing when Solvit suffered travel sickness and ran last in the Schweppes Cup at Caulfield, but indicated Murdoch did not lack a sense of adventure.

The gelding first came to Moonee Valley the following Spring, this time fit and able to dispose of a handy field of "milers" in the Waterford Crystal Mile. By the time of his return visit, for the 1993 Cox Plate, Solvit had notched his first Group 1 success, leading throughout to win the New Zealand Stakes over 2000m at Ellerslie the previous Autumn. On that occasion he beat The Phantom Chance, but in the Cox Plate he was unable to hold that horse at bay, although he beat home the rest quite comfortably.

His effort convinced Murdoch he was capable of winning the race, so from that moment she planned his preparations with the sole purpose of having him at his peak come Cox Plate day, 1994. After a mixed Summer campaign, during which he won the Group 1 Action Stakes at Ellerslie but ran off the track after leading into the straight in the Ranvet Stakes at Rosehill, Solvit went for a spell. Given he'd beaten all but the winner in the '93 Cox Plate, Murdoch, after toying with the idea of going to Melbourne for the Feehan Stakes at Moonee Valley in mid-September, saw no reason to change his lead-up into the 1994 running of the championship.

Once again, he kicked off with a 1200m opener at Foxton (2nd), followed with run in a 1400m Group 2 at Hastings (2nd) then had his final prep race in the Group 2 Kelt Stakes over 2000m at Hastings. The previous year, Solvit had finished second in the Kelt to the very, very talented Calm Harbour. He struck no such opposition this time and led throughout to win easily. Afterwards jockey David Walsh declared, "Whatever beats him in the Cox Plate, wins."

Murdoch and Solvit arrived in Melbourne a week before the Cox Plate and set up camp at Mornington. There a shetland named Roseanne took over the Solvit-minding duties, which had been attended to at home by a pony named Jack.

A hot field lined up for the 73rd running of the weight-for-age Classic. Among the runners were the classy import Jeune; Caulfield Cup placegetters Alcove and Tenor; weight-for-age star Durbridge; and the 1993 Victoria Derby winner Redding. In addition, for the first time Hong Kong was represented by River Verdon, and adding to the class was the old veteran himself, Rough Habit.

Murdoch was confident. As she pointed out later, the previous year Solvit had some niggling problems; this time he was in perfect fettle. For all of that, he was largely unwanted by punters and drifted to start at 10-1, the favorite was Jeune at 3-1.

Most big races are planned, either by trainers or jockeys, or both. Although he suggested otherwise, privately Walsh believed Solvit would lead, and his rivals did too. So if Walsh was stunned when Solvit missed the start by a length, his fellow jockeys were just as surprised not to see him in front.

With not much effort, Solvit was soon able to slide past three-year-old St. Covet into the lead racing towards the 1400m mark, and from that point he was always going to be the horse to beat.

It was far from easy though, for on several occasions in the last 400m it appeared he might be run down. Redding and Alcove made strong runs at him, but Solvit lifted. Then Rough Habit, incredibly a 50-1 chance, lunged between horses to stake a late claim. This year though Solvit was not to be denied. Plumbing the depths, he stuck his blinkered head out to win by half of it. Justice!

As a foal, Solvit was a tough little customer, so much so the stud grooms felt he should be called Samson. Mischievously though, they dubbed him Simpson.

The nickname stuck, but on Cox Plate day, 1994, Solvit was indeed Samson.

1995 – 'O' IS FOR OCTAGONAL AND OUTSTANDING

JOHN HAWKES ... Even "Mr Unflappable" was excited about Octagonal's potential.

Almost from the moment he entered the Karaka sale ring there was an expectation the brown, almost black, Zabeel colt would be a top racehorse.

Jack and Bob Ingham took a gamble paying $210,000 for a horse by an unproven sire, but it was a calculated one. He was a fine type, a classic type in fact, according to the Ingham's bloodstock manager Trevor Lobb.

And he was from an outstanding broodmare, Eight Carat, who'd already produced the winners of seven Group 1 races.

The moment of truth came in mid-December, 1994, when the cleverly named Octagonal made his racecourse debut in a run-of-the-mill juvenile race at Rosehill. Coming to the turn the colt was last in a field of 10, and hanging. The truth, it seemed, was less than palatable.

Two hundred metres later it was as edible as ice cream. Switched to the outside by jockey Michael Evans, Octagonal exploded into action and proceeded to treat his rivals with utter disdain. His winning margin of almost three lengths momentarily stunned his usually unflappable trainer John Hawkes. "He's a very good horse, a very good horse," were the only words he could muster, but he kept repeating them.

How good? Well, four months later Octagonal won the Group 1 AJC Sires Produce Stakes after being beaten a whisker by Flying Spur in the Golden Slipper Stakes. And less than 12 months later the colt stamped himself a champion in the making by outgunning the very versatile, very classy Mahogany to win the 1995 Cox Plate.

Yet it took almost another season of racing for Octagonal to become a cult hero among racegoers; the "Big O" badges and banners didn't start appearing until around the time of his AJC Derby win in April the following year.

Such is the extent of the Ingham's racing empire, at the beginning of each season scores of two-year-olds will be tried

1995
(Saturday, October 28. Attendance: 38,077)

$1,500,000 plus $6,500 trophies Weight for Age 2,040m

1.	**OCTAGONAL**	J. R. Hawkes	48.5	*R. S. Dye*	15/2
2.	**Mahogany**	D. L. Freedman	59kg	*G. Hall*	5/1
3.	**Station Hand**	P. C. Hayes	59kg	*D. Gauci*	20/1

Winning details

Margin: ½ nk x 2 len. **Time:** 2:06.38 (record new track) 14 started.

Breeding: Zabeel – Eight Carat – Pieces Of Eight (b c 3)
Owner: Woodlands Stud Syn. (Mgrs J.H. & R. W. Ingham)

Winner's Colors: Cerise

Winning Numbers: 14, 3, 5

ALSO RAN

Jeune	P. C. Hayes	W. Harris	59	9/2
Seascay	P. C. Hayes	D. Taggart	59	50/1
Mr Marconee	J. R. Lynds	L. Cassidy	59	16/1
Just Apollo	S. C. Rainford	R. Ealden	56.5	125/1
Pakaraka Star	G. W. Gulliver	V. Colgan (a)	59	50/1
Danewin	R. H. Thomsen	D. Oliver	57	7/2ef
Star Dancer	B. J. Wallace	G. Cooksley	59	66/1
Danarani	J. B. Cummings	P. Payne	54.5	15/1
Stony Bay	G. Waterhouse	L. Dittman	57	33/1
Solvit	M. J. Murdoch	D. Walsh	59	25/1
Our Maizcay	G. L. Searle	B. York	48.5	7/2ef

Scratched: Nick's Joy

OH FOR THE 'BIG O' ... Shane Dye on Octagonal (outside) and Greg Hall on Mahogany go to the line head and head in a thrilling finish to the 1995 Plate. Octagonal had won again in a close outcome, as if he knew where the post was. – Picture: HWT

and tested, many to be discarded, some to achieve a measure of success, a relative few to make names for themselves.

When the season began in 1994, trainer John Hawkes had 150 youngsters on the books. He always believed Octagonal the one most likely to succeed, but it was with justification he gave the colt his "best of" nomination when the season ended.

Approaching the Spring, the Inghams and Hawkes planned Octagonal's early three-year-old campaign, and agreed he should be aimed at the Cox Plate. Despite Octagonal being beaten first up by the very ugly but very, very speedy Our Maizcay in the 1200m Roman Consul Stakes at Rosehill, Hawkes was more than happy with the performance. "It proves to me he has come back in great order," he said.

The colt backed up his trainer by winning his next two starts, over 1300m in the Heritage Stakes at Rosehill, and over 1400m in the Stan Fox Stakes at Randwick. A week later, Melbourne racegoers saw Octagonal for the first time when he stepped out in the Group 1 Caulfield Guineas, renewing his rivalry with Our Maizcay.

The Kiwi colt is living testament to the fact a horse does not have to look good to be good. Short coupled and short necked, he nevertheless came to the Guineas unbeaten in five starts for the season. Octagonal's scoreline with Our Maizcay stood at one all, the local colt having beaten the visitor in the Todman Slipper Trial the previous Autumn.

The Caulfield Guineas was never a contest. Our Maizcay jumped to the front, dictated the terms, and then shot away at the top of the straight to win by three lengths. Octagonal raced back in the ruck, and never came into the race until the last 200m when he finished strongly into third place, just behind Ravarda.

Despite the defeat, Hawkes didn't waver from the plan to run Octagonal in the Cox Plate. "I think the weight-for-age horses are susceptible this year. A good three-year-old is always hard to beat at weight-for-age," he said.

While Hawkes had no problem with it, jockey Darren Gauci did. Told by Hawkes he could ride Octagonal a kilo over at 49.5kg, Gauci needed to lose two kilos in 36 hours to keep the mount. He didn't, and Shane Dye, who'd been on stand-by to ride the colt, took the mount, assuring Hawkes he'd be able to make the allotted weight of 48.5kg, which later proved to be a crucial factor.

Although a number of good horses had indifferent form going into the 1995 Cox Plate, enough were racing well enough to provide Octagonal with stiff

> Told by Hawkes he could ride Octagonal a kilo over at 49.5kg, Gauci needed to lose two kilos in 36 hours to keep the mount. He didn't, and Shane Dye, who'd been on stand-by to ride the colt, took the mount, assuring Hawkes he'd be able to make the allotted weight of 48.5kg, which later proved to be a crucial factor.

opposition. Our Maizcay was there, albeit on trust at the distance; the defending champion Solvit had won his lead-up race; former top flight three-year-old Danewin was coming off a Caulfield Stakes win, and the 1993 Victoria Derby winner Mahogany was out to justify a highly unorthodox preparation given him by trainer Lee Freedman.

To dwell upon Mahogany just for a moment, his only Group 1 success as a four-year-old, a season which saw him suffer serious back problems, had come first-up in the Lightning Stakes over 1000m at Flemington in the Autumn.

Freedman was convinced Mahogany raced best fresh, and therefore decided he would have only one start before the Cox Plate, in the Craiglee Stakes at Flemington, seven weeks before the Moonee Valley engagement. He ran a super race, being beaten only a half neck by Jeune, also a Cox Plate contender.

It's funny how big occasions can affect people. In the week leading up to the Cox Plate, Hawkes remained confident Octagonal could win; come the day, he began to have second thoughts. In the tense moments leading up to the race Hawkes wondered whether the colt was seasoned enough. "He's the best horse I've trained," he said, "and he'll run his heart out. But he still might be a bit immature."

Luck in racing is worth a fortune. Octagonal had neither good nor bad luck in the Cox Plate, but by racing near the back of the field he was able to get a clear run when it counted.

Danewin, equal 7-2 favorite with Our Maizcay, had the good luck to slot into a perfect position early, but the shocking bad luck to be trapped behind the rapidly tiring Our Maizcay approaching the home turn, when he appeared to be coasting.

Mahogany had the good fortune to slip through on the inside to lead at the 200m, but perhaps the bad luck to run into a three-year-old for whom defeat was not an option.

As he would later prove time and time again, Octagonal seemed to know where the winning post was, and after a thrilling duel with the older galloper gained the upper hand in the last few strides to win by a half neck. Whether he could have done it with an extra kilo, we'll never know.

The following week, Octagonal was unluckily beaten in the Victoria Derby. The following Autumn he was all but unbeatable, in succession winning the Canterbury and Rosehill Guineas, the Mercedes Classic and the AJC Australian Derby.

Down on form the following Spring, he still managed to win the Underwood Stakes at Caulfield, and those who'd idolised him in early 1996, returned in force with their banners and cerise-painted faces (Octagonal's silks were that color) when in the Autumn of 1997 he won the Chipping Norton Stakes, the Australian Cup, and, for the second year running, the Mercedes Classic.

Retired to the Ingham's Woodland Stud in the Hunter Valley, Octagonal was accorded a very high status as a sire, when his services were sought by a French stud, thus making him the first Australian "shuttle" stallion.

His progeny were eagerly sought at the 2000 yearling sales. Those that possess only a bit of his ability will be good horses, for Octagonal raced himself into the rare category of being one of Australia's all-time great horses.

1996 – THE WIN MADE IN HEAVEN

BART CUMMINGS ...
the tear in his eye after
Saintly's Plate win "must
be hay fever".

Amid the shouting and the tumult that greeted Saintly's win in the 1996 Cox Plate, one man shed a silent tear.

Rarely does master trainer Bart Cummings reveal his inner feelings, and this momentary breach in his defences was quickly shored up with a typical one-liner. "Must be hay fever," he muttered.

Quite clearly though, Saintly's narrow, gutsy win stirred something in the great man that countless big race wins over four decades had failed to do. Many believe it might finally have erased memories of Cummings' disastrous Cups King Syndicate in the late 1980's that left him $20 million in debt.

Most likely that was part of it, but Cummings must have taken enormous pride in the fact he was the breeder and a part-owner of the striking chestnut, as well as being his trainer. Another cause for the emotion was the knowledge one of his co-owners was Dato Tan Chin Nam. Dato Tan, a long time associate, did not desert Cummings in his time of need, a point the trainer was keen to make in the heady aftermath of the Cox Plate win.

Saintly is by Sky Chase, once trained by Cummings, out of All Grace, raced and trained by Cummings. Three moves back in her pedigree is Dark Queen, the dam of Cummings' only previous Cox Plate winner Taj Rossi. Then, of course, there was the Beadman factor. Darren Beadman had had an on-off relationship with Saintly the previous season. He won the Carbine Club Stakes and the Australian Cup on him at Flemington, but rode Octagonal to beat the Cummings-trained horse three times in Sydney during the Autumn.

Come the Spring, Beadman had the choice of both mounts, but to commit to one would mean missing out on the other. It was generally thought he would stick with Octagonal, so it came as something of a surprise when he chose Saintly. He had some quite practical reasons for choosing Saintly, but Beadman, a devout Christian, also admitted to having sought divine guidance, hence Saintly became known as "The Horse from Heaven".

At the beginning of the Spring, Cummings had nominated two major targets for Saintly, the Cox Plate and the Melbourne Cup, and in doing so went against his own precedent. Not one of Cummings' previous nine Melbourne Cup winners had even run in the Cox Plate.

Saintly began his

1996
(Saturday, October 26. Attendance: 36,190)

$1,500,000 plus $11,500 trophies Weight for Age 2,040m

1.	**SAINTLY**	J. B. Cummings	57kg	D. Beadman	5/1
2.	**Filante**	J. Denham	57kg	L. Dittman	9/4ef
3.	**All Our Mob**	G. Waterhouse	59kg	S. Marshall	20/1

Winning details

Margin: Hd x ½ nk. **Time:** 2:05.73 (record) 8 started.

Breeding: Sky Chase – All Grace – Sir Tristram (ch g 4)
Owner: J. B. Cummings, Dato Tan Chin Nam, Dr C. P. Lim, E.H.K.Tong & T. Tan

Winner's Colors: Black, white check, yellow sleeves, black & white checked cap

Winning Numbers: 4, 5, 2

ALSO RAN

Juggler	G. Waterhouse	S. King	59	9/4ef
Octagonal	J. R. Hawkes	D. Gauci	57	13/2
Crying Game	A. Johnson	R. Griffiths	57	66/1
Anthems	J. R. Hawkes	S. Dye	48.5	7/1
Adventurous	G. Waterhouse	G. Boss	48.5	20/1

All started

campaign in late August, running on strongly but well beaten into second place by Filante in the 1400m Warwick Stakes. Filante had the best of him again in the 1600m Chelmsford Stakes at Randwick, but when stepped up to the 1900m of the Hill Stakes at Rosehill, Saintly found top form and quite easily accounted for Nothin' Leica Dane.

As has been seen, it was quite common in the early days for Cox Plate aspirants to come through the AJC Metropolitan Handicap, but the practice had all but disappeared. Not only did Cummings resurrect it, he decided to give Saintly a warm-up for it in the Craven Stakes at Randwick two days before. The hot favorite at 4-13, Saintly naturally was expected to win, but shocked just about everyone by failing to outstay the tearaway leader Adventurous, despite heading him inside the 200m.

Cummings though wasn't too disappointed. "I thought he tried very hard. He didn't shirk his task at any stage," he said. He might have felt tempted to trot out the same line after the Metropolitan, in which Saintly again loomed up to surely have the race in his keeping, only to weaken this time into third place, behind the Gai Waterhouse-trained pair Hula Flight and Nothin' Leica Dane.

He didn't, but with even Beadman now expressing some doubts about Saintly's maturity, Cummings admitted there was some cause for concern. "We'll press on though," was his optimistic comment.

Many attributes have taken Cummings to the top of the training tree, not the least of them his attention to detail. He remained puzzled by Saintly's two defeats and was intrigued when Beadman mentioned the fact that on both occasions the gelding's saddle had slipped backwards. "We think that may have been part of the reason he was beaten," Cummings said. "But in the Cox Plate? You watch. He'll come around the outside and storm home."

Prophetic words.

During the Autumn, Beadman had been using a thin, rubber girth on Saintly, but it had been stolen, at about the same time as Saintly's form began to slip. The theory gained credence when Saintly, his saddle firmly in place, reeled off several cracking gallops at Flemington. His final workout, two days before the Cox Plate, was described by some trackmen as a winning gallop, yet still Filante and Juggler were preferred to him in the betting market.

All Our Mob, second in the Epsom Handicap, was also given some chance, but few were prepared to pin their faith in the defending champion Octagonal, whose Spring form apart from a battling Underwood Stakes win had been lack-lustre.

Once again, the race itself rose to the occasion. Rounding the turn any one of four horses could have been nominated the winner, with Filante on the rail, Juggler and All Our Mob tackling him, and out wide Saintly making the corner looking like a speedway jalopy.

"He half screwed when I hit him," Beadman explained later. "As soon as I stopped hitting him he stretched out again – that was the difference."

In a slogging finish, Filante was in front just metres from the post, and in fact his connections thought they had won. But with raking strides Saintly surged up on the outside to gain the day by a head. Beadman did a "star jump" off his back, then in his victory speech gave "all of the glory to God". It was a genuine call, as was Cummings' acknowledgement in his few words of Dato Tan's support.

Quite possibly we never saw the best of Saintly. At his next start, he was authoritative in winning the Melbourne Cup, picked up a virus on the trip over and couldn't run in the Japan Cup, then scored a brilliant win first up in the Orr Stakes in early February.

Soon after a bowed tendon prematurely brought to an end the career of a very high class, very genuine galloper.

1997 – BART HATCHES A RIPPER PLAN

Those who availed themselves of the 40-1 offered about four-year-old mare Dane Ripper winning the 1997 Cox Plate could consider themselves good judges.

Just the fact master trainer Bart Cummings considered running her in the race should have been enough for her to start at no more than half those odds.

There are probably occasions when Cummings does something on a whim, but you can bet they are few and far between. Invariably there is a sure method to his apparent randomness, and such was the case with Dane Ripper.

As Michael Hedge pointed out in *Class Racehorses -1998* Cummings' "sense of theatre is as well developed as is his ability to train racehorses".

What appeared to be a spur-of-the-moment decision, to run the four-year-old in the weight-for-age championship instead of in a lesser event on the program, was in fact a well thought out plan.

This, despite Dane Ripper never having won beyond 1500m, and never having contested a weight-for-age race. For all that, Dane Ripper neither lacked for quality nor ability, having won the Group One Stradbroke Handicap at Eagle Farm the previous June.

A big, long striding bay, her breeding, too, was of the highest class, being by the world-renowned stallion Danehill, out of the Group 1 winning mare Red Express. Her three wins as a two-year-old included the 1200m Group 3 Mercury Classic at Kembla Grange, highly promising for a filly whose physique suggested time would improve her.

Dane Ripper had only one start in the Spring of 1996 before developing leg problems. Wisely, Cummings decided to spell the filly for six months and it probably was the making of her.

In eight starts through the Autumn and Winter, Dane Ripper never missed a place, and her Stradbroke win was the mark of a very good horse indeed. She ended her Winter campaign on a winning note, in the Winter Stakes on a heavy track over 1500m at Eagle Farm in mid-June.

Cummings was of the opinion Dane Ripper, despite her size and bulk, performed best if her runs were spaced. Thus she raced only three times in the lead-up to the Cox Plate.

Resuming over 1100m at Rosehill in late August,

1997
(Saturday, October 25. Attendance: 35,658)

$1,500,000 plus $15,500 trophies Weight for Age 2,040m

1.	**DANE RIPPER**	J. B. Cummings	54.5kg	*D. Oliver*	40/1
2.	Filante	J. Denham	59kg	*J. Cassidy*	11/8f
3.	Vialli	P. O'Sullivan	59	*G. Childs*	16/1

Winning details

Margin: 1½ len x 1¼ len. **Time:** 2:07.65 9 started.

Breeding: Danehill – Red Express – Sovereign Red (b m 4)
Owner: Pitt Place Pty Ltd Syn (Mgr Mrs J. M. Codner)

Winner's Colors: Yellow, black sleeves, yellow armbands, black cap

Winning Numbers: 7, 1, 4

ALSO RAN

Encounter	C. Connors	R. S. Dye	48.5	9/2
Moss Downs	C. McNab	B. York	59	40/1
Schubert	P. C. Hayes	L. Cassidy	49.5	7/1
Juggler	G. Waterhouse	D. Beadman	59	15/2
Alfa	J. B. Cummings	S. King	57	5/1
Tarnpir Lane	C. Brown	G. Eades	57	10/1

All started

she finished second, then two weeks later finished mid-field in the Research Plate over 1200m, again at Rosehill. Dane Ripper didn't race for three weeks before finishing mid-field in the Doncaster Handicap, and that was it as far as racing was concerned. Floated to Melbourne the mare spent the next three weeks on the track, significantly doing a lot of her preparatory work at Moonee Valley.

In the care of Cummings' astute track rider Joe Agresta, Dane Ripper was taken from Flemington to the Valley to gallop on no less than four occasions, each time working over 1600m and sprinting home her last 600m. At this stage, Cummings had indicated that her mission was more likely to be the Waterford Crystal Mile on Cox Plate day than the feature race.

At the "Breakfast with the Stars" gallops on the Tuesday morning, Dane Ripper was ridden in a gallop by Agresta, and worked quite brilliantly. Still, there was some surprise when it was announced she had accepted for the Cox Plate.

Explaining this apparent switch of plans at a press conference later, Cummings claimed that after the gallop Agresta said to him, "You've got her in the wrong race, boss," to which Cummings replied, "We'll soon fix that, Joe."

As Hedge revealed, Dane Ripper's successful assault on the race had in fact been planned and executed with great care and precision. Cummings admitted as much when he said: "The thing was she may have been balloted out had there been a capacity field. There's no point in saying anything unless you know."

Even before the Moonee Valley gallop the acceptance cheque already had been written out, and top jockey Damien Oliver had been engaged to ride her. Opposing Dane Ripper in the Cox Plate was an assortment of gallopers who ranged from being classy to very good, but, with the possible exception of the three-year-old Encounter, could not be considered outstanding.

Filante, runner up to Saintly the previous year, was the favorite on the strength of an easy win in the Yalumba Stakes at Caulfield, where other Cox Plate contenders Alfa and Tarnpir Lane had filled the minor placings.

Veteran Juggler, third in the '96 Cox Plate was there, along with New Zealand's Kelt Stakes winner Moss Downs, but the main challenge was expected to come from Encounter who had posted four successive wins including one against the older horses (including Filante and Juggler) in the George Main Stakes, and a courageous win in the Caulfield Guineas.

Jockeys riding favored horses in big races are under enormous pressure. Conversely for those riding long shots, it is an everything to gain, nothing to lose situation. Oliver freely admits to feeling absolutely no pressure as he took Dane Ripper into the stalls for the start of the Cox Plate, and he consequently rode what is best described as a "peach" of a race.

Encounter cost himself his chance by over-racing in the lead, and Filante's chances certainly were not helped when Schubert made a lightning move at the 900m to go after the leaders. Jim Cassidy on Filante was forced to go earlier than planned, and found himself in the lead before the home turn. Meanwhile, Oliver had Dane Ripper sitting back off the pace, content to play his luck and try for an inside run.

This came when Filante rolled away from the rail upon straightening up, and producing the sprint that claimed her the Stradbroke, Dane Ripper burst through to win running away. It was an emotion-charged win for the mare's owners, Joy Codner and her daughter Gae, who bred Dane Ripper from their Group One winning mare Red Express. It was husband and father Ron Codner who introduced the family to racing, but sadly he died in 1995.

"He would have been so proud today," wife Joy said during the presentation.

At her only other Spring start Dane Ripper ran fifth in the Mackinnon Stakes on a heavily biased track, but she returned to Melbourne in the Autumn for two notable victories.

The first came in the St. George Stakes at Caulfield, when she defeated Australian racing's new superstar, Melbourne and Caulfield Cups winner Might And Power, fair and square over 1800m.

It set the stage for a clash of the titans in the Australian Cup over 2000m at Flemington, but it came to nothing when Might And Power suffered a minor injury and was scratched on race morning.

Had he run he would have needed to be at his absolute peak to have beaten Dane Ripper, who produced her trademark acceleration to win in a canter by 4½ lengths.

However, the Cox Plate victory will forever be remembered as her greatest success – and while on paper it might have appeared to have been a lucky last minute decision, in truth, the victory was only further evidence of the forethought of the training genius, Bart Cummings.

1998 – A MIGHTY DISPLAY OF POWER

The 1998 Cox Plate saw a display of equine power and public adulation that had old-timers comparing it to Tulloch's Plate some 30 years earlier.

Might And Power led from start to finish in one of the most stunning victories recorded not only at Moonee Valley, but in any race. On his winning time of 2:03.7, Might And Power was a lengths better winner than the revered Bart Cummings-trained Saintly, who had run a record (on the new Strathayr surface) of 2:05.73. Saintly's win had been described as being made in Heaven, as apart from his name, his jockey Darren Beadman swapped his saddle soon after for a career in the Ministry. The Almighty was also a very strong factor in the 1998 success, too. The winner was named after a hymn by his deeply religious owner, Mr Nick Moraitis, and the Cox Plate was the last of the holy trinity of Victorian races won by Might And Power after his successes in the Caulfield and Melbourne Cups the previous year.

If that wasn't enough to cement his greatness, the fact that it was widely reported that Might And Power had become the first horse since Phar Lap to win the Cox Plate the year after winning the Melbourne Cup, seemed more complimentary (as is the case when any horse is compared with Phar Lap). Unfortunately, the report didn't add that not many Cup winners had fronted up in the Cox Plate the following year.

However, this should not detract from what was an amazing victory, which Moonee Valley Chief Executive Paul Brettell summed up nicely when he said: *"This is one you can tuck away for the grandkids."*

In season 1996-97, Might And Power was an immature three-year-old, but that didn't stop him finishing second to Intergaze in the Canterbury Guineas and fourth behind Ebony Grosve in the AJC Australian Derby. In his final start for the season he hinted at what was to come with a six-length win in the Group 3 Frank Packer Plate over 2000m at Randwick.

First-up in the Spring of 1997, Might and Power stormed home to win over 1200m at Warwick Farm; then finished second twice, in the Tramway Handicap and the Shannon Quality.

It was form good enough to see him start a 15-4 favorite for the Epsom Handicap, but he ran into a traffic jam in the

Following on from the "win made in Heaven" for Saintly the previous year, the Almighty was also a very strong factor in the 1998 success, too. The winner was named after a hymn by his deeply religious owner, Mr Nick Moraitis and the Cox Plate was the last of the holy trinity of Victorian races won by Might And Power after his successes in the Caulfield and Melbourne Cups the previous year.

1998
(Saturday, October 24. Attendance: 38,514)

$1,510,000 plus $16,000 trophies Weight for Age 2,040m

1.	**MIGHT AND POWER**	J. Denham	58kg	J. Cassidy	8/11f
2.	**Northern Drake**	K. Man	56.5	G. Childs	100/1
3.	**Tycoon Lil**	C. Jillings	54	R. S. Dye	11/2

Winning details

Margin: 1¼ len x nk. **Time:** 2:03.54 (record) 11 started.

Breeding: Zabeel – Benediction – Day Is Done (b/br g 5) **Owner:** N. Moraitis

Winner's Colors: White, grey sash, pink striped sleeves, grey cap

Winning Numbers: 1, 8, 9

ALSO RAN

Dodge	J. R. Hawkes	B. Prebble	56.5	25/1
Catalan Opening	J. B. Cummings	D. Oliver	58	16/1
Doriemus	D. L. Freedman	G. Hall	58	20/1
Dracula	J. R. Hawkes	L. V. Cassidy	48.5	10/1
Batavian	G. Rogerson	P. Johnson	58	50/1
Gold Guru	L. M. Macdonald	P. Payne	56.5	12/1
Kenwood Melody	W. H. Mitchell	C. Munce	48.5	9/1
Super Slew	F. Thomas	C. Reith	58	100/1

All started

Randwick straight and finished eighth, albeit climbing all over the leaders on the line to be less than three lengths from the winner, Iron Horse.

The loss cost jockey Brian York the mount on Might And Power in Melbourne and allowed Jim Cassidy to come in from the cold reaches of a two-year suspension, courtesy of the "Jockey Tapes" affair, to partner the bold galloping bay in two of the most memorable wins in turf history.

Old-timers, who watched him crack a smart Caulfield Cup field by seven and a half lengths in course record time, were moved to compare him with the mighty Tulloch. Tulloch though didn't lead all the way, but the burst of acceleration he displayed to power away from the field in 1957 was mirrored by Might And Power, whose whirlwind charge down the Caulfield straight was nothing short of awesome.

Two weeks and three days later he surpassed even that effort. To win the Melbourne Cup after leading and being continually challenged over the last 2000m remains as one of Australian racing's greatest performances.

No sign here of the Caulfield Cup brilliance – just a sheer bloody-minded refusal to surrender. Even in the final stride he denied a determined lunge by the great stayer Doriemus to win by a nose.

A race-eve injury to Might And Power prevented a showdown with 1997 Cox Plate winner, Dane Ripper, in the Australian Cup in the Autumn, but the gelding finished the season with four straight wins, three of them at Group 1 level.

He began the new season with the Cox Plate as his main mission and won two of his four lead-up races, the Group 2 Chelmsford Stakes at Randwick in September and, two weeks before his Moonee Valley assignment, the Group 1 Caulfield Stakes.

The consensus among the trainers, jockeys and scribes was that Might And Power's effort had put him in the same class as two of Tommy Smith's champions, Tulloch and Kingston Town. Tulloch created an Australian record in running 2:01.1 for the 1¼ miles of the 1960 Cox Plate, which was seen by a record crowd of 50,670 (many of whom, it is said, tossed their hats into the air as a show of appreciation). Kingston Town, of course, holds another Cox Plate record, having won the race three times on end from 1980.

Quite apart from the record-breaking time run by Might And Power, there were legitimate comparisons with Tulloch's year when it came to crowd reaction, too. Fedoras not being fashionable, the faithful were wearing suits or T shirts and jeans as they flocked to the fence to pay homage as Might And Power's owner, Mr Nick Moraitis, went onto the track to lead back his champion. Moraitis was so overwhelmed by the win and the public reaction that he kept raising both his arms as if he were praising some Divine being. In addition, he slapped the hands of the faithful lining the fence while they chanted their mantra of *"Nick, Nick, Nick"* or *"Might And Power, Might And Power."*

Such was the spirit of the occasion that the normally silent Jack Denham, the 74-year-old trainer of Might And Power, was moved to make a rare, short public address. He said the victory was his greatest moment in racing, particularly after finishing second with Filante the two previous years. Apart from crowd reaction – which also extended to trainer Denham – another "Tulloch-day" similarity was the size of the crowd. No, it wasn't 50,000 plus as it had been in 1960, but the roll-up of 38,514 was the biggest since 1974.

The story of the race was that it was all over after going for 300m. Shane Dye on second favorite Tycoon Lil had stated publicly that the only way he could beat Might And Power was to try to get him in a pocket and keep him there until the sprint home. Jim Cassidy had other ideas on the 8/11 favorite and went to the front soon after the jump and dictated the pace throughout. Halfway down the straight it appeared as if 100/1 outsider Northern Drake would make a race of it, but Cassidy and Might And Power were just kidding as they dug deep to win by two lengths.

Cassidy said after the race that he knew at the 800m that the other runners had to put up at that stage, or lose. He looked around at that point and then really set the gelding going, running the final 800m in 47.98 seconds, continuing the momentum right through to the final stages, clocking the last 200m in 12.1 seconds.

As chief steward Des Gleeson commented after: "He's the best stayer I've seen and he did it all by himself."

1999-2000 — SUPER MARE HAS HER DAY IN THE SUN

There was drama and intrigue aplenty on the eve of the 1999 Cox Plate, which promised to be one of the best contests for decades.

Two runners were under a cloud while a third, Northern Drake, who had finished second in the race the year before, was announced as a non-starter after going lame.

The focus of the race was the star three-year-old Redoute's Choice. Trained by Rick Hore-Lacy, the colt had started only six times, yielding four wins including Victoria's main two-year-old, the Blue Diamond Stakes. In the new season he showed his class by winning first-up in the Group 1 Manikato Stakes (1200m) at Moonee Valley and he then took the 1600m Caulfield Guineas. The Cox Plate was to decide if he was an exceptional three-year-old against some real class opposition.

However, on the eve of the race Hore-Lacy sent shivers down the spine of Moonee Valley officials when he declared that the colt would not run if the predicted rain occurred. While officials kept looking over their shoulders for any cloud build-up, Northern Drake was announced as a non-runner. He had been in doubt with a leg injury early in the week, recovered from that, but then developed lameness in the other foreleg.

Days earlier there had been further worries over Redoute's Choice after a track gallop at Moonee Valley. A very relaxed horse, he simply didn't want to stretch out when he went on his own and Hore-Lacy was forced to send him around for a second time over a sharp 600m with a galloping companion to get him to raise a sweat.

Also of concern was whether the Plate's first international runner – the Dermot Weld-trained Make No Mistake – would take his place in the race, which was part of the Emirates World Series for the first time. Make No Mistake had arrived in a blaze of publicity to take home Australasia's greatest weight-for-age spoil, in much the same manner as Weld had done years earlier with Vintage Crop in the Melbourne Cup.

Only two days before the Plate however, there was gloom in the Weld camp when it was announced

You learn a bit after winning races such as 10 Melbourne Cups, six Caulfield Cups and three Cox Plates and Bart Cummings, who did not have a runner, was spot-on in his prediction.

He was emphatic that Sunline would lead and defy others to run her down.

1999
(Saturday, October 23. Attendance: 32,397)

$1,8000,000 plus $16,000 trophies Weight for Age 2,040m

1.	SUNLINE	T. McKee	54kg	G. Childs	6/1
2.	Tie The Knot	G. Walter	58kg	R. S. Dye	4/1
3.	Sky Heights	C. Alderson	56.5	D. Oliver	11/2

Winning details

Margin: 1½ len x 1¾ len . **Time:** 2:05.40 11 started.

Breeding: Desert Sun – Songline – Western Symphony (bm 4)
Owner: T. J. McKee, T. A. Green and Mrs H. M. Lusty

Winner's colors: Pale blue, red and yellow striped sleeves, yellow cap

Winning Numbers: 8, 1, 6

ALSO RAN

Testa Rossa	D. Lawson	E. Wilkinson	48.5	14/1
Redoute's Choice	R. Hore-Lacy	C. Munce	48.5	7/2f
Intergaze	R. Craig	C. Carmody	58	13/2
The Message	J. Ralph	B. Prebble	58	160/1
Make No Mistake	D. K. Weld	P. Smullen	58	15/1
Lahar	P. Cave	G. Hall	55.5	125/1
Inaflury	C. Alderson	L. Cassidy	54	8/1
Commands	J. R. Hawkes	C. Brown	48.5	201

Scr: Northern Drake

that Make No Mistake had pulled up sore after a gallop because of a stone bruise. Farriers eventually remedied the problem with a special shoe designed to take pressure off the bruised hoof allowing the Irish galloper to take his place in the field.

The day also dawned bright with little sign of rain, which meant Hore-Lacy, too, was happy – but not as happy as MVRC officials.

Redoute's Choice, as good as he was, was really up against some "big guns" in what was to be his toughest test to date.

These included the brilliant mare Sunline, the seasoned and classy campaigners Tie The Knot and Intergaze, Caulfield Cup winner Sky Heights and stalemate Inaflury, who had been third in the Caulfield Cup.

Interestingly, while Hore-Lacy wanted the rain to stay away, the Sunline camp wanted it to rain to improve the chances of their quality front-running mare.

All week the talk had been of Redoute's Choice emulating the feats of the brilliant three-year-olds Octagonal, Red Anchor and the filly Surround with pre-post markets all having the colt on the top line of betting. Bart Cummings did not have a runner in the race – but he was prepared to say very publicly that he did not think Hore-Lacy's horse would win. You learn a bit after winning races such as 10 Melbourne Cups, six Caulfield Cups and three Cox Plates, and it appears the public at large were prepared to listen to Cummings, who was emphatic that Sunline would lead and defy others to run her down.

The mare's co-trainer Trevor McKee, who prepares the horse with his son Steven at Taranaki (NZ), had been saying for months that Sunline – a winner of nearly $2.5 million leading up to the Cox Plate – was the best mare in Australasia. In her Plate lead-up she had won the Warwick Stakes before finishing second in the Theo Marks Quality (1300m) and the George Main Stakes (1600m). At her final outing she was a good fourth in the Epsom which had primed her perfectly for the Cox Plate journey.

When betting on the Plate opened there was evidence of the possible Cummings' influence, with Sunline opening favorite on the Tote while Redoute's Choice was a clear favorite with bookmakers.

As Cummings predicted, Sunline hit the front soon after the start with jockey Greg Childs dictating terms for the entire journey. Chris Munce on Redoute's Choice settled just behind him and coming to the home turn the pair looked set to fight out a thrilling finish. Then Childs released the brakes, and as game as he was, Redoute's Choice had no answer and began to drop back. Childs gave his mount a kick and she shot clear into the straight and it was obvious that the race was all over at that stage.

Tie The Knot began to make ground and, although he finished resolutely, he was never going to make up the leeway to finish 1½ lengths behind Sunline, while Caulfield Cup winner Sky Heights also finished on stoutly to be a further 1¾ lengths back. The success made it Cox Plate victory number three for the New Zealand training centre of Taranaki, which produced the winners Bonecrusher (Frank Ritchie, 1986) and the Phantom Chance, who won the race for Colin Jillings in 1993.

It was the first success in the race for Childs who had finished second on Let's Elope in 1992 only to be relegated to fifth on protest; was third on Vialli in 1997 and had been second on Northern Drake the previous year.

Make No Mistake knocked up to beat only three runners home and it was obvious that his hampered preparation meant that Australian racegoers did not see the best of the Irish Group winner. However, Weld said that he had treated the trip as a "learning experience" and that he would be back for another tilt.

One rider who had mixed feelings after the race was Larry Cassidy who had an arrangement with the McKee's that he rode Sunline in Sydney while Childs had the mount in Melbourne.

In the topsy-turvy world that is racing, the Cox Plate provided Child's opportunity for glory, while Cassidy beat only one runner home on Inaflury.

As they say, that's racing.

Sunline returned to New Zealand within days of her win, but barely had time to draw breath before she was back to her winning ways first-up over 1400m in a Group 2 at Pukehoe in late November. This run was a necessary prelude to taking on some of the best horses in the world in the big Group 1 international, the 2000m Hong Kong Cup at Sha Tin. She showed a lot of fight to lead early in that event, but had run her race after hitting the home turn, and finished seventh.

This time she returned home for a proper spell and was off the scene for nearly three months before resuming in scintillating style at the Sydney autumn carnival taking the 1400m Group 2 Apollo Stakes (a distance over which she was never beaten in her entire career) and she then carried 60kg to take the Group 1 Coolmore over a further 100 metres.

Carrying the steadier of 57.5kg in the Doncaster Handicap, the mighty mare was unable to repeat her three-year-old winning effort, finishing second, a neck behind the John Hawkes-trained Over. She had her revenge next start, this time at weight-for-age, when Over finished third behind her in the All Aged Stakes, giving Sunline three wins in four post Cox Plate starts, to end her four-year-old campaign with six wins and three seconds in 11 starts.

With Cox Plate number two on the agenda, she resumed in Melbourne – and at Moonee Valley – at the start of the 2000-2001 season to stroll home by more than three lengths in the 1200m Group 1 Manikato Stakes. Thereafter she made it a winning hat-trick in taking the Memsie (1400m) and Feehan (1600m) Stakes, but failed by a half head (at 4-9 favourite) in the Turnbull Stakes (2000m) at Flemington, posting her third defeat over the distance.

Given her good form at Moonee Valley, where she was unbeaten in four starts (including a 2000m win), punters were prepared to overlook the narrow Flemington loss with the result Sunline was marked as hot favourite to make it Cox Plate number two.

RACING TO RECORDS ... Sunline's seven length winning margin in 2000 equalled the record set by Dulcify in 1979 and saw her become the first horse in Australasia to win more than $6 million and take over from Octagonal as Australasia's greatest stakeswinner. – Picture: Colin Bull

But as always, there were doubters. One was Glen Boss, on second favourite Sky Heights, who had been an easy winner of the 2000m Yalumba Stakes at Caulfield two weeks earlier. Boss said he would be on Sunline's back throughout the race. He said he was going to chip away at her all the way and never let her out of his sight. On paper, such pre-race hype suggested it would be an exciting tussle between the 11/8 favourite and the 4/1 second pick. Adding to the intrigue was that Sunline had proven vulnerable over 2000m at Flemington at her latest run and Boss's pressure tactics had the potential to make her more susceptible.

But Sunline's rider Greg Childs had his own plan, which was to render useless the intended ploy by Boss – or any other rider – to bring Sunline undone.

Boss's plans faltered at the start when Sky Heights missed the jump slightly, whereas Sunline left the gates smartly and was up with the leaders, albeit wide from her outside barrier, going out of the straight the first time. Childs was content to keep her off the fence up with the leader The Message until Sunline coasted to the front with 800m to go. Thereafter it was a procession. Childs increased his lead to three lengths at the 600m mark and after turning for home the only interest was by how far she would win.

The margin was seven lengths from Caulfield Cup winner Diatribe with Referral a nose away third.

Rather than being put under pressure, Childs had turned the tables, with every other runner being put to the test from the 1000m.

Her victory equalled the record winning margin set by Dulcify in 1979 and saw Sunline become the first horse in Australasia to win more than $6 million and take over from Octagonal as Australasia's greatest stakeswinner. Prior to winning the $1.18 million first prize, her earnings totalled just over $5.1 million for 20 wins and five seconds in 28 starts. She also joined illustrious company in becoming only the second mare in history to win successive Cox Plates, after Flight, who had done so in 1945-46.

Childs said post-race that he was concerned he might have gone too early when he went to the front at the 800m, but had done so in order to keep her travelling comfortably, as co-trainer Trevor McKee said he didn't want Sunline to ruin her chances by pulling. And while Childs admitted some concern at that point, McKee's feelings were exactly the opposite, with him saying that the way she was travelling at the 800m "she would have to fall over to lose". He said it was by far her best performance in any 2000m race she had contested and she had appreciated being on her own outside the hustle and bustle for most of the way.

First thoughts of trainer McKee, who revealed he had knocked back big overseas offers for the mare in the preceding weeks, was to be back at the same time and same place next year, to match Kingston Town's Cox Plate treble, achieved in 1980-82. The immediate mission though, was the big Hong Kong international meeting in mid December.

For the vanquished, it was a race to just forget. Boss, who finished second-last on Sky Heights, said his mount could never have beaten Sunline while Jim Cassidy, who finished fifth on Skoozi Please, told reporters that while he was travelling well, when he saw how well Sunline was travelling at the 800m, "it broke my heart".

"I now know what it must have been like to race behind Might And Power," Cassidy said.

Stephen Baster, on early leader The Message,

2000
(Saturday, October 28. Attendance: 34,071)

$1,820,000 plus $20,000 trophies Weight for Age 2,040m

1.	**SUNLINE**	T. McKee	55.5kg	G. Childs	11/8f
2.	Diatribe	G. Hanlon	58kg	C. Williams	15/1
3.	Referral	S. Englebrecht	58kg	L. Cassidy	125/1

Winning details

Margin: 7 len x Nose. **Time:** 2:07.70 13 started.

Breeding: Desert Sun – Songline – Western Symphony (bm 4)
Owner: T. J. McKee, T. A. Green and Mrs H. M. Lusty

Winner's colors: Pale blue, red and yellow striped sleeves, yellow cap

Winning Numbers: 10, 9, 4. **Barriers:** 13, 6, 4.

ALSO RAN

Oliver Twist	B. Mayfield-Smith	P. Payne	58	30/1
Skoozi Please	G. Rogerson	J. Cassidy	56.5	15/1
Testa Rossa	D. Lawson	B. Prebble	56.5	9/1
The Message	J. Ralph	S. Baster	58	125/1
Fubu	C. Brown	M. Gatt	48.5	50/1
Tie The Knot	G. Walter	D. Beadman	58	6/1
Show A Heart	B. Miller	C. Munce	49	12/1
Shogun Lodge	B. Thomsen	D. Oliver	56.5	14/1
Sky Heights	C. Alderson	G. Boss	58	4/1
Beat The Fade	J. B. Cummings	J. Patton	54	125/1

All started.

VALLEY OF THE KINGS

said that he would have needed a towrope to keep up with Sunline after she went past him, while Darren Bedadman said of third favourite Tie The Knot, that he was the first horse beaten.

Sunline had only a brief let up in New Zealand before resuming with a 1400m Group 2 win at Pukehoe to have her right for Hong Kong, where she was to contest the 1600m mile race. This time she made amends for her previous Hong Kong effort, in leading all the way to narrowly beat local hero Fairy King Prawn.

Another international run came at the World Cup meeting in Dubai in March 2001. Initial plans were for her to run in the $6 million World Cup on dirt but after a trip to Dubai, trainer McKee preferred the $2 million Dubai Duty Free over 1800m on turf. Sunline led in that race but was passed at the 200m and had to settle for third behind French star Jim And Tonic and the Hong Kong hero Fairy King Prawn.

Returning to Melbourne in the Spring of 2001, she finished second in two Moonee Valley runs over 1200m and 1600m, but recorded wins in the 1400m Memsie Stakes at Caulfield and, importantly, over the 2000m of the Turnbull Stakes, which she had been unable to achieve the previous year.

Favourite at $2.80 to equal Kingston Town in completing a Cox Plate treble, she again set the pace for most of the way before being collared by Northerly, who grabbed her close to the post in a three- way tussle with Viscount. The trio was racing tight at the finish which resulted in three protests – Sunline (second) against Northerly (first) and third-placed Viscount against both Sunline and Northerly. All three were dismissed, costing Sunline a place in Cox Plate history.

But she was still given another chance to complete the race treble, by returning for a fourth Cox Plate in 2002 after a close second to Lonhro in the 2000m Yalumba Stakes at Caulfield. As usual, Sunline set the pace in the Cox Plate before being collared by Northerly after turning from home. As usual she stuck on, but had to settle for fourth after Defier and Grandera grabbed her in the dying stages.

While she failed to equal Cox Plate history she had nevertheless achieved equine immortality in many other areas. An Australian and NZ Hall of Famer, she was a three-time Australian Horse of the Year and a dual winner of the NZ equivalent. Winner of a record $11.3 million, she had the amazing record of 32 wins – 13 of them Group 1 - and 12 placings in 48 starts and had raced herself into Australasian turf lore.

Sent to stud, she had four foals, none of whom got close to matching their mother.

Sunline was sadly put down in April 2009 after suffering from the debilitating foot disease laminitis for many months, and was buried at Ellerslie racecourse in NZ.

2001-02 — THE NORTHERLY BUSTER BLEW THEM ALL AWAY

For the first time in memory, sections of the crowd booed rather than cheered the Cox Plate winner in 2001.

New Zealand mare Sunline, the Cox Plate darling of the two previous years, was attempting to equal the trio of race wins achieved by Kingston Town in 1980-82 and punters had sent her out a 7/4 chance to make Cox Plate history.

Rising Perth star Northerly had spoilt the party in a controversial finish which was to involve three protests, and many racegoers vented their disappointment when the head-on film of the events in the straight were screened around the course.

It mattered not that Northerly was an Australian horse, the Kiwi super mare had become a Moonee Valley favourite over the years and many in the crowd wanted to see her achieve Cox Plate super-star status.

Once again she had led the strong field – which included German internationals Silvano and Caitano – and had bullocked on strongly in the straight, only to be caught in a skirmish with Northerly and Viscount near the line, to be beaten by ¾ of a length for second, with Viscount a long head away.

Then came the aftermath. The head-on film had shown Viscount, who had been following Sunline for most of the way, appeared to be squeezed between her and Northerly when the West Australian gelding made his run from third place and loomed up to the lead inside the 100 metres. Sunline also seemed affected when she threw her head up near the 50m and it was no surprise when the protest siren sounded.

Kerrin McEvoy on third placed Viscount lodged objections against both Northerly and Sunline, while Childs protested against Northerly. It was a case of irony for former West Australian jockey Damien Oliver on Northerly. The previous week Oliver had hoped to win the Caulfield Cup on Sky Heights, when he (unsuccessfully) protested against New Zealand mare Ethereal. Now it was a case of hoping to keep the race against two protests, one from the rider of a New Zealand mare.

It was all in the

2001

(Saturday, October 27. Attendance: 38,081)

$2,050,000 plus $20,000 trophies Weight for Age 2,040m

1.	*NORTHERLY	F. Kersley	58kg	D. Oliver	5/2
2.	*Sunline	T. McKee	55.5kg	G. Childs	7/4f
3.	*Viscount	J. R. Hawkes	48.5kg	K. McEvoy	11/1

*PROTEST: 3rd against 1st & 2nd dismissed: protest 2nd against 1st dismissed.

Winning details

Margin: ¾ len x Lng hd . **Time:** 2:05.84 8 started.

Breeding: Serheed (USA - North Bell – Bellwater (FR) (bg 5)
Owner: Mrs J. A. Kersley, N. G. & Mrs S. M. Duncan, R. G. Sayers, P. M. Bartlett, T. M. Patrizi and I. F. Grijusich.

Winner's colors: Yellow, black Maltese cross, quartered cap

Winning Numbers: 1, 7, 8. **Barriers:** 3, 8, 1.

ALSO RAN

Silvano (GER)	A. Wohler	A. Suborics	58	6/1
King Keitel	P. Jenkins	B. York	58	40/1
Universal Prince	E. B. Murray	J. Sheehan	56.5	15/4
Caitano (GB)	A. Schutz	A. Starke	58	80/1
Referral	R. S. Englebrecht	C. Brown	58	66/1

All started.

TOUCH AND GO NEAR THE POST ... Damien Oliver steers Northerly past Viscount (pink silks) with Sunline's head just visible on the inside and then had to survive a protest from the riders of both horses before becoming the first West Australian horse since Aquanita in 1962 to win the Cox Plate. – Picture: Colin Bull

stewards' hands whether Sunline would equal Kingston Town's feat and some in the crowd were letting the stewards know their feelings in advance.

Northerly was the rising star of the Melbourne spring that year. Prepared in Perth by former star harness driver and trainer Fred Kersley, he had won one of two races in his home state in 1999-2000, the year Sunline won her second Cox Plate. After winning three races in Perth in the new season, Northerly came to Melbourne in the autumn of 2001, winning the $1.2 million wfa Australian Cup in record time at Flemington. (His rider that day was Greg Childs!) Kersley now knew he had a horse capable of mixing it with the best and wasted no time in testing Northerly in the best company when he returned to Melbourne in his five-year-old season.

Northerly was back at Moonee Valley in September 2001 and beat odds-on favourite Sunline by a long head over 1600m in the Group 2 Feehan Stakes at weight-for-age; followed by Group 1wins in the Underwood Stakes at Caulfield and the 2000m of the Yalumba Stakes there. Kersley had been considering a Caulfield Cup start with Northerly but opted for the Cox Plate because of the wfa conditions and the distance. Kersley knew that Sunline was a crowd favourite, but also knew his horse was in perfect condition leading into the trainer's first Cox Plate meeting.

As Kersley and connections waited patiently for stewards to resolve the protest, there was one part-owner more anxious for two reasons, back in Perth. This was Ron Sayers, whose daughter was getting married that afternoon. Sayers and his daughter watched the race on television some 90 minutes before the wedding – and then had to wait some while stewards deliberated. When the protest siren sounded the father of the bride thought he might have to seek more assistance from the priest!

Another part-owner, Ian Grijusich was also anxiously awaiting the outcome at Moonee Valley, intending to tell Damien Oliver a secret once the result was declared. Like Northerly's trainer and owners, Oliver was also a West Australian, and he admitted later that he was feeling very emotional about the West Australian links when he came back to scale. What Grijusich was to tell him would only add to those emotions; being the fact that Grijusich's father had trained a horse which ran in the race in which Oliver's jockey father Ray was killed in a racefall at Kalgoorlie in 1975 when Damien was only three. He had deliberately avoided telling Damien about the connection so as not to upset him before the race.

Soon Oliver and the Northerly clan were cock-a-hoop when stewards dismissed both protests and Northerly became the first West Australian-trained horse since Aquanita in 1962 to win a Cox Plate.

It was then that Kersley admitted he would have been very surprised had the decision gone the other way, given that Northerly had come from behind both Sunline and Northerly and still beaten them.

John Hawkes, trainer of Viscount, said the Press would not be able to publish his comments.

But Kerrin McEvoy at least had a comment for the public record, saying he had no doubt Viscount should have won had not first, Northerly, and then Sunline, caused inconvenience to his mount.

Greg Childs also had a snipe at Northerly saying that while Sunline was beaten by a better horse on the day, the situation was not helped when Northerly shifted in on Sunline.

The best of the German runners was Silvano, who held on for fourth after looking a contender when in the company of the first three placegetters on the turn. Unfortunately he could not match pace with the trio on straightening. Compatriot Caitano never looked a contender and beat only one home.

Having put Perth racing firmly on the map, Northerly disappointed at home in his one run there after the Cox Plate before being spelled. Starting a hot 5/4 favourite he could finish only 11th in the Group 1 Railway Stakes (1600m) at Ascot before being turned out. The victor that day, Old Comrade, would become a thorn in his side in another big race down the track.

Back in Melbourne for the autumn of 2001, Northerly was 6/4 favourite when he resumed in the Group 1 C. F.Orr Stakes but was beaten by just over a length into second place by Bakarda. He was back to his best at his next start, also at Caulfield, when he turned the tables on Old Comrade in winning the Group 2 St George Stakes.

Next up was the race he'd won the previous year, the Australian Cup at Flemington, for which Northerly was at 4/5 to make it a double. This time Old Comrade had the edge at the end of the 2000m Group 1 worth $1.2 million, bringing Northerly's autumn campaign to an end, but Kersley would be back in spring.

He opened his Melbourne spring campaign in the Memsie Stakes but could finish only fourth after trying to savage Fields Of Omagh in the run. On better behaviour the following week, he took the 1600m Group

IN ELITE COMPANY ... Jockey Patrick Payne and connections head back to scale after Northerly became only the fourth horse to win the Caulfield Cup-Cox Plate double in the same year, joining Tranquil Star (1942), Rising Fast (1954) and Tobin Bronze in 1967. – Picture: Colin Bull

VALLEY OF THE KINGS

2 Craiglee Stakes followed by Group 1 success in the Underwood Stakes. On a roll, he completed the hat-trick by scoring narrowly in the 2000m Turnbull Stakes at Flemington. He had been ridden by Greg Childs in these three wins and started $5.50 favourite the following week for what would be the jockey's first Caulfield Cup success.

Next up was the Cox Plate, and despite his great spring association with Northerly, there was no doubt that Childs was going to remain loyal and stick with Sunline, who to date had provided two wins and a second for him in the Cox Plate.

Despite his outstanding

2002
(Saturday, October 26. Attendance: 38,325)

$3,000,000 plus $20,000 trophies Weight for Age 2,040m

1.	NORTHERLY	F. Kersley	58kg	P. Payne	3/1ef
2.	Defier	G. Walter	58kg	C. Munce	7/1
3.	Grandera	S. Bin Suroor	58kg	F. Dettori	8/1

Winning details

Margin: 1 len x Lng nk . **Time:** 2:06.27 9 started.

Breeding: Serheed (USA) - North Bell - Bellwater (FR) (bg 6)
Owner: Mrs J. A. Kersley, N.G. & Mrs S. M. Duncan, R. G. Sayers, P. M. Bartlett, T. M. Patrizi & I. F. Grljusich.

Winner's colors: Yellow, black Maltese Cross, quartered cap.

Winning Numbers: 1, 4, 3. **Barriers:** 5, 6, 3.

ALSO RAN

Sunline	T. McKee	G. Childs	55.5	5/1
Fields Of Omagh	T. McEvoy	D. Oliver	58	16/1
Lonhro	J. Hawkes	D. Beadman	56.5	3/1 ef
Ustinov	J. B. Cummings	S. Arnold	56.5	40/1
Bel Esprit	J. G. Symons	K. McEvoy	48.5	9/1
Assertive Lad	G. Waterhouse	J. Cassidy	58	50/1

All started

form, Northerly was up against another smart foe apart from Sunline; the Sydney star and Caulfield Guineas winner Lonhro. His lead-up form included wins in the Group 2 Chelmsford Stakes (1600m) at Randwick and the 2000m of the Group 1 Yalumba at Caulfield at his Melbourne debut that spring when he narrowly beat Sunline.

Come Cox Plate day punters could not split Lonhro and Northerly, with them sharing favouritism at 3/1 equal ahead of Sunline on the second line at 5/1. Adding to the intrigue of the race was the first appearance of a Godolphin runner in the race, with Frankie Dettori wearing the famous all blue colours on Grandera. Touted as the best 2000m horse in the world, Grandera was heavily backed in the fortnight preceeding the race once it was learned he was making the trip. The fact that Detorri had decided to ride in the Cox Plate for Godolphin ahead of partnering Prix de l'arc de Triomphe winner Marienard in the US Breeders Cup – run on Cox Plate day - was a significant factor in the big betting support.

A winner of Group 1s in three different countries, Grandera's price tumbled from 12/1 to 5/1 in days preceding the Plate but he was marked at 8/1 by punters on race day. Importantly, a win in the Cox Plate would see Grandera win the World Series of Racing title.

With Childs back on Sunline, Patrick Payne had the mount on Northerly. Riding a perfect race, he had the sit in second place behind Sunline and had moved up to her approaching the home turn. He overhauled the mare halfway down the straight to hold off a fast finishing Defier and Grandera, with Sunline clinging onto fourth.

The win saw Northerly become only the fourth horse to win the Caulfield Cup-Cox Plate double in the same year, behind Tranquil Star (1942), Rising Fast 1954) and Tobin Bronze in 1967.

Questioned immediately after the race about a possible Melbourne Cup start – he had 60kg in the race after being penalised 2kg for his Caulfield Cup win – Kersley said it would be asking too much for the six-year-old.

Winner of the Australian Cup again at Flemington in the autumn of 2003, Northerly also had three runs in Sydney with seconds in the Group 1 Ranvet and BMW.

The iron warrior was then beset by injury suffering a torn tendon in his off-fore, requiring an immediate spell. Back after a year off, he resumed with a creditable fourth in Perth in August 2004 but then disappointed in two Melbourne runs, bowing out after finishing midfield in the 2000m Turnbull Stakes.

It was all over for the Perth iron horse who won $9.3 million for 19 wins – nine Group 1s - and nine placings in 37 starts to become Australasia's second-highest stakes-earner. Named the Australian Racehorse of the Year in 2003, he was also inducted into the Australian Racing Hall of Fame in 2010.

> "Then he missed the start in a crack field and I thought 'that's it, forget him'. But I still kept one eye on him and the other eye on the entire field, how I don't really know!
>
> "When he took off from last at the 400m I thought, 'run home hard mate, cover yourself in glory, run in the top five if you can'.

For a horse costing only $50,000, Fields Of Omagh proved himself among the most durable - and successful – competitors in the W. S. Cox Plate.

He started five times in Moonee Valley's "Australasian weight-for-age championship" for the amazing record of two wins, a second, a third and a fifth. These races alone netted earnings of $4.7 million out of his total winnings of almost $6.5 million.

Moonee Valley proved a great venue for the gelding with him also starting four times in the Group 2 Feehan (Dato Tan Chin Nam) Stakes there for a win, a third a fourth and a fifth. Taking those into account, his winnings at the track totalled just under $5 million.

His Cox Plate record equals that of another iron horse, Tranquil Star, who also contested the race five times on end between 1941-45 for a similar record to that of Fields Of Omagh, for two wins, a second, a fourth and a fifth.

His Moonee Valley record aside, Fields of Omagh – who earned the nickname FOO – also featured strongly in other feature events. Other Group wins came in races such as the Futurity and the Eclipse Stakes, while he also finished within a half neck of Northerly in the 2002 Caulfield Cup. He was also placed in big races such as the Yalumba, C. F. Orr, Toorak and Turnbull stakes. FOO also ran against world class company in Dubai, Japan and Hong Kong, but his overseas record failed to match his Australian feats. The bottom line though, was that FOO, who twice overcame ligament injuries, was a relentless competitor. Though punters appreciated his Cox Plate fight, they rarely liked his chances, marking him between 15/1 and 20/1 in each of his Plate races.

He was bought by former racing journalist cum bloodstock expert Murray Bell for the No Big Deal Syndicate, co-managed by racecaller Bryan Martin. Martin asked Bell, who had proven he had a good eye for horses, to purchase a colt and a filly for the syndicate. His first choice was a Belotto filly called Muffin McLay, for $31,000. (She earned about $6,500 after winning a maiden at Kyneton.)

Bell's other purchase was a colt by 1987 Cox Plate winner Rubiton out

2003
(Saturday, October 25. Attendance: 30,109)

$3,000,000 plus $20,000 trophies Weight for Age 2,040m

1.	**FIELDS OF OMAGH**	T. McEvoy	58kg	S. King	16/1
2.	**Defier**	G. Walter	58kg	P. Payne	10/1
3.	**Lonhro**	J. Hawkes	58kg	D. Beadman	4/7 fav

Winning details

Margin: Nk x ½ len . **Time:** 2:07.61 8 started.

Breeding: Rubiton- Finneto - Ceretto (IRE) (b g 6)
Owner: No Big Deal Syndicate (Mgrs B. Martin & M. Bolton),
M. J. O'Connor, A. Cork, A. Sorrell & E. J. LeGrand

Winner's colors: Royal blue, gold diamond, diamond sleeves and cap

Winning Numbers: 3, 2, 1. **Barriers:** 6, 8, 7.

ALSO RAN

Zagalia	T.C. Conners	G. Childs	54	30/1
Clangalang	G. A. Ryan	C. Brown	56.5	9/2
Shower Of Roses	G. Waterhouse	C. Munce	54	12/1
Natural Blitz	D. Harrison	K. McEvoy	56.5	16/1
Paraca	A. Balding	N. Rawiller	54	66/1

All started

of Finetto, being offered by well-known Victorian breeder Martin O'Connor. The colt had been passed in for $45,000 at the sale Bell was attending, but he liked the look of the colt and made a closer inspection.

"He rang me and said it had a bump on its knee, but it shouldn't cause any problems," Martin said.

"Martin O'Connor told me he needed $50,000 for the horse, so I told him we would proceed if he joined the syndicate of owners, which meant he also had to take a share in Muffin McLay.

"He agreed, so like others in the group, he had a share in a filly who won a few thousand and in a gelding who won $6 million. As they say, that's the luck of the draw in racing."

When it came to naming their new colt, a name came to Martin when he was thumbing through the English Time Form ratings magazines.

"The name of an Irish horse called Fields Of Omagh jumped out of a page," Martin said.

"I remember I used to love the name of one of Colin Hayes' horses called Flanders Fields. It was a great name to use in a racecall and the name Fields Of Omagh had the same effect."

Placed in the hands of Peter Hayes (his brother David was in Hong Kong) at Lindsay Park in the Barossa Valley, Fields Of Omagh was gelded in his two-year-old season and did not race. He won twice at Sandown in eight runs during his first preparation in 2001. During this period Peter Hayes was tragically killed in a light aircraft crash, resulting in Lindsay Park foreman Tony McEvoy becoming head-trainer and taking over the preparation of FOO.

Under him FOO hinted what was in store when he came back from a spell in the spring with five wins on end, four at city tracks in Adelaide and Melbourne before his campaign came to a forced end when the gelding hurt his near-fore suspensory after winning the Group 3 Eclipse Stakes in late November 2001.

Careful treatment saw Fields Of Omagh back in action at the start of the 2002 season; his standouts were a win in the Feehan and a half neck second to Northerly in the Caulfield Cup, after which he was fifth in his first Cox Plate.

Injury struck again in the autumn of 2003; this time Fields of Omagh hurt his off-fore suspensory. Spelled for six months, he fronted up again in the spring of 2003. At his first run back he finished last of 18 over 1400m at Caulfield, but jockey Kerrin McEvoy told connections the run had been good under the circumstances. Puzzled, they asked why, and McEvoy explained that FOO was having some issues with his feet. This was later discovered to have been caused by tight racing plates. Re-shod, he finished a much improved second two weeks later in the Toorak Handicap with Steven King in the saddle. While that was a lot better performance, two runs from a spell was hardly a regular lead-up to a race like the Cox Plate; but that is where FOO found himself two weeks later, again under Steven King.

All the rage for the race was the brilliant Sydney champion Lonhro, who was in peak form with four group wins on end – the Warwick, Chelmsford and George Main Stakes in Sydney and then in the Group 1 Yalumba (Caulfield) Stakes at Caulfield a fortnight before the Cox Plate. Considered Australia's best horse, it was little wonder he was at 4/7 while FOO appeared to be just making up the numbers at 16/1 in the field of eight. Lohnro had started 3/1 equal favourite in the Cox Plate the year before to finish sixth, (one place behind Fields of Omagh) after ruining his chances when he reared in the barriers.

But John Hawkes was a confident trainer in 2003 saying Lonhro was primed for his "grand final",

Jockey Darren Beadman was also on a high, having had a careless riding suspension for his previous win on Lonhro at Caulfield reduced by a day, so he could ride in the Plate. But he had to pay for that day's grace, being fined $30,000.

"It's not about money, it's irrelevant; it is about being able to ride Lonhro," a relieved Beadman said. But considering first prize in the Cox Plate was just over $2 million, earning the winning rider a minimum of $100,000, having to pay a $30,000 fine seemed like a win.

McEvoy made particular effort to ensure the horse was right for Cox Plate number 2. He had sent Fields Of Omagh back to the Lindsay Park stables after his second in the Toorak Handicap, allowing McEvoy around two weeks to fine tune the horse in the hilly terrain there. This followed a tactic trainer Colin Hayes had used successfully before Almaarad took the 1989 Cox Plate.

On Cox Plate day, Fields Of Omagh had the race in his sights just before the home turn when he led the rest of the field up from third place to early leaders Paraca and Shower Of Roses. Despite his light preparation, FOO stayed on strongly in the wet conditions and was able to hold off Defier by a neck with Lonhro a half length away.

Steven King had planned the tactics after watching videos the day before, intending to take up a prime position near the lead and force runners to come around him from the turn. The win gave King the third leg of Victoria racing's elusive "Group 1 Triple Crown", after winning the Caulfield and Melbourne Cups on Let's Elope in 1991.

Neither Darren Beadman nor John Hawkes had any excuses for Lonhro's disappointment, with a Hawkes saying the stallion had every chance but was "not good enough" on the day.

While the big FOO syndicate were jumping out their skins, syndicate co-manager and Moonee Valley racecaller Bryan Martin was bounding down the stairs from his grandstand eyrie, to join his co-owners.

"Everything had gone to the script, we had watched all the videos the day before with Tony Mc Evoy and Steve King and knew exactly where we had to be coming to the turn," Martin said.

"I told Steve make sure he had a length up his sleeve when Lonhro and Defier came at him. I knew they would come hard.

"Steve did that and turned it into a dogfight, and the horse kept finding.

" I beat the owners out of the stand and beat the chief steward into the enclosure and I had come down from the broadcast box and 6 flights!"

But the Cox Plate journey for Fields of Omagh was far from over. He was back again the following year in 2004 for tilt number three, setting

2006
(Saturday, October 28. Attendance: 34,276)

$3,100,000 plus $40,000 trophies Weight for Age 2,040m

1.	FIELDS OF OMAGH	D. A. Hayes	58kg	C. Williams	20/1
2.	El Segundo	C. W. Little	58kg	D. Gauci	3/1
3.	Pompeii Ruler	M. Price	56.5kg	C. Newitt	14/1

Winning details

Margin: Nose, lng hd . **Time:** 2:06.89 12 started.

Breeding: Rubiton- Finneto – Cerreto (IRE) (b g 9)
Owner: No Big Deal Syndicate (Mgrs B. Martin & M. Bolton), M. J. O'Connor, A. Cork, A. Sorrell & E. J. LeGrand

Winner's colors: Royal blue, gold diamond, diamond sleeves and cap

Winning Numbers: 2, 4, 11. **Barriers:** 7, 10, 9.

ALSO RAN

Aqua D'Amore	G. Waterhouse	K. Fallon	55.5	25/1
Our Smoking Joe	D. L. Freedman	D. Beadman	58	15/1
Miss Finland	D. A. Hayes	Ms L. Cropp	46	9/1
Apache Cat	G. Eurell	G. Childs	56.5	40/1
Casual Pass	M. Ellerton	N. Rawiller	58	25/1
Lad Of The Manor	R. Hoysted	D. Nikolic	58	12/1
Red Dazzler	M. Price	J. Cassidy	56.5	25/1
Racing To Win	J. O'Shea	G. Boss	56.5	11/4f
Grey Swallow	D. Sutton	S. King	58	10/1

Scr: Honor In War

MOMENTS FROM GLORY ... Craig Williams ranges up to eventual close runner-up El Segundo en route to Plate win number two for Fields of Omagh. – Picture: Colin Bull

up the challenge after winning a Listed Race in Adelaide at his third run from a spell. FOO again acquitted himself well, when, ridden by Danny Nikolic, he earned $500,000 when second behind three-year-old Savabeel after settling midfield and making his run from the turn.

He also had only a sparse lead-up the following year when he was placed in both the Group 2 Feehan stakes and Group 1 Yalumba Stakes at his second and third runs from a spell before tackling the Cox Plate for the fourth time in 2005. This time he had to again settle for a placing – though in the best of company, when third behind champion mare Makybe Diva – adding a further $220,000 to his Moonee Valley stakes tally.

Now nine, he had one last Hurrah in him for the Moonee Valley championship, to equal the five starts set by Tranquil Star in the 1940's.

Again, he had had only three preparatory runs, being unplaced in all of them. Frankly, on that form, and because of his age – no nine-year-old had won the race - his chances seemed forlorn. It was announced well beforehand that this would be the gelding's swansong for his 31 owners.

But they had the chance to dream once more with their tenacious gelding, this time under the care of David Hayes who had returned from Hong Kong. And sitting in the saddle was Craig Williams, who had been most commonly linked with stablemate, star filly Miss Finland, who had won the Thousand Guineas and would go on to take the Oaks and the Cadbury Guineas. Miss Finland was also in the Cox Plate but Williams was unable to make her weight of 46kg, so New Zealand's Lisa Cropp had the mount on the 9/1 chance while Williams was on the stable's 20/1 hope.

Two runners dominated the betting - El Segundo, who had won the Memsie and Underwood Stakes, and the Sydneysider Racing To Win, who had dual Group 1 successes in the Epsom Handicap and George Main Stakes. The latter headed the market at 11/4 with El Segundo marginally longer at 3/1.

On settling, Racing To Win was in touch with the leaders out wide, while El Segundo was last, just behind Fields Of Omagh.

Approaching the home turn, El Segundo had improved markedly to be in third place with Fields Of Omagh also rallying to get in touch, being on the extreme outside as the field, led by Pompeii Ruler, fanned for home. Next thing FOO and El Segundo were challenging for the lead halfway down the straight and the judge had to call for a photo to split Fields Of Omagh, El Segundo and Pompeii Ruler on the line.

Maybe he was over-excited or conscious of bias, but Martin was a caller who generally gave his verdict on the likely winner in such close finishes. This time he remained silent.

"This was the most emotional day of all. We had decided the day before that he would be retired, win lose or draw. He had done his job and he had given us so much joy, this was certainly his swansong.

"I was so emotional I cried a little when he led them onto the track and the applause came for him.

"I knew I had to hold it together for me and everyone involved, as well as for the racecall.

"Then he missed the start in a crack field and I thought 'that's it, forget him'. But I still kept one eye on him and the other eye on the entire field, how I don't really know!

"When he took off from last at the 400m I thought, 'run home hard mate, cover yourself in glory, run in the top five if you can'.

"Then he simply exploded in the last 250m. He had never gone quicker in his life and he nosed out El Segundo.

"I thought he may have just won but discretion took over. I did not want to be wrong especially on this occasion. The relief when the number was posted was extraordinary. Our family emotions were already so high, as my son Tim and his partner Louise announced their engagement the night before.

"FOO gave us the greatest ride in life one could ever imagine and he was the nexus of creating Living Legends. A horse can change your life forever!"

While Martin had kept his counsel on declaring the result, he let fly once FOO's No. 2 went into the frame.

"He's got it. He's done it," he called excitedly on the on-course broadcasting system when FOO got the verdict by a nose. He then broke his 2003 record of bounding downstairs from the broadcast box to ground level.

The never-say die gelding had made it Cox Plate win number two for himself and for David Hayes, who had prepared Better Loosen Up 16 years earlier.

For the vanquished there was disappointment. El Segundo had been in front just before and moments after the line, but jockey Darren Gauci and connections vowed they would come back to fight another day.

For FOO, it was a fairytale farewell with him becoming only the 11th multiple winner of Australasia's greatest weight-for-age race, earning him immediate retirement in the Living Legends complex for retired horses near Sunbury, Victoria.

It was a rest, well-earned.

2004 — THE "I TOLD YOU SO" PLATE

Those who failed to back the winner of the 2004 Cox Plate either didn't read newspapers or listen to radio or watch television. Or, simply didn't believe trainer Graeme Rogerson.

In a break from the usual taciturn attitude of horse trainers – who generally prefer to keep their opinions to themselves, or at best, give mono-syllabic responses to a horse's chances – Rogerson was positively effusive.

He told everyone at every media opportunity that three-year-old Savabeel was one of the best horses he had ever had and that the colt would win.

Rogerson's performance was akin to that of the legendary Tommy Smith at his spruiking best. Smith, a record-holding seven-time winner of the Cox Plate, made an art form of promoting himself and his horses in all major races – with justifiable results.

But Rogerson's tip fell mostly on deaf ears, evidenced by the fact that Savabeel started at the big odds of $15 to become the first three-year-old since Octagonal in 1995 to win the weight-for-age championship.

While Moonee Valley Racing Club was no doubt extremely grateful for the string of headlines in the week-long race lead-up, some people were more suspicious that Rogerson was simply "talking up" the value of the colt in an attempt to sell him. And, considering Rogerson bred the horse and was also the major part-owner of the colt, there were reasons aplenty for him to keep the horse in the headlines!

In the end it was Rogerson who had the last laugh, with the value of the colt increasingly dramatically after the Plate success – and once again Rogerson was not backward in letting people know the worth of the Zabeel colt.

A two-year-old winner at his first start in February 2004, Savabeel's only other success before the Cox Plate had been in the Group 1 Spring Champion Stakes against other three-year-olds three weeks before the Plate. Rogerson said after the Moonee Valley win that Savabeel's value had rocketed from $10 million to $20 million because of his Plate triumph – and,

Rogerson had said he considered the colt to be the best horse in Australia. He had proved the knockers wrong in winning the Cox Plate and in his mind he was up to both the Derby and the Melbourne Cup. And it was not as if Rogerson was talking off the top of his head in the heat of the moment after the Cox Plate. He had in fact entered Savabeel for the Melbourne Cup four months earlier and he had been handicapped on 47kg.

2004
(Saturday, October 23. Attendance: 32,187)

$3,000,000 plus $20,000 trophies Weight for Age 2,040m

1.	SAVABEEL	G. Rogerson	48.5kg	C. Munce	14/1
2.	Fields Of Omagh	T. McEvoy	58kg	D. Nikolic	15/1
3.	Starcraft	G. Newham	56.5kg	G. Boss	7/2

Winning details

Margin: Len, lng nk . **Time:** 2:06.88 13 started.

Breeding: Zabee l (NZ) - Savannah Success – Success Express (USA) (br c 3)
Owner: G. A. Rogerson, B. Reid, M. J. Whitby, W. A. Choy & M. J. Achurch

Winner's colors: Red, dark blue sleeves, green armbands

Winning Numbers: 13, 4, 7. **Barriers:** 6, 7, 1.

ALSO RAN

Grand Armee	G. Waterhouse	D. Oliver	58	4/1
Regal Roller	C.McDonald	M. Flaherty	58	12/1
Delzao	G. Kavanagh	S. King	56.5	40/1
King's Chapel	M. Walker	D. Beadman	56.5	16/1
Elvstroem	A. Vasil	N. Rawiller	56.5	13/4f
Elegant Fashion	D. A. Hayes	G. Mosse	55.5	8/1
Paolini	A. Wohler	E. Pedroza	58	30/1
Our Egyptian Raine	G. Begg	C. Brown	55.5	30/1
Miss Potential	W. Borrie	R. Jones	55.5	150/1
Natural Blitz	D. Harrison	S. Baster	58	100/1

All started

CONFIDENCE GALORE ... apart from the spruiking by trainer Graeme Rogerson, jockey Chris Munce also believed Savabeel was a top chance going on his Spring Champion Stakes win at Randwick. – Picture: Colin Bull

considering Rogerson owned 40% of him, who in his position wouldn't have miss the opportunity to keep talking up the colt?

His immediate reaction after Savabeel became the first three-year-old to win the race in nine years since Octagonal - another son of Zabeel - was: "I don't think I'll be selling him.

"I might stand him (as a stallion) myself. He's a once-in-a-lifetime horse. He's done it at both ends and has beaten the best, just like I said he would."

And the promotion didn't stop there. Such was Rogerson's faith in his colt, he said punters should back up on Savabeel the following week in the Victoria Derby.

This time however, his prediction fell short of the mark. Savabeel, who started $3.30 equal favorite in the Derby had his colors lowered by co-favorite, the WA star, Plastered.

That performance put a dent in another of Rogerson's post Cox Plate predictions – being that Savabeel would also run in the Melbourne Cup, a comment probably influenced by the fact that the Cox Plate win had made Savabeel exempt from any Melbourne Cup ballot.

Rogerson had said he considered the colt to be the best horse in Australia. He had proved the knockers wrong in winning the Cox Plate and in his mind he was up to both the Derby and the Melbourne Cup. And it was not as if Rogerson was talking off the top of his head in the heat of the moment after the Cox Plate. He had in fact entered Savabeel for the Melbourne Cup four months earlier and he had been handicapped on 47kg.

Chris Munce, who had won the Spring Champion Stakes on Savabeel at Randwick before the Cox Plate, was back on board at Moonee Valley. And he was only there because of the confidence he had in his mount after the Sydney win. This was because Munce had promised himself that he would not waste hard again to ride a three-old in the Cox Plate after the stress he went through to ride Show A Heart at 49kg when he finished 10th in 2000.

It was expected that Savabeel would settle back in the field, but Munce elected to go forward early, settling behind pacesetters Regal Roller and Miss Potential. He moved to the lead on entering the straight to last by a length from the previous year's winner Fields Of Omagh with Starcraft a close-up third. Munce said he made the move for home knowing that with no weight (48.5kg) on his back it was up to the others to catch him. 2003 winner Fields Of Omagh tried hard to do that, but trainer Tony McEvoy said it was impossible for the seven year to concede nearly 10kg to the winner over the final stages. But in what proved to be a chilling prediction, McEvoy said it would not be the last Cox Plate run for the horse.

Bookmakers did Paul Makin, the big-betting owner of third placegetter Starcraft, a big favour. They quoted Starcraft second favourite at 7/2 – half a point below the price at which Makin had said he would have a $1 million bet on his horse.

Favourite Elvstroem, who started at 13/4 on the strength of three Group wins on end – in the Gr 1 Underwood and Gr 2 Turnbull Stakes before also taking the Caulfield Cup - finished 8th after suffering a chequered run, particularly when making a run near the 800m. He showed that form all wrong when he stepped out next for a great fourth behind Makybe Diva in the Melbourne Cup.

As mentioned earlier, Savabeel missed that race after his Derby defeat, but Rogerson still had big plans in store for him in the autumn of 2005. He mapped out an ambitious program of four Group 1 races in Melbourne and Sydney. His best effort was a first-up second in the Orr Stakes at Caulfield, but he finished well back in his other three runs in the Futurity Stakes, Cadbury Guineas and the Queen Elizabeth Stakes at Randwick. Thereafter he was retired to stud in 2005, having earned $2,760,000 with three wins and four placings in 13 starts. It proved to be a handsome return for part-owner Rogerson, who had bought the colt for $400,000.

Not surprisingly, there was a story behind Rogerson purchasing the colt. He revealed he had phoned another super salesman, well-known retailer Gerry Harvey, of Harvey Norman fame, some years earlier, saying he needed some cash. He suggested that Harvey should buy his mare Savannah Success with the Zabeel colt (Savabeel) at foot. Harvey paid $1.4 million for the mare and foal and then on-sold the foal through his 2003 Magic Millions sale ring, with Rogerson paying $400,000 for it.

While it proved a bargain buy for Rogerson, not surprisingly, the master trader Harvey also did well out of the deal. A colt by Red Ransom out of his new mare was sold by Harvey for $1.55 million in 2006 and a Redoute's Choice colt out of Savannah Success sold for $1 million two years later. The sales deal turned out to be a win-win deal for all parties.

2005 — SHE PROVED HERSELF A DIVA ON COX PLATE DAY, TOO!

Ability-wise, she was long odds-on, probably around $1.10 if a market were framed on that score. But then there were the imponderables which could only be answered in the race. How would the dual Melbourne Cup winner, renowned for her dourness, handle the pressure-cooker atmosphere of the 2040m at the tight Moonee Valley circuit, where she had never won before?

Makybe Diva® laid claim to be the best mare in Australian history – a reputation confirmed after her third Melbourne Cup 10 days later - when she toyed with her rivals to win one of the most memorable Cox Plates in 2005 and become Australia's top money-earner in the process.

She achieved all manner of records and adulation from all quarters in a win described by Lee Freedman "as big as it gets for me" (to that stage).

Conjecture before the race was this. Ability-wise, she was long odds-on, probably around $1.10 if a market were framed on that score. But then there were the imponderables which could only be answered in the race. How would the dual Melbourne Cup winner, renowned for her dourness, handle the pressure-cooker atmosphere of the 2040m at the tight Moonee Valley circuit, where she had never won before? There were plenty in the field who could serve it up to her and perhaps she would have trouble under full pressure in negotiating the tight home turn.

Bookmaker Mark Read also suggested jockey Glen Boss could also be a factor, saying his winning strike rate was not as high as it could have been and his confidence could be at an ebb.

So on the combination on the score of ability and the imponderables, bookies put up $2.25, only to be hit by punters big and small, with the result that when the starting stalls opened she was a $2 chance. By the time they were at the home turn, her price was long odds-on and bookies knew their payout queues were going to be long.

While the pressure tactics did occur - with the result that eight of the 14 runners were fanned out on the turn, with Makybe Diva out six from the rail heading for home – there was never a doubt about her handling the track and coping with the hub-bub. She showed she could respond to anything her rivals applied but Freedman admitted he thought "the needle on the petrol gauge was knocking on empty when she came into the straight".

2005
(Saturday, October 22. Attendance: 33,153)

$3,000,000 plus $25,000 trophies Weight for Age 2,040m

1.	**MAKYBE DIVA**	D. L. Freedman	55.5kg	G. Boss	Evens fav
2.	Lotteria	G. Waterhouse	54kg	C. Munce	20/1
3.	Fields Of Omagh	D. A. Hayes	58kg	S. King	16/1

Winning details

Margin: 1¼ len, ½ hd . **Time:** 2:09.27 14 started.

Breeding: Desert King (IRE) -Tugela (USA) – Riverman (USA) (b m 7)
Owner: Emily Krstina (Aust) Pty Ltd Syndicate (Mgr: T. Santic)

Winner's colors: Royal blue, white stars, red and white checks and checked cap

Winning Numbers: 10, 12, 6. **Barriers:** 4, 8, 10.

ALSO RAN

Sky Cuddle	P. Moody	G. Childs	55.5	100/1
Lad Of The Manor	R. Hoysted	B. Johns	58	8/1
Confectioner	D. A. Hayes	C. Williams	58	20/1
Super Kid	J. Moore	N. Rawiller	58	20/1
God's Own	J. B. Cummings	S. Baster	48.5	7/1
Xcellent	M. Moroney	M. Coleman	56.5	12/1
Greys Inn	M. De Kock	W. Marwing	58	25/1
Tosen Dandy	H. Mori	M. Yoshida	58	200/1
Desert War	G. Waterhouse	L. Cassidy	58	20/1
Outback Prince	A. Cummings	D. Beadman	56.5	100/1
Hotel Grand	A. Cummings	J. Ford	48.5	20/1

All started

NOTHING COULD MASK THEIR DELIGHT ... Elated owner Tony Santic leads in his super mare while jockey Glen Boss and the Clerk of Course also join in the spirit of occasion in their Makybe Diva ® masks. – Picture: Colin Bull

Jockey Glen Boss knew that from the turn it was just a matter of heading for victory after shrugging off everything they had thrown at her.

Boss said he couldn't believe it when the pressure started at the 1000m mark.

"It played into our hands. When they wanted some eyeball-to-eyeball stuff that far out, we were certainly prepared to answer the challenge."

Boss said he had not anticipated this to occur at that point and although it was not part of his game plan, he figured his mount would be the only survivor from it all.

"Fancy taking on the nation's best stayer with 1000m to go? The horses that tried to go with her dropped out and ran nowhere.

"She gave everything she had – and nothing can beat her when she is in that mood.

"She went through the brick wall as usual. She put them away from the home turn."

Boss said he knew he would win from that point and could hear the crowd roaring all the way down the straight. (Passengers on a flight between Melbourne and the Gold Coast also shared in the action, with the captain putting the race on through the inflight speaker system!).

Earlier Makybe Diva had only three behind her on settling with the leaders slackening off the pace 1400m from home. Jockey Mike Coleman who had Xcellent in near last pace was unhappy with the pace and set out for the lead near the 1000m, which was the signal for the rest of the field to make the forward charge.

Fields of Omagh and Lotteria were soon in the thick of things and at the 600 metres this pair was joined by Confectioner and Makybe Diva out wide striving for the lead with Desert War and Hotel Grand on their inside.

(Even Chief Steward Des Gleeson was in awe of the mare's run, saying he never thought he would see the day when the winner of the Cox Plate was eight wide near the 600m mark).

It was clear coming to the home turn that the battle was over, with Boss taking a peep at the runners on his inside and outside before unleashing the mare for the run home.

"She just hit the pedal and it was over in moment," he said.

To the deafening roar of the stand Makybe Diva lasted by 1¼ lengths from the Gai Waterhouse trained Lotteria with grand old Cox Plate campaigner Fields of Omagh a head away third. It was the eight-year-old's fourth appearance in the race which he won in 2003 before finishing second behind Savabeel the following year.

Boss was punching the air with delight as he returned to scale and the crowd lapped it up, with the large throng in the stand and near the presentation area clapping and cheering, not wanting to lose the moment. It was described by veteran sports writer Ron Reed as "the greatest moment in Australian sport for the year".

Freedman and owner Tony Santic were awestruck. It was an amazing turnaround in a week for Freedman, who had lost his star stayer Mummify the week before when he broke down badly just after the line when third in the Caulfield Cup the previous Saturday.

"I don't think this country has seen a better horse in the last 30 or 40 years," he said of Makybe Diva.

"No horse will ever repeat her feat of two Melbourne Cups, a Sydney Cup, a BMW, an Australian Cup and a Cox Plate."

He said she was the best horse he had ever trained – high praise considering he had trained in excess of 100 Group 1 winners including those of four Melbourne and Caulfield Cups and Golden Slippers and has had the likes of Naturalism, Alinghi, Mahogany and Super Impose through his yard. He modestly added that the credit belonged to the horse – not him – as she was so easy to train.

Before the race the club had distributed 10,000 cardboard masks in Makybe Diva's colors. Santic had his own upmarket version, which almost hid the tears he shed as he met the mare in the winning enclosure.

He admitted his only worry had been on the turn when Boss had to go wide to reel in the leaders who had tried to outrun the mare. But it was only a fleeting concern after he saw Boss looking around to check he had all the runners covered.

In winning, Makybe Diva established all manner of records.

- She became Australasia's greatest stakes winner of all time with earnings of $11,426,685 ahead of dual Cox Plate winners Sunline ($11,351,607) and Northerly ($9,340,950)
- She was the only mare to win the Melbourne Cup-Cox Plate double and only the third horse behind Phar Lap (1930-31) and Might And Power (19997-98) to achieve the feat.
- She joined Tranquil Star as the only the second seven-year-old mare to win the Cox Plate.
- She was the only mare to win the Australian Cup-Cox Plate double, joining the company of illustrious gallopers Dulcify (1979); Saintly (1996) and Northerly (2001).
- She became the only mare to win the BMW - Cox Plate double, joining Kingston Town (1980); Bonecrusher (1986) and Might And Power (1998).

Rival trainers were effusive in their praise of the winner. While describing the run of runner-up Lotteria as "outstanding" Gai Waterhouse said her horse had been beaten by a champion, "the best stayer you will see".

David Hayes, who prepared Fields Of Omagh, had been absent in Hong Kong for some years and had not seen a lot of Makybe Diva, but said he was now on her bandwagon, calling her a "superstar".

Glen Boss had the final say, declaring he was just the lucky one on her back and that he was "in awe of her and what she can do".

And 10 days later the mighty mare was to make racing history, by becoming the first horse to win the Melbourne Cup for the third time, producing amazing scenes at Flemington. Course broadcaster Greg Miles got it exactly right announcing as Makybe Diva went over the line that "the champion becomes a legend".

HOOFNOTE: Former Cox Plate darling Sunline gave birth to her second foal (by Zabeel) at Coolmore Stud in NSW on the same day Makybe Diva was stealing her thunder by becoming Australasia's biggest stakes-earner

MAKYBE DIVA is a registered trade mark of MAKYBE Racing & Breeding Pty Ltd.

2007 – HE WAS FAR FROM A SECOND-RATER

In a bitter blow, six-year-old El Segundo lived right up to his name in the 2006 Cox Plate. El Segundo is the Spanish word for second, and this is where he finished – by only a nose – behind Fields Of Omagh in a three-way photo finish.

Making the result even harsher was that El Segundo appeared to be in front just before and just after the line.

Stung by the narrow defeat, owners Don Howell, Ian Hickey, Philip Murphy, Andy Evans and Paul McNamee agreed over a consoling drink after the race that they would return in 2007 and be celebrating instead. They were soon joined by trainer Colin Little.

"An hour after the race, after defeat had set in, we just started to think about the following year," Little said.

Remarkably, they were triumphant in their return 12 months later, though, unfortunately for him, Gauci was not part of the winning equation.

"It was no fault of Darren's that he missed the winning ride the following year," Little said.

"He did nothing wrong when he only just lost and not one of the owners made any specific comments to me on why Darren was replaced. They pay the bills and it is their right to put on any jockey they want.

"They simply wanted to start afresh, and in fact selected Damien Oliver to ride the horse in future campaigns. He rode him a few times the following autumn for wins in the Carlyon Stakes and the (Gr. 1) Orr Stakes and they were expecting him to take the Cox Plate ride".

But, like El Segundo's owners, Oliver too, was soon to have a change of heart.

"Just as the owners are entitled to change their mind, jockeys have the same right," Little said.

So come Cox Plate day Oliver was committed to

His instructions for Nolen in his Cox Plate debut were for him to be patient.

"I told him to treat it as just a normal race, to bide his time and not go for home too early. Too often jockeys have a rush of blood at the half mile and I didn't want him to fall into that trap.

"I knew my horse could put quick sectionals together and I didn't want Luke to be sucked into going to soon".

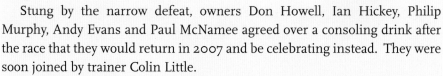

2007
(Saturday, October 27. Attendance: 34,561)

$3,00,000 plus $50,000 trophies Weight for Age 2,040m

1.	EL SEGUNDO	C. W. Little	59kg	L. Nolen	6/1
2.	Wonderful World	J. B. Cummings	57.5kg	N. Rawiller	40/1
3.	Haradasun	A. J. Vasil	57.5kg	D. Oliver	4/1

Winning details

Margin: 2 len, ½ len . **Time:** 2:06.33 13 started.

Breeding: Pins – Palos Verdes (NZ) – Oak Ridge (FR) (b g 6)
Owner: D. W. Howell, I. G. Hickey, P. Murphy, A. Evans & P. McNamee

Winner's colors: Gold and black stripes, red sleeves and cap

Winning Numbers: 1, 8, 6. **Barriers:** 7, 6, 4.

ALSO RAN

Miss Finland	D. A. Hayes	C. Williams	55	3/1f
Devil Moon	M. Kavanagh	H. Bowman	55	13/2
Eskimo Queen	M. Moroney	C. Newitt	55	25/1
Divine Madonna	M. Kavanagh	D. Dunn	56.5	12/1
Zipping	G. Rogerson	D. Nikolic	59	25/1
Efficient	G. Rogerson	S. Arnold	57.5	8/1
Lad Of The Manor	S. Stout	G. Childs	59	30/1
Niconero	D. A. Hayes	B. Rawiller	59	40/1
Marasco	F. Kersley	M. Rodd	59	25/1
Magic Cape	S. Ritchie	B. Shinn	57.5	80/1

All started

FIRST TIME LUCKY ... Luke Nolen followed instructions perfectly to win the Cox Plate on El Segundo at his first ride in the race. – Picture: Colin Bull

the Tony Vasil-trained Haradasun providing Luke Nolen with the opportunity for his first Cox Plate ride – and on a 6/1 third favourite.

(Oliver's mount was second favourite at 4/1, a point longer than Miss Finland. Gauci did not have a mount.)

Nolen, stable rider for Peter Moody, had ridden El Segundo in three races prior to the Cox Plate after Oliver moved on. Their biggest success in the lead-up had been to win the Group 2 Dato Chin Nam (Feehan) Stakes at the Valley two starts before the Plate. This was a great pointer to their chances, with eight earlier Cox Plate winners having won the weight-for-age Feehan, in which El Segundo narrowly beat Haradasun.

Little said it was a good confidence-booster to have beaten Haradasun, considering his horse was "slightly underdone".

"To know that he had been able to beat one of his main Plate rivals and that there was a bit of improvement in him gave us reason to be bullish", Little said.

Another good omen was the record of horses who had finished second in the Cox Plate going on to win the race the following year.

Beginning with runner-up Easingwold in the first Cox Plate in 1922, six second-placed runners went on to win the championship 12 months later, the others being Hydrogen, Dhaulagiri, Our Poetic Prince, Super Impose and Solvit.

Omens aside, Little admitted that he was confident going into the race because of the condition of his horse.

"The previous year we had galloped El Segundo at the Valley on the Tuesday before the Plate and he was flat for a couple of days afterwards. I initially thought he might have done too much on the Tuesday but he came out days later for that gallant second.

"We also galloped him on the same Tuesday in 2007 and he ran the same time as the previous year. But this time, instead of being flat after the workout, he was bristling with energy. He was certainly in better shape than the previous year.

"And going on what he had done after being flat in 2006, we had reason to be more hopeful in 2007. We didn't want to appear cocky but we knew we had a better horse than the previous year."

"He'd had a better preparation, was stronger horse and was in perfect shape. We had reason to be bullish that we could make amends for 2006," Little said.

His instructions for Nolen in his Cox Plate debut were for him to be patient.

"I told him to treat it as just a normal race, to bide his time and not go for home too early. Too often jockeys have a rush of blood at the half mile and I didn't want him to fall into that trap.

"I knew my horse could put quick sectionals together and I didn't want Luke to be sucked into going to soon".

Nolen heeded the advice perfectly. He was among the leading group on settling behind pacesetters Miss Finland, Devil Moon, Haradasun and Wonderful World. Nolen was happy to bide his time midfield down the back straight and when Haradasun went to the front at the 1000m Nolen clicked his mount into sixth, travelling comfortable.

With the sprint right on at the 500m Nolen inched into fourth place behind the leading group of Wonderful World, Haradasun and Devil Moon, just waiting to pounce as the field rounded the turn, as if Little's instructions of "stay patient" were ringing in his ears.

Approaching the turn Nolen knew it was now the time to turn on the power. He loomed up three-wide to Wonderful World and Haradasun and as they hit the straight the race was over and in a matter of strides. In top flight, El Segundo careered away to win by two lengths from Wonderful World with Haradasun a further half length astern.

It was a copybook ride but a modest Nolen said: "I was always in a nice spot. The whole race went to script nicely. We just fell into a nice spot three back and one out and the horse did the rest".

(But stewards saw things differently and were to suspend him for 11 meetings for causing interference to Wonderful World as he surged to the lead.)

As they had vowed the previous year, this time the gelding's owners were celebrating but Don Howell joked to journalist Mark Harding that after the 2006 loss he "went home, into a dark room and they released me about three weeks ago".

Any hopes of El Segundo lining up for a Cox Plate repeat in 2008 were soon thwarted, after he bowed a near-side tendon in trackwork, forcing him to be spelled for more than a year. He did eventually make it back to the track in January 2009 but was unplaced in two runs. Turned out because of another niggle in his near foreleg, he resumed his spring campaign once again in the 1200m Aurie's Star Handicap at Flemington.

In previous campaigns he finished last of eight in the Flemington sprint en route to winning the 2005 JRA Cup and the Yalumba (Caulfield Stakes); in 2006 he was second in the Aurie's Star before winning the Memsie and Underwood Stakes before his Cox Plate second and in 2007 he was third in the Flemington prelude on his way to winning the Cox Plate.

Omens were good then when he finished third in the 2009 Aurie's Star. He lined up again in the Dato Chin Nam and this time finished fifth of 10 which set him up for a third crack at the Cox Plate. This time El Segundo settled near last. No doubt heeding instructions from the previous year Nolen began moving up closer to the leaders approaching the home turn. Once there, El Segundo unleashed his customary finishing burst but this time he had to settle for fourth behind subsequent dual Plate winner and Bart Cummings-trained star, So You Think.

Back for another campaign in the autumn of 2010, Little was planning a start in the Ryder Stakes at Rosehill and had been working El Segundo the reverse way to acclimatise him, and noticed that he was not as comfortable galloping in that direction.

He chose the 1200m Newmarket Handicap at Flemington as the gelding's first-up run but he ran probably the worst race of his career, finishing 15th of 19. Little was mystified by the run and put it down to the fact that the gelding had appeared uncomfortable in some of his new training gallops. Regardless, El Segundo took his place in the Ryder, but suffered another tendon injury in the run. This time it was in the off-fore, the opposite leg to that he hurt in 2007, and he was retired immediately.

"It was sad because he had been a part of my family for six years and was a life-changing horse for us," Little said.

"You wait 40 years for a horse like him. They only come along once in a lifetime."

But the old warrior, a winner of just under $4 million for 12 wins and eight placings in 44 starts, has not been lost to racing.

He now acts as a "minder" at Amarina Farm in the Hunter Valley calming down yearling colts after they have been weaned.

Little do the precocious colts realise that their gentle guardian – who will give those who misbehave a nip or gentle head nudge to keep them in line - was once one of Australia's toughest combatants.

2008 – WHAT A DIFFERENCE A YEAR MAKES!

What a difference a year made for Flemington trainer Mark Kavanagh and his stable star Maldivian.

After the disappointment of Maldivian being scratched at the barrier in the 2007 Caulfield Cup, the pair were kings of the track, with Kavanagh celebrating his biggest-ever win, after Maldivian triumphed in the 2008 W. S. Cox Plate 12 months later.

While he was celebrating wildly after the Moonee Valley success, Kavanagh had shown great restraint following Maldivian's withdrawal under dramatic circumstances a year earlier. Maldivian had gone into the 2007 Caulfield Cup as hot favourite, following two impressive middle distance wins on end – one by more than four lengths over 2040m at Moonee Valley and then by 1¼ lengths in Group 1 Yalumba Stakes (2000m) a week before the Cup.

Punters had backed the five-year-old into the shortest priced Caulfield Cup runner for 41 years, with him being at only $2.50 (6/4) just before the start. But seconds before the field was to be despatched, the gelding reared and struck himself on a television audio strut on the top of his stall and had to be withdrawn, being led back to scale with blood freely flowing down his head, neck and chest.

It was a bitter blow, not only for Kavanagh and connections, but for racing in general, that such a seemingly simple incident could have such dire consequences. But Kavanagh remained stoic and refrained from publicly lambasting racing officials, who had permitted an audio aerial required for the live race telecast, to be bolted on top of Maldivian's stall, and it was that piece of equipment which inflicted the injury when Maldivian reared.

Fast forward 12 months and Kavanagh's demeanour was exactly opposite to that at Caulfield, after Maldivian led throughout in Australasia's 'weight-for-age championship', to post his first win in his seven-start Spring campaign. In contrast to his Caulfield Cup price, this time he was at the good odds of 10/1, being on the fourth line of betting, after finishing midfield in both the 2000m Turnbull Stakes and the Caulfield Cup in his preceding runs.

2008
(Saturday, October 25 . Attendance: 34,072)

Of $3,000,000 plus $50,000 trophy Weight for Age 2,040m

1.	MALDIVIAN	M. Kavanagh	59kg	M. Rodd	10/1
2.	Zipping	J. D. Sadler	59	D. Nikolic	6/1
3.	Samantha Miss	K. Lees	47.5kg	G. Boss	7/2f

Winning details

Margin: Len, sht nk . **Time:** 2:06.92 12 started.

Breeding: Zabeel (NZ) - Shynzi (USA) - Danzig (USA) (b g 6)
Owner: Pakistan Racing Syndicate (Mgr J. M. Ricciardo)

Winner's colors: Lime, Black Horse Head motif, Lime and Black Horse Shoes Cap

Winning Numbers: 2, 3, 12. **Barriers:** 6, 5, 2.

ALSO RAN

Zarita	P. Hyland	D. Dunn	55.5	30/1
Theseo	G. Waterhouse	N. Rawiller	59	15/1
C'est La Guerre	J. Sadler	S. Arnold	57.5	20/1
Alamosa	M. Price	C. Newitt	57.5	10/1
Gallant Tess	D. Payne	C. Brown	57	30/1
Princess Coup	M. Walker	O. Bosson	57	15/4
Master O'Reilly	D. O'Brien	V. Duric	59	12/1
Sirmione	J. B. Cummings	D. Oliver	59	12/1
Raheeb	A. J. Cummings	B. Shinn	59	40/1

All started

FAMILY FUN ... Isobel Kavanagh, her husband trainer Mark and son Levi with Maldivian after his win.
– Picture: Colin Bull

In an endeavour to fire him up for what would be his last run that Spring, Kavanagh made two important changes - first he put the gelding over log jumps in a change to his training routine, and then he applied blinkers.

Schooling horses over jumps to sharpen them up is a tactic which has been used successfully by many top trainers in recent years. Trainer Mike Moroney did this with Brew days before he won the Melbourne Cup in 2000, as did Graeme Rogerson with Efficient days before he won the 2007 Melbourne Cup.

Kavanagh had sent Maldivian over four log jumps in the centre of Flemington, and after appearing bewildered the first time round, the gelding quickly learned the routine of jumping over them on the second circuit.

The irony was not lost on Kavanagah – himself a former jumps jockey in South Australia. He joked that cable tv was being installed in his stables and he might put on some of his old jumping tapes for Maldivian to learn from.

Added to that change in routine was the application of the blinkers, which Kavanagh said was the last trick he had up his sleeve in an effort to get Maldivian to show the form which had made him such a headline horse the previous year. Even though he had won his only two previous runs at Moonee Valley – both over the same 2040m as the Cox Plate – those successes had been the previous year and the gelding had been struggling in top class company prior to the 2008 Plate.

But Kavanagh believed he had the necessary tricks up his sleeve to make it third time lucky for the Zabeel gelding at the Valley. He said the use of blinkers with the breed was a "tried and true formula" and he had been waiting for the optimum opportunity to use the gear.

His prediction proved spot on with jockey Michael Rodd dictating the terms throughout, kicking to the front from barrier rise to go with the Theseo, well clear of the rest of the field, in the mid-stage.

This pair had things their own way until Zipping became the first to emerge from the pack to move up to third approaching the school. Maldivian was still travelling comfortably in front rounding the home turn when favourite Samantha Miss – attempting to become the first filly to win the race since Surround in 1976 - made a fleeting run at him. Fresh from four Sydney wins on end, between 1200m and 1600m, she began to fade in the run home and had to be content with the minor placing. Zipping, who had begun to take up the field to the leaders at the 600 metres, fought on well to finish second. Theseo, who had gone early with Maldivian, tired and finished fifth.

Elated winning jockey Michael Rodd said all credit belonged to Kavanagh, who had "turned the horse around".

"He couldn't stay last week (when ninth in the Caulfield Cup) and now he's won a Cox Plate only a week later."

Kavanagh said "everyone has been telling me how to train Maldivian", but he had stayed focused and had implemented the two tactics which he always intended to employ, and they had done the trick.

"We had him tuned up today and we played our last trump card with the blinkers. There was nowhere to go after today," he said in a post-race television interview.

It was the second big win for Kavanagh during the afternoon after taking the major Victoria Derby prelude, the Group 2 AAMI Vase, with rising star and Caulfield Guineas winner Whobegotyou (who was to finish second to 100/1 chance Rebel Raider in the Derby.)

2009-10 – HE MADE EVERYONE THINK TWICE

Handsome four-year-old stallion So You Think had the image and following of a rock star as he made his way onto the track for the 2010 W. S. Cox Plate.

And, for good reason, as Australasia's weight-for-age championship was his test of the season after a faultless lead-up, resulting in four wins on end.

Here he was at only his 10th start – and not even actually four-years-old - attempting to win Cox Plate number two.

He had surprised somewhat 12 months earlier at only his fifth start to win the championship under Glen Boss by an easy 2½ lengths from Manhattan Rain and Zipping. With two wins and a second to his credit coming into the Plate, it was not surprising that the then three-year-old was rated a 12/1 chance against top company in 2009, headed by Feehan Handicap and Yalumba Stakes winner Whobegotyou, who was also unbeaten in four starts at Moonee Valley.

But what a difference a year had made. In 2010 the son of High Chapparal was right under the spotlight back at Moonee Valley, considered a certainty to take Plate number two. While bookmakers had him marked at odds of 2/1 on – the equal sixth shortest priced Cox Plate runner in history – one corporate bookmaking company considered him such a sure thing it paid out winning bets on him before the race!

In an unprecedented move, the company paid out $250,000 worth of win bets on So You Think five days before the race was run. The company's chief executive, Matthew Tripp, said the result was a foregone conclusion and he wanted his customers to enjoy their winnings in advance.

Tripp said that as a bookmaker he knew there was no such thing as a "sure thing" in racing, but he considered So You Think winning the Cox Plate was as close as anyone could get. One lucky punter received $77,000 having placed $7000 on So You Think some months earlier.

So while some punters didn't have to wait for the result, there were plenty of

> "You want to know how special he is? If I'm having a bad day, I'll go in his box with him. After that, I'm having a good day.
> "Does that explain it to you?"

2009
(Saturday, October 24 . Attendance: 31,780)

Of $3,000,000 plus $50,000 trophy Weight for Age 2,040m

1.	SO YOU THINK	J. B. Cummings	49.5kg	Glen Boss	12/1
2.	Manhattan Rain	Gai Waterhouse	49.5kg	Craig Williams	20/1
3.	Zipping	John Sadler	59kg	Steve Arnold	11/1

Winning details

Margin: 2½ len, long neck . **Time:** 2:03.98 13 started.

Breeding: High Chaparral (IRE) - Triassic (NZ) - Tights (USA) (b/br c 3)
Owner: Dato Tan Chin Nam & Tunku Ahmad Yahaya

Winner's colors: Black and white checks, yellow sleeves, black and white checked cap

Winning Numbers: 14, 13, 2. **Barriers:** 7, 13, 2.

ALSO RAN

El Segundo	C. W. Little	L. Nolen	59	15/1
Scenic Shot	D. Morton	S. Scriven	59	20/1
Whobegotyou	M. Kavanagh	D. Oliver	57.5	7/4f
Heart Of Dreams	M. Price	C. Newitt	57.5	13/2
Rock Kingdom	G. Waterhouse	N. Rawiller	57.5	15/1
Black Piranha	C. Karakatsanis	T. Angland	59	20/1
Road To Rock	A. Cummings	G. Schofield	59	20/1
Vision And Power	J. Pride	H. Bowman	59	20/1
Speed Gifted	D. L. Freedman	D. Dunn	59	10/1
Nom De Jeu	M. Baker	M. Rodd	59	66/1

Scr: Sir Slick

LOOK WHO'S BOSS ... jockey Glen Boss knew he had the race in his keeping on So You Think at the turn into the straight in 2009. – Picture: Colin Bull

other bookmakers looking to the heavens, with So You Think having dominated the carnival, costing them dearly to that stage.

The colt's name and pictures appeared everywhere in the race lead-up, hardly surprising considering he had won his only three runs that spring.

The sequence began over 1400m in Group 2 level at Caulfield when, under new rider Steve Arnold, So You Think beat a strong field including Shoot Out, Typhoon Tracy and Whobegotyou in the Memsie Stakes in late August. Punters took bookmakers to the cleaners and his odds of 11/2 were an absolute luxury in light of what was to come.

His next assignment was a much tougher task in the 1800m Group 1 Underwood Stakes. This time he was 7/4 on but was more impressive, scoring by just over two lengths, from stablemate Dariana. By now, the Cox Plate was looking to be at his mercy. The race looked to be even more in his keeping after So You Think's next effort in the 2000m Yalumba Stakes, in which he strolled home by an effortless 3¼ lengths at 5/2 on.

In the Yalumba the race was over in a twinkling when jockey Steven Arnold took off inside the 600m and thereafter was never troubled to beat Alcopop and Whobegotyou. Arnold said that the horse was a lot more relaxed than he had been in the Underwood, but had just "powered" to the front. Arnold said the Cox Plate looked an ideal next start after such a performance.

The stallion was now odds-on for the Cox Plate.

All the while, trainer Bart Cummings was providing training acumen to his Melbourne foreman Reg

Fleming from his Sydney hospital bed, where he had been confined for some weeks after injuring his pelvis in a fall.

Cummings had plans for So You Think to emulate the feats of another former champion Saintly, who took the Cox Plate-Melbourne Cup double in 1996. At that stage, Fleming considered Saintly was superior to So You Think, but he conceded that So You Think was heading in the right direction.

And that direction was Moonee Valley on October 23 for Cox Plate number two at only his 10th start.

It was all lights, camera and action with everyone associated with So You Think in the week's lead-up.

Cummings track rider Joe Agresta, paid a special tribute to So You Think, saying that apart from being a champion, such was his status, that he was a "horse of a generation".

Jockey Arnold also got into the act, saying that So You Think was so special, he wiped his feet before he got onto the horse.

And foreman Reg Fleming had an emotional response to a question from Herald-Sun racing writer Matt Stewart, who sought Fleming's opinion about the stallion. It was just a straight-from-the-heart reply, which meant so much more than any conjured response:

"You want to know how special he is?

If I'm having a bad day, I'll go in his box with him.

After that, I'm having a good day.

"Does that explain it to you?"

But Sydney trainer Gai Waterhouse, who had just won her first Caulfield Cup with Descarado, was having none of the So You Think hoopla. She said bookmakers – and the public - had it wrong and that her brilliant mare More Joyous was the runner most likely to succeed.

The four-year-old mare had won eight races straight – and had hit the Cox Plate in peak form with Group 1 wins in the George Main Stakes at Randwick and in Caulfield's Toorak Handicap with the big weight of 58kg. Bookmakers were not as convinced, marking her mare 13/2 on the second line of betting.

Now right under the spotlight – unlike the case 12 months earlier at Moonee Valley – So You Think was the shortest priced Cox Plate favourite for more than 40 years at the odds of 2/1 on to give Cummings his fifth winner in the race.

Now recovered, Cummings was on hand on race day with So You Think's owner, the billionaire Malaysian chess master, Dato Chin Nam, famous for his chessboard silks with yellow sleeves and a chessboard cap.

While So You Think had led throughout in 2009, Jockey Nash Rawiller decided to employ the same tactics on More Joyous, to ensure that So You Think had to do plenty of work with his 57.5kg. Approaching the 600m More Joyous was still in front, and Rawiller admitted later that he thought at that stage that his tactics might have flattened the favourite. Moments later So You Think gave the pair windburn as Arnold released the brakes and decided to go for home.

The race was over in a matter of moments as So You Think careered to the front to hold off the evergreen Zipping, who was coming again near the line by 1¼ lengths with Whobetyou a long head away third. More Joyous finished fifth. Fourth placegetter was Shoot Out, ridden by Corey Brown. The pair had been in the

2010
(Saturday, October 23 . Attendance: 31,546)

Of $3,000,000 plus $50,000 trophy Weight for Age 2,040m

1.	**SO YOU THINK**	J. B. Cummings	57.5kg	S. Arnold	1/2f
2.	**Zipping**	R. E. Hickmott	59kg	N. Hall	16/1
3.	**Whobegotyou**	M. J. Kavanagh	59kg	M.Rodd	14/1

Winning details

Margin: 1¼ len, long hd . **Time:** 2:07.45 13 started.

Breeding: High Chaparral (IRE) - Triassic (NZ) - Tights (USA) (b/br h 4)
Owner: Dato Tan Chin Nam & Tunku Ahmad Yahaya

Winner's colors: Black and white checks, yellow sleeves, black and white checked cap

Winning Numbers: 5, 1, 2. **Barriers:** 5, 6, 10.

ALSO RAN

Shoot Out	J. Wallace	C. Brown	57.5	12/1
More Joyous	G. Waterhouse	N. Rawiller	55.5	13/2
Avienus	M. Webb	C. Williams	57	150/1
Wall Street	J. Lynds	M. Coleman	59	20/1
Captain Sonador	R. Milne	G. Boss	57.5	100/1
Trusting	J. Thompson	J. Cassidy	57.5	40/1
Luen Yat Forever	P. Choi	D. Dunn	59	100/1

All started

THERE, THERE, SETTLE DOWN ... Trainer Bart Cummings gives owner and great mate Dato Tan Chin Nam a gentle pat on the head to calm him down after win number two by So You Think. – Picture: Colin Bull

news by the sudden death days earlier of Shoot Out's regular jockey Stathi Katisidis, and Brown had worn Katsidis's breeches in the race.

But all honours were with So You Think, who, after only 10 starts, had emulated the feats of champions like Phar Lap, Tobin Bronze, Kingston Town, Sunline and Northerly as a dual winner of Australasia's greatest weight-for-age race.

Even the taciturn Cummings admitted the effort was "pretty good", but he was having none of So You Think being the best horse he'd ever prepared comments.

"That's being disrespectful to the good horses I've had before like Galilee, Let's Elope, Saintly, but he is getting up there now.

"It takes a special horse to win a Cox Plate, it takes a great horse to win two."

Arnold said he was expecting more competition from the backmarkers before he went up to More Joyous and he had plenty in reserve as he ranged next to the mare.

At that stage he decided to "turn the gas on now" and admitted that So You Think bottomed out about 50 metres before the line.

"But he's an exceptional horse and I'm just rapt to be on him', Arnold said.

Times showed just why So You Think had to peter near the line, as he came home his final 600 metres in an astounding 34.92 seconds, faster than the 35.26 run by sprinting queen Black Caviar, considered the world's best sprinter, in a 1200m race earlier in the day.

So You Think was immediately made a short priced Melbourne Cup favourite, and who was surprised, considering he had the backing of 12-time race winner Bart Cummings to get him to the post.

The previous year, Cummings had aimed him at the Group 1 Emirates Stakes over 1600m at Flemington after So You Think had won the Cox Plate as a three-year-old.

Ridden by Cox Plate winning jockey Glen Boss, So You Think could finish only second in the Emirates following his all-the-way win in the Cox Plate, which had completed a Group 1 Melbourne spring treble for Cummings, who had also won the Toorak Handicap with Allez Wonder and the Caulfield Cup with Viewed, who had won the Melbourne Cup the previous year.

Cummings left the Cox Plate riding tactics in 2009 to Boss, who surprised with his front-running move which paid off handsomely with him winning by 2½ lengths, to give the jockey his second Cox Plate win after that of Makybe Diva four years earlier.

Cummings knew after that win that he had a champion in the making, but as usual, he let others do the talking.

Boss said he knew at the top of the straight that he would win.

"What about Bart? Unbelievable," he said on dismounting.

"I had to pinch myself at the top of the straight, I just couldn't believe it. He's (Cummings) just extraordinary, extraordinary, there's nothing else you can say."

But, like everyone else, he was unable to pinpoint the reason for Cummings' prowess.

"He's just Bart, that's all, he's just Bart," Boss said.

A postscript to the 2010 Cox Plate was that So You Think was set to do a Saintly and run in the Melbourne Cup. It was considered by many to be a big quest, with bookmakers questioning whether the four-year-old would handle the 3200m, particularly considering he had not raced beyond the 2040 metres of the Cox Plate.

In a bid to teach him to settle, Cummings ran So You Think in the 2000m Mackinnon Stakes the week after the Cox Plate. The horse settled easily in the field and then exploded away to win as he liked by nearly four lengths.

Three days later he was 2/1 favourite for the Melbourne Cup, and after fighting for his head around the back turn, fought on well to finish third behind international star Americain.

Days later he was gone from Cummings' stable, having been bought by Coolmore Stud for amounts reported to range from $30 million to $60 million, leaving Cummings and stable staff shattered.

Australia had lost a champion, who in only two short seasons had included two Cox Plates in eight wins and three placings in 12 starts before his actual fourth birthday, for earnings of around $5.7 million. He was now to be a horse of the world, with an excited Aidan O'Brien awaiting the arrival of the Australian champ to run him in some of Europe's greatest races.

So You Think quickly lived up to expectations overseas, winning his first two Group races in Ireland and was then beaten a neck in the Prince Of Wales's Stakes at Royal Ascot. He then won the five-horse Group 1 Coral Eclipse at Sandown Park and followed up with another Group 1 in the Irish Champion Stakes at Leopardstown.

And he did make it to the world's greatest weight-for-age race, where he was a fast-finishing fourth behind German filly Danebream in the Prix de l'Arc de Triomphe, after being well back early.

2011 — WILLIAMS RIDING IN THE PINK

Jockey Craig Williams was on the cusp of Australian riding history after winning the 2011 Tatts Cox Plate on outsider Pinker Pinker.

That feature win followed his success the previous week on Southern Speed in the Caulfield Cup, which saw him join George Young, Bill Duncan, Scobie Breasley, Harold Badger and Jim Johnson to win the Caulfield-Moonee Valley Group 1 Spring double.

(As it transpired the saga of Williams in the spring of 2011 became a story of its own. In between his Caulfield and Moonee Valley successes had been another feature win for Williams on French stayer Dunaden in the Geelong Cup, after which he was booked to ride the six-year-old in the Melbourne Cup. So impressive had been the Geelong win that Dunaden was marked into second favourite for the Melbourne Cup, giving Williams a prime chance of becoming the first rider to win Melbourne's Group 1 spring "triple crown". Days later Williams was suspended by stewards for 10 meetings – which included the Melbourne Cup - on a careless riding charge in a minor race at the Bendigo Cup meeting on October 26. After losing an appeal to the Racing Appeals and Disciplinary Board on the Friday before the Melbourne Cup, Williams then appeared before the Victorian Civil and Administrative Tribunal on the day before the Cup. Once again he was refused permission to take the Cup mount on Dunaden. Williams then was at the movies when the Melbourne Cup was being run but soon began receiving text messages confirming his worst nightmare – Dunaden, with French rider Christophe Lemaire in the saddle, won the Cup, costing Williams a place in Australian racing history.)

Pinker Pinker, trained by former Olympic equestrian Greg Eurell, gave Williams his second Cox Plate after having taken it on Fields Of Omagh in 2006.

It was the first Plate success for Eurell, who had made his name a couple of seasons earlier with the brilliant sprinter Apache Cat, a winner of 19 races – eight of them Group 1s – for earnings of just over $4.5 million.

But despite such heady wins as two Doomben Ten Thousands, a Cadbury Guineas, Australia Stakes and a Lightning Stakes with Apache Cat, and

2011

(Saturday, October 22. Attendance: 30,959)

Of $3,000,000 plus $50,000 trophies Weight for Age 2,040m

1.	PINKER PINKER	G. Eurell	55.5	C. Williams	25/1
2.	Jimmy Choux	J. Bary	57.5	J. Riddel	11/2
3.	Rekindled Interest	J. Conlan	57.5	D. Dunn	9/1

Winning details

Margin: 1¼ len, half nk . **Time:** 2:05.39 14 started.

Breeding: Reset- Miss Marion (Success Express) (b m 4)
Owner: M. D. Kirby Nominees Syndicate (Mgr: Mrs J Gazdowicz)

Winner's colors: Royal blue, royal blue and tangerine striped sleeves and cap

Winning Numbers: 11,5, 9. **Barriers:** 11,9,3.

ALSO RAN

Wall Street	J. Lynds	D. Beadman	59	80/1
Secret Admirer	G. Begg	B. Avdulla	55.5	12/1
Efficient	R.Hickmott	S. King	59	18/1
King's Rose	P.Moody	L.Nolen	55.5	10/1
Helmet	P. Snowden	K. McEvoy	49.5	7/4f
Sincero	S. Farley	C O'Brien	57.5	25/1
Glass Harmonium	M. Moroney	D. Oliver	59	9/1
Playing God	N. Parnham	S. Parnham	57.5	70/1
Shamrocker	D. O'Brien	S. Arnold	55.5	50/1
Avienus	M. Webb	B. Rawiller	57	70/1
Lion Tamer	M. Baker	H. Bowman	57.5	12/1

Scr: Descarado, Yosei

IN THE PINK ... Craig Williams was in rare big-race form when Pinker Pinker gave him a Cox Plate win after success in the Caulfield Cup. – Picture: Colin Bull

competing for Australia in the 1984 Los Angeles Olympics, Eurell said winning the Cox Plate had topped them all.

Pinker Pinker scored by 1¼ lengths from second favourite Jimmy Choux with Rekindled Interest (9/1) third. Heavily backed Darley runner Helmet (7/4 fav.) faded to finish eighth after leading the field for most of the way.

Pinker Pinker, whose best wins had been twice at Group 2 level and had been twice placed in Group 1 company in the Epsom and AJC Oaks, was among a group of four horses who came under the scrutiny of the MVRC committee to fill the last two positions in the final field. The committee had to decide from Avienus, Pinker Pinker, triple Group 1 winner Yosei and Victoria Derby and Melbourne Cup winner Efficient, who had been off the scene through injury and had been unplaced in only two runs in the spring of 2011 since winning the Turnbull Stakes two years earlier.

The committee put Efficient and Pinker Pinker into the field with many observers surprised that the latter had gained a run ahead of Yosei, who was made second emergency. This was because Yosei had won more Group 1s than any other Australian horse in the 2011 Cox Plate field and was ranked ninth on the final list of 16 acceptors. Further, it was the first time that a triple Group 1 winner had been excluded from a Cox Plate field. (Yosei's trainer Stuart Webb said he had been told by the committee that this was because of Yosei's poor form over 2000 metres.) In another surprise, Avienus, whose best form had been a win in Group 2 company, was made first emergency ahead of Yosei. As it transpired, Yosei had to be scratched because of a leg injury and after the Gai Waterhouse-trained Descarado was also pulled out, Avienus gained a run. But, after all the pre-race conjecture, the end result certainly countered those critics of the MVRC committee's decision to place Pinker Pinker in the field.

And while this may have appeased the committee, the result was generally a blow for punters, with the mare starting at the big odds of 25/1 after touching 30/1 at one stage. But that would not have been the case had they been privy to a conversation between Williams and Eurell after trackwork earlier in the week. Williams said the mare had worked perfectly at Moonee Valley on the Tuesday at the special pre-Plate gallops and later in the week he visited Eurell and minutely went through what he believed would happen in the race.

"He was really confident," Eurell said.

A pending storm caused some disruption at the start of the race but, once it was underway, as planned,

Williams settled midfield with favourite Helmet and Underwood Stakes winner Lion Tamer setting the early tempo.

Pinker Pinker dropped back towards the tail of the field with some 800 metres to go and began her forward move from the 600 metres, with Williams content to bide his time on the inside waiting for an opening. Sticking to the rails, Pinker Pinker was right on the leaders rounding the turn and after Jimmy Choux got the better of Helmet near the 200 metres, Williams, who had enjoyed a perfect rails run, set out after the new leader.

"A run just came for me on the fence, so I took it," Williams said. "She was really game in between horses. She raced like a tough old gelding in the end. She deserved to win."

While Jimmy Choux was clear on straightening, Williams quickly shook up Pinker Pinker, despite thinking that the bird had flown.

"On straightening my focus was to run down Jimmy Choux. Once I gave her a reminder, she exploded when the race was there to be won," Williams said.

Eurell was unable to immediately take in what the win meant to him. He said that the 1984 Olympic Games, where he competed in the individual and team showjumping, had been the pinnacle, but the Cox Plate success was "unbelievable".

Pinker Pinker, who had the lowest earnings of any of the Cox Plate runners, having won some $665,000 for five wins and four placings in15 starts, saw her earnings soar almost three-fold with the first prize of $1.8 million.

It was a fitting reward for the patience of part-owners David and Carol Kirby. It was the first Group 1 success for the Kirbys, who had been racing horses for some 40 years. Eurell had paid $120,000 for Pinker Pinker for them after the mare had been passed in at the Inglis sales.

Eurell said the Kirbys had asked him to look at a couple horses at the sale but Pinker Pinker was the one they most wanted.

Jockey Jonathan Riddell, who rode Plate runner-up Jimmy Choux, said it was scary hitting the front when his mount was travelling so well.

"I had a lovely run, I used him a little bit early but once I dropped my hands I was purring.

"I think I got beaten by a better run on the day rather than the better horse. Match them up again and I think we beat her," Riddell said.

Dwayne Dunn on third-placed Rekindled Interest had a simple explanation for his minor placing – "We just ran into a traffic jam on the home bend".

Kerrin McEvoy, who finished 8th on early leader Helmet said he was travelling comfortably between the 1200m and the 600, but he was unable to match Jimmy Choux when he challenged from there. "It's fair to say he didn't see the trip out strongly," McEvoy said.

And while Helmet's performance was a disappointment for Darley, the stable did have some success in the race, with Pinker Pinker being by the Darley stallion Reset.

New Zealander Lion Tamer, a Victoria Derby winner, had to be euthanised when he broke a hind leg after pulling up.

The other main attraction on Cox Plate day 2011 was the appearance of super sprinting mare Black Caviar, who made it 15 wins on end in easily winning the Schweppes Stakes by six lengths at odds of $1.03.

The big Valley crowd was rapturous, and Black Caviar's jockey Luke Nolen said he was a bit overwhelmed by the reaction.

"It's Cox Plate day but it seems like she's really the star of the show," he said.

And on this Cox Plate day, she was!

2012 – NOT QUITE, BUT ALMOST A WALK IN THE PARK

If nothing else, the 2012 Sportingbet Cox Plate proved that hype has never been the key to winning anything, nor has a tendency to ignore the bleeding obvious.

As usual, months beforehand, many different horses were talked up as being likely to capture the wfa championship. At various stages top-liners such as Atlantic Jewel, Manighar, More Joyous, Green Moon, Pierro and All Too Hard were given the nod, and the feeling was it could be one of the best Cox Plates ever.

Perhaps it didn't turn out to be quite that, but it still attracted a class field. Even though Ocean Park, a little pocket rocket from New Zealand, had flown under the radar early in the piece, you can bet that when he powered down the centre of the Moonee Valley straight to overhaul Black Caviar's younger half-brother, All Too Hard, there were some shrewd punters rubbing their hands.

Hindsight is a wonderful thing, but there were signs in the late summer and autumn that the then three-year-old colt had the credentials to be a Cox Plate horse. And, as we will see, his standing was confirmed just 50 minutes before the big race.

A very early hint about the colt's ability was that his trainer, a quietly spoken Matamata horseman named Gary Hennessy, who generally bought yearlings for Hong Kong businessmen Andrew Wong and Stephen Yan, deviated from his usual pattern with Ocean Park.

By Thorn Park out of the Zabeel mare Sayyida, Ocean Park cost Hennessy $150,000 as a yearling, but even as he was bidding for the colt the trainer had a premonition. "You get a feeling for horses when you've been around them for a while," Hennessy, a second generation trainer, said. "I've had a lot of horses for Andrew and Stephen, but they've always gone to Hong Kong. Ocean Park was different. I can't explain why, but when I bought him I knew he was something special."

After winning the

The Cox Plate Breakfast barrier draw, held the Tuesday before the race, has embraced a novel twist in recent years whereby the horse's name is drawn, and connections can pick their own barrier. The first of the 14 horse names out of the barrel in 2012 was More Joyous, and a beaming Gai Waterhouse strode to podium and selected.......barrier 11.
The shocked gasp that rippled through the assembled throng was nothing compared to the reaction of More Joyous' colourful millionaire owner, John Singleton.

2012
(Saturday, October 27. Attendance: 30,175)

Of $3,000,000 plus $50,000 trophies Weight for Age 3YO+ 2,040m
First $1,800,000 and trophies of $35,000 to owner, $4800 to both the trainer and jockey and $5400 to strapper; 2nd $440,000; 3rd $220,000, 4th $130,000, 5th $110,000; 6th, 7th & 8th $100,000.

1.	**OCEAN PARK**	G. Hennessy	57.5kg	G. Boss	5/1
2.	**All Too Hard**	M. W. & J. Hawkes	49.5kg	C. Munce	8/1
3.	**Pierro**	Gai Waterhouse	49.5kg	C. Brown	9/2

Winning details

Margin: Nk, 3¼ len . **Time:** 2:04.14 14 started.

Breeding: Thorn Park - Sayyida (Zabeel) (b h 4)
Owner: A. Wong, S. Yan & G. Hennessy

Winner's colors: Violet, white crossed sashes and sleeves, red cap

Winning Numbers: 9, 13, 12. **Barriers:** 9, 3, 7.

ALSO RAN

Ethiopia	P. Carey	Rhys McLeod	57.5	16/1
Shoot Out	C. Waller	H. Bowman	59	16/1
Southern Speed	L. Macdonald & A Gluyas	L. Nolen	57	40/1
Green Moon	R. Hickmott	C. Williams	59	4/1f
Proisir	G. Waterhouse	C. Newitt	49.5	9/1
Sincero	S. Farley	M. Rodd	59	30/1
Happy Trails	P. Beshara	K. McEvoy	59	60/1
More Joyous	Gai Waterhouse	N. Rawiller	57	15/2
Linton	J. Sadler	S. Arnold	59	100/1
Glass Harmonium	M. Moroney	J. McDonald	59	80/1
Rekindled Interest	J. Conlan	D. Dunn	59	25/1

All started

Group 3 Wellington Stakes (1600m) at Trentham in January, Ocean Park failed by a neck to hold off outstanding filly Silent Achiever in the Group 3 Waikato Guineas (2000m) in early February. While Ocean Park was given a six week let-up, Silent Achiever franked the form with wins in the Group 2 Avondale Guineas, and then against the males in the New Zealand Derby.

Both horses headed across the Tasman, with Ocean Park making his Australian debut in the Randwick Guineas. He was slowly away, was knocked from pillar to post, and did well to finish midfield, less than three lengths from the winner, Mosheen.

At his next start Ocean Park, ridden for the first time by Glen Boss, came up against Silent Achiever and the very talented Waterhouse-trained three year-old Laser Hawk in the 2000m Rosehill Guineas. Boss freely admits his was a terrible ride, not helped by some misinformation – he took off at the 800m, was five wide around the home turn, and was in front way too early – nevertheless Ocean Park failed by only a half neck to keep Laser Hawk at bay, and still finished a long head to the good of Silent Achiever. Two weeks later he was all set to run in the Australian Derby, but was scratched on race morning after becoming cast in his box. Laser Hawk ran third in the classic, and Silent Achiever an unlucky sixth.

Boss was already singing Ocean Park's praises, going so far as to say the colt was a "budding superstar". But once Ocean Park was home in a spelling paddock at Matamata it was a case of out of sight, out of mind.

And when, on the final day of the Randwick autumn meeting, More Joyous, unbeaten two year-old Pierro and the unbeaten Atlantic Jewel all won, and were nominated as likely Cox Plate aspirants, as was the weight-for-age star of the Sydney carnival, Manighar, Ocean Park was not even yesterday's news. So much so, that when the first genuine markets were framed for the Cox Plate, in August, Ocean Park was $31. Early favourite was Atlantic Jewel at $4.50, but less than a week later she was out with a tendon injury.

Early the autumn, Gai Waterhouse predicted she'd win the Cox Plate with one of a couple of stars. Her crystal ball gazing appeared to be on track when Pierro, who captured the two-year-old Triple Crown, won his first start as a three-year-old, and champion mare More Joyous had little more than a working gallop in a successful start to her spring campaign.

Across the Tasman, in early September, Ocean Park made his seasonal debut in the Group 1 Makfi Challenge Stakes (1400m) at Hastings. He looked to be hopelessly boxed in with 300m to run, but found an opening late and produced an amazing turn of foot to win pulling up.

The eye-catching effort caused his Cox Plate price to be more than halved, and, when he came from another seemingly hopeless position to win the Group 1 Underwood Stakes (1800m) at Caulfield at his next start, people just had to take notice. The bookies certainly paid heed, promoting him to be the Cox Plate second favourite at $6, behind Pierro at $4.50 and ahead of More Joyous at $7. Another contender emerged when Lloyd Williams' six-year-old Green Moon, runner-up in the 2011 Caulfield Cup and winner of the Blamey Stakes in the autumn, impressed by winning the 2000m Turnbull Stakes at Flemington.

At the same time a potential Cox Plate winner in Manighar was lost through injury, and then, on Caulfield Guineas day, the Waterhouse challenge began to look a bit wobbly. Pierro, an almost unbackable favourite for the Caulfield Guineas, couldn't hold off the challenge of All Too Hard, and 40 minutes later More Joyous endured a torrid run before finishing fourth in the Toorak Handicap. Earlier in the day, Ocean Park was workmanlike in beating Alcopop to win the Caulfield Stakes, but Glen Boss was adamant he wouldn't swap the Cox Plate ride for another. "He needed the run," he said.

The Cox Plate Breakfast barrier draw, held the Tuesday before the race, has embraced a novel twist in recent years whereby the horse's name is drawn, and connections can pick their own barrier. The first of the 14 horse names out of the barrel in 2012 was More Joyous, and a beaming Gai Waterhouse strode to podium and selected.......barrier 11.

The shocked gasp that rippled through the assembled throng was nothing compared to the reaction of More Joyous' colourful millionaire owner, John Singleton. "I love Gai but this is madness," Singo fumed. "If this was a normal race and not the Cox Plate, the horse would be scratched and the trainer sacked."

Waterhouse explained her choice by saying More Joyous didn't like being "cluttered up", and from barrier 11 would avoid the early scramble for the fence. As for Singleton's outburst she dismissed it as just "a lover's tiff."

Still, the "tiff" continued through until race eve, when Waterhouse, in a "Dear John" letter, apologised to her long-time friend and owner for her decision. It was just the sort of story a PR department prays for; certainly no-one at the Moonee Valley was complaining.

Come the day, More Joyous was a drifter to $8.50 to the fourth line of betting with punters settling on Green Moon as the one most likely at $5, just shading Pierro at $5.50.

Despite threatening not to, Singleton turned up to see More Joyous run, but he was still not on speaking terms with Waterhouse.

Only two horses firmed in the betting. All Too Hard came in from $10 to $9, and Ocean Park from $6.50 to $6. The money for him perhaps could have been influenced by the result of the race preceding the Cox Plate, the Schweppes Crystal Mile. The winner, who was last on the home turn but swept down the centre of the track to score running away, was none other than Silent Achiever, the horse Ocean Park had battled with earlier.

When the Plate field jumped away all eyes were on More Joyous, to see if she could overcome the wide barrier. As it turned out she couldn't, but for all of work she had to do, there still remains a niggling doubt about her being able to run a genuine 2000m.

It was expected Proisir, the third of Waterhouse's runners, would make the running, so it was a surprise when the reigning Australian Derby champion, Ethiopia, kicked through to lead the field out of the straight. Eventually Proisir was able to head him, but it ensured the race was run at a genuine tempo.

Sweeping towards the home turn Ethiopia ran past Proisir, but he was under pressure and, at that moment, the horse looking most likely was All Too Hard. Making full use of the colt's 49.5kg, jockey Chris Munce kicked a couple of lengths clear. Out in the middle of the track the violet and white colours of Ocean Park were looming ominously. To his great credit, All Too Hard did not surrender meekly, and it was only in the last 100m that the New Zealander gained the upper hand to score by a neck.

"Once he saw the bunny when we straightened up, he just let go," was the way Boss aptly described it.

Despite all of the lead-up conjecture, the fact is, the three best horses were the first three home, the minor placing going to Pierro, albeit over four lengths from the winner. For Boss it was his third win in the Cox Plate, after Makybe Diva in 2005 and So You Think, when that horse notched the first of successive victories in 2009. It was also a third Cox Plate in four years for New Zealand's Windsor Park Stud, which stands Thorn Park and stood So You Think's sire High Chaparral for a number of seasons.

2013 — AWARD FOR SHAMUS WAS A JUST REWARD

The Cox Plate field of 14 is decided on the Tuesday morning before the race and Shamus Award was an acceptor minutes before closing time, along with Chris Waller's consistent wfa performer Foreteller. There were 15 acceptors, and it came as no surprise that Shamus Award was reduced to being the first emergency. He was included in the barrier draw though, and landed perfectly in gate three.

Trainer Danny O'Brien was stony-faced as he waited in the third placegetter's stall for his colt, Shamus Award, after the 2013 Caulfield Guineas.

The Snitzel three-year-old, last into the straight, had finished powerfully to be beaten 2½ lengths into the minor placing, and it was very clear O'Brien believed he should have won.

It wasn't just the thought of the colt having missed out on a career boosting Group One contest that had the Flemington trainer seething. He also reckoned Shamus Award, still a maiden, now would have little hope of getting into the 2013 Cox Plate field.

Many would have scoffed at the colt being considered as a Cox Plate hope, but for O'Brien, Australia's premier weight-for-age race had always been a target.

As he and the connections of Shamus Award drowned their sorrows at dinner that evening, none could have imagined that two weeks later they would be popping champagne corks!

Not only did Shamus Award make it into the Cox Plate field, he won it, becoming the first maiden to do so since the race began in 1922. Much was made of this, with some suggesting he shouldn't have been allowed to run.

This focus on the colt being a maiden seemed to blind more than a few to the fact that even a cursory glance at his form would have revealed him to be a very, very good horse who, in many of his eight starts, all but one of them at Group or Listed level, had been without one of racing's most vital ingredients – luck.

Shamus Award, was bought for $230,000 at the Inglis Easter Sale in 2012 for prominent owners Sean Buckley and Vern Oldfield.

2013
(Saturday, October 26. Attendance: 30,986)

Of $3,000,000 plus $50,000 trophies Weight for Age 3YO+ 2,040m
First $1,800,000 and trophies of $35,000 to owner, $4800 to both the trainer and jockey and $5400 to strapper; 2nd $440,000; 3rd $220,000, 4th $130,000, 5th $110,000; 6th, 7th & 8th $100,000.

1.	**SHAMUS AWARD**	D. O'Brien	49.5kg	C. Schofield (a)	$21
2.	**Happy Trails**	B. Cozmanis	59kg	D. Dunn	$12
3.	**Fiorente**	G. Waterhouse	59kg	B. Shinn	$8

Winning details

Margin: ½ hd, lg nk . **Time:** 2:05.27 14 started.

Breeding: Snitzel - Sunset Express (Success Express, USA) b c 3
Owner: P S Buckley & G & C Pastoral Co Pty Ltd, Mgr: V C Oldfield

Winner's colors: Black, emerald green chevrons, white and emerald green seams, sleeves, black and green striped cap

Winning Numbers: 15, 2, 3. **Barriers:** 3, 2, 15.

ALSO RAN

Foreteller	C. Waller	C. Newitt	59	$21
Super Cool	M. Kavanagh	C. Brown	57.5	$18
Side Glance (UK)	A. Balding	C. Williams	59	$41
Seville	R. Hickmott	H. Bowman	59	$31
It's A Dundeel	M. Baker	J. McDonald	57.5	$4 fav
Long John	P. Snowden	K. McEvoy	49.5	$7
Green Moon	R. Hickmott	B. Prebble	59	$12
Mull Of Killough	J. Chapple-Hyam	S. Arnold	59	$41
Puissance De Lune	D. Weir	B. Melham	59	$5.5
Masked Marvel	R. Hickmott	M. Rodd	59	$31
Rekindled Interest	J. Conlan	M. Zahra	59	$51

Scr: Atlantic Jewel

RIDING ON HOPE ... Chad Schofield had only hope riding with him on Shamus Award over the concluding stages. – Picture: Colin Bull

"Sean had talked about giving me couple of horses, and the first one that turned up was Shamus Award," O'Brien explained.

The O'Brien stable generally likes to be patient with young horses, and only starts them as two-year-olds if they do everything right. Shamus Award was one of those.

By coincidence he had his first start on Cox Plate day, 2012, and finished third in an Inglis 2YO after over-racing. At his second start, at Flemington in the Maribyrnong Stakes, he again raced fiercely after being kicked up out of the barrier.

Shamus Award wore blinkers in those first two outings, a mistake according to his trainer. "I think he could have won both those races – that he didn't was a combination of a bad ride and my decision to put the blinkers on."

Still, the colt had shown enough to suggest he was above average, so O'Brien began planning an autumn campaign that centred around the 1400m Sires Produce Stakes at Flemington.

After finishing third first up over 1100m at Caulfield in early February, Shamus Award ran fifth in the Blue Diamond Stakes, where he found a few of his rivals just too sharp.

The colt ran a cracking race in the Sires, but perhaps was in front a shade too soon, and was run down on the line by the Sydney-trained filly Twilight Royale. Although disappointed O'Brien reckoned the signs were good. "I felt that when we got him back at three, at 1600 and even 2000m, he'd be right up there with the best three-year-olds," he said.

It was an interesting thought, given Shamus Award's breeding. He's by the former champion sprinter Snitzel, out of the Success Express mare, Sunset Express, who didn't win beyond 1400m.

But, said O'Brien, you can sometimes miss horses by just focusing on their pedigrees. "We do a lot of testing with our horses to see where they might get to – on the treadmill with heart rate monitors, lactate testing, stuff like that – so we've got a pretty good profile of what an elite mile, mile and quarter horse is.

He said Shamus Award had always profiled as a horse that would run a good mile. "And if you are good, solid miler you can step up to a mile and quarter too."

Also in the colt's favour was the fact Snitzel had sired an Oaks runner-up (Aliyana Tilde) and broodmares by Success Express had produced Cox Plate winners Savabeel and Pinker Pinker.

"The Caulfield Guineas was the target in the spring, but the Cox Plate was always on the radar," O'Brien said.

Shamus Award kicked off his spring campaign with an unlucky second behind Cauthen in the 1200m McKenzie Stakes at Moonee Valley. Behind him in third place was Darley runner Long John.

Two weeks later Shamus Award went to a 1400m listed race at Flemington and ran seventh after getting his tongue over the bit.

O'Brien had two things in mind when he saddled up Shamus Award – this time with a tongue tie – in the Group 2 Stutt Stakes at Moonee Valley on AFL Grand Final eve.

That it was a 1600m race was significant. "I wanted to give him two runs at the mile in case he did go to the Cox Plate, and it also gave us the chance to go to the Valley again," O'Brien said.

Shamus Award should have won the Stutt, instead of being beaten a short half head by Divine Calling. Ridden by Craig Williams, he was taken on in the lead for the first 800m, had to take up the running before the turn, then suffered interference in the last 100m.

The colt took no harm from his hard run and O'Brien was confident enough to tell his connections that if he drew a good barrier in the Caulfield Guineas he couldn't see him being beaten.

"I thought he'd lead, and there would be no pressure. Unfortunately two things happened – Craig Williams, who knew the horse really well, was suspended, and then we drew wide (barrier 11)".

Glen Boss rode Shamus Award at Caulfield, and after travelling 200m found himself five and six wide, and seemingly not sure whether to press on or rein back. As the field started the climb towards the 1200m pole his mind was made up for him, and he took hold. At no stage was he able to get closer than four wide, and rounding the turn he was right off the track in last place and standing the leader (and eventual winner) Long John the best part of six or seven lengths.

Running on relentlessly the colt had more than halved that margin at the finish, with Boss shaking his head as they crossed the line. "I don't know what happened – an incredible run," Boss told the trainer.

O'Brien was, in his own words, gutted. Here he had a horse whose Guineas run was similar to those of Octagonal (3rd) and So You Think (5th), who both went on to win the Cox Plate, but because Shamus Award was still a maiden probably wouldn't get into the field.

Earlier the same afternoon the Mark Kavanagh-trained mare Atlantic Jewel had made a one-act affair of the Caulfield Stakes, to become a solid $3 favourite for the Moonee Valley showpiece. Others high up in the Cox Plate market were Underwood winner It's A Dundeel and the Gai Waterhouse-trained import Fiorente, runner-up in the 2012 Melbourne Cup and winner of the Feehan Stakes at the Valley in mid-September.

Also in the betting was Puissance De Lune, trained by Darren Weir, while Long John's Guineas win had put him into the mix as well.

The Cox Plate field of 14 is decided on the Tuesday morning before the race and Shamus Award was an acceptor minutes before closing time, along with Chris Waller's consistent wfa performer Foreteller.

There were 15 acceptors, and it came as no surprise that Shamus Award was reduced to being the first emergency. He was included in the barrier draw though, and landed perfectly in gate three.

The marbles were barely back in their case when news came through that what Kavanagh thought was just a minor knock to Atlantic Jewel's off fore-leg during trackwork that morning was, in fact, a tendon injury. She was out (and subsequently retired).

"All of a sudden we were in the field, had the draw, had the rider and had the horse spot on," O'Brien said.

Getting a class jockey for a three-year-old in the Cox Plate is always a problem, given they only carry 49.5kg. But O'Brien had always had 19-year-old Chad Schofield in mind for his colt.

The teenage son of former South African and now top Sydney jockey Glyn Schofield had shown so much early promise in the harbour town that trainer David Hayes brought him to Victoria to be his stable rider, and had seen his faith in the youngster rewarded in spades.

That Shamus Award was a maiden was a stumbling block for many, but the facts were that here was a very classy three-year-old, with no weight and the capability of leading, or at the very least being handy all the way.

Come raceday, It's A Dundeel was the favourite at $4, Puissance De Lune was $5.50 and third in the betting at $7 was Guineas victor Long John, whom $21 chance Shamus Award should have beaten at Caulfield.

Trusting his judgement O'Brien he gave Schofield no firm instructions, other than to "let him roll to the winning post, and work it out from there. I did say he'd have to give him a rest at some stage, given he was going to the 2000m for the first time."

Schofield rode a composed and brilliant race. He jumped the colt cleanly and held the rail in the run to the post the first time, with Puissance De Lune pulling on his outside, and Long John out three wide.

Racing down the Dean Street side from the 1600m Schofield was able to hold up in front, even though he now had Super Cool on his outside. At this point Blake Shinn on Fiorente found himself three wide, and allowed his horse to stride up to sit outside Shamus Award passing the 1000m.

Running towards the home turn it looked as though Fiorente might have his younger rival's measure, but Shamus Award was in for the fight. "Three (600m) from home he picked up the pace and was full of running," Schofield said.

At the top of the straight the colt kicked away from Fiorente, but wider out the Turnbull Stakes winner Happy Trails was coming quickly. "I looked at the big screen a couple of times in the last 100 and saw Happy Trails flying home," said Schofield. "I just hoped we could stick on." They did, by a half head.

Schofield became only the third apprentice rider to win the Cox Plate, and the first since Brent Thomson on Fury's Order in 1975. The result brought up O'Brien's 15th Group One win in 18 years.

Happy Trails had run a mighty race and stamped the Turnbull form, while game Fiorente was to win the Melbourne Cup 10 days later. Side Glance, who finished sixth, was the best of the European visitors, and franked the form by taking the Mackinnon Stakes at Flemington a week later.

It's A Dundeel didn't have much luck, but it's likely his chance went by the wayside when the hoof injury left him with five weeks between runs, while Puissance De Lune was found to be lame post- race, and missed the rest of the spring.

With odd exceptions only top class horses win the Cox Plate. Some might argue, but in our eyes Shamus Award was NOT an exception.

2014 – ADELAIDE WAS THE IDEAL INTERNATIONAL 'DEBUTANT'

Always the best weight-for-age contest in Australia, the Cox Plate finally achieved the international prominence it deserved when Adelaide, an overseas colt with an Aussie name, became the first foreign raider to take the race in 2014.

It was the moment the Moonee Valley Racing Club and Cox Plate fans had been waiting some 20 years for, ever since a long, loping stayer from the other side of the world propelled Australian racing into the global racing spotlight in 1993. And if anyone at Moonee Valley had harboured a notion of what would be the perfect 'first international' Cox Plate win, they couldn't have wished for anything better than the win of Adelaide.

- He was not just any horse, but a colt – Adelaide was still a three year-old by Northern Hemisphere time – who was trained in Ireland, was a Group 1 winner in the US, had won and been placed at Group level in Ireland, England and France, and hadn't missed a place in just seven starts.
- The person who prepared him was not just any trainer, but Aidan O'Brien, arguably the best trainer in the world who, from the legendary Ballydoyle stables in Tipperary, has sent out the winners of hundreds of Group races, among them five Epsom Derbys, four English Oaks, 11 Irish Derbys, four Breeders Cups Turf, a Prix de l'Arc de Triomphe .... and oh, three Champion Hurdles at Cheltenham.
- Adelaide's jockey was not just any rider either. Ryan Moore was considered the best jockey in the world, with Group 1 wins in 10 different countries in races such as the Epsom Derby, Prix de l'Arc de Triomphe, the Japan Cup and the Breeders Cup Turf.
- Neither were the owners an anonymous bunch, but rather an influential group that included members of the powerful Coolmore clan,

2014
(Saturday, October 25. Attendance: 28,216)

Of $3,000,000 plus $50,000 trophies Weight for Age 3YO+ 2,040m
First $1,800,000 and $35,000 trophy. 2nd $440,000; 3rd $220,000, 4th $130,000, 5th $110,000; 6th, 7th & 8th $100,000.

1.	**ADELAIDE (IRE)**	A.O'Brien IRE	56	R. Moore	$8
2	**Fawkner**	R. Hickmott	59	N. Hall	$4.40f
3.	**Silent Achiever**	R. James	57	N. Rawiller	$26

Winning details

Margin: Sht nk, ½ hd . **Time:** 2:03.76 14 started.

Breeding: Galileo (IRE) – Elletelle (IRE) (Elnadim USA) bh 4
(to Southern Hemisphere breeding)
Owner: Mrs J. Magnier, W.H. Webb, Mrs J. Murray,
Mrs J. Ingham, D. Smith, M. Tabor & Mrs T. Magnier

Winner's colors: Royal blue, red sash, white cap

Winning Numbers: 11, 2, 9. **Barriers:** 13, 4, 11.

ALSO RAN

Side Glance (GB)	A. Balding	J. Spencer	59	$21
Foreteller	C. Waller	T. Berry	59	$31
Happy Trails	P. Beshara	D. Oliver	59	$12
Criterion	D. Payne	J. McDonald	57.5	$6
Sweynesse	J.O'Shea	C. Schofield	49.5	$17
The Cleaner	M. Burles	S. Arnold	59	$15
Wandjina	Ms G. Waterhouse	D. Yendall	49.5	$31
Sacred Falls	C. Waller	Z. Purton	59	$8.5
Royal Descent	C. Waller	G. Boss	57	$11
Almalad	Ms G. Waterhouse	C.Newitt	49.5	$31
Guest Of Honour (IRE)	M Botti	C. Williams	59	$80

All started

REWRITING THE RECORDS ... Ryan Moore races into history when Adelaide, far left, became the first international runner to win Australia's premier weight-for-age race. – Picture: Colin Bull

the likes of Tom Magnier, his mother Sue and Michael Tabor, along with John Ingham, a member of one of Australia's most successful racing families.

For a race that boasts a never-ending list of great trainers, outstanding jockeys and above all, champion horses, it was the ultimate result. For the icing on the cake, it was a spell-binding contest that saw eight horses cross the line with less than two lengths between them.

That it was an Irish horse that broke the Cox Plate's international 'duck' was, in its way, symbolic, for it was another horse from that country, Vintage Crop, trained by the maestro Dermot Weld, which heralded the beginning of a whole new (global) era in the rich history of Melbourne's spring carnival. When Irish jockey Mick Kinane produced the big chestnut with a withering run to take the 1993 Melbourne Cup, the eyes of the world, rather than the just those of Australia, became focused on racing 'Down Under', and in the following years equine raiders were sent from countries near and far to do battle with the local champions.

Almost immediately after Vintage Crop thrust Melbourne racing into the spotlight, the Cox Plate also became a target, with the dual Hong Kong Gold Cup winner River Verdon finishing down the field in 1994. However, the Cox Plate had to wait until 1999, a year after English horse Taufan's Melody took the Caulfield Cup global, for its next international runner, Dermot Weld's Make No Mistake, which finished eighth.

Weld's participation seemed to reignite international interest, and from 2001 through to 2005 each running of the Cox Plate boasted one or more overseas combatants, from the likes of the UK, Germany, Hong Kong and South Africa. Godolphin's classy weight-for-age performer, Grandera, ran third behind Northerly in 2002, but the others made little impression.

Perhaps relegated to the 'too hard' basket, the Cox Plate fielded only two international runners in the next eight years, but in 2014 three of them (Adelaide, Side Glance and Guest of Honour) faced the starter, and it was the horse most likely who produced a truly memorable performance to re-write the Cox Plate history book, and give both O'Brien and Moore their first Australian Group 1.

The 2014 Cox Plate had a number of scripts running, and the tale of Adelaide was only one of them. In pre-race discussions, the acclaimed visitor and a host of other high profile entrants often had to play second fiddle to a rough and ready nag from Tasmania. His name was The Cleaner, and the vision his name conjured up was pretty close to the truth.

There's nothing punters love more than a front-runner, a horse who goes out and runs his rivals off their feet. The Cleaner did more than that; he also ran them out of their heads. His knockabout trainer, 65-year-old Mick Burles, bought him for $10,000 as a yearling – a real upstart, a 'smart-arse', is how he described him – and after making a bit of a name for himself in Tassie, the gelding started winning races on the mainland, several of them at the Valley.

Mick and his three mates who owned the horse, were quite happy to keep picking up what they could get, but when he won a 1600 metre race at Moonee Valley in August they began to dream that perhaps he could win a Cox Plate. Proof that, perhaps, they weren't dreaming after all, came in the wfa Dato' Tan Chin Nam Stakes over 1600 metres at Moonee Valley in early September, when The Cleaner led throughout to beat Cox Plate hopefuls Mourinho and Foreteller. Right there and then the Tassie boys said, 'why not'?

The decision to send Adelaide to Australia was much longer in the making.

"The Cox Plate is one of your big championship races, a world class race. We had always been very aware it," O'Brien said. "But it is hard to get a horse that fits the right profile."

It was Coolmore Australia chief, Tom Magnier, who convinced O'Brien that Adelaide was THE horse, and he and some other Australians, including Ingham, backed their faith in the colt by buying into him late in July, 2014. Three weeks later Adelaide rewarded them with a comfortable win in the $530,000 Group 1 Secretariat Stakes over the Cox Plate distance on a tight-turning, left-hand track not unlike Moonee Valley, at Arlington in Chicago. A few days later O'Brien confirmed Adelaide's trip to Melbourne, but given the circumstances of the trainer's previous Australian experience – he was grilled by Racing Victoria Chief steward Terry Bailey after his three runners in the 2008 Melbourne Cup finished in the last four – there were still a few sceptics.

Not so the bookmakers, who'd always kept Adelaide safe in the market. The colt was around $26 in first markets but quickly firmed to $21 and then $15 when he completed his Cox Plate preparation with a cracking run in the Prix Niel over 2400 metres at Longchamp on September 14. Ridden by Moore in that race, Adelaide was locked in on the rails for almost the entire length of the straight. He eventually obtained a clear run less than 200 metres from the post - at that stage giving the leader the best part of five lengths – and charged home to finish third, beaten less than two lengths.

The day prior to the Prix Niel, the Peter Moody-trained Dissident had just beaten Lloyd Williams' 2013 Caulfield Cup winner, Fawkner, in the Makybe Diva Stakes at Flemington, and they shared Cox Plate favouritism at $10. (Dissident subsequently was injured and missed the race). It was Fawkner's first start for six months, but indicated Williams' somewhat unorthodox preparation – he would have only one more start before the Cox Plate – was on track. Things were hotting up, and the prospect of a fairytale Cox Plate gained momentum when The Cleaner won the JRA Stakes over 2050m at the Valley on Grand Final eve.

Adelaide, along with a planeload of spring carnival hopefuls, arrived in Melbourne around lunchtime on October 11, and went into quarantine at the Werribee International Horse Centre. At about the same time, across the other side of town at Caulfield, Fawkner galloped into Cox Plate favouritism when he beat a class field, most of which were heading for Moonee Valley, in the Caulfield Stakes.

Now, only the traditional barrier draw breakfast was left to influence things, and it did. Fawkner and the 2014 Australian Racing Club Derby winner, Criterion, draw well in four and six respectively, but Adelaide drew 13 and The Cleaner the outside barrier in the 14 horse field. The Cleaner's camp was nonplussed, and Tom Magnier put a brave spin on Adelaide's alley, saying, "The draw probably isn't ideal, but he's travelled well and the lads at the track (Werribee) are very happy with him. The race is right up there with the best in the world; we're delighted to be here and very excited". Then he added, "but it's a huge ask."

It was, made even harder by Adelaide having to carry 56kg, by virtue of him being considered a 4YO under Southern Hemisphere breeding time. But despite all of this he still had plenty of admirers, many of them perhaps mindful of O'Brien's comments a few days before the race. The impending Breeders Cup series in the US prevented him coming to Melbourne, but he was reported as saying he believed Adelaide to be a comparable 3YO to his stable star, Australia, winner of the 2014 Epsom and Irish Derbys. As the field went to the post Fawkner was the $4.40 favourite, Criterion was a $6 chance, and Adelaide was third pick at $8.

When the gates flew open things unfolded as expected, with Stephen Arnold pushing forward from the outside barrier on The Cleaner to try to claim the lead. But, as they turned out of the straight and headed down past the 1500 metres, the Tassie champ was still four wide, as the three-year-olds Wandjina and Almalad, along with Side Glance, pushed up inside him. The Cleaner eventually got to the rail, but it took some work.

Nick Hall on Fawkner secured a beautiful trail behind the leaders, but Moore on Adelaide found himself with no option other than to slot in behind the entire field. "We had several plans and we didn't really do any of them," he said later. "He jumped slowly and I went back to any plan I could think of."

Moore was helped by his firm belief that Adelaide was the best horse in the field, and by a thorough knowledge of the race, courtesy of having watched, over and over, a decade of Cox Plate races. He knew that despite the strong early gallop the pace would come off at some stage, and he was ready for it. Swinging into the back straight he set off three wide, and slowly and steadily worked his way into the race. "I was going around them, but I was able to make my ground smoothly, and keep a fairly constant speed," he explained.

Racing down the side, past the 600 metres, The Cleaner went for home, but on the turn he was struggling, and there was a line of horses across the track. Fawkner was looming ominously out three wide, while the widest of all was Adelaide. Moore said later he'd watched vision of the great Makybe Diva coming 'six wide' to win the Plate in 2005, so being out there didn't concern him. Also, and this is important, he had absolutely no doubt his mount would be very strong to the line.

And he was. As Andrew Garvey wrote in the Age, "What might otherwise have looked like an outrageous charge around the field turned out to be pure genius, given Moore's knowledge of the horse under him."

O'Brien wasn't there to share the moment, but he did call Moore before the race. He inquired about the weather, and the track rating, and then told his jockey, "Have a good day and enjoy yourself."

That he did, but at no stage during the post-race celebration was he anything other than polite ... and humble. As a long press interview came to a close, one interviewer wished Moore well and said, "You've got a place in Australian history now." Moore looked him in the eye and said, "No, I would say the horse has."

Much, much later on that night, as the Coolmore crowd and their Australian partners celebrated an amazing victory, the phone rang.

"Send him home ... I want him home on the next plane." It was O'Brien, apparently quite serious, no doubt keen to get a horse as good as Adelaide back into the bosom of Ballydoyle, particularly in light of Australia having been retired to stud.

It didn't happen. Adelaide was soon transferred into the stables of ace Sydney trainer Chris Waller, to be trained for the multi-million dollar Championship races at Sydney's autumn carnival.

Oh, and if you are wondering how the Cox Plate winner came to be named, the answer is simple. Sue Magnier, incidentally the daughter of legendary Irish trainer Vincent O'Brien (no relation to Aidan), who names most of the Coolmore thoroughbreds, spent some time living in the South Australian capital.

ACKNOWLEDGMENTS

This book would not have been possible when first published in 1999 without the co-operation of the Committee and staff of Moonee Valley Racing Club, in particular former office bearers, Chairman Geoff Torney; Chief Executive, Paul Brettell; Racing Manager, Fred Fox; Membership Manager, Judith Fitzmaurice; Assistant Racing Manager, Vin Lowe and Glenyse Buckley. Other club identities who also assisted greatly were former Chairmen, Bill Stutt and Norman Carlyon; Chief Executive, Ian McEwen and long-time staffers George Nye and Keith Upton.

The publishers and authors are also most appreciative of the assistance of the Herald & Weekly Times Limited (HWT) for permission to reproduce many photographs herein and for the contribution of photographer Colin Bull.

Thanks go too, to Lyn Kirkwood, for her research prowess; and to former racing editors, Jack Elliott of The Herald and Rollo Roylance of The Sporting Globe for their assistance in putting history into perspective.

References include MVRC archival material; various newspaper articles from *The Herald (Sun); The Sun News Pictorial; The Age; The History Of the Australian Thoroughbred Vols 1 & 11* (Harold Freedman, Andrew Lemon) Southbank Communications Group; *The Melbourne Cup* (Maurice Cavanough) Lloyd O'Neill Pty Ltd/ Jack Pollard Pty Ltd; *The Caulfield Cup* (Maurice Cavanough) Jack Pollard Pty Ltd; *A Century Galloped By* (John Pacini) Globe Press Pty Ltd; *First Tuesday In November* (D. L. Bernstein) Heinemann; *Notable Australian/New Zealand Thoroughbreds* (Mary Mountier, Douglas M. Barrie & Graeme Clark) Alister Taylor Publishers; *From Go to Whoa* (Peter Pierce, Rhett Kirkwood) Crossbow; *From Tote to CAD* (Max Anderson & Pierre Cochrane) Julius Poole & Gibson Pty Ltd; *The King* (Graeme Kelly) The Australian Bloodhorse Review; *They're Racing!* (Garrie Hutchinson), Viking, Penguin Books Australia; *Class Racehorses, Australia and New Zealand* (Vols 1-16), AAP Information Services Pty Ltd; *Miller's Guide* (Editor, Dennis Huxley), Miller Form.

ABOUT THE AUTHORS

RHETT KIRKWOOD, a multiple award winner for racing journalism, worked on newspapers before transferring to Public Relations and Marketing.

He began at The *News* in Adelaide followed by *The Sun News Pictorial* and *The Herald* in Melbourne, where his hobby of racing became his vocation.

He scripted the videos *This Fabulous Tuesday* (on the Melbourne Cup) and *The Dominators* (on trainers Colin Hayes, Bart Cummings and Tommy Smith) and he was co-author of the racing book, *From Go To Whoa*.

Another book, written in conjunction with Brian Meldrum, was an updated version of Maurice Cavanough's original history of the Melbourne Cup. He also wrote the 150 year history of Flemington and the VRC with former VRC CEO, Rod Johnson.

In America, Kirkwood unearthed previously unseen photographs of Phar Lap's 37 wins, resulting in him producing the book, *"The Phar Lap Collection"*. He was also a producer of the video, *"Phar Lap – The People's Champion"*.

In his leisure time, he and his wife, Lyn, are often found at the racetrack.

BRIAN MELDRUM was the Managing Editor – Racing, at the *Herald and Weekly Times* in Melbourne.

He began his journalistic career at the *Kyabram Free Press* in 1965, moving to Melbourne in 1970 to become a racing writer for the *Sun News Pictorial*.

Apart from living and working in England in the mid-1970's, Meldrum has been involved in racing journalism for almost 30 years.

He has won numerous awards, including the prestigious Bert Wolfe Award for racing excellence, on two occasions.

Together with his wife Gillian, and three daughters Anna, Fiona and Eleanor, he lives in Melbourne's south-east, close enough to the racecourses and golf courses that cater for his twin passions.